Date Due

M I S C O N C E I V I N G
C A N A D A

MISCONCEIVING CANADA

The Struggle for National Unity

Kenneth McRoberts

Toronto New York Oxford
Oxford University Press
1997

Oxford University Press
70 Wynford Drive, Don Mills, Ontario M3C 1J9

Oxford   New York
Athens   Auckland   Bangkok   Bombay
Calcutta   Cape Town   Dar es Salaam   Delhi
Florence   Hong Kong   Istanbul   Karachi
Kuala Lumpur   Madras   Madrid   Melbourne
Mexico City   Nairobi   Paris   Singapore
Taipei   Tokyo   Toronto

and associated companies in
Berlin   Ibadan

Oxford is a trademark of Oxford University Press.

Canadian Cataloguing in Publication Data
McRoberts, Kenneth, 1942–
  Misconceiving Canada : the struggle for national unity

Includes bibliographical references and index.
ISBN 0-19-541233-8

1. Federal government – Canada. 2. Canada – English-French relations.
3. Quebec (Province) – History – Autonomy and independence
movements. 4. Canada – Politics and government – 1963–1984.*
5. Canada – Politics and government – 1984–1993.*
6. Canada – Politics and government – 1993–   .* I. Title.

FC98.M37 1997   971.064   C97-930480-6
F1027.M37 1997

Text & Cover Design: Brett Miller
Cover Illustration: Brett Miller
Formatting: Linda Mackey

To Susan

TABLE OF CONTENTS

LIST OF TABLES

ACKNOWLEDGEMENTS

Literally speaking, the origins of this book go back to the winter of 1991, when I gave a Robarts Lecture in Canadian Studies at York University. Prepared in the wake of the collapse of the Meech Lake Accord, the book was my first attempt to make sense of Canada's increasingly serious predicament, and the particular role that the Trudeau strategy has played in producing it. Subsequent events, such as the Charlottetown fiasco and the astonishingly close 1995 Quebec referendum result, only seemed to confirm my thinking.

More generally, however, this book reflects a far longer process of observation and analysis that began in 1965 when, as a graduate student, I worked as a research assistant with the Royal Commission on Bilingualism and Biculturalism. It is a sad commentary on Canadian political life that over the years we have become steadily less and less able to address, let alone answer, the questions about the relationship between Quebec and English Canada that were so openly debated in the 1960s.

In the course of preparing the manuscript I had the indispensable assistance of a series of students in York's political science graduate program: Robert Boucher, Jean-Guy Bourgeois, Jonathan Carson, Peter Graefe, Gerald Kernerman, Michael Rutherford, and Panayotis Sarantakis. A large number of individuals read and commented on portions of the manuscript: Harry Arthurs, Michael Behiels, André Blais, Alan Cairns, Barbara Cameron, John Harles, Gad Horowitz, Paul-André Linteau, Marie McAndrew, Kenneth McRae, Daniel Marien, Patrick Monahan, Michael Oliver, Claude Ryan, Jeffrey Simpson, George Szablowski, and Hugh Thorburn. In true collegial fashion, Reg Whitaker read virtually the whole manuscript and offered invaluable comments. In addition, André Burelle, Tom Kent, and Gordon Robertson kindly granted lengthy interviews. Needless to say, these individuals do not all agree with the arguments that I make in this book. I remain responsible for errors of fact.

The manuscript was superbly edited by Freya Godard, with an eye to both maintaining editorial standards and rendering the text comprehensible and readable. At Oxford University Press, Phyllis Wilson, Ric Kitowski, and Jane McNulty oversaw the production of the book with both care and efficiency, after Euan White had made the initial arrangements. Finally, my wife, Susan Chapman, to whom this book is dedicated, supported the process throughout in countless ways. She understood better than anyone else just why this book was so important to me.

INTRODUCTION

What Went
Wrong?

In the fall of 1996, the prospects for Canada look bleak; of the many 'unity' crises that Canada has known, this one is undoubtedly the worst. The November 1995 referendum on Quebec sovereignty produced the smallest of victories for the forces of federalism: 0.06 per cent, or 54,288 votes; it could easily have gone the other way. Moreover, surveys have regularly indicated that in a new referendum the Yes vote could prevail. If there ever was a last chance for Canada this would seem to be it.

Yet, despite the efforts of some, no real progress has been made in resolving the issues that led to this state of affairs. Indeed, many Canadians remain deeply confused about why this crisis emerged in the first place. As a result, a kind of fatalism has set in. As survey after survey demonstrates, the clear preference of both Quebec francophones and anglophone Canadians is that Quebec should remain part of Canada, within a 'renewed federalism'. Yet Canada's political leaders seem singularly unable to arrange such a 'renewal'.

Thus, to many Canadians outside Quebec as well as Quebeckers,[1] Quebec sovereignty seems to have become inevitable, if not in the short term then in the middle or long term. To be sure, the Quebec government would still have to win a new referendum. But the chance that sovereignty would be rejected seems to depend on the difficulty the current Quebec government might have in retaining the solidarity of Quebec francophones or on their apprehension about the economic costs of sovereignty. The possibility that a No vote might result from Canadians' actually resolving their differences seems remote.

Indeed, it is difficult to see how the divisions between Quebec francophones and their fellow Canadians can be bridged. Never has there been so much animosity. Prominent members of one group regularly charge the other with prejudice, intolerance, and even racism. Beyond that, all attempts to find a formula of accommodation, whether the minimalist Meech Lake Accord or the all-encompassing Charlottetown Accord, have ended in failure.

Yet separation is not inevitable; even now, it might still be possible for Canadians to resolve their differences. As this book will attempt to show, solutions do exist. The problem lies in politics: the weight of past failures, the presumptions that have been injected into our institutions, and, in particular, the vision of Canada that remains predominant in the federal government.

First, however, we need to establish what went wrong. We can hope to find a way out of the crisis only if we know why we are in it. The main purpose of this book is to uncover the origins of the present crisis. In doing so, it will show that our present predicament was not inevitable: after all, for close to 100 years the Canadian polity had been reasonably stable.

The argument of this book is that the roots of the present crisis lie in decisions made in the 1960s. More specifically, they lie with Pierre Elliott Trudeau's 'national unity' strategy, at the centre of which was an attempt to implant a new Canadian identity. 'National unity', it was presumed, meant that all Canadians must see their country and their place in it in exactly the same way.

In particular, this meant persuading Quebec francophones to abandon their historical attachment to the notion of a distinct francophone national collectivity, centred in Quebec and firmly linked to the Quebec government. Through such measures as official bilingualism and a constitutionally entrenched charter of rights, francophones were to be incorporated into Canada as a whole and to adopt a vision of Canada that included multiculturalism and the equality of the provinces.

As this book will show, the national unity strategy failed abysmally to change the way Quebec francophones see Canada. Indeed, the attachment of Quebec francophones to Quebec as their primary identity is stronger than ever, and they are more determined than ever that Quebec be recognized as a distinct society.

It is ironic that the national unity strategy, although conceived primarily in relation to Quebec, has had its main impact, not in Quebec, but in the rest of the country and has transformed the way many English Canadians think of Canada. As such elements of the Trudeau strategy as a charter of rights, multiculturalism, or the equality of the provinces have become central to English Canadians' view of Canada, so they have destroyed any willingness to recognize Quebec as a distinct society. Indeed, within the Trudeau strategy these principles were intended to negate Quebec's claim to recognition.

In short, a strategy designed to produce unity has instead produced division, and on a huge scale. It has also destroyed the basis on which the stability of the Canadian polity had rested and on which a new reconciliation might have been developed.

Yet, the Trudeau strategy was not the only one that was presented to

Canadians in the 1960s. Trudeau's predecessor, Lester Pearson, had been struggling with considerable success to develop a national unity strategy that accommodated Quebec nationalism, rather than trying to undermine and supplant it. In that respect it was rooted in the historical traditions of Confederation. Moreover, Pearson's approach was endorsed by both the other federal parties. But after Trudeau's election as prime minister, his approach to national unity soon became the dominant one in the federal government, and enormous resources and energies were mobilized on its behalf. In the federal arena it was soon the only legitimate approach to the national unity question; in effect, it had become a new orthodoxy.

Even today, many Canadians are reluctant to conclude that their country has been ill served by the Trudeau strategy. After almost 30 years, the alternative approaches that were pursued by the Pearson government and charted by the opposition parties are largely forgotten. Moreover, the vision of a bilingual, multicultural Canada is a generous one that has mobilized the best instincts of much of a generation of English Canadians. Much more than being just a route to national unity, it has become for many English Canadians the very basis for defining justice and equality.

Thus, many English-Canadian commentators continue to celebrate Trudeau's contribution to Canadian unity. If the strategy has been less than fully successful, they claim, the problem lies with errors in implementation rather than with the basic conception. Or its unifying potential was undermined by the electoral opportunism of Brian Mulroney and the power-grabbing premiers who joined with him in the Meech Lake misadventure. They may have failed to undo Trudeau's constitutional legacy, thanks in large part to Trudeau's personal intervention, but their actions and statements served to resurrect antagonisms and whet appetites that the Trudeau government had put to rest. So, the argument goes, if only federal and provincial politicians had not departed from the strategy that Trudeau had formulated and put in practice, we would not be in our present predicament.

If it was somehow possible to hold such views before the 1995 Quebec referendum, surely it is impossible now. Clearly, the time has come for a critical reappraisal of the Trudeau strategy for national unity and the direction in which it has taken Canada. Only on this basis can we hope to find ways to take the country beyond its present crisis. That is the purpose of the chapters that follow.

My study begins by exploring the deep historical roots of the conception of Canada that Trudeau and his colleagues attempted to change. In particular, Chapter 1 shows how francophones have long seen themselves not only as a distinct collectivity but, for over two centuries, as a collectivity rooted in Quebec. Inevitably, that has meant seeing Confederation on a dualist basis, as the creation of two founding peoples, with Quebec as the centre of the francophone people.

Historically, English Canadians saw Confederation very differently, starting from the premise that they were part of a British nationality that transcended Canada. At the same time, English-Canadian leaders came to see Canada itself as a 'compact' among the colonies that formed it. To that extent, there was the basis of a common framework through which English Canadians and French Canadians could understand Canada. They might disagree over precisely who the parties to the compact were—whether colonies and provinces, or nations and 'races'—but at least Confederation itself was a compact among collectivities, however defined.

In the 1960s, the rise of a new nationalism in Quebec forced the federal political élites to re-examine the relationship between Quebec and the rest of the country. At first, as Chapter 2 shows, they searched for ways to accommodate the nationalist demands for a new relationship. The Liberal government of Lester Pearson led the way. Not only did Pearson himself openly recognize Canada's dualist foundations and the central place of Quebec within them, but he appointed a royal commission to determine how Canada might become an 'equal partnership between the two founding races'. He and his colleagues also developed an 'asymmetrical' view of Canadian federalism, by which the Quebec government was able to assume responsibilities that in the rest of the country remained with the federal government. Both the Progressive Conservatives and the New Democratic Party formulated similar policies on Quebec, in the process radically departing from their own traditions. Prominent English-Canadian intellectuals were closely involved in these endeavours. One could even talk of a consensus among English-Canadian élites on the accommodation of Quebec nationalism.

Yet, as Chapter 3 will show, by the late 1960s the consensus had been replaced by the new national unity strategy formulated by Pierre Trudeau. The strategy was itself rooted in a world-view that was based on Trudeau's very distinctive personal experiences. Indeed, Trudeau's vision of Quebec and of Canada was not shared by most Quebec francophones, though he had been struggling for years to change the way his fellow francophones saw Canada and themselves. It is partly for this reason that, in his campaign for the leadership of the Liberal Party, he could not count on the automatic support of his Quebec colleagues, many of whom were quite uneasy about Trudeau and his attitudes toward Quebec and Canada. None the less, with his selection as party leader (and hence prime minister) and his subsequent election, Trudeau was able to persuade English Canadians that his vision of Canada and his strategy for achieving it were in fact 'what Quebec wanted'. The effort to implement that strategy was to dominate the next 15 years of Canadian political life and to leave a lasting imprint on our institutions.

The centre-piece of the national unity strategy was official bilingualism, the subject of Chapter 4. After examining the recommendations of the Royal Commission on Bilingualism and Biculturalism, we see how the implementation of federal language policy was shaped by Trudeau's individualism and conception of national unity. In particular, this meant an insistence that the policy be applied as uniformly as possible throughout the country with minimal concessions to the enormous regional differences in language use. In the process, significant recommendations of the B&B Commission were ignored. More important, by calling for official bilingualism, not just at the federal level, but at the provincial level as well, the Trudeau government's language policy contradicted the Quebec government's attempts to provide necessary support to the French language in Quebec and placed demands on the other provinces for linguistic measures that were not warranted by their situations. In effect, to a much greater extent than necessary, the language policy divided Canadians and worked against its underlying purpose of Canadian unity.

A second component of the Trudeau strategy was multiculturalism. Once again the deliberations of the B&B Commission are the starting point. Chapter 5 shows how the commission's conception of biculturalism had built upon the established French-Canadian understanding of Canada, rooted in dualism and the distinctiveness of Quebec. In rejecting biculturalism and basing its policy on multiculturalism, the Trudeau government was seeking to rein in Canadian dualism by reducing it to language alone. Rather than two cultures, let alone societies or nations, Canada was composed simply of individuals, of whom some spoke English, others French, and some both languages. The notion of a multicultural Canada has gained strong adherents outside Quebec, especially among Canadians of neither British nor French origin and members of 'visible minorities'. But it has been largely rejected by Quebec francophones as a definition of their place in Canada.

Finally, the Trudeau government tried to reform Canada's political institutions to make them accord better with its vision of the country. Beyond strengthening the symbols and practices of Canadian sovereignty, this meant asserting the role and visibility of the federal government as the 'national' government of all Canadians. But in particular it meant giving Canada a constitution that would better embody the Trudeau vision. Chapter 6 shows how the Trudeau government was singularly successful in achieving this objective. Indeed, the Constitution Act, 1982, conforms precisely to the priorities that Trudeau had enunciated in 1967, not only patriating the constitution but inserting a bill of rights, with language rights as the centre-piece. At the same time it does not contain the elements that other parties had wanted but Trudeau did not, such as changes in the division of powers.

More fundamentally, the Constitution Act, 1982, was passed without the consent of the Quebec legislature. For that reason, as I show, it was opposed by a broad range of federalists in Quebec, including the leader of the Liberal Party. In effect, this crowning measure of the national unity strategy directly violated the basic view of Canada, including the notion of a 'double compact', held by generations of francophones. Negating the historical bases of French-Canadian allegiance to Canada, it created a split among Quebec federalists that is still very much with us.

The two principal attempts to remedy this major failing, the Meech Lake Accord and the Charlottetown Accord, are the subject of Chapter 8. Both of them ran up against the deep loyalty to the Trudeau vision outside Quebec and were defeated by it. Although the Meech Lake Accord was modest in scope, its 'distinct-society' clause managed to violate every principle of the Trudeau vision and was thus unacceptable to most English Canadians. Given the open and acrimonious conflict between English Canada and French Quebec that resulted, any hope that the Meech Lake Accord might achieve the national reconciliation that its framers had intended was destroyed well before the Accord fell victim to the three-year ratification deadline.

The Charlottetown Accord was much more comprehensive, but, reflecting the fact that the Quebec government had not been involved in its formulation until the very end, it sought to render the content of Meech more compatible with the Trudeau vision. At the same time, changes made in the final negotiations so that it would be less objectionable to Quebec, such as the weakening of Senate reform, undermined support in western Canada, ensuring that in the subsequent referendum it was strongly defeated there as well as in Quebec. I will show that Quebec's demands might have been met in ways that were compatible with western Canadian aspirations, such as asymmetrical arrangements, but only by violating the Trudeau vision. Public frustration with the Charlottetown débâcle was seen in the 1993 federal election, which saw the rise of the Bloc Québécois and Reform, and the collapse of the Progressive Conservatives.

As Chapter 9 argues, the 1995 Quebec referendum with its near victory of the Yes vote can only be seen as proof of the failure of the Trudeau strategy. Indeed, the No side's razor-thin victory apparently was made possible by Jean Chrétien's last-minute promises to undertake measures that themselves contradicted the Trudeau vision.

Yet, in the wake of the referendum the federal government has been unable to deliver meaningfully on those promises. Indeed, given its roots in the Trudeau vision, its efforts in this direction have little credibility. Unable to devise an effective strategy for 'renewing' Canadian federalism so as to strengthen francophone support for the federal order, the Chrétien government and many federalist opinion leaders have turned to attempting to make the alternative of sovereignty unattractive. There could be no clearer evidence than this of the inadequacies of the national unity strategy.

The final chapter begins with a review of this critical reassessment of the strategy and its consequences for Canada. It then maps out some of the routes to resolving the crisis that become available once that strategy has been abandoned: formalizing asymmetry within Canadian federalism, revising language policy on a territorial basis, recasting Canada as a multi-national confederation, and so on. Whether any of this can be done, however, is an open question.

Yet, if Quebec should opt for sovereignty it will be important to remember that Canadians and Québécois need not become the worst of enemies, as some have claimed, and would still have common interests that needed protection. I will explore ways of doing this. In the last analysis, as this book shows, a vote for sovereignty is not inevitable but would be the result of errors and miscalculations that were made, often with the best of intentions, by our political class. In particular, it would have stemmed from a national unity strategy that was based on a misconception of Canada.

PART ONE

Two Visions
of Canada

CHAPTER 1

The First Century: Separate Nationalities

From the beginning, English-speakers and French-speakers have seen Canada in fundamentally different ways. At the time of Confederation, most anglophones saw themselves as members of a British nationality that transcended the boundaries of the new Dominion, whereas most francophones identified with a *canadien* nationality that fell considerably short of these boundaries. By the same token, the ways in which they understood the basic terms of Confederation were fundamentally contradictory, and continued to be so. To this day anglophones and francophones have different, indeed incompatible, visions of Canada.

The attachment that most francophones feel to Canada has been mediated through their continued primary attachment to a more immediate, distinctly francophone society, itself a national community. Moreover, they have tended to see this collectivity as rooted in Quebec. Indeed, the link between francophones and the territory of Quebec was formalized in 1791, through the Constitution Act that established Lower Canada as a distinct colony. Historically, francophones have been divided over the precise boundaries of their national community. Whereas many have limited it to Quebec, others have extolled the idea of a *nation canadienne* that extends throughout Canada wherever francophones are present. Some have even gone further, imagining an *Amérique française* that included parts of the United States inhabited by Franco-Americans. Few, though, have seen their nation as the whole of Canada.

For that matter, the very term *Canadien* emerged long before Confederation. With the transformation of New France into a British colony, *Canadien* was appropriated to designate all residents of the colony, francophone and anglophone alike. Francophones then began to call themselves *Canadiens français*. Yet the ambiguity persisted: for many francophones, *Canadien* continued to designate their own distinctly francophone society.

Historically, anglophone Canadians have seen themselves, and Canada, very differently. Initially, most of them saw themselves first and foremost as members of a larger collectivity that subsumed Canada: the British Empire. Indeed, this was the primary basis of a sense of nationality. Sir John A. Macdonald captured a strong popular sentiment when he declared in 1891, 'A British subject I was born and a British subject I will die.'[1] Confederation was itself quite consistent with that imperial sentiment since it had been encouraged by the British Colonial Office. The Confederation project did imply an incipient Canadian nationalism, but this new nation was to be an integral part of the Empire. To quote Sir John A. again, the new Canada was to be 'a British nation under the British flag and under British institutions'.[2]

Some anglophones, of course, also identified strongly with their historic colonies. In particular, Maritimers hesitated to link their futures with Canada, fearing that their economic interests would be subordinated to those of the other provinces. For that matter, the residents of Upper Canada (modern-day Ontario) had themselves functioned as a separate entity from 1791 until the creation of the United Canadas in 1840.[3] For them, a primary purpose of Confederation was to escape 'domination' by Lower Canada. But there was an important difference between these colonial identities and the *canadien* identity: they were not based on a sense of nationality. For most anglophones, nationality remained British.

With time, and the decline of Britain, the sense of a British nationality atrophied. By and large, it was replaced with a new conception of a Canadian nationality, directly attached to the Canadian state and unmediated by any previous identity. Few anglophones have felt any attachment to a distinctly English-Canadian nationality.

To be sure, the involvement of native peoples with Canada has also stemmed from their membership in a prior collectivity, but until quite recently native peoples were not in a position to force their claims upon the Canadian political scene. If only because of their much larger numbers, francophones (at least in Quebec) have always been able to do so.

THE ROOTS OF NATIONALITY

The sense of distinct nationality that francophones brought to Confederation had taken form decades before, borne of the struggles between francophones and anglophones in Lower Canada. It was based on a collective identity as *Canadiens* that had been firmly established during the French regime.

The *canadien* identity seems to have emerged quite spontaneously. The various French regional identities that colonists brought to New France gradually merged into a common *canadien* identity, just as their various vernaculars merged into a common French dialect.

This process was fostered not only by palpable cultural differences from, and open conflict with, the aboriginal population and the rival English-speaking colonists, but also by simple isolation from metropolitan France. It was further strengthened by struggles for power and status between the permanent residents of the colony (or *habitants*) and the metropolitan Frenchmen who monopolized the positions of authority—ecclesiastical, political, and military—in the colony. Certainly this process of 'identity formation' was not fostered or even sanctioned by the colonial authorities.

At the same time, of course, New France did not produce a nationalist movement seeking autonomy from France in the name of the *Canadiens*.[4] That was precluded not only by the colony's economic dependence on France, but also by the absolutist ethos that reigned in the colony. Nor did the mere fact of Conquest produce a nationalist movement.[5] That was not to come until several decades later.

None the less, the sense of collective identity among the *Canadiens* and their attachment to their cultural distinctiveness were sufficient to frustrate the British plans for the new colony. Under the Royal Proclamation of 1763, the Catholic Church would have lost its legal status and privileges, the seigneurial system would have been eliminated, and the common law would have replaced the civil law of the *ancien régime*. The first colonial Governor quickly concluded that this assimilationist strategy could not succeed, and the Proclamation was never enforced.

The Origins of Dualism

Twelve years later, the colonial authorities switched to the opposite policy of formally recognizing and legally entrenching the distinctive *canadien* institutions. Under the Quebec Act the Church's legal privileges (including the right to collect tithes) were restored, the seigneurial system was re-established, and the civil law was adopted for the colony. In this way, the Quebec Act laid the basis for Canadian dualism. Even today, supporters of Canadian dualism begin with the Quebec Act as they construct their cases.

At the same time, the dualism of the Quebec Act was purely cultural: at the urging of clerical leaders, an elected representative assembly was not established in the colony. More fundamentally, this cultural dualism was profoundly conservative, restoring as it did the quasi-feudal privileges of the Church and seigneurs. But that situation did not last long, for the clamouring of a growing anglophone merchant class and an emerging *canadienne* petite bourgeoisie of liberal professionals resulted in the Constitution Act of 1791.

Linking Culture and Territory

The Constitution Act granted representative institutions to the British colony and divided it into Lower Canada and Upper Canada. Although, strictly speaking, the division was territorial, the rationale was to accommodate cultural dualism. In the words of the British colonial secretary, its main purpose was to reduce 'dissensions and animosities' among two 'classes of men, differing in their prejudices, and perhaps in their interests.'[6] The measure served to link francophones with a specific territory. In the words of the historian George F.C. Stanley, the Act 'was to give renewed vigour to the idea of French Canadian separateness. It provided the French fact with a geographical as well as a political buttress.'[7] Once established, this buttress was to prove unmovable.

At the same time, the separation of the 'two classes of men' was not complete, and in Lower Canada, the francophone majority and anglophone minority were soon embroiled in a dispute over control of the colony's political institutions. In the new legislative assembly the *canadien* majority, led by an increasingly assertive petite bourgeoisie, challenged the predominance of executive bodies in which anglophones were in the majority. Fuelling the steadily growing struggle was a conflict of economic interests between the anglophone colonial bourgeoisie and the predominantly agrarian *Canadiens*, with their liberal professional leaders. But the struggle was also due to periodic attempts by anglophone leaders to advance the old dream of assimilation by eliminating separate francophone schools or reuniting Upper and Lower Canada.

By the early 1800s, these conditions had produced a full-fledged nationalist movement that claimed the status of nation for the *Canadiens* and demanded more power for Lower Canada's representative assembly and greater autonomy for the colony itself from Britain.[8] Although, during the 1830s, this struggle for democracy enlisted some members of Lower Canada's anglophone population, it remained quite distinct from a comparable popular movement developing in Upper Canada. The armed insurrections that broke out in both colonies in 1837 were themselves dualist, functioning separately under two very different leaders: Louis-Joseph Papineau and William Lyon Mackenzie.

With the defeat of the rebellions, the British authorities gave Lord Durham the task of determining the cause of the insurrection and devising prescriptions to ensure it would not happen again. In his report, which he wrote in 1838, Durham saw French-English dualism as the heart of the problem. In an oft-quoted passage Durham declared: 'I expected to find a contest between a government and a people; I found two nations warring in the bosom of a single state: I found a struggle not of principles but of races.'[9]

Accordingly, while recommending that responsible government be granted, he proposed that the two colonies should be merged into one—the United Canadas.

The purpose of the second recommendation was to eliminate the cultural underpinning of dualism. Citing the assimilation of Louisiana's French-speakers as a model, Durham declared: 'The only power that can be effectual at once in coercing the present disaffection, and hereafter obliterating the nationality of the French Canadians, is that of a numerical majority of a loyal and English population.'[10] Expressing the belief in the superiority of British civilization that pervaded the British ruling class and that perhaps followed logically from his own liberalism,[11] Durham insisted that in any event such an assimilation would be to the benefit of the *Canadiens*: 'There can hardly be conceived a nationality more destitute of all that can invigorate and elevate a people, than that which is exhibited by the descendants of the French in Lower Canada, owing to their retaining their peculiar language and manners. They are a people with no history, and no literature.'[12]

The United Canadas: Formalizing Dualism

In one of the greatest ironies of Canadian history, not only did cultural dualism survive union, but the political institutions of the new United Canadas soon evolved a most elaborate scheme of political dualism. Indeed, the French-Canadian attachment to the United Canadas, with its cultural and political security, was to complicate greatly the subsequent transition to Confederation, and the memory of this dualism was to affect how French Canadians evaluated the development of Confederation.

In fact, this new assimilationist strategy had little chance of success. As William Ormsby noted, 'The assimilation of French Canada would have been difficult, if not impossible, in 1791—fifty years later it was an entirely unrealistic objective.'[13] The colonial governors soon realized this; their masters in London took much longer to do so.

Unfortunately, from the point of view of the assimilation policy, the link between French Canadians and a specific territory could not be completely eliminated. If the two Canadas had been fully merged and seats in the new common legislature awarded according to representation by population, Lower Canada would have had considerably more seats than Upper Canada. Accordingly, Upper and Lower Canada were maintained, under new names—Canada West and Canada East.[14] They were assigned equal numbers of seats. Only English was to have official status in the new legislature.

Durham and the British colonial authorities had incorrectly assumed that the English Canadians in the new legislature would be sufficiently cohesive to exploit their numerical preponderance and form a reliable government. But divisions soon developed among the English Canadians over responsible government, which the British refused to grant. As a result, the initial Conservative government was soon defeated by defections to Robert Baldwin's Reform caucus. In the name of responsible government, it formed a coalition with French Canadians under Louis-Hyppolyte Lafontaine, who had been briefly involved in the 1837 insurrection. Although the colonial secretary in London was furious, he finally had no choice but to accept a government formed of this Baldwin-Lafontaine coalition.

Beyond the issue of responsible government, the English Canadians of Canada West and Canada East were also separated by the inevitable economic rivalry between Toronto and Montreal. And Canada West was divided by a host of internal issues.[15]

Finally, as Douglas Verney has shown, the British colonial authorities apparently felt obliged to allow Quebec's public service, with its predominantly French-Canadian clientele, to continue providing services in French. Nor did they eliminate the Quebec civil law or the Church's responsibility for education. Thus, the United Canadas maintained separate senior administrative positions, such as provincial secretaries, commissioners of Crown lands, and deputy superintendents of education.[16]

Given this intractable social reality, the United Canadas developed an elaborate set of practices.[17] First, thanks in part to the dualism in administrative structures, the ministries were themselves dual. There were separate superintendents of instruction and ministers of public works for Canada East and Canada West. There were even dual prime ministers.

Second, the capital actually shifted between Canada East and Canada West. During its first session, in 1841, the new legislature decided that the capital should alternate between Quebec City and Toronto,[18] but after that, repeated efforts to agree on a permanent site failed. During the 1840s, Kingston and Montreal were also used as capitals. In 1849 the legislative assembly decided that the capital should alternate between Quebec City and Toronto every four years. Although this arrangement must have produced major administrative costs and delays,[19] a contemporary did allow that the 'perambulating system' also brought benefits: 'It had undoubtedly the effect of making not only the public men but all men of large affairs in either province very much better acquainted with the state of things and the temper of the people in Quebec and Ontario, respectively, than they were ever before or since.'[20]

Third, the provision that all records of the United Canadas legislature should be in English only was eliminated in 1848. Fearful of rising French-Canadian discontent, the Canadian governor had already called for such a move in 1845. But his recommendation provoked the extreme displeasure of

Prime Minister Sir Robert Peel. Three years passed before the British parliament finally repealed the offensive provision. In 1849 the Governor, Lord Elgin, began the practice of reading the Throne Speech in both English and French.[21]

Finally, within the Union legislature a certain presumption developed that a measure affecting one of the sections would not be adopted unless a majority of the members of that section were in favour. During the Confederation debates, Sir John A. Macdonald was to claim this had been a rigorous practice of the legislature: 'We have had a Federal Union in fact, though a Legislative Union in name.'[22] However, over the years there were a good many occasions when this presumed 'double-majority' convention was not followed.[23] In the mid-1840s leaders of the French-Canadian caucus had tried, unsuccessfully, to establish the principle that the government should itself be constructed on the double-majority principle.[24] Lower Canadian and Upper Canadian seats in the Executive Council would be controlled by whatever party had the legislative majority in that section. None the less, at least among the French-Canadian members there was a belief that the affairs of the United Canadas should be guided by the notion of double majority.

It is striking to see how far dualistic practices were extended, given not only the assimilationist intent that lay behind the United Canadas but the requirements of parliamentary procedure. For instance, according to established practice only one minister could be appointed prime minister. Thus, as Verney recounts, the leaders of the Upper Canadian and Lower Canadian partners in the government, who usually held the position of attorney general, would simply decide which one of them the governor should appoint first (prime) minister (later, they assigned the title to a third member).[25] In practice, however, they functioned as co-leaders.

None the less, by the 1850s the very dualism that endeared the United Canadas to the French Canadians of Canada East became intolerable to much of the Canada West political leadership. Changes in population had a lot to do with it. Just as the population statistics had commended to the British and Upper Canadians the premise that Lower Canada should have no more seats than Upper Canada, so the population statistics undid the premise. The 1851 census demonstrated that Canada West's population had become substantially larger than Canada East's. Canada West's Reform leaders were rapidly converted to the logic of 'rep by pop', and their old alliance with the French Canadians of Canada East fell apart. Indeed, in their effort to preserve the existing structure, French-Canadian leaders found themselves allied with Canada West's Tories. The new alliance was able to form governments during the 1850s, but in Canada West pressure for a new regime built steadily.

The demands by Canada West for rep by pop and French-Canadian resistance led to frequent deadlocks, and a series of governments failed to maintain confidence.

In a fierce denunciation of dualism, Reform leader George Brown declared in 1864: 'We have two races, two languages, two systems of religious belief, two systems of everything, so that it has become almost impossible that, without sacrificing their principles, the public men of both sections could come together in the same government. The difficulties have gone on increasing every year.'[26] At the time, Brown was advocating a new federalism for the United Canadas in which power would be almost totally devolved to separate legislatures. Shortly after, he joined his long-standing political rivals to embrace a new strategy for escaping the structures of dualism: the incorporation of the United Canadas in an enlarged British North America.

As the forces for Confederation gathered, French-Canadian leaders viewed the prospect of change with alarm. Despite the original intent of union, it had served the French Canadians well. They had been able to force the British authorities to abandon the goal of assimilation and even to accept the formal recognition of French in the United Canadas legislature. Rather than dissolving Quebec in a larger system, the United Canadas had afforded Quebec considerable administrative and even legislative autonomy. Finally, with its far-reaching application of the principle of duality, 'union' had given the French-Canadian nation a semblance of equality with English Canada. In fact, between 1848 and 1864, the dual ministries had always had a French Canadian as one of their heads.[27] It would prove difficult to abandon such a practice. Indeed, the experience of the United Canadas and its example of dualism continued to shape French-Canadian political ambitions and notions of justice long after the new regime of Confederation was in place.

For English Canadians, however, the very idea of duality had been thoroughly discredited by the final years of the United Canadas. Not only was a serious application of dualism rendered irrelevant by the changes in population, but the United Canadas had been proven to be unworkable.

CONFEDERATION: FROM DUALISM TO FEDERALISM

The leaders of the movement for Confederation had no interest in applying the principle of dualism. In the new Canada, French Canadians and Quebec would be very much in the minority. Indeed, for many English Canadians the very reason for Confederation was to escape the stalemates and the alleged subordination to French-Canadian interests that had come to characterize the United Canadas. As a result, there is little trace of dualism in the British North America Act. To be sure, French is given equal status with

English in the federal Parliament and courts, as well as in the legislature and courts of Quebec. But there is no provision for the hyphenated ministries of the United Canadas. And Quebec representation in the House of Commons was to be based on its population.[28] In the Senate it was fixed at one-third.

By the same token, in his famous proclamation of the new 'political nationality' to be created through Confederation, the leader of French-Canadian supporters, George-Étienne Cartier, avoided any forthright evocation of dualism. He insisted that this nationality would be purely political and thus would be fully compatible with the 'diversity of the races'. But in describing this racial diversity, he declared: 'In our own Federation we should have Catholic and Protestant, English, French, Irish and Scotch, and each by his efforts and his success would increase the prosperity and glory of the new Confederacy.'[29]

Yet such was the sense of nationality and fear of English-Canadian domination among the French-Canadian élites that they were not prepared to abandon dualism unless another formula, namely federalism, was applied in its place. In fact, as we have seen, a form of federalism had already emerged during the United Canadas. Not only had Lower Canada retained its distinctiveness, as Canada East, but on some occasions the double-majority principle had been observed, giving Lower Canada effective autonomy in matters that affected it alone.

It was clear that federalism was the price of Confederation, given French-Canadian attitudes, although even then, the liberal *Rouges* were likely to remain opposed. And the Maritime leaders, fearful of dominance by Upper and Lower Canada, were seizing on federalism as a way to protect their own autonomy.

Indispensable as federalism may have been to securing the necessary support for Confederation, however, the major English-Canadian promoters of the new Canada were most reluctant to embrace it. They wanted a strong government. After all, the leading force for Confederation was the English-Canadian bourgeoisie, which wanted a government with the capacity to underwrite its ambitious engineering projects, such as the construction of railways.[30] And for many English Canadians the threat of military invasion from the United States seemed to warrant the strongest possible government.

Thus, for Upper Canadians in particular, federalism was at best a regrettable concession imposed by Quebec and, to a lesser degree, the Maritimes. In 1865 Sir John A. reiterated his oft-stated preference for a 'legislative union':

> [But] we found that such a system was impracticable. In the first place, it would not meet the assent of the people of Lower Canada, because they felt

that in their peculiar position—being in a minority, with a different language, nationality and religion from the majority . . . their institutions and
their laws might be assailed, and their ancestral associations . . . attacked and
prejudiced.

Second, he noted: 'We found too, that . . . there was as great a disinclination
on the part of the various Maritime provinces to lose their individuality, as
separate political organizations, as we observed in the case of Lower Canada
herself.'[31]

Nevertheless, he confidently predicted in a famous private letter that
within a lifetime the province would be absorbed into the federal domain.[32]
Indeed, according to some sources, at the final round of constitutional negotiations in London Macdonald tried once again to secure a unitary system.
In this, he had the support not only of most of his anglophone colleagues but
of the British colonial authorities as well. Only a threat by George-Étienne
Cartier to return to Canada and mobilize support against this last-minute
change prevented it from being carried through.[33]

Not surprisingly, given their desire for a strong central government,
many of the English-Canadian participants in the Confederation debates
betrayed a quite confused idea of what federalism represented. P.B. Waite says
of the authors of the Quebec Resolutions:

> The word 'federal' was used to describe the Quebec plan, not because it
> defined the proposed relations between the central and the provincial gov-
> ernments, but because it was the word the public was most familiar
> with. . . . The French Canadians and the Prince Edward Islanders insisted
> that the constitution be federal, and the constitution was certainly called
> federal; what it was really intended to be was another matter.[34]

Indeed, when Macdonald declared at one point in the debates that the new
regime would be based on 'the well understood principles of federal government', the ensuing elaborations by his supporters showed that most members of his coalition thought that federalism had to do with different bases of
representation in the Senate and the House of Commons![35]

The terms of the BNA Act closely reflect this balance of forces and attitudes. The new regime did give Quebec a government of its own, restoring
what had been lost in 1840. Once again, French Canadians would have a legislature in which they would form the clear majority. But this concession to
French-Canadian demands was heavily circumscribed.

First, over the fierce objections of many French-Canadian supporters of
Confederation, measures were included to protect the interests of Quebec's

English-speakers.[36] That is why the BNA Act guaranteed the status of English in Quebec's legislature and courts.[37] There is no comparable measure protecting the French-Canadian minorities of the other provinces. Similarly, protection of Quebec's English Canadians was also the primary reason why the Act protects denominational schools in both Quebec and Ontario.[38] In addition, the Act has special provisions to protect the representation of Quebec's English-Canadian districts in the Senate and the Quebec legislature.[39]

Second, the division of powers outlined in the Act is heavily weighted in favour of the federal government. To be sure, the provinces were assigned jurisdictions that bore directly upon Quebec's distinctive cultural institutions: education, civil law, solemnization of marriage, health, and so on. Thus, in areas crucial to their survival, French Canadians would not have to rely on a government responsible to a primarily English-Canadian electorate. However, owing to the predominance of the English-Canadian bourgeoisie in the Confederation movement, the federal government was given the critical jurisdictions affecting Canada's economic life, as well as exclusive access to the primary source of revenue, indirect taxes. Moreover, provision giving Ottawa broad responsibility for 'peace, order and good government' and possession of all jurisdictions not exclusively assigned to the provinces was clearly intended to ensure that the federal government would play the pre-eminent role.

Indeed, Ottawa was granted prerogatives that are directly at odds with the federal principle. In particular, it was given the right to 'disallow' legislation already passed by provinces and to instruct a lieutenant-governor to 'reserve' legislation passed by a provincial legislature until such time as federal cabinet should consent. By some readings, the system is not federal at all.[40]

All this did not stop the proponents of Confederation in Quebec from promoting the new regime as a decidedly federal one that would give Quebec a strong government of its own. Indeed, some of the rhetoric has a familiar ring to it. To quote one leading *bleu* newspaper, 'In giving ourselves a complete government we affirm the fact of our existence as a separate nationality, as a complete society, endowed with a perfect system of organisation.'[41] On the day of Confederation's birth, the same newspaper declared: 'As a distinct and separate nationality, we form a state within the state. We enjoy the full exercise of our rights and the formal recognition of our national independence.'[42]

In fact, it was apparently the need to make the new regime acceptable in Quebec that led its authors to dub it a 'confederation'. To quote one authority: 'Federation' and 'confederation' seem to have been deliberately used to confuse the issue. It is clear that there was a certain amount of camouflage. . . .

The object was to carry the proposals.'[43] By any reasonable standard the system was definitely not a confederation, which would imply that the provinces possessed exclusive sovereignty and Ottawa's authority was delegated to it by them. Even its credentials as a federation were far from clear.

Nevertheless, it was on the basis of its promise of federalism that the new regime was accepted in Quebec. Even at that, among the 49 French-Canadian delegates attending the Quebec Conference, only 27 voted in favour of the proposal. The rest voted against.[44] Their reason for doing so had been expressed well during the debates by the *rouge* leader, Jean-Baptiste-Eric Dorion:

> I am opposed to the scheme of Confederation, because the first resolution is nonsense and repugnant to truth; it is not a Federal union which is offered to us, but a Legislative union in disguise. Federalism is completely eliminated from this scheme, which centres everything in the General Government. . . . In the scheme we are now examining, all is strength and power, in the Federal Government; all is weakness, insignificance, annihilation in the Local Government![45]

It appears that many English Canadians also saw Confederation in those terms. As Waite observes,

> the French Bleus thought it was [a federation], but for a powerful majority of others Confederation was an attempt to put aside the insidious federal contrivances that had grown up within the Union of Canada, to relegate the questions that had caused them to the care of *subordinate, local* legislatures, and to establish at Ottawa a strong, cohesive, sovereign, central government [emphasis added].[46]

In short, federalism may have been the only basis upon which French Canadians were prepared to give up the dualism of the United Canadas, but its status in the new Confederation was precarious indeed. Over the following decades, political leaders and commentators, especially francophone, frequently called for a return to the 'spirit of Confederation'. But it is clear that more than one spirit presided at the deliberations that led to Confederation. From the outset, anglophones and francophones had very different understandings of the political order that had been created.

The First Few Decades

As was to be expected, there was virtually no application of the duality principle in the new federal government beyond the provisions of the BNA Act for the use of English and French in Parliament and federal courts. First, the

United Canadas' practice of two first ministers was definitively abandoned: in inviting Sir John A. Macdonald to become first minister, the governor-general was careful to specify that Sir John A. alone would be prime minister. Indeed, Lord Monck declared: 'I desire to express my strong opinion that in future . . . the system of dual First Ministers which has hitherto prevailed, shall be put an end to.'[47] Apparently this statement provoked no protest among French-Canadian politicians.[48]

The question of titles was quite a different matter. When Monck recommended that Macdonald be knighted, George-Étienne Cartier refused to accept the lesser title recommended for him, calling it a slight to French Canadians.[49] Eventually, Cartier got his wish. Dualism may have been relegated to the margins of Canadian politics, but French Canadians were not prepared to see it dismissed from the symbolic realm as well.[50] (Of course, Cartier's personal vanity was also a factor.[51])

Second, none of the other cabinet positions was dual. In fact, of the thirteen places in Sir John A.'s first cabinet, only four were held by Quebeckers (three of whom were French Canadian). As W.L. Morton has noted, this was significantly fewer than what the French-Canadian proportion of the Canadian population would have warranted. For that matter, the United Canadas cabinets had always contained *four* French Canadians.[52] Although Cartier was a senior member of the cabinet, as was in keeping with his personal status and long-standing relationship with Macdonald, the other two French Canadians received relatively minor positions.[53]

Third, in Parliament, Quebec's new diminished status followed the terms of the BNA Act. In the House of Commons, where rep by pop was to prevail, Quebec was given 65 of 181 seats. In the Senate, Quebec held 24, or one-third, of the seats.

Finally, the capital no longer alternated between English and French Canada. It was established permanently in Ottawa, overlooking the Ottawa River from the Ontario side.

The organization of the new federal government clearly showed that for Quebec, and its French Canadians, the price of gaining its own provincial government was to lose any claim to dualism in the organization of the common government, beyond the BNA Act's section 133 obligations for the use of French in Parliament and the federal courts.

With time, however, some trappings of dualism appeared in federal institutions. In the twentieth century, the federal Liberal party has alternated between English-Canadian and French-Canadian leaders, though without declaring openly that it was bound to do so.[54] Similarly, the first Canadian governor-general, Vincent Massey, was succeeded by a French Canadian, Georges Vanier; subsequent federal governments have followed this alternation principle. However, these various office holders were not expected to act as representatives of their linguistic group.

Moreover, there was never any suggestion that dualism should be applied to decision making as it was in the United Canadas. The proportion of francophones and Quebeckers in the cabinet was roughly equal to their proportions of the Canadian population, and, in particular, there is no evidence that francophone ministers or Quebec ministers were able to exercise a veto. Perhaps the most significant concession to dualism lies in the provision of the Supreme Court Act, 1875, that two of the six Supreme Court justices should be from the bench or bar of Quebec and in the practice of reserving appeals from Quebec for panels in which Quebec justices are in a majority.[55]

As it happened, the new Quebec provincial government paid greater deference to the principle of dualism, owing to the economic and political strength of its English-Canadian minority. Not only were the provisions of section 133 duly observed in Quebec, but English was used, along with French, as a language of service to the public. Indeed, some documents were routinely published in English only.

Beyond that, English Canadians enjoyed a numerical presence in provincial cabinets that greatly exceeded their share of the population. From 1867 to 1897, three of the six or seven cabinet members were usually anglophones. In fact, two anglophones were premier for a short time. The Speaker of the Legislative Council (the appointed upper body) was usually an anglophone.[56] Moreover, anglophones were well represented in senior portfolios. In fact, the minister of finance was almost always an English Canadian, who reportedly was usually selected by the Bank of Montreal.[57]

Dualism was also the rule in the new province of Manitoba created in 1870. Here it was due to the fact that anglophones and francophones (largely Métis) were almost equal in numbers. This dualism was to be short-lived. By the 1890s the francophone proportion (including Métis) had fallen to about 10 per cent of the population and English was made the sole language of the Manitoba legislature.[58]

In short, with Confederation dualism persisted primarily in Quebec itself rather than in federal institutions. Rather than a complement to federalism, dualism was a way of blunting federalism, preventing the domination of provincial institutions that would have followed from French Canadians' overwhelming demographic preponderance in the new province. Moreover, it seemed, dualism was acceptable only to protect anglophone minorities, not francophone ones.

On the other hand, as Confederation took form, federalism became quite robust—far more so than many of the Fathers of Confederation, especially Upper Canadian, had anticipated or would have wanted. It was to be expected that French-Canadian élites in Quebec would value Quebec's full autonomy as a province. For them, federalism was the great compensation for the loss of dualism in Canadian institutions. At first, however, the expression of provincialism was muted by the dominance of the Quebec provincial legislature by *bleu* allies of the Conservative government in Ottawa.[59]

The wariness about Canadian domination with which the Maritimes had viewed Confederation ensured that they would be strongly attached to their provincial governments. Indeed, a year after Confederation the Nova Scotia legislature passed a resolution calling for the repeal of the new arrangement.[60]

It was perhaps less predictable that Ontario's provincial government would become a leading champion of provincial autonomy, given the aversion that many Upper Canadians participating in the Confederation debates seemed to have had for federalism. None the less, some Upper Canadians had in fact developed a strong loyalty to their region before Confederation.[61] Beyond that, Ontario's autonomism was fuelled by class conflict between Ontario farmers and lumbermen, on the one hand, and financial interests allied with Ottawa, on the other.[62] All this was reinforced by partisan conflict between Liberal administrations in Ontario and the Conservative federal government[63] and by the normal self-interest of political élites in the importance of their governments. These factors all combined to make the Ontario government, especially under Oliver Mowat, a leader in defending provincial jurisdiction and powers.[64]

Indeed, Oliver Mowat joined forces with Quebec premier Honoré Mercier to convene the first interprovincial conference in 1887, which five of the seven provinces attended (Conservative-controlled British Columbia and Prince Edward Island declined). Held in Quebec City, the conference approved of 22 resolutions calling either for constitutional changes to limit federal powers, such as abolition of its 'quasi-unitary' powers, or for increased federal subsidies and access to sources of revenue.[65]

The ultimate evidence of the extent to which the federal principle had taken hold was the celebration by provincial leaders of a new doctrine to justify provincial autonomy: the compact theory of Confederation. The theory was first elaborated in the early 1880s by a Quebec judge, T.J.J. Loranger, who expressed alarm at the threat to specifically French-Canadian interests posed by federal encroachments on Quebec's provincial autonomy. Loranger declared, 'The confederation of the British Provinces was the result of a compact entered into by the Provinces and the Imperial Parliament which, in enacting the British North America Act, simply ratified it.'[66] From this it followed that there could be no enhancement of federal powers without the consent of all the provincial governments.[67] The theory was quickly embraced by Quebec Premier Honoré Mercier, who elaborated it at the 1887 interprovincial conference. In fact, it became a basic tenet of the political leadership of most provinces. By the end of the century: 'It would be difficult to find a prominent politician who was not willing to pay at least lip-service to the principle of provincial rights and its theoretical underpinning, the compact theory.'[68]

THE REVIVAL OF DUALISM

In embracing the concept of federalism, Mowat and other English-Canadian provincial leaders did not, however, embrace the spirit in which French Canadians viewed it. For most French Canadians the ultimate purpose of Quebec's provincial autonomy was to protect their cultural distinctiveness. For English-Canadian leaders the purpose of provincial autonomy was quite different. Indeed, time would show that they were quite prepared to use provincial autonomy against the distinctiveness of French-Canadian minorities in their own provinces.

At the time of Confederation, French-Canadian leaders from Quebec had little concern about any French-Canadian communities in other parts of the Dominion. Ever since the Constitution Act created a distinct Lower Canada in 1791, it was in Quebec that French Canadians sought to maintain their nationality.[69] The union of Lower Canada with Upper Canada had not led Quebec's French Canadians to extend their notion of a *canadien* nation. To be sure a certain number of Quebec French Canadians did emigrate to Ontario, and the diocese of Ottawa was part of the Church's Quebec province.[70] But the focus of Quebec's French-Canadian leaders remained centred on Quebec. Thus, the main virtue of the United Canadas for Quebec lay in the extent to which, through the development of dual ministries and a certain application of the double-majority principle to legislative decision making, Lower Canadians (and the *canadien* majority) were able to exercise some autonomy.

During the Confederation debates there had been no French-speaking participants from Canada West or the Maritime colonies. And of course no provisions were adopted to protect French language rights in the other provinces. Only denominational rights were protected, and that was essentially the indirect result of the campaign of English Canadians in Quebec to protect their position. The French-Canadian delegates were preoccupied with Quebec's status since protecting the *canadien* nation meant securing the autonomy of Quebec.

None the less, as Arthur Silver has demonstrated, a series of events forced French Canadians in Quebec to take account of the fate and tribulations of

French-Canadian communities beyond their borders. In 1871 the New Brunswick legislature passed a statute preventing local school boards from supporting denominational schools. Although the act did not specifically refer to the province's *Acadiens*, Quebec's French-Canadian leaders did become concerned about this treatment of fellow Catholics. Then, in 1885 Ontario forced its unilingual French schools to become bilingual. As members of these minorities took their complaints to Ottawa for redress, Quebec's French Canadians became more aware of their fate.[71]

Events in Manitoba were to have the most powerful impact on Quebec. In 1870 the Métis leader Louis Riel led a rebellion against the terms under which the Red River settlement had become British territory, subject to transfer to Canada. In the process, Riel was responsible for the execution of an English-Canadian opponent. In the 1880s, Riel was at the centre of a new Métis uprising, which was finally put down in 1885. Riel was sentenced to hang and, after the mobilization of Ontario opinion in favour of execution and of Quebec opinion against it, he was indeed executed.

As Silver carefully details,[72] immediately after Confederation French Canadians still had no particular interest in the Canadian North West and were largely opposed to annexation of its territory. However, they developed a certain sympathy for Riel in 1870, especially after they began to see the Ontario campaign against Riel as a campaign against French Catholics. Even then, Riel and his followers were still seen as 'savages'.[73] Their success in obtaining French language rights under the Manitoba Act of 1870 made them useful allies, but they were not fellow French Canadians. During the 1870s, a debate over whether Ottawa should grant amnesty to the participants in the Red River rebellion aroused French Canadians to a clearer identification with the Métis cause.

However, when in 1885 Riel was sentenced to hang, emotions in Quebec reached a fever pitch. Believing that Riel was basically insane and that, in addition, the conditions of the Métis constituted extenuating circumstances, French Canadians tended to see the sentence as an expression of English-Canadian hatred for all French-speaking Catholics. With the hanging, emotions exploded. French-Canadian newspapers declared: 'The death of Riel is an impious declaration of war, an audacious defiance hurled at the French-Canadian race' and 'We all know that they'd have liked to slit all our throats, to kill all of us French Canadians.'[74]

By allowing the execution to take place, the Macdonald government had confirmed that, under Confederation, Quebec French Canadians could not count upon the federal government to protect their interests. In a confrontation between the two linguistic groups, the English-Canadian majority was bound to prevail at the federal level. French Canadians could rely only on the Quebec government to embrace their interests.[75]

Coupled with these developments beyond Quebec's borders, a series of events in Canada's external relations underscored further the inability of French Canadians to make their positions prevail in the federal government. Canada was being called upon to participate in imperial military ventures, and many English Canadians welcomed these opportunities to express their identity as British North Americans. French Canadians, however, tended to reject such ventures, seeing themselves as members of a distinct *canadien* nationality.

First, at the turn of the century Britain called upon Canada to commit Canadian troops to fight in the Boer War. English Canadians were favourable; French Canadians were strongly opposed. Although he first relied on volunteers, Prime Minister Wilfrid Laurier did send a contingent of regular Canadian troops in 1899.

Second, in response to British pressure, Laurier created a small Canadian navy in 1910. While English-Canadian Conservative politicians denounced it as too small, French-Canadian nationalists called it a dangerous move that would make participation in imperial wars inevitable.

Most important of all, during the First World War the federal Union government of Robert L. Borden imposed conscription for overseas service, evoking a tidal wave of protest in Quebec. Before imposing the measure, Borden had called a federal election, in which his government won only three seats in Quebec.

As if that were not enough, the question of French-Canadian minority rights outside Quebec emerged once again. In 1912, just before the war, Ontario passed Regulation 17, which restricted French-language education, and in 1916 Manitoba abolished bilingual schools.

A 'DOUBLE COMPACT'

It was clear that the established version of the compact theory was no longer an adequate protection for French-Canadian interests, since the provinces could evoke it to fend off criticism of their treatment of French-Canadian minorities or federal intervention to force a remedy. And it was no defence against untoward actions of the federal government in its own jurisdictions, whether it be the hanging of Riel or the commitment of Canadians to imperial military adventures.

It fell to Henri Bourassa, the leading French-Canadian nationalist at the turn of the century, to reformulate the theory. This new version was to become deeply rooted in Quebec and to shape fundamentally the crisis in which Canada now finds itself.

In 1902 Bourassa presented the notion of a 'double compact'. Reaching back to the United Canadas, he seized upon its dualism, arguing that it constituted a moral premise of Confederation:

> The imperial statute which the current government has given us is only the force of a double contract. One was concluded between the French and the English of the old province of Canada, while the aim of the other was to bring together the scattered colonies of British North America. We are thus party to two contracts—one national and one political. We must keep a careful eye on the integrity of these treaties.[76]

Thus, beyond a 'political' contract, to which all the provinces were party, there was a 'national' contract, which was the exclusive product of the United Canadas. The substance of the two contracts differed. Apparently the national contract guaranteed French-English duality whereas the political contract protected French Canadians from the imposition of imperial military obligations by their English-Canadian compatriots.[77]

There is in fact a certain plausibility to the notion of a dualistic contract that was distinctive to the United Canadas and its successors. Historian George C.P. Stanley has shown how statements by leading Upper Canadian politicians demonstrate that, for many of them, 'the mutual acceptance of equality of status was a vital and fundamental principle of the constitution; that it constituted, if not an unbreakable pact, at least a gentleman's agreement between the two racial groups which went to make up the population.'[78] Not surprising is Lafontaine's 1849 declaration of support of 'the principle of looking upon the Act of Union as a confederation of two provinces.' More striking is Sir John A. Macdonald's 1861 claim that 'the Union was a distinct bargain, a solemn contract' and his reference in 1865 to the 'Treaty of Union' between Lower and Upper Canada.[79] (Considering that the creation of the United Canadas was imposed by the British authorities in an effort to assimilate the francophones, this was a remarkable reinterpretation of the arrangement.)

To be sure, as they entered into discussions with Maritime leaders about a new Confederation, the leaders of the United Canadas began to refer to a pact between territorial units as opposed to 'races'.[80] But even then the notion of compact remained a primarily 'Canadian' one, which did not have the same resonance for the Maritime participants. And for the Canadians it retained its 'bi-racial' connotations since it was 'in its origin, a racial concept'. In short, there was a certain basis to Henri Bourassa's claim that there existed a national compact formed in the United Canadas and guaranteeing cultural duality.[81]

Of course, Bourassa did not claim that the terms of the compact could be directly derived from the British North America Act, the formal text of Confederation. Neither did Stanley, for that matter. Rather Bourassa (and Stanley) pointed to 'the spirit of the constitution'. For Bourassa it would be foolish to rely exclusively on a detailed exegesis of the Act's provisions without considering the origins of British constitutionalism and 'the particular circumstances that preceded and surrounded the signing of the federal pact.'[82] As Ramsay Cook argues, 'Bourassa's cultural compact was, in the last analysis, a moral compact.'[83]

Yet how could such a cultural compact be applicable throughout the whole of Canada? Bourassa had offered a second line of reasoning in 1905, during a debate over whether minority rights should be recognized in the creation of Alberta and Saskatchewan. Referring to section 93 of the BNA Act, which guarantees denominational schools, Bourassa said it was intended to guarantee that 'a man, in whatever province of Canada he may choose to be his abode, can rest assured that justice and equality will reign and that no matter what the majority may attempt they cannot persecute the minority.'[84] He acknowledged that this contract was unwritten but argued that it dated as far back as the Quebec Act of 1774. He pointed out, moreover, that the territory upon which the two provinces were to be established had been bought with the money of all Canadians, Catholic and Protestant, English-Canadian and French-Canadian.[85]

Two additional points about Bourassa's vision of dualism must be stressed. First, if the notion of a cultural compact was developed largely in response to the use that some governments had made of their provincial autonomy at the expense of their French-Canadian minorities, it was not to diminish, let alone replace, the long-standing notion of a compact among all the provinces.[86] After all, Quebec still remained the heart of French Canada, and Quebec's provincial autonomy was the indispensable first defence of French Canada's interests. In Bourassa's words, Quebec was 'the particular inheritance of French Canada'.[87] Thus, the two ideas remained together in an uneasy co-existence.[88] The contract was a double contract.

In fact, within one formulation of the double contract, the cultural compact was derived from Quebec's provincial autonomy. In 1912 Bourassa argued that, since the main purpose of federalism was to preserve French Quebeckers' nationality as French Canadians, then the possessors of that nationality should have a 'right to equality throughout the whole of this confederation'.[89]

Second, while strongly committed to the extension of French language rights throughout Canada, Bourassa insisted that the two cultures must remain separate and distinct. His opposition to Canada's participation in imperial military ventures had made him a strong Canadian nationalist, but his nationalism rested on a particular conception of Canada. He did not see it as a single undifferentiated nation. Rather, as his reformulation of the compact theory suggests, he saw Canada as composed of two distinct collectivities. As Bourassa declared in 1912, he was seeking not 'some bastard fusion of the two races, in which they would lose their distinctive qualities and characteristics, but a fruitful alliance of the two races, each one remaining distinctly itself, but finding within the Canadian confederation enough room and liberty to live together side by side.'[90]

In fact, partly because he saw Canada in such rigorously dualist terms Bourassa was not prepared to support Canadian independence from Britain. Despite his fierce opposition to British imperialism, he had to recognize that Canada was not ready for independence because 'a more open clearer agreement' did not exist between the "races".'[91]

In the course of a famous response to Jules Tardival, a turn-of-the century French-Canadian separatist, Bourassa declared:

> The nation which we wish to see developed is the Canadian nation, composed of French Canadians and English Canadians, that is to say a nation of two elements separated by language and religion and by the legal arrangements necessary for the preservation of their respective traditions, but united by a sentiment of brotherhood in a common attachment to a common country.[92]

Thus, Bourassa was careful to stress that the two 'elements' were 'separated' by language and religion, as well as by the 'legal arrangements' necessary to preserve them.

However sincere may have been Bourassa's attachment to Canada, his vision had little resonance with English Canadians, most of whom were unsympathetic to his fierce rejection of imperial military obligations. At the time few English Canadians embraced his notion of a cultural compact.[93] The compact theory had become deeply rooted among English-Canadian politics, but only as a compact among provinces.

In Quebec, however, the notion of a double contract, in which an interprovincial compact was coupled with a national compact between the two founding peoples, became firmly entrenched. Most French-Canadian constitutional scholars were convinced of its existence and vigorously defended it in exchanges with their English-Canadian colleagues.[94] It was invoked regularly by Quebec's political élites. When the Quebec provincial government of Maurice Duplessis passed a law in 1953 authorizing the creation of a royal commission (the Tremblay Commission) on constitutional questions, it began the law with the statement:'Whereas the Canadian Confederation, born of an agreement between the four pioneer provinces, is first and above all a pact of honour between the two great races which founded it.'[95] By the same token, in its report the commission duly affirmed the notion of a double compact.[96]

By some accounts, the notion of dualistic compact had by then become a basic premise of all francophones in Quebec. In 1958 the dean of francophone sociologists, Jean-C. Falardeau, declared that however much English Canadians might dismiss such a notion, 'the sociologically significant and important fact' is that since the end of the nineteenth century French Canadians have understood Canada in those terms:

> It became a persistent theme, articulated in various forms by French Canada's religious and political leaders right up to the present day. Whether or not English-Canadian commentators and legal scholars find it acceptable, it will persist as one of the most tenacious elements of the way in which French Canadians understand the history of their Canada.[97]

It is clear that during the first century of Confederation English Canadians and French Canadians became rooted in fundamentally different conceptions of the country they shared. For many English Canadians, Canada was simply the North American expression of a British nationality. After all, the institutions created through Confederation had been carefully fashioned on that assumption. As Confederation developed, it took on much more of a federal form than had been expected. Indeed, by the late 1800s, the English-Canadian political élites generally agreed that Confederation itself was based on a compact among the provinces. But the predominant sense of nationality was British, and the symbols of the Canadian political order remained resolutely so.

For their part, the francophones of Quebec continued to view Canada in terms of their own nationality as French Canadians or *Canadiens*. And this nationality was firmly anchored in the territory and political institutions of Quebec. Formally established in 1791, through the Constitution Act, this link between French Canadians and Quebec had persisted without interruption. Even the forced merger of Quebec with present-day Ontario had not shaken the bond; indeed union had reinforced it. Involvement in Confederation, and concern with issues beyond Quebec's borders, had not broken this link either: Quebec remained 'the particular inheritance' of French Canadians. Instead, francophone leaders had been led to portray Quebec as central to a dualistic racial compact, supplementing the notion of a provincial compact now firmly established in English Canada.

With the turn of the century, Henri Bourassa and other French-Canadian leaders had started to contest openly Canada's identification with Britain and British nationality and to champion a Canadian nationhood. In this, they matched an emerging sense among English Canadians of a distinctly Canadian nationality. Yet these two conceptions of Canadian nationhood were fundamentally different. For the French-Canadian political and intellectual élites, any idea of a Canadian nationality was rigorously rooted in cultural dualism. Canada was a 'bicultural pact' and Quebec was a partner to that pact. The emerging sense of Canadian nationalism in English Canada had no room for such notions. Indeed, it had little patience for compacts of any kind, whether between races or among provinces.

AFTER THE SECOND WORLD WAR: COMPETING NATIONALISMS

During the Second World War, these competing notions of nationality led to a bitter struggle over the issue of conscription for overseas military service. As a 1942 Canada-wide referendum clearly established, anglophones were overwhelmingly in favour while francophones were opposed, claiming that they had no obligation to fight Britain's wars. None the less, the federal government did send some conscripted soldiers overseas. After the war, the contradiction in definitions of nationality gave rise to a new struggle, between Ottawa and Quebec City.

Ottawa as the 'National' Government

There were a variety of reasons why the federal government began to assert its new role as the 'national' government of Canada. Among many English Canadians, if not French Canadians, pride in the exploits of Canadians in the Second World War heightened the sense of Canadian nationality, as did Britain's post-war decline. During the war, Ottawa had already assumed unprecedented predominance over the provinces. Citing the demands of war, it had deployed emergency powers and persuaded the provinces to allow it to monopolize personal and corporate tax. As the war came to an end, federal officials naturally wished to preserve their new power. Finally, the Keynesian doctrines of economic management and elaboration of a welfare state provided a tailor-made rationale for Ottawa to remain the primary government. Both the depression that followed the First World War and the Great Depression of the 1930s were cited as examples of what might happen if the federal government were to relinquish its new-found ability to steer the Canadian economy and society.

In the post-war years Ottawa took a series of steps to formalize Canadian nationhood. In 1946, the Canadian Citizenship Act was passed, making Canadian citizenship distinct from the status of British subject. In 1949 the Supreme Court was made the final court of appeal in all matters, and the right of Canadians to take cases to the Judicial Committee of the Privy Council was abolished. In 1952 a Canadian was appointed governor-general for the first time. The term 'Dominion' was quietly discarded,[98] and the federal government increasingly referred to itself as the 'national' government.

By the same token, Ottawa elaborated a complex of social programs, based on the notion that all Canadians were entitled to certain minimum public benefits wherever they might live. As the 1944 Speech from the Throne declared:

> Plans for the establishment of a national minimum of social security and human welfare should be advanced as rapidly as possible. Such a national minimum contemplates useful employment for all who are willing to work; standards for nutrition and housing adequate to ensure the health of the whole population; and social insurance against privation resulting from unemployment, from accident, from the death of the bread-winner, from ill-health and from old age.[99]

This agenda amounted to no less than a 'new National Policy', to use Donald Smiley's evocative phase.[100]

At the same time, the federal government became more active in supporting distinctively Canadian cultural production, as a way of reinforcing the national identity of Canadians. In 1949, it established a Royal Commission on National Development in the Arts, Letters and Sciences, declaring in an order-in-council, 'It is in the national interest to give encouragement to institutions which express national feeling, promote common understanding, and add to the variety and richness of Canadian life.'[101] The commission had a single chair, Vincent Massey, even though in Quebec it was often dubbed 'the Massey-Lévesque Commission', suggesting that commissioner Georges-Henri Lévesque was co-chair. The commission called upon the federal government to undertake two major new initiatives to support national cultural life: to create a Canada Council to foster cultural activity and to establish a program of federal grants to universities. Both were adopted during what was, in Claude Bissell's words, 'a period of intense nationalism and pride'.[102]

This new conception of Ottawa as a national government meant a very different relationship with the provincial governments. If Ottawa was to meet

new responsibilities to maintain national standards in such areas as social policy and post-secondary education, it would have to act in jurisdictions that
had been assigned to the provinces under the BNA Act and from which, up
to that point, Ottawa had been largely absent. In part, this was accomplished
through conditional grants that Ottawa made available to the provincial governments on condition that they be devoted to designated programs and
abide by conditions set by Ottawa. But it also meant that the federal government was providing funds directly in areas of provincial jurisdiction to
individuals, as in the case of family allowances, and to institutions, as in the
case of grants to universities. To do all this Ottawa tried to maintain its
wartime role as exclusive collector of income tax, a source of revenue that,
under the BNA Act, it shared with the provinces. In short, the provinces were
to be assigned a subordinate place in 'the new National Policy'.[103]

As the federal government pursued these goals, sometimes in the face of
fierce opposition from some provinces, it was quite prepared to challenge
long-standing notions about the prerogatives of the provincial governments.
The compact theory had long been rejected by federal officials. Accordingly,
during the 1940s Ottawa began to call upon the British parliament to make
amendments to the BNA Act, which remained a British statute, without first
obtaining the approval of the provincial governments. In each case, it argued
that, since the changes did not affect provincial responsibilities, prior approval
by the provincial governments was not necessary. Each of the requests was
granted. Two of them, including the amendment governing Newfoundland's
union with Canada, were made over Quebec's objections. Finally, in 1949
Ottawa obtained an amendment to the BNA Act giving it the power to alter
unilaterally certain parts of the Act that, it contended, did not affect the
provinces.[104] In effect, Ottawa rendered moot the essential premise of the
compact theory: that the constitution was, in its entirety, a pact among the
provinces that could not be altered without their consent.

Despite Quebec's consistent opposition to Ottawa's initiatives, the later
ones in fact had been the work of a French-Canadian Prime Minister, Louis
St Laurent. Of mixed parentage and completely bilingual and bicultural,[105]
Louis Stephen St Laurent saw Canada in resolutely individualist terms, dismissing any notion of a dualist Canada composed of distinct collectivities:

> He saw the relationship between French and English Canadians not on a
> group, but on an individual basis, as citizens of the same state, with equal
> rights. He described his concept of Canadian citizenship as 'a situation of
> absolute equality, equality not only in the text of our constitutional laws but
> practical equality in the daily application of these texts, in the real situation
> of each individual . . . in his everyday relations with his fellow citizens.[106]

From the outset of his career in federal politics, St Laurent had explicitly rejected the compact theory of Canada, flatly declaring in 1943, as justice minister, 'Confederation was not really a pact among the provinces.'[107] Hence, he regularly insisted that Ottawa had the right to change unilaterally parts of the constitution that did not directly involve the provinces. Once he even appeared to confirm that Parliament had the power to eliminate application of section 133 regarding the use of English and French, although he was clearly opposed to such a measure.[108] In a famous 1954 Quebec City speech in which he denounced Quebec separatism and proclaimed that francophones were fully able to compete with other Canadians, St Laurent scandalized Quebec nationalists by declaring that 'the province of Quebec can be a province like the others.'[109]

With St Laurent as prime minister, appealing to an incipient Canadian nationalism, asserting Ottawa's pre-eminence as the national government, and proclaiming Ottawa's constitutional powers, the federal government's challenge to the predominant French-Canadian view of Canada could not have been clearer. In many ways St Laurent's tenure clearly presaged that of a later prime minister of similar background, Pierre Elliott Trudeau.

Quebec: The National Government of French Canada

The concerted post-war effort of Ottawa to assume the mantle of Canada's national government reinforced Quebec City in its historical role as government of the French-Canadian nationality, which had become well established during the first few decades of this century.

The dualism of post-Confederation Quebec had begun to decline as the government became a more clearly francophone institution. The economic predominance of Quebec's anglophone minority remained very much intact, but its political élites gravitated to Ottawa. After 1920 anglophone representation in the cabinet was limited to two members, and after 1994 all finance ministers were francophones.[110]

Moreover, the various crises over the status of francophones outside Quebec and Canada's imperial military obligations had a marked effect on Quebec's provincial politics. Reaction against the hanging of Louis Riel had resulted in the election of Honoré Mercier's Parti national, born from an infusion of the provincial Liberal Party with French-Canadian nationalists. Anger at the imposition of conscription during the First World War had in 1918 led to a resolution in the provincial legislative assembly proposing that Quebec leave Canada if this should be the wish of the rest of the country.[111] More important, it had sealed the fate of the provincial Conservative Party.

Having failed to win power in 1931, despite the onset of the Depression and the best efforts of a populist party leader to exploit resentment against the English-Canadian 'trusts', the Conservatives joined with French-Canadian nationalist forces. In 1933, Conservative leader Maurice Duplessis entered into a formal alliance with Action libérale nationale, a group of nationalists and discontented Liberals. Consolidated under Duplessis's firm leadership, and dubbed the Union nationale, this coalition won control of the Quebec government in 1936. After losing power in 1939, the Union nationale was re-elected in 1944, partly by exploiting the French-Canadians' anger at conscription during the Second World War. Confirmed in his nationalist vocation, Duplessis found plenty of ammunition in the need to respond to Ottawa's post-war campaign to become a national government and to intervene in areas hitherto left for the provinces.

The most important elaboration of Quebec's role as the national government of French Canada was in fact a direct response to a federal initiative. The report of the Massey Commission provoked the Duplessis government to appoint a royal commission on constitutional problems, commonly known as the Tremblay Commission. After years of deliberation, the Tremblay Commission produced a voluminous report offering not only a diagnosis of the conflicts within Canadian federalism and an outline of the responsibilities which rightly belong to Quebec, but a statement of the underlying nature of French-Canadian society.[112]

The Tremblay Commission's deeply conservative view of French-Canadian society set the tone of the report as a whole, which was based on the assumption that French Canada was by nature a Catholic society in which the role of government should be limited by the historical reliance upon private institutions. Thus the recommendations concentrated on limiting the power of the federal government rather than expanding that of the Quebec government. On this basis, the constitutional framework established in 1867 was quite satisfactory, as long as Ottawa retreated from the many intrusions into provincial jurisdictions that had begun in the post-war years.

Although its constitutional position may have been conservative, as was its view of French-Canadian society, the commission offered a strong challenge to Ottawa's claim to be a national government. If 'nation' was to be understood in sociological terms, then Ottawa's claim was a clear threat to the French-Canadian nation, which was centred in Quebec. If 'nation' was to be understood politically, then the Quebec government had as much claim to national status as Ottawa.[113] Moreover, the commission's demand that the federal government should defer to the provinces in social and cultural policy[114] threatened much of the edifice of programs and services that Ottawa was developing in the name of the Canadian nation.

The Duplessis government demonstrated in quite concrete terms how Ottawa's efforts to establish national programs could be undermined by

Quebec's own claims to national status. During the 1950s, the Quebec government simply refused to participate in a number of conditional-grant programs that Ottawa offered to the provinces. These included grants regarding hospital insurance, vocational training, forestry, civil defence, and the Trans-Canada Highway[115]. In addition, the Duplessis government ordered Quebec universities to refuse the direct grants that the federal government established in 1951. The funds that the universities would have received simply accumulated in Ottawa until 1960, when Ottawa and Quebec City agreed to allow Quebec to recover through a federal tax abatement the money intended for universities.

To be sure, this tactic was highly effective in blunting Ottawa's plans, but it was a costly one for the Quebec government. By one estimate, Quebec's non-participation in conditional-grant programs cost it $82,031,000 in federal funds, or $15.60 per capita of the Quebec population, in the fiscal year 1959/60 alone.[116] Only a government that was not itself committed to rapid expansion of the role of the state could contemplate using it. During the 1960s, Quebec governments were to use other strategies, which were even more threatening to Ottawa's plans.

The Duplessis government's refusal to participate in federal programs demonstrated the potential for conflict that lay in the federal government's post-war assumption of the mantle of national government. It also dramatically revealed how the understanding of Canada held by French-Canadian élites differed from that of their English-Canadian counterparts. For, by and large, Quebec's francophone élites supported the Duplessis government in its vigorous defence of provincial autonomy and in the claim to national status that underlay this defence.[117] In the rest of Canada, political and intellectual élites instead were quite favourable to Ottawa's new initiatives. For that matter, Quebec was the only provincial government that refused to take part in federal shared-cost programs.

In short, during the post-war years the federal government challenged in a way it never had before the established French-Canadian understanding of Canada. In the name of its new role as the seat of the Canadian nation, the federal government began to develop the symbols of a distinctly Canadian nation, to construct an edifice of social, economic, and even cultural programs designed to develop and strengthen the Canadian nation, and to establish national standards of social services that all Canadians, as Canadians, could expect as a basic right. Inevitably, this entailed involvement in provincial jurisdictions. By and large, English-Canadian élites and public opinion welcomed the new power that Ottawa was assuming and the nationalist discourse upon which it rested. Only in Quebec was there resistance, as francophone élites defended the historical notion of a distinctly French-

Canadian nation and of the Quebec government as protector of that nation. Clearly, the new Canadian nationalism which Ottawa was articulating had the potential to divide English Canadians and French Canadians more profoundly than ever before.

The post-war years had also revealed another phenomenon in the person of Louis St Laurent. Given his own bicultural roots, St Laurent found especially congenial the idea of a distinctly Canadian nationality and Ottawa's role as a national government. At the same time, he could be broadly dismissive of the predominant French-Canadian understanding of Canada, to the point of declaring that Quebec was simply 'a province like the others'. In these ways, the first prime minister raised in a bicultural milieu was also a portent of things to come.

From the outset English-Canadian and French-Canadian élites viewed Confederation in very different ways, owing to the profound differences in historical experience, sense of nationality, and central preoccupations that they brought to the new arrangement. As a result, at the time of Confederation they held radically opposed understandings of the nature of the new regime. If they supported it, they did so for very different reasons.

The differences were to persist. The English-Canadian understandings of Canada were to change, as the notion of a British nationality gave way in the post-war years to that of a distinctly Canadian nationality. Despite the fierce determination of many English-Canadian Fathers of Confederation to establish a unitary system, as Confederation developed, most English-Canadian élites became clearly wedded to federalism and even to the notion that it rested upon a historical compact. Yet, however much English-Canadian views of Canada may change, they remained fundamentally different from those of French Canadians, who continued to be firmly committed to a French-Canadian nationality. For them, federalism had a different purpose, the defence of culture as opposed to regional or economic interest, and the compact that underlay it had to be understood as a 'double compact'. Ultimately, Confederation could not erase the French-Canadian belief in dualism as a basic principle both of political organization and of justice.

Yet the notions of federalism and compacts at least provided French-Canadian and English-Canadian élites with a common discourse: they simply interpreted the concepts differently. The post-war years demonstrated the reaction that could arise in Quebec if these concepts should be challenged by a federal government that claimed for itself the title of 'national' government.

CHAPTER 2

The 1960s:
Coming to Terms
with Duality and
Quebec Nationalism

The 1960s were marked by an open dialogue and debate about the nature of Canada that died with the end of the decade, not to be repeated in the 25 years since. During the 1960s francophone and anglophone Canadians confronted, in a way they never had before, their fundamentally divergent conceptions of Canada. The trigger for that process was, of course, developments in Quebec.

CHANGES IN QUEBEC: FORCING ENGLISH CANADA TO TAKE NOTICE

As we have seen, most French-Canadian notions of Canadian dualism had always afforded a privileged status to Quebec as the centre of the francophone collectivity. In the early 1960s, this pre-eminent status of Quebec was made much more explicit as nationalist thought and strategies were fundamentally recast.

The New Liberal Nationalism
The very definition of the nation began to change: in place of a 'French Canada', defined in ethnic terms and present throughout Canada wherever people of French descent continued to speak French, intellectual and political leaders referred to the nation as 'Quebec', a territorial entity consisting of the province of Quebec. Although the Quebec nation was to be predominantly French-speaking, it would be difficult to base it on ethnicity. This gradual shift to a territorial conception of nation was due, in turn, to the ascendancy of notions of social and political organization that were difficult

to accommodate in the older idea of a French-Canadian nation: those of a modern, secular society.

However sanctified a rural agrarian society might have been in traditional nationalist thought, its fate had long been sealed. The modernization of French-Canadian society was already under way at the turn of the century.[1] By the 1930s, Quebec had become a predominantly urban, industrial society. If French Canada was to survive, it would be as a modern society. Only in Quebec, where French-speakers were the overwhelming majority, was it possible to imagine the full economic, social, and cultural institutions of a modern society functioning in the French language. Even in Quebec the construction of a fully modern francophone society was a daunting task given both the limitations of the Church-controlled private institutions that continued to dominate education, health, and social services and the extent to which ownership and management of the Quebec economy remained largely in the hands of anglophones. Only through intervention by the state could these constraints be overcome. By definition, the state that would modernize the francophone nation had to be a state that was itself under the control of francophones: the government of Quebec. In short, the Quebec government had to become the *moteur principal* of the new Quebec nation.

Sociologically, the conversion of Quebec nationalism to the goals of modernity was due to the multitude of changes in French Quebec society that had been under way during the first part of this century: urbanization, industrialization, the emergence of mass media, and, in particular, the rise of new social classes. The bearers of the ideology tended to be a new middle class of intellectuals, academics, administrators, and other salaried professionals.[2] In their campaigns to have the Quebec state assume more active roles, the new middle class could usually count on the strong support of organized labour.

In ideological terms, the transformation of nationalist discourse resulted from the long-delayed triumph of liberalism in French Quebec. In the early 1800s liberal conceptions of political authority and the role of the Church had been proclaimed by French-Canadian liberal professionals. They had contributed to the abortive rebellions of the 1830s. But with the failure of the rebellions and the subsequent dominance of the Church in French Quebec, political and social liberalism was very much on the defensive. The modernizing processes of this century fostered a resurgence of liberal forces. By the 1950s, francophone intellectual and social leaders were decrying the anti-democratic tendencies of the Duplessis regime and calling for an expansion in the social and economic responsibilities of the Quebec state.[3] With the election in 1960 of the Liberal government of Jean Lesage, in which the francophone new middle class was a major presence, liberal forces had a new foothold in the Quebec state and the period of the Quiet Revolution began.

Many of the greatest achievements of the Quiet Revolution can be seen only as expressions of liberal ideals. Educational reform involved not only the creation of a Ministry of Education and construction of a complete public system, but a concern with social equality in public institutions, as with the CEGEPs' combination of pre-university and vocational education. Electoral practices were fundamentally reformed by establishing the autonomy of the Director General of Elections, reducing disparities in the sizes of constituencies, and regulating party finances through measures, such as reimbursement of electoral expenses, that were then among the most progressive in Western democracies.[4] In the overhaul of labour relations, the right to strike was granted in the public sector, for the first time in North America.

At the same time, the discourse of the Lesage government was also resolutely nationalist. The government proclaimed that the Québécois had to become 'maîtres chez nous'—'masters in our own house'. The nationalization of private electrical firms to create a comprehensive public hydro utility was justified on a variety of grounds, but certainly one of them was the desire to reduce anglophone dominance of the upper levels of the Quebec economy. It was primarily in this way that the nationalization would bring about the 'libération économique' of Quebec.

In effect, the Quiet Revolution represented a new departure for Quebec: the combining of nationalism with liberalism. Most observers have interpreted the Quiet Revolution in precisely these terms.[5] Yet, for one prominent observer, Pierre Elliott Trudeau, such a combination of nationalism and liberalism was logically impossible. Upon his rejection of the Quiet Revolution would hang much of the future of Canadian politics.

Once it had become predominant among French Quebec's intellectual and political leaders, the new liberal nationalism virtually dictated a radical re-examination of Canada's political structures. Within the new understanding of Quebec and its needs, old Canadian ways of doing things that had always been sore points for Quebec's leaders now became intolerable. And their long-standing assumptions about Quebec and its place in Canada now had to be made explicit.

The Need to Restructure Canadian Federalism

Once the francophone leaders had fully embraced modernity and could in fact claim that, at least in Quebec, their society already possessed the defining traits of modernity, the old ideals of dualism and equality with the rest of

Canada took on a new urgency. As a modern society, francophone society could settle for no less than full equality with its anglophone partner. Moreover, since this modernity achieved its fullest expression in Quebec the demands for equality between francophone Canada and its anglophone equivalent tended to focus on Quebec.

The central place of the Quebec government in the project of a modern francophone society gave a greatly expanded meaning to the long-standing claim that Quebec was not 'a province like the others'. As the fundamental institution of the Quebec nation, the Quebec government could not have the same status as the other provinces. Indeed, the Lesage government systemically replaced the term 'la province du Québec' with 'l'État du Québec'. Not only did the project of a modern Quebec nation require that the Quebec government be confirmed in the status of a national government, but it meant that the Quebec government's powers and resources had to be greatly expanded so that it could assume its new responsibilities.

In short, the new liberal Quebec nationalism gave rise to demands that the Canadian political order be refashioned to conform better to the Canadian duality and the centrality of Quebec within it. In part, this involved symbolic recognition of these two premises, making explicit for all Canadians what had always been understood among francophones. But it also entailed major structural changes in federal institutions and in the place of Quebec in the federal system. In both cases, however, the goal of most Quebec nationalists was to redefine the Canadian relationship, not to terminate it.

These objectives were embraced, in one form or another, by each of the three premiers of Quebec during the 1960s. For Jean Lesage, the preferred formula was a *statut particulier*. In an address in Vancouver in 1965, Lesage insisted that however the status of French might be improved in federal institutions, French Canadians: 'feel that in Quebec there is a government that is able to play an irreplaceable role in the development of their collective identity, their way of living, their civilization, their values. . . . I believe there is nothing wrong, far from it, in recognizing this fact as one of the fundamental elements of Canada's future.'

He noted, 'We are already on the way . . . to establishing the beginnings of a particular status for Quebec' to which might be added new powers, such as relations with other countries. All this was necessary because the Quebec government, 'for historical and demographic reasons, will assume, in addition to the responsibilities that normally belong to a provincial government these days, the special function of being the instrument through which the French-Canadian community affirms itself.'[6]

For Daniel Johnson, the focus initially was more on restructuring Confederation on a bi-national basis. In his 1965 best-selling book, *Egalité ou indépendance*, Johnson wrote, 'This [new Canadian] constitution should, in my opinion, be conceived so that Canada is not only a federation of 10 provinces but a federation in which two nations are equal in law and in fact.'[7]

As premier, however, Johnson insisted upon additional powers for Quebec, declaring at the 1968 constitutional conference: 'Given the insights of our history, the French Canadians of Quebec, who constitute 83 per cent of the francophone population of Canada, cannot be expected to entrust the leadership of their social and cultural life to a government where their representatives are in the minority and, in addition, are bound by ministerial responsibility and party discipline.'[8]

Similarly, at a constitutional conference in 1969, Jean-Jacques Bertrand insisted that Ottawa's proposals for official bilingualism missed the fundamental problem, that of equality between two nations, one of which is centred in Quebec:

> For the French Canadians of Quebec what is important is not the ability to speak, as individuals, their language in the regions of the country where it has little chance of being understood; it is the ability to live collectively in French, to work in French, to build a society in their image; it is the ability to organize their collective life according to their culture.[9]

None of these three premiers was separatist, nor were their two political organizations, the Quebec Liberal Party and the Union nationale. But they were all committed to a major restructuring of Canadian federalism so as to accommodate the new Quebec.

By the same token, during the 1960s most of Quebec's francophone intellectuals contended that the new Quebec nationalism required an extensive restructuring of the Canadian political order. André Laurendeau, the intellectual leader of his generation, who, as we shall see, became co-chair of the Royal Commission on Bilingualism and Biculturalism, believed that the Canadian crisis could not be resolved without a major change in Quebec's constitutional position.[10] Claude Ryan, Laurendeau's successor as editor of Le Devoir, tirelessly promoted the same objective. In 1967 he produced a two-volume supplement to Le Devoir in which 40 experts assessed the concept of special status. Neither Laurendeau nor Ryan was a separatist. Laurendeau had definitively abandoned separatism in his youth, partly from apprehension over the excesses of nationalism.[11] Ryan is a life-long federalist; indeed, as head of the Quebec Liberal Party he was a leader of the federalist forces in the 1980 referendum.

The Limited Strength of Separatism
To be sure, the social and political upheavals of the late 1950s and early 1960s did produce an authentically 'separatist' movement calling for Quebec to

become a fully sovereign state, with little or no economic links to the rest of Canada. Separatist leaders such as Pierre Bourgault, Marcel Chaput, and André D'Allemagne and their Rassemblement pour l'indépendance nationale captured the attention of the English-Canadian press, as did the mail-box bombings by members of the Front de libération du Québec. Moreover, their activities were often referred to by Quebec's political leaders who, seeking a refashioning of the Canadian political order, claimed that rejection of their demands would strengthen the hand of the separatists and lead to the end of Canada.

None the less, separatism remained a minor force throughout the 1960s. Opinion surveys indicated that public support for Quebec independence remained low, averaging 8 per cent in the early 1960s and 11 per cent from 1968 to 1972.[12] Two separatist parties, le Ralliement pour l'indépendance nationale (RIN) and le Ralliement national (RN), did run candidates in the 1966 provincial election, but none was successful; between them the two parties received only 9 per cent of the popular vote[13].

In 1967 René Lévesque adopted the goal of Quebec sovereignty but in a way that assumed a comprehensive continuing relationship with the rest of Canada—indeed he called it a 'new Canadian union'.[14] For that reason, his option had considerably more public appeal than the independence of the RN and RIN.

In sum, during the 1960s, processes of economic and social change within French Quebec, dating back to the turn of the century, had their long-delayed impact and Quebec's political and intellectual leadership mobilized around the project of a modern society. The project was to be a liberal one, the construction of a secular, pluralist society, but it was also a national project, that of the Quebec nation.

For many Quebec francophones, this new Quebec nationalism made several long-standing aspects of the Canadian political order intolerable, such as the under-representation of francophones and the French language in Ottawa and the denial of French-language rights in all provinces but Quebec. Clearly, for Canadian dualism to have any meaning, these matters had to be addressed.

However, the new nationalism involved much more. After all, it was driven by the project of completing the construction of a modern francophone society in Quebec. Of necessity it called for a change in the status and powers of Quebec. To most of Quebec's political leaders this was quite compatible with a continuing Canadian relationship. Indeed, they believed it could be accommodated within a federal order. But it did require that Quebec's specificity be recognized in a new way.

ENGLISH CANADA: GROWTH OF CANADIAN NATIONAL FEELING

For its part English Canada also was becoming increasingly confirmed in a new Canadian nationalism.[15] Unlike Quebec nationalism, this nationalism lacked a clearly defined notion of a people or a national society. And until the late 1960s it lacked a thorough analysis of Canada's economic and cultural dependence on the United States. By and large, the new Canadian nationalism was limited to politics, in particular the status and attributes of the Canadian state.

This growing Canadian nationalism was partly fuelled by the international situation. During the late 1950s, Canada had assumed prominence in the United Nations as a broker among nations and a peacekeeper, culminating in Lester Pearson's part in resolving the Suez crisis. The steady decline of Great Britain had been confirmed by John Diefenbaker's failure to renew trade relations with Great Britain.[16] At the same time throughout the 1960s the US position of world dominance fostered a host of conflicts in relations with its peripheral northern neighbour: the extraterritorial application of US trade laws, American desire to maintain nuclear armed missiles in Canada, Canada's reluctance to support the American intervention in Vietnam, and growing reaction against the predominance of US interests in the Canadian economy.

The strengthening among English Canadians of a Canadian nationalism was also the result of developments in the Canadian state. As we saw in the previous chapter, from the late 1940s onward, Ottawa had drawn upon a new Canadian nationalism to legitimize state actions in a wide range of areas. Acting upon the recommendations of the Massey Commission, the federal government created the Canada Council, which has been crucial to the emergence of an indigenous professional arts community.[17] Through a series of new social measures it sought to define basic services to which all Canadians were entitled. By the same token, it undertook to give greater coherence to the notion of Canadian citizenship.

In quite different ways, the governments of John Diefenbaker and Lester Pearson continued this practice of refashioning federal political institutions to support and incarnate this growing Canadian nationalism. Diefenbaker may have been more solicitous than his Liberal predecessors of the British connection, but his adoption of a Canadian Bill of Rights was the culmination of a long-standing personal campaign to make the rights and privileges of Canadian citizenship explicit. As for Lester Pearson, the adoption of a distinctive Canadian flag was one of his most enduring achievements as prime minister; certainly it was among the hardest won.[18]

The common emphasis of both Canadian and Quebec nationalisms upon the state, but different states, was to complicate greatly the possibility of any accommodation of Quebec within a continuing Canadian relationship. The older, French-Canadian, nationalism had been largely focused on private, Church-related institutions. Thus, the nation could be advanced in ways that did not impinge at all on the Canadian political order. With the new nationalism, focused on the Quebec state, a questioning of that order was inevitable. And with the growing Canadian nationalism, focused on the Canadian state, English Canadians were much less disposed to enter into such a debate.

To be sure, the contradiction might have been eased or even avoided if English-Canadian political and intellectual leaders had been prepared to embrace the idea of a distinctly English-Canadian nation, as many Quebec nationalists urged them to. But until the late 1960s few English Canadians were prepared to do so. Their nationalism remained an essentially political nationalism, centred on the Canadian state. From that perspective, the new Quebec nationalism was necessarily a problem and a threat. As the poet and academic Douglas LePan wrote in 1966: 'We in Ontario have never thought of ourselves, or of English-speaking Canada, as a nation because we thought that there was one nation, Canada, to which both we and our compatriots in French Canada belonged.'[19]

None the less, many English-Canadian political and intellectual leaders struggled earnestly during the early and mid-1960s to find ways to accommodate Quebec's new aspirations, however troubling and frustrating they may have been. In the process, all three federal parties adopted positions that in one fashion or another, responded directly to these demands.

THE EARLY YEARS: LOOKING FOR A FORMULA TO ACCOMMODATE QUEBEC NATIONALISM

The process of addressing Quebec's demands was led by the Liberal party. The Liberals, of course, had been responsible for the massive post-war expansion of the federal government with its assumption of the mantle of national government. And we have seen how Prime Minister St Laurent flatly rejected Quebec's claim to distinctiveness.

The Liberal Government of Lester Pearson
In the early 1960s, however, while his party was still in opposition, Liberal leader Lester Pearson actively sought to fashion a means of accommodating Quebec's new demands. Though Pearson had been a prominent member of the Liberal cabinets of the 1950s, he had been preoccupied with Canada's

foreign relations. Thus, he was less imbued than other Liberals with the post-war centralist notions.[20] Moreover, his international experience had made him more disposed to recognize the need to respond to forces of social and political change, as did the perspective he acquired through his early years as a professor of history. And his successes in international diplomacy had strengthened his belief that conflict should be resolved through conciliation and accommodation. In short, he was singularly well equipped to initiate new approaches to the Quebec question.

In this enterprise, Pearson could draw upon Quebec francophones in the party, such as Maurice Lamontagne, Jean-Luc Pepin, and Maurice Sauvé,[21] who, though deeply committed federalists, were in touch with the new nationalist currents in Quebec. Beyond that, two of Pearson's English-Canadian advisers had known Jean Lesage for many years. Tom Kent, Pearson's main political adviser, had become acquainted with Lesage in the 1950s through work on fiscal questions. And Gordon Robertson, who, when Pearson became prime minister served under him as clerk of the Privy Council, had been Lesage's deputy minister when the latter was federal minister of natural resources. Together, Kent and Robertson not only gave Pearson a direct contact to Lesage but helped to fashion Pearson's attempts to find an accommodation with the Quebec government.[22]

Pearson was obviously uneasy with the new Quebec nationalism and the ways in which Lesage was responding to it.[23] But as he related in his memoirs, he saw that only by directly accommodating it could separatism be undermined:

> The intensity of [national feeling in Quebec] made it clear that if we failed to contain and destroy separatism by coming to terms with the Quiet Revolution, that if we failed to treat Quebec as the heart of French culture and French language in Canada, as a province distinct in some respects from the others, we would have the gravest difficulty in holding our country together.[24]

So upon assuming office in April 1963, Pearson moved quickly to set a new tone in the Quebec-Canada relationship. In part, Pearson's strategy involved reinforcing dualism within the Canadian political order. Central to this effort was the Royal Commission on Bilingualism and Biculturalism, which he created in 1963. The idea of a commission had originally been suggested by André Laurendeau, a leading Quebec intellectual and editor of *Le Devoir*, whom Pearson named as co-chair and chief executive officer.[25] If only to persuade Laurendeau to accept the position, Pearson had given the commission a mandate (in fact, prepared by Maurice Lamontagne) that far exceeded such nominal forms of dualism as language practices in the federal government. The commission was

> to inquire into and report on the existing state of bilingualism and bicul-
> turalism in Canada and to recommend what steps should be taken to *develop*
> *the Canadian Confederation on the basis of an equal partnership between the two*
> *founding races*, taking into account the contribution made by other ethnic
> groups to the cultural enrichment of Canada and the measures that should
> be taken to safeguard that contribution.[26]

Moreover, the commission's inquiry should go beyond the federal government alone to examine the impact that 'private organizations' had on bilingualism and biculturalism (at Laurendeau's insistence) and the extent to which the provincial systems of education enable students to become bilingual.[27]

Beyond the commission's mandate, its very structure was deeply rooted in the ideal of dualism. The co-chairs were a francophone and an anglophone: Laurendeau and Davidson Dunton, president of Carleton University. Of the other original members, three were francophone (two from Quebec) and three were anglophone (two from central Canada). In addition to these eight members, there were two representatives of 'the other ethnic groups' that were integrated into one or the other 'official' cultures: a French-speaking Polish Canadian and an English-speaking Ukrainian Canadian.[28] Similarly, the bureaucracy of the commission had anglophone and francophone co-secretaries along with an anglophone director of research and a francophone special consultant on research.[29]

At the same time, Pearson saw the need to respond directly to Quebec's demands for recognition of its specificity. He straightforwardly embraced the underlying claims of Quebec nationalists when, addressing a meeting of the Canadian French-language Weekly Newspapers Association at Murray Bay, Quebec in 1963, he declared: 'While Quebec is a province in this national confederation, it is more than a province because it is the heartland of a people: in a very real sense it is a nation within a nation.' Similarly, in a January 1964 interview, Pearson said on English-language CBC television that Quebec was: 'in some vital respects not a province like the others but the homeland of a people.'[30] Both of those statements drew national attention and were subsequently referred to by leaders in the other federal parties, whether positively or negatively, as authoritative statements of the Liberal position.[31]

Pearson also elaborated the notion of a 'co-operative federalism' in which Quebec would be able to assume a role different from the other provinces, provided that the same opportunity was made available to the other provinces. He explained in his memoirs:

> We might make provision for Quebec to develop *de facto* jurisdiction in certain areas where she desired it most. Although the federal government had to retain intact certain essential powers, there were many other functions of government exercised by Ottawa which could be left to the provinces. By forcing a centralism perhaps acceptable to some provinces but not to Quebec, and by insisting that Quebec must be like the others, we could destroy Canada. This became my doctrine of federalism. I wanted to decentralize up to a point as the way to strengthen, indeed to establish and maintain, unity.[32]

On this basis, the Pearson government entered into a wide variety of federal-provincial arrangements that enabled Quebec to take full responsibility for programs that in the rest of the country were managed jointly by the federal and provincial governments or even by Ottawa alone. Known as 'contracting out', the arrangement had in fact been included in the Liberals' 1963 election platform at the instigation of Maurice Sauvé.[33] Each of the arrangements was made available to all the other provinces, but Quebec was the only one to use the opportunity. The formula was applied to a large number of programs where Ottawa and the provinces would share the cost.

The framework for the arrangement was spelled out in the Established Program (Interim Arrangements) Act of 1965, which was itself based on an agreement reached between Ottawa and Quebec City the previous year. Under the Act, provinces choosing to opt out of a program would be able to recover the funds on their own, thanks to an extra abatement on the federal personal income tax. The provinces were required to undertake that during an interim period they would both maintain the programs and provide the federal government with audited accounts of the expenditures they were devoting to them. In fact, under the 1964 agreement Quebec even pledged that it would not dismantle the programs even after the interim period had expired.[34] To that extent the arrangement amounted to a formality: the nature and scale of programs remained intact. Yet, as Tom Kent was to write many years later, 'A federation . . . rests on getting its formalities right.'[35]

The 'contracting out' formula was even applied to exclusively federal programs, such as the youth allowance and student loan programs that Ottawa established in 1964.[36] The most prominent instance was, of course, the Canada Pension Plan. In 1964 Ottawa had declared its intention to establish a national contributory plan. At a stormy federal-provincial conference in Quebec City, the Quebec government presented its own plan for a pension scheme. Moreover, it threatened not to support the constitutional amendment that would be necessary for the federal government to operate its program. After protracted discussions, including secret bilateral negotiations between Ottawa and Quebec City, all governments agreed on a compromise by which provincial governments would be able to 'opt out' of a federal pension program; the terms of the federal program were themselves modified so as to be more attractive to the provinces, lessening the likelihood that any province would withdraw. In turn, Quebec agreed to the necessary constitutional amendment. Under the legislation establishing the Canada Pension Plan, the plan would not operate in a province if, within a specific period of time, its government declared that it intended to establish a program of its own. Quebec was the only province to do so.[37]

Not surprisingly, Jean Lesage proclaimed the outcome of the pension plan issue to be a victory: 'I used all means that Providence has given me so that Quebec, in the end, would be recognized as a province with special status in Confederation. And I have succeeded.'[38]

Given the current English–Canadian attitudes toward Quebec, it is striking how the arrangement also met with general approval outside Quebec. *The Globe and Mail* declared, '[Pearson] appears to have pulled a political triumph out of the teeth of disaster.'[39] In the House, NDP Leader Tommy Douglas was highly congratulatory; John Diefenbaker was generally approving, though he used the opportunity to deride the Pearson government for the inadequacies of its original scheme.[40] For the members of the Pearson government who had been involved in the negotiations, the agreement ended a crisis that they believed had threatened to destroy the country.[41] This view was shared by Stanley Knowles, a member of the Opposition and a close student of pension questions:

> I felt it was one of the best examples of co-operation between Canada and Quebec, between English and French Canada, or English Canada and French Quebec. . . . Negotiating that kind of an agreement so that face was saved on both sides and nobody lost anything [was a great achievement] . . .
> I think Confederation was saved at that point. I think there was a risk of Confederation coming apart at the seams over that whole social security package, and that was avoided, and avoided successfully.[42]

In effect, the predominant English–Canadian reaction was one of relief, as this first confrontation with Quebec nationalism had been resolved.

A reaction against the accommodative strategy did begin to build in some areas of the federal government. In the spring of 1964, Al Johnson, the new assistant deputy minister of finance with responsibility for federal-provincial relations, began a concerted campaign to eliminate contracting out.[43] He enlisted the support of Mitchell Sharp, who became minister of finance after the election in November 1965.

Mitchell Sharp had opposed the concept of contracting out ever since it was adopted as party policy in 1963, believing that tax rates should be standard across the country.[44] Moreover, his opposition to contracting out was strengthened by the influence of a newcomer to the federal scene, Pierre Trudeau, who vigorously rejected contracting out or any other special arrangement with Quebec. Rather than the Pearsonian search for accommodation, Trudeau argued for a very different strategy for the Quebec question: confronting Quebec nationalism head on and avoiding special arrangements for the province. In his memoirs, Sharp relates that he was greatly impressed during a cabinet committee in 1966 when, for the first time, he heard Trudeau, who was attending as Pearson's parliamentary secretary, argue that policies that result in a special status for Quebec were but a slippery slope to separation.[45]

Still, according to some officials of the time, the contracting issue may not have been the main reason that Finance demanded a change in fiscal arrangements. For some key players, including deputy finance minister R.B. Bryce, the opposition to shared-cost arrangements may have had much more to do with taking control of the federal government's finances by reducing the burden of federal transfer payments to the provinces. In effect, the presumed need to standardize fiscal arrangements could be a convenient argument for simply cutting back on the financial commitments.[46] In the case of post-secondary education, standardizing arrangements meant converting the provinces to *Quebec's* special arrangement of tax abatements and ending the transfers they had become used to.

Whatever its motives, Finance was well-placed to make its arguments prevail since it had primary responsibility for defining the federal position on fiscal relations with the provinces. Thus, in September 1966 Finance Minister Mitchell Sharp announced that the federal government was moving away from shared-cost programs, in the process eliminating the very basis of contracting out. In return for taking over the largest of the programs, the provinces would receive additional income tax points. But otherwise, Sharp said, Ottawa would not continue its past practice of 'making room' for the provinces through tax abatements. The provinces would have to raise the necessary funds themselves.[47]

None the less, even though Finance had succeeded in its campaign against contracting out, it had not changed the minds of the architects of asymmetry, Tom Kent and Gordon Robertson.[48] Kent had already left the Prime Minister's Office at the end of 1965 to become deputy minister to

Jean Marchand in the new Department of Manpower and Immigration. In 1967 Kent and Marchand ended job training grants to the provinces and introduced a new scheme by which Ottawa arranged for training services itself, by entering into contracts with the provinces or with private parties. But the policy was not part of any new tough strategy with Quebec. In fact, Ontario was the most opposed to it.[49] At first, Ottawa and Quebec City struggled over control of manpower policy in the province, but the dispute was resolved through the creation of a joint Quebec-Ottawa committee, which in turn established a *special role* for Quebec in manpower programs.[50]

On the other hand, Gordon Robertson, who remained clerk of the Privy Council, had resisted Finance's campaign and argued in favour of contracting out. This is made clear in Al Johnson's account of an exchange with him in early 1966:

> Mr Robertson pointed out that our reasoning with respect to shared-cost programmes was based upon the assumption that contracting-out was 'a bad thing'—that it would lead to an associate state. He said he was not inclined to accept this proposition: he thought contracting-out might well give Quebec the special status she seems to want, for symbolic reasons, and that, having accomplished this she might be deterred from asking for further measures which would make manifest, in Quebec, the special status which that province enjoyed.[51]

Despite this argument with Finance over contracting out, Robertson did not renounce the notion of asymmetry as a way of dealing with Quebec.[52]

Most important, it does not appear that Pearson himself abandoned his belief that Quebec needed to be accommodated through special arrangements.[53] As long as he was prime minister, that remained part of his approach to the Quebec question. Some commentators have claimed that Pearson had been disabused of these ideas by Pierre Trudeau. Not only did Trudeau's position as Pearson's parliamentary secretary give him an advantageous position from which to persuade Pearson to accept his views, but these views were being echoed by Marc Lalonde, who became Pearson's chief policy adviser in April 1967.[54] However, Pearson's close associates dismiss the notion that Trudeau had such influence with Pearson. They contend that as long as he was prime minister, Pearson took his cue from Jean Marchand, whom he regarded as his Quebec leader, and whom he wanted to succeed him as prime minister. Of a more pragmatic bent than Trudeau, Marchand did not have the same objections as Trudeau to special arrangements for Quebec, nor did he share Trudeau's visceral antagonism to Quebec nationalism.[55]

By 1967 Pearson and his close associates were becoming concerned that Quebec's demands were too great to be met through the ad hoc, non-constitutional arrangements they had been pursuing. They would have to tackle constitutional revision. Trudeau's campaign against asymmetry and a distinct role for Quebec was beginning to have an influence on English-Canadian public opinion; Pearson's new policy adviser, Marc Lalonde, was arguing along the same lines. None the less, Pearson declared an openness to specific arrangements for Quebec. In the fall of 1967 he said in a speech in Montreal, 'I believe that particular provisions for Quebec, as well as for other provinces where required to ensure the fulfilment of particular needs, can be recognized and secured in the constitution without destroying the essential unity of our Confederation.'[56]

As justice minister, Trudeau had a crucial part in the preparations for the first federal-provincial constitutional conference, which Pearson convened in February 1968. In particular, the order of priorities which the federal government set, starting with entrenchment of a charter of rights, shows Trudeau's influence.[57] Yet, as prime minister, Pearson was still in charge of the question. Indeed, by all reports he was quite uncomfortable with the highly abrasive style that Trudeau adopted at the conference. When Trudeau, as justice minister, engaged Quebec premier Daniel Johnson in a fierce debate, Pearson found Trudeau's behaviour inappropriate and brought the exchange to an end.[58] In sum, throughout his tenure as prime minister, Pearson instinctively considered accommodation, rather than confrontation, to be the proper way of handling the Quebec question.

The two other main federal parties also became committed to trying to find a way of accommodating the new Quebec nationalism. The processes that led the Progressive Conservatives and the NDP in these new directions were similar. Both parties were electorally weak in Quebec and needed to make themselves more attractive to Quebec voters. This meant overcoming the legacy of decades of estrangement from Quebec. In each case, the parties were pulled in this direction by Quebec nationalists who actively challenged them to recognize the new Quebec, provoking but overcoming considerable resistance. The new receptiveness to Quebec nationalism was of course limited by the Canadian nationalism that most English Canadians shared. None the less, it was a radical change from the traditional positions of each party. The two parties may have had their own reasons for adopting their new policies, but the intellectual and political climate of the early and mid-1960s allowed and even encouraged them to do so.

The Progressive Conservatives: Struggling with 'Two Nations'
Until Diefenbaker's electoral victories, the Progressive Conservatives had been effectively excluded from Quebec for decades. After the conscription

crisis during the First World War, the Conservatives had secured on average 7.8 per cent of Quebec's seats and 27.1 per cent of its popular vote. Diefenbaker's tenure as prime minister, from 1957 to 1963, did not really improve that state of affairs—even though in 1958 the Conservatives had won 50 seats in Quebec.

The Diefenbaker government undertook some not insignificant reforms to recognize dualism in federal institutions, such as simultaneous translation in the House of Commons and Senate and bilingual pay cheques in the federal public service. With the appointment of Georges Vanier as Governor-General after Vincent Massey, Diefenbaker established the principle of alternating this office between anglophones and francophones.[59] And in 1959 Diefenbaker entered into an agreement with Quebec Premier Paul Sauvé that ended the six-year stand-off precipitated by Maurice Duplessis's refusal to allow Quebec universities to accept federal grants.[60] That had been the first time that Quebec opted out of a federal spending program with compensation, and the arrangement laid the groundwork for the whole edifice of *de facto* special status for Quebec that the Pearson government created in the 1960s.

None the less, as prime minister, Diefenbaker articulated a vision of Canada that rejected any notion of Canadian duality let alone the distinctiveness of Quebec. Throughout his political career, he championed the ideal of an 'unhyphenated' Canadianism in which cultural differences were, by definition, immaterial. As he explained in his memoirs, the primary motive behind his long struggle to establish a Canadian bill of rights had been 'to assure Canadians, whatever their racial origins or surnames, the right to full citizenship and an end to discrimination. This was basic to my philosophy of "One Canada, One Nation."'[61] In 1961 he even ordered the Dominion Bureau of Statistics to introduce the category 'Canadian' as a possible response to the census question on ethnic origin. He reversed the order in light of protests from francophone nationalist groups, which feared that it would threaten the idea of a distinct French-Canadian nationality and might cause the size of the French Canadian population to be underestimated.[62]

Beyond that, Diefenbaker's discomfort with a specifically French-Canadian perspective affected relations with the French-Canadian members of his caucus.[63] Upon his election in 1957, Diefenbaker appointed only one francophone to his cabinet; even after winning his majority in 1958, and having far more francophones to choose from, he appointed only six, and to largely minor positions.[64] In the 1963 election, in which the Pearson Liberals were victorious, the Conservatives won only eight seats in Quebec. Two years later, the result was the same.

After Diefenbaker was defeated in 1963, forces within the PC party embarked upon efforts to refashion the image and policies of the party so as to attract support in French Quebec. For many members, of course, that entailed replacing its leader. In April 1965, the party's ostensible Quebec lieutenant, Léon Balcer, left the party after failing to secure a leadership convention and declaring that Diefenbaker 'is genuinely against French Canada'.[65] Finally, in 1967, these efforts culminated in both an extended debate over the Quebec question and a leadership convention. The party emerged with general adherence to a new strategy regarding Quebec, premised on the notion that Canada is composed of 'two nations', and a new leader prepared to put this strategy into effect.

In August 1967 the party held a 'thinkers' conference' at the Maison Montmorency in Courville, Quebec.[66] Invited to give a 'major address' on the constitution, Marcel Faribault, a prominent Quebec financier and legal expert, tried to confront the essentially English-Canadian conference participants with neo-nationalist trends in Quebec. He argued that, given the French-Canadian understanding of the term 'nation', there is 'nothing in the two nation concept that is opposed to a federal political regime.' And, reviewing Claude Ryan's proposals for a special status for Quebec, Faribault announced, 'With the best will in the world it is impossible for me to find anything in this program that is revolutionary, anti-federalist or *a fortiori* separatist.'[67]

Frustrated by the apparent intransigence that had greeted his address, Faribault spoke to the conference participants a second time, further underlining the strength of nationalist currents in Quebec and effectively demanding that the participants respond to them:

> Now, what about particular status? . . . Don't you realize that this is the evolution? Are you unable to realize that this is what is happening to the country? . . .
>
> The same way the question of the two nations is no longer debatable in the Province of Quebec. Admit that you will put . . . admit that you must put, at the preamble of a new Constitution, something which will be the recognition that there are in this country two founding peoples. *You put that down.* We might translate it in French 'two nations'. You will translate it, two 'founding races or people' if you want. We cannot say 'people' because '*people*' in our case doesn't mean nation, the same way as 'nation' in English doesn't mean '*nation*' [emphasis in original].[68]

Faribault's second intervention had the desired effect: the participants of the constitution committee approved a summary statement that does indeed refer to Canadian duality in the terms he suggested. Calling for a national conference on the constitution, the statement declared that the constitutional change should take into account:

> That Canada is and should be a federal state.
> That Canada is composed of two founding peoples (deux nations), with historical rights who have been joined by people from many lands.
> That the constitution should be such as to permit and encourage their full and harmonious growth and development in equality throughout Canada.[69]

The French phrase 'deux nations' was inserted into this English-language text for clarity.[70]

The committee ignored Faribault's challenge to address the concept of special status. Indeed, others had issued the same challenge much more pointedly. In fact, York University historian Paul Stevens had proposed to the constitutional committee that Quebec be granted complete jurisdiction over housing, manpower, and social welfare, participate directly in the administration and programming of the CBC and have some responsibilities in external relations. Quebec MP Martial Asselin had enthusiastically supported Stevens's proposal.[71] But no hint of such arrangements appears in the final statement.

For that matter, the concrete proposals accompanying the statement's endorsement of 'two founding peoples (deux nations)' treated duality in purely linguistic terms, calling for 'complete equality of language rights for French and English throughout Canada, subject only to the practical necessary adjustments within the several provinces'.[72] The statement did, however, embrace the conception of Canada that underlay the demands of Quebec nationalists, and that was enough to infuriate John Diefenbaker, who was still leader of the party and still a potential candidate at the party leadership convention scheduled for September. He proclaimed, 'Montmorency was not representative of Conservative thinking in his country. . . . There's only one Canada. Only one nation, one national idea, and one national dream.'[73]

The convention was to demonstrate that a broad consensus had in fact developed in the party to the effect that Canada is composed of two nations, however defined and whatever the institutional implications. In the days preceding the convention, a study group approved the Montmorency report with hardly any dissent and the PC national policy committee gave its approval without difficulty.[74] So as to avoid a fight on the floor over the two-nations question, the convention organizers agreed that the policy committee would simply report its decisions to the convention; there would be no debate or vote.

Diefenbaker, however, tried to force the issue. He used his address as party leader to call upon the delegates to renounce the policy and, to that end, presented himself as a last-minute candidate for re-election. There were some expressions of support for Diefenbaker's position: the Saskatchewan delegates endorsed it and the Alberta premier and BC attorney-general telegraphed their approval.[75] But the convention debate did not take place, though as a partial concession, the organizers agreed that the report would be tabled rather than presented without debate to the convention, as had been originally planned.[76] After coming a distant fifth on each of the first three ballots, Diefenbaker withdrew from the race. The notion of two nations was explicitly endorsed in the convention addresses of most of the leading candidates: Fleming, Fulton, Hees, McCutcheon, Roblin, and Stanfield.[77]

Clearly, there were limits to this new PC consensus on the notion of two nations. Its proponents were usually careful to rule out any notion of separate state structures. Faribault and others had placed great store in the increasingly tenuous argument that, unlike English Canadians, French Canadians saw the term 'nation' in essentially cultural and social terms. As we have seen, during the 1960s, nationalist leaders in Quebec had come to give the state a central place in their idea of nation. English-Canadian proponents of two nations tended to see French Canada rather than Quebec as the 'other' nation and to hedge about the existence of an English-Canadian nation. None the less, the party had come far indeed from the 'one Canada' of John Diefenbaker. It had embraced a dualist conception of Canada that had been proposed by leaders of Quebec itself and that offered the basis for a new relationship with Quebec nationalism.

The new party leader had repeatedly expressed sympathy for a distinctive place for the Quebec government in Canadian federalism. Just before the convention, an article by Robert Stanfield containing the following passage had appeared in *Le Devoir:* 'The Quebec situation presents certain distinctive aspects. Quebeckers feel that, in order to achieve their aims and ambitions, they must be given more authority over economic and social affairs in their province. I don't think any solutions that we will find for the problems of our federation will be able to ignore this feeling in Quebec.'[78] And speaking before the convention's policy committee, Stanfield said he disliked the term 'special status' but then outlined 'some kind of different arrangement in the distribution of authority, in respect to social and economic matters' for Quebec.[79] On that basis, he obtained the endorsement of Claude Ryan, editor of *Le Devoir,* for leader of the party and, in the following year, for prime minister.[80]

THE NDP: 'TWO NATIONS' AND 'SPECIAL STATUS'

Like the Progressive Conservatives, the NDP had a heavy legacy in Quebec to overcome. Its predecessor, the CCF, had never been able to establish a base in French Quebec, where it faced the combined opposition of the clerics, who attacked its Protestant roots, and French-Canadian nationalists, who attacked its centralist predilections. Indeed, to the extent the CCF had any support in Quebec, it was in the English-Canadian community in Montreal. The prominence in the party of such figures as F.R. Scott, son of an Anglican bishop and lifelong supporter of a strong federal government, only confirmed the claims of the party's French-Canadian detractors.[81] A primary reason for replacing the CCF with a new party had been to overcome this deficiency in Quebec. Beyond that, the prospect of a new social democratic party had attracted a good number of Quebec francophone union leaders and social activists who were at the same time deeply involved in the new Quebec nationalism. They were determined to secure a place for themselves and their ideas within the new party.[82] Thus, from the outset the party was under strong pressure to try to come to terms with the new Quebec nationalism.

Before the party's founding convention in 1961, the Quebec NDP members and sympathizers held a colloquium to formulate common positions and reached agreement on three principles: the affirmation that Canada is composed of two nations, the need for a renewed and decentralized federalism, and recognition of Quebec's right to self-determination. It was agreed that for tactical reasons the last proposition would not be explicitly put to the convention. On this basis, the Quebec delegates submitted a resolution to the party's National Committee requiring that in all NDP official documents the term 'federal' or 'Canadian' should be used in place of 'national' and that 'Confederation', 'country', or 'Canada' should be used instead of 'nation'.

Initially, the National Committee rejected the proposition. In response to protests from Quebec, the leadership agreed to modify the party program, but not the party's constitution, along those lines. At the convention, the committee persisted in this refusal. Speaking for the Quebec delegation, Michel Chartrand insisted that, since French Canadians form a distinct nation, the application of 'national' to the federal NDP would be incomplete, unacceptable, and assimilationist. The counter-attack was led on behalf of the party leadership by Eugene Forsey, who declared, 'Canada is composed of two ethnic groups but not two nations.'[83] Confronted with this open debate, the leadership relented; the party's statutes committee adopted the Quebec position.

The next day, the Quebec delegation succeeded in having the draft party program modified to its satisfaction. In particular, a revised section begins with the declaration: 'The New Democratic Party declares its belief in federalism, the only system that can assure the joint development of the two nations which originally joined together to create Canadian society, as well as the development of other ethnic groups in Canada.'[84] To be sure, this general statement of principle offered no indication of what types of institutional arrangements were warranted.[85]

During the 1960s, the NDP worked its way to a formal endorsement of a distinctive place for Quebec within the federal system. Once again, this came about largely at the prodding of the Quebec caucus. In 1965 the selection of a promising new Quebec leader, Robert Cliche, together with the acceleration of the constitutional debate forced the party leadership to address the Quebec question in more concrete terms.

The initial formulation alluded to a special role for Quebec but also insisted that 'certain basic matters had to be left to the jurisdiction of the federal government'; it drew up a list of such 'matters' that effectively undercut any enhancement of Quebec's position.[86] When the proposal met with widespread criticism from Quebec nationalists and a Quebec NDP convention failed to adopt it,[87] a new, stronger version was presented, and approved, at the party's third federal convention, in July 1965. At the same time, the convention adopted a series of resolutions that would have entailed centralization of power in Ottawa.[88]

None the less, the party leadership began to use the term 'special status' to denote the party's position on Quebec. In addressing Parliament in 1966, NDP leader Tommy Douglas declared:

> We believe that a Canadian constitution must be sufficiently flexible to give the federal government the necessary power to provide for equality of treatment and equality of opportunity for all Canadians, while at the same time recognizing a special status for the province of Quebec in terms of language, culture and the civil code, in keeping with the principle of the equal partnership of the two founding races.[89]

Finally, at its fourth biennial convention in 1967, the party responded to prodding from the editor of Le Devoir, Claude Ryan, by overwhelmingly approving a description of special status, formulated by Charles Taylor:

> In fields of government which touch a community's way of life—fields such as social security, town planning, education and community development—Quebec must have the right and the fiscal resources to adopt its

own programmes and policies in place of those designed and financed by
the federal government. At the same time, the federal government must be
able to play an increased role in these fields where this is desired by the people of other provinces.[90]

During the 1968 election campaign, Tommy Douglas vigorously
defended this position:

> The NDP takes the position that we must have a strong federal government.
> It must have power it has never had before to grapple with modern prob-
> lems that are conspicuously beyond the grasp of the provincial and munic-
> ipal governments. . . . Thus, it may mean that in any area such as education
> and housing, where Quebec feels that a strong federal power may erode
> provincial rights, it may be necessary to have two programs—one for
> English-speaking Canada and one for Quebec.[91]

NDP campaigners argued that the federal government would not be able to
extend its activities in ways that were urgently needed unless Quebec was
permitted to exempt itself, at least to some degree, from such measures. By
recognizing special status, they argued, 'Canadians elsewhere can seek federal
action in these fields without creating misunderstanding, frustration and
intolerable strains to our confederation.'[92] By the same token, party leaders
blamed Trudeau's alternative of official bilingualism for the creation of 'poi-
sonous antagonisms', especially in western Canada.[93]

There is evidence that the party activists themselves supported these
efforts to accommodate Quebec nationalism. According to Alan Whitehorn's
survey of NDP convention delegates, 63.9 per cent supported a 'special status'
for Quebec in 1971. This support fell substantially during the 1970s.[94]

During the 1960s, all three major federal parties made a sustained effort to
understand the new Quebec nationalism and to devise constitutional formulas and structures that would accommodate it. The Liberal Party, under
Lester Pearson, took the lead in this process, launching a national inquiry into
the conditions needed to create 'an equal partnership between the two
founding races' and building an asymmetrical federalism that in effect provided Quebec with a distinctive status. The PCs adopted a dualistic conception of Canada that repudiated the 'one Canada' of John Diefenbaker. And
the NDP formally adopted both a 'two nations' vision of Canada and a 'special status' for Quebec.

To be sure, no party was fully united around these positions. John
Diefenbaker had fought a bitter rearguard resistance to the PC's new position.

The decision of the NDP founding convention that the party constitution recognize two nations precipitated Eugene Forsey's departure and alarmed Frank Scott and Pierre Trudeau;[95] the party's subsequent endorsement of special status for Quebec was denounced by Ramsay Cook and Kenneth McNaught.[96] None the less, the leaders and many members of all three parties were committed to a new approach to the Quebec question, designed to accommodate nationalist demands.

ENGLISH-CANADIAN INTELLECTUALS

Parallel processes were taking place among English-Canadian intellectuals. Some actively promoted the new effort to find an accommodation of Quebec nationalism within Canadian federalism. English-Canadian academics had been prominent in such events as the Progressive Conservatives' Montmorency conference, where the historian, Paul Stevens, had presented a blueprint for Quebec special status. Charles Taylor and others had played similar roles in the NDP.

Other English-Canadian intellectuals went one step further, attempting to lay the basis for a distinctly English-Canadian nationalism, centred on an English-Canadian nation.[97] Unlike the predominant Canadian nationalism, with its emphasis on the formal status of the Canadian state, this new strand of nationalism saw the nation in social, cultural, and economic terms and was informed by a critical analysis of American imperialism. Rather than a merely political entity, the nation was also a social and cultural collectivity. The primary goal of the new nationalism was not to maintain the Canadian federal system but to emancipate the nation from American domination. From that perspective, the nation could be readily envisaged as English Canada, rather than Canada as a whole, and Quebec nationalism could be an ally, rather than a threat. On this basis, the logic of two nations would no longer be one-sided.

Gad Horowitz, for instance, regularly used the pages of *Canadian Dimension* to make the case for an English-Canadian nationalism. In 1965 he wrote in an article called 'The Future of English Canada':

> The greatest threat to the existence of Canada is not the autonomist drive of Quebec. It is the weakness of the will to nationhood in English Canada. . . .
>
> There is no way of avoiding an autonomous Quebec. Quebec demands and deserves autonomy. She will have autonomy within confederation, or there will be no more confederation. . . . The obvious solution to Canada's difficulties would appear to be a federal government which is weak in relation to Quebec, but strong in relation to the other provinces— in other words, a 'special status' for Quebec within confederation.[98]

At the same time, such academics as George Grant, Kari Levitt, and Mel Watkins were offering a comprehensive critique of Canadian economic and cultural dependence on the United States.[99] Together with the reaction against the influx of Americans into Canadian universities in the 1960s, these writings were to be the basis for a more clearly defined form of Canadian nationalism, focused upon American imperialism.

In sociological terms, this more clearly defined form of Canadian nationalism was propelled by social forces in English Canada not unlike those that championed the new Quebec nationalism. As in Quebec, the clearest social base of the new Canadian nationalism was a rapidly growing class of salaried professionals, composed of intellectuals, teachers, artists, and administrators.[100]

The organizational base for the idea of an English-Canadian nation, and the systematic application of the two-nations thesis, came with the rise of the Waffle Movement in the New Democratic Party. An informal grouping of leftists, the Waffle published a manifesto in August 1969, under the title 'For an Independent Socialist Canada'. Under the leadership of two academics, Mel Watkins and Jim Laxer, the Waffle sought to enlist the NDP as a whole in its campaign against American imperialism. On the Quebec question, the Waffle manifesto declared:

> A united Canada is of critical importance in pursuing a successful strategy against the reality of American imperialism. Quebec's history and aspirations must be allowed full expression and implementation in the conviction that new ties will emerge from the common perception of 'two nations, one struggle'. Socialists in English Canada must ally themselves with socialists in Quebec in this common cause.[101]

During the 1960s, discussion about Canadian unity was marked by an extraordinary willingness to examine new and unconventional approaches. The Liberal government of Lester Pearson may have provided the lead, but both opposition parties became involved in the effort to find a way to accommodate the new demands of Quebec nationalists, as did many English-Canadian intellectuals. In fact, one leading political observer, Anthony Westell, claimed that by 1967 the idea of particular status for Quebec had become fairly conventional within Quebec and that 'it was accepted in some measure by many English Canadians in the political capital of Ottawa and the communications capital, Toronto.'[102]

In a very few years that was no longer true.

CHAPTER 3

Trudeau and the New Federal Orthodoxy: Denying the Quebec Question

Not all the English-Canadian political and intellectual élites supported the effort to accommodate Quebec neo-nationalism. By the mid-1960s some federal officials were trying to reverse the Pearson government's experiments with asymmetry. Prominent members of both the Progressive Conservative and New Democratic parties had vigorously opposed the new directions their parties had embarked on. Still, through most of the 1960s these remained minority positions.

By the end of the 1960s, the effort to accommodate Quebec nationalism was over and was to remain so for decades to come. Instead, all three parties were united around a strategy of confronting and undermining Quebec nationalism. This radical reversal was made possible by a new political phenomenon: a francophone from Quebec who insisted that accommodation of Quebec nationalism was unnecessary, wrong-headed and, in fact, immoral. In its place, he proposed to incorporate Quebec francophones into a new pan-Canadian identity.

Pierre Elliott Trudeau's vision of Canada was not shared fully by most of his fellow Quebec francophones. Nor did it correspond to the way in which most English Canadians understood their country. Yet ultimately it was to have a profound impact on Canadian politics. Indeed, it has become so deeply incorporated into Canada's most important political institutions, especially the constitution, that all attempts to depart from it, such as the Meech Lake Accord, have ended in débâcle.

THE ROOTS OF TRUDEAU'S POLITICAL WORLD-VIEW

To a very considerable extent, the distinctiveness of Trudeau's political vision can be traced to the distinctiveness of his life, which had begun in circumstances very different from those of most Canadians, francophone or anglophone.

As the son of a French-Canadian father and an English-Canadian mother of Scottish descent, Trudeau acquired a degree of bilingualism that is rare not only in Canada, but in any country. The result was profound: he was unable or unprepared to identify exclusively with either English Canada or French Canada. Instead he fastened upon the supremacy of the individual. To a much greater extent than most Canadians, he had a compelling reason to do so.[1]

Especially important to Trudeau's intellectual and political development was his youthful ambivalence toward and eventual estrangement from French Canada. According to Clarkson and McCall, the early death of Trudeau's father reinforced his ambivalence about French Canada: English became the primary language of the household and the customs of his French-Canadian relatives increasingly seemed odd.[2] Trudeau's general milieu remained francophone, but he used the intellectual and moral élitism of his classical college, Collège Brébeuf, as 'a useful disguise for his general unease and his mounting ambivalence about being a French Canadian.'[3] Soon after his father's death he took the unusual step of beginning to speak international French, as well as adopting his mother's maiden name as his middle name.[4]

This estrangement from French Canada grew as Trudeau pursued his university studies. After an intellectually deadening stint earning a law degree at l'Université de Montréal, he entered Harvard, where he found himself woefully unprepared by his studies in French Canada's leading institutions. Identifying himself on his residence door as 'Citizen of the world', he immersed himself in English-language social science and philosophy, studying with some of the leading American scholars of the period. After Harvard, he went to Paris, where he spent only eight months, enjoying the city but disappointed by the courses at l'École libre des sciences politiques. Finally, he went to the London School of Economics, which he found much more stimulating, especially the teachings of Harold Laski, a leading socialist theorist.[5]

In 1949 Trudeau returned to Montreal, confirmed in his individualism but also familiar with the latest developments in American and British social science, with post-war liberal thought, and with Keynesian notions of economic management and the welfare state. He was even more estranged from French Quebec than before.[6] On the other hand, his training and worldview, as well as a certain anglophilia, should have made him a perfect recruit for the federal government, where he took a position with Privy Council Office in 1949. Yet, here too, he felt marginal.

Not only was Trudeau frustrated with the minor tasks that were assigned to him in the PCO, but he felt excluded by the pervasiveness of anglophones in the upper levels of the federal government. In fact, he and the other French Canadians in the federal bureaucracy even referred to themselves by a code name, 'les Grecs', to denote their inferior status.[7] Trudeau had been confronted with his French-Canadian roots. He may still have seen himself as a citizen of the world, but there appeared to be no place for him in the federal government.

Freeing Quebec from its 'Backwardness'

Trudeau remained uncomfortable with French Quebec. It simply did not measure up in terms of the post-war liberal world-view in which he had been confirmed. His only recourse was to *change* Quebec society—an exceedingly ambitious undertaking that was to become his personal mission.

Trudeau was confirmed in this mission by his recent conversion to the Catholic doctrine of personalism, with its emphasis on personal responsibility and social action. To quote Clarkson and McCall:

> He would return to his people and call them into the twentieth century. . . . He would transcend their cultural parochialism, their political backwardness, even their 'lousy French', through the loftiness of his motives and the clarity of his mind. He could be an intellectual worker-priest among the *habitants* of French North America, pitting himself against the élites of the province.[8]

Upon returning to Montreal, Trudeau devoted himself to confronting French Canadians with their 'backwardness', and showing how they might escape it. He co-founded *Cité libre*, a journal of opinion intended to disseminate his liberal critique of Quebec society. And he used more popular media, such as the weekly *Le Vrai*, for which he wrote a series of articles that tried to make the rudiments of liberal democratic thought intelligible to the average French Canadian. He even tried to establish political movements, with such names as Rassemblement provincial des citoyens and Union des forces démocratiques, that would educate French-Canadian voters in the true significance of the democratic vote.

For Trudeau, the dismal quality of Quebec's political life was the most flagrant of its deficiencies. In an article called 'Some Obstacles to Democracy in Quebec', he described a political culture that tolerated massive corruption and the arbitrary use of state power because it did not comprehend the basic premise of democracy: that sovereignty must reside with the people. The *ancien régime* heritage of New France, the anti-democratic manipulations of an authoritarian clergy, and the fundamental corrosiveness of nationalism had conspired to prevent French Canadians from realizing that sovereignty should reside with them and that governments should be accountable to them. They thought that

> government of the people by the people could not be *for* the people, but mainly for the English-speaking part of that people; such were the spoils of conquest. . . . They adhered to the 'social contract' with mental reservations; they refused to be inwardly bound by a 'general will' which overlooked the racial problem. Feeling unable to share as equals in the Canadian common weal, they secretly resolved to pursue only the French-Canadian weal, and to safeguard the latter they cheated against the former.[9]

By the same token, Trudeau insisted that since French Canadians saw the state as beyond their control, they could not appreciate its potential for improving their social and economic conditions.

Nor had French Canadians developed a proper respect for the rights of the individual. This required the vigilant defence of political liberties not only against the arbitrary actions of the state but also against groups of citizens who try to use the state to impose their views. In a polemic published in *Cité libre* in 1962 he referred to 'civil liberties having survived in the province of Quebec thanks only to the Communists, the trade unions, and the Jehovah's Witnesses, and to English and Jewish lawyers and the judges of the Supreme Court in Ottawa.'[10]

Finally, and most important of all, French Canada was imprisoned by nationalism. Indeed, the corrosive effects of nationalism were at the root of all the many manifestations of Quebec's 'backwardness'. As elsewhere, nationalism was the enemy of democracy, individual rights, and social and economic justice. In the caustic analysis of Quebec society that formed the first chapter of *La Grève de l'amiante*, Trudeau argued that in Quebec, nationalism had corrupted the Church's social doctrine:

> As a result, the Church's social doctrine, which in other countries opened the door to the democratization of peoples, the emancipation of workers and social progress, in French Canada was invoked in support of authoritarianism and xenophobia. And, worse still, this doctrine made it impossible for us to resolve our problems. . . . It rejected any solution that worked for our 'enemies': the English, Protestants, materialists, etc.[11]

Indeed, opposition to nationalism was the leitmotiv of Trudeau's writings. The untrammelled expression of emotion in politics and the enemy of reason, nationalism was, throughout the world, the source of intolerance and the cause of horrendous wars.[12] Needless to say, such an intense rejection of nationalism and of ethnically or culturally defined collectivities came naturally to someone who himself did not feel a clear membership in any such collectivity.

Rejecting the Quiet Revolution

The 1960s presented Trudeau with a paradox: through the Quiet Revolution, Quebec was rapidly building the liberal, progressive society that he had been beseeching it to create, but nationalism, which he had seen as the abiding obstacle to such change, was stronger than ever; in fact, the leaders of the Quiet Revolution claimed to be guided by a *liberal* nationalism.

For Trudeau, this was an impossibility. As a general phenomenon, nationalism was hostile to liberal values. Nationalism in Quebec could never escape the fundamentally conservative social and political assumptions that had always governed French-Canadian nationalism. Given its intrinsic ethnic roots, it could never become a 'territorial nationalism'.[13] Trudeau was thus quick to claim that the Quiet Revolution had become a victim of counter-revolutionary sectarianism.[14]

His argument seemed forced, for the accomplishments of the Quiet Revolution were too substantial to be dismissed so easily. Certainly, he did not persuade many of his fellow Québécois, not even all his *Cité libre* collaborators. As Gérard Bergeron put it, Trudeau could never see what was 'trudeauiste' in the Quiet Revolution.[15] In short, Trudeau remained marginal to Quebec, even as it was being transformed.

Trudeau was naturally troubled by the continuing attempts of Lester Pearson, Jean Lesage, and so many others to find an accommodation of Quebec nationalism within the Canadian federal system, believing that such an enterprise could only lead to disaster. The logic of nationalism was invariably one of secession and the construction of a separate nation state.[16] Thus, the various schemes for *statut particulier* and similar arrangements either were themselves separatist or were simply naive: by strengthening nationalism they would inevitably lead to separation.

By the early 1960s, Trudeau was pondering a new strategy: returning to Ottawa. Perhaps by establishing a strong presence in the federal government he and like-minded francophones would be able to present the Québécois with an alternative to the nationalism of the Quebec government and lead them out of their fixation upon Quebec. To do that, however, he and his colleagues would have to assume positions within the federal government; they would have to run for election.

To the extent Trudeau had been associated with any political party it had been the CCF and its successor, the NDP. But it was obvious that the NDP was not going to form a government in the foreseeable future. The Liberals, on the other hand, who were the Official Opposition, could entertain such hopes, and the Pearson leadership was actively seeking prominent francophone recruits. They were especially interested in Jean Marchand, former leader of the Confédération des syndicats nationaux and member of the B&B Commission. But Marchand insisted that he must be accompanied by others, namely his friend Pierre Trudeau and the journalist Gérard Pelletier.

There were complications, however. Trudeau, in particular, had been highly critical of Pearson's position that Canada should use American nuclear warheads and had expressed his views in bitter *Cité libre* articles. The issue was sufficient to preclude his running in the 1963 election.

By the 1965 election the warheads issue had receded. Moreover, the Pearson Liberals were in power. They were still keen on recruiting Marchand—but Trudeau was another matter. After all, in his denunciations of accommodation with the Lesage government and its neo-nationalism, he was directly attacking the very policy that the Pearson government had been pursuing. This was not lost on such architects of the policy as Maurice Lamontagne, who actually discouraged Trudeau from running.[17] Eventually, they bowed to Marchand's insistence that he would go to Ottawa only if Trudeau and Pelletier could accompany him. Even then, there was an embarrassingly long delay while Liberal party organizers looked for a seat in which Trudeau might run. Finally, rather than a predominantly francophone riding, as Trudeau had wanted, they settled on the heavily anglophone, and affluent, riding of Town of Mount Royal.

Although Jean Marchand insisted that Trudeau (and Pelletier) should accompany him to Ottawa, even he did not fully share Trudeau's views on Quebec nationalism. After the election, in which all three were successful, Jean Marchand reportedly advised Pearson not to appoint Trudeau as his parliamentary secretary, warning that Trudeau was a poor guide to contemporary Quebec.[18]

The Trudeau Vision of Canada

Trudeau went to Ottawa with a coherent set of views not just on Quebec and its place in Canada, but on political life in general. He had developed a very distinctive understanding of the values that should animate the Canadian polity and of the ways in which its institutions should be organized. Thus, during the years leading up to his assumption of the prime ministership he was able to present Canadians with a radically new vision of their country.

At the centre of Trudeau's political world-view was, of course, his indi-vidualism. There could be no doubt that the individual should be supreme and that all collectivities were suspect. But Trudeau's individualism was a peculiarly demanding one. Rooted in the Catholic doctrine of personalism, it stressed personal responsibility and the use of one's own abilities to per-form 'good works'. It was an individualism that excluded self-indulgence; in fact, it could call for public service and a political career.[19]

Coupled with this individualism was an abiding commitment to human rights. If the individual is to be free he or she must enjoy the political and legal capacity to exercise that freedom. By and large, Trudeau saw these rights in quite conventional, and rather naive, terms. Citizens, he presumed, could actually hold their governments responsible through the simple act of voting. Indeed, if they did not use that right properly, they simply got the govern-ments they deserved.[20] His writings suggested little appreciation of the capacity for independent action that the state afforded political leaders.[21] (Of course, his career as prime minister was to suggest otherwise.) Nor did his writings reveal a well-developed sense of economic and social rights.

In another respect, however, Trudeau's notion of human rights was quite unconventional, for he insisted that, in the case of Canada, human rights extended beyond conventional notions of legal, political, and even social rights, to incorporate linguistic rights: 'In a country such as ours, with its two founding linguistic groups, the preservation of individual rights also must mean the guarantee of the linguistic rights of both groups.'[22]

Trudeau had very definite ideas as to how human rights should be safe-guarded. In the case of Canada, the traditional legal and conventional bases were insufficient. Nothing less than a formal charter of rights, entrenched in the constitution, would do. As early as 1955 Trudeau had advocated the con-stitutional entrenchment of a bill of rights,[23] of which a central purpose was the protection of language rights.[24] Indeed, in his address as justice minister to the Canadian Bar Association in 1967, Trudeau presented entrenchment of language rights as the virtual solution to Canada's national unity problems:

The language provisions of the British North America Act are very limited. I believe that we require a broader definition and more extensive guaran-tees in the matter of recognition of the two official languages. . . . I venture to say that, *if we are able to reach agreement on this vital aspect of the over-all prob-lem, we will have found a solution to a basic issue facing Canada today* [emphasis added].[25]

The corollary to Trudeau's insistence on the primacy of the individual was, of course, a strong opposition to nationalism. Not only was he fiercely critical of French-Canadian nationalism, but he was also hostile to any other nationalist ideology that championed an ethnic or culturally defined collectivity. Indeed, he equated nationalism with emotion. For him nationalism could have no material base and thus had no place in politics, which should be based upon reason.

In Trudeau's writings, federalism took pride of place as the strategy for creating a politics of reason. Drawing on the works of the nineteenth-century British writer, Lord Acton, Trudeau hailed federalism as a superior form of organization that has the promise of replacing the emotion of nationalism with reason. Federalism could bring together societies, even nationalities, that would not otherwise share the same political system, thereby avoiding the excesses of the nation state. By their very logic, federal systems must be based on accommodation and continual bargaining:

> Federalism is by its very essence a compromise and a pact. It is a compromise in the sense that when national consensus on *all* things is not desirable or cannot readily obtain, the area of consensus is reduced in order that consensus on *some* things be reached. It is a pact or quasi-treaty in the sense that the terms of that compromise cannot be changed unilaterally.[26]

Ultimately, federalism must privilege reason over emotion as the basis for political action and decision making.

On other occasions, Trudeau offered another route to a politics of reason: functionalism. This seemed to involve the technocratic notions of systems management and planning that were making their rounds in the 1960s. Indeed, they became a staple of the early years of the Trudeau government, though in Ottawa, as elsewhere, their credibility was short-lived. Trudeau's ideas about federalism had more lasting power.

Trudeau did acknowledge that in some instances reason might be insufficient to hold a federation together, and there might be a temptation to resort to nationalism. To be sure, in a multinational federation this might not be a narrow ethnic nationalism but it would still be nationalism. Such a strategy, he insisted, would probably be counter-productive:

> If the heavy past of nationalism is relied upon to keep a unitary nation-state together, much more nationalism would appear to be required in the case of a federal nation-state. Yet if nationalism is encouraged as a rightful doctrine and noble passion, what is to prevent it from being used by some group, region, or province within the nation? If 'nation algérienne' was a valid battle cry against France, how can Algerian Arabs object to the cry of 'nation kabyle' now being used against them?[27]

This, then, was the great virtue of multinational federations. In the last analysis, they could be held together only by reason.

As his political career progressed and he became more directly involved with the problem of sustaining the Canadian polity, Trudeau began to develop a second alternative to nationalism: the notion of a shared political community or a 'just society'.[28] But whatever the strategy or formula to be used, the promise was the same: to transcend narrow nationalisms and make it possible for different groups to live in harmony in the same political order.

On this basis, Trudeau could in fact offer a compelling new vision of the nature and purpose of the Canadian polity. Canada could be no less than an example for the whole world. If this should be true, then Canadians had a moral responsibility to overcome their divisions and, in particular, defeat the forces of Quebec nationalism. Much more was at stake than the mere survival of Canada. The real issue was the fundamental issue of politics everywhere: defence of reason, threatened by the forces of emotion. Trudeau's vision of Canada had a strong element of 'rational messianism', to use Reg Whitaker's phrase.[29]

If Pierre Trudeau's vision of the country was expressed far more clearly than that of most aspiring politicians, it was also far more personal than most. Rather than devices designed to attract supporters or ingratiate him with voters, Trudeau's writings were nothing less than an attempt to reconceive Canada on the basis of his own beliefs. As Gérard Bergeron has written, 'from his own personal make-up, he extrapolated the model of the ideal Canadian citizen'.[30]

In effect, his vision of Canada constituted the terms upon which he was prepared to accept Canada and Canadians. Trudeau made it clear on a variety of occasions that if Canadians would not conform to the model he had constructed, then they had no interest for him. In an interview with Anthony Westell of the *Toronto Star* in February 1969, he declared:

> If I don't think that we can create some form of a bilingual country, I am no longer interested in working in Ottawa. If I want to work as an English-speaking person I'll look for a job in another country or I'll go and work in Europe or I'll look for a job in Washington. . . . What attaches me to this country is the belief that the French language can have certain rights. I think it's true for many French Canadians who believe in federalism. . . . It's the only view that can make any sense.[31]

Clearly, the vision of Canada that Trudeau had so carefully and eloquently constructed differed radically from the way in which most Canadians saw their country. This was true even of French Canadians. Despite some superficial similarities, the Trudeau vision was in fact quite removed from mainstream French-Canadian thought. But most English Canadians did not know that.

The Trudeau Vision and French Canada

As Chapter 1 demonstrated, the established French-Canadian conception of Canada was rooted in a pervasive dualism. Most clearly delineated in the double-compact theory of Henri Bourassa, it saw Canada as composed of two distinct collectivities. In Bourassa's terms, Canada was 'a fruitful alliance of the two races, each one remaining distinctly itself'. At the same time, the province of Quebec had a special role as the centre of the francophone collectivity as 'the particular heritage of French Canadians'.

This understanding of Canada had become firmly entrenched among French Quebec's political and intellectual élites. And it had been duly affirmed by Quebec provincial governments. In the process, it had come to be shared by most Quebec francophones as a given of political life.

Trudeau's vigorous defence of language rights throughout Canada fell squarely within that tradition and was in perfect continuity with Henri Bourassa's campaigns against Ontario's Regulation 17. On this basis, Ramsay Cook could write in 1971, 'Bourassa's position is best and most fully represented today by those French Canadians who follow Prime Minister Trudeau.'[32]

Trudeau's dualism, however, went no further, and in fact he rejected the underlying spirit of dualism as it was generally understood in Quebec, including Henri Bourassa's basic premises. Indeed, despite the claim of some writers that in attacking Quebec neo-nationalism Trudeau was reiterating the pan-Canadian ideas that Henri Bourassa had first advocated,[33] Trudeau's main writings of the period, such as the pieces assembled in *Federalism and the French Canadians*, contain only cursory references to Bourassa.[34] Their intellectual inspiration lay elsewhere, most notably with the turn-of-the-century English political theorist, Lord Acton.

Trudeau's defence of language rights was based not upon the historical claims of collectivities, or races, but upon individual human rights. He was quite explicit that if there was a case for French language rights, which he strongly believed to be so, it was due to numbers. And other groups, with no pretense to historic claims, might make the same claim should numbers favour them as well: 'Historical origins are less important than people generally think, the proof being that neither Eskimo nor Indian dialects have any kind of privileged position. On the other hand, if there were six million people living in Canada whose mother tongue was Ukrainian, it is likely that this language would establish itself as forcefully as French.'[35]

In fact, Trudeau was explicitly opposed to granting legal recognition to a francophone collectivity. He was strongly critical of the B&B Commission's notion of biculturalism, especially as it was developed under André Laurendeau. Biculturalism may have been in close continuity with Henri Bourassa's vision of Canada, but it was not part of his.

Finally, Trudeau was vehemently opposed to any enhanced recognition of Quebec as the primary base of francophones, including the steps the Pearson government had taken in this direction. In 1966 he declared, 'Federalism cannot work unless all the provinces are in basically the same relation to the central government,'[36] and in 1968 he proclaimed, 'Particular status for Quebec is the biggest intellectual hoax ever foisted on the people of Quebec and the people of Canada.'[37] Indeed, in 1967 he even used a vulgarism ('connerie') to describe special status.[38]

In effect, Trudeau was attempting to redefine Canadian dualism, drastically reducing its meaning. Rather than a dualism of collectivities it was one of individuals who happen to speak one of two different languages. Nor was this dualism rooted in geography. It was to extend throughout Canada as a whole once language rights were recognized.

Trudeau's version of dualism offered a strategy for undermining the older notion of dualism, and the special significance it bestowed upon Quebec. Through his brand of linguistic dualism Quebec would be reduced to 'a province like the others'. If minority language rights were protected throughout Canada, then the French-Canadian nation would stretch from Maillardville in British Columbia to the Acadian community on the Atlantic coast:

> Once you have done that, Quebec cannot say it alone speaks for French Canadians. . . . Mr Robarts will be speaking for French Canadians in Ontario, Mr Robichaud will be speaking for French Canadians in New Brunswick, Mr Thatcher will speak for French Canadians in Saskatchewan, and Mr Pearson will be speaking for all French Canadians. Nobody will be able to say, 'I need more power because I speak for the French-Canadian nation.'[39]

In effect, Trudeau was calling upon Quebec francophones to change fundamentally the way in which they see Canada, to cease looking to the Quebec government as the protector of their distinctive interests, and to place their confidence in the federal government instead. As Jeremy Webber has observed: 'As [Trudeau] would often tell Quebecers, they had to choose between two alternative—and not complementary—objects of allegiance: Quebec or Canada. Although Trudeau's administration preached respect for provincial jurisdiction, when it came to allegiance he used the language of a unitary state.'[40]

The dominant francophone view of Canada and of the central role of the Quebec government had deep historical roots. Indeed, the notion that francophones had to place their confidence primarily in the Quebec government, with its largely French-Canadian electorate, had been established in 1791, with the creation of Lower Canada. And it had been reinforced time and again as francophones struggled with their anglophone compatriots over basic questions, including the very recognition of the French language. Now, thanks to the neo-nationalist leadership of the Lesage government, the notion of dualism, centred in Quebec, was more deeply rooted than ever. Trudeau could not simply wish away two centuries of history, however eloquent his vision of a linguistic equality that stretched from coast to coast. Besides, his vision simply lacked credibility, for most francophones knew that their language and their collectivity could never have the strength in the rest of the country that it enjoyed in Quebec.

Thus, when Trudeau launched his bid for the leadership of the Liberal party, he and his vision of Canada had limited appeal to Quebec francophones; among the intellectual élites the rejection was massive and open. Symptomatic was the position taken by *Le Devoir* editor, Claude Ryan, whose commitment to federalism was beyond dispute but who had long insisted that there must be an accommodation of Quebec nationalism. Accusing Trudeau of being 'dangerously rigid and haughty', he endorsed Paul Hellyer for the Liberal leadership, after Mitchell Sharp became unavailable.[41] At election time, Ryan noted that unlike the rigid and intransigent Pierre Trudeau, Robert Stanfield had made a sustained and honest effort to comprehend the Quebec question. Moreover, in choosing Marcel Faribault as his Quebec leader, Stanfield demonstrated that he was prepared to risk displeasing English-Canadian opinion. Thus, he declared his support, as a general rule, for Conservative rather than Liberal candidates.[42]

The unease of francophone intellectuals about Trudeau and his diffidence toward Quebec was only confirmed in February 1968, when Trudeau, who was appearing on CBC English-language television, first attacked the nationalist intellectuals and then in effect ridiculed the whole of Quebec society by denouncing the quality of French spoken in Quebec: 'I don't think Ottawa should give one single whit of power to the province of Quebec until it has shown the rest of Canada it can teach better language in its schools.' Some Quebec nationalists, he said, spoke 'awful French' and they wanted 'to impose this lousy French on the whole of Canada'.[43]

Among provincial political élites, there was open resistance. Not surprisingly, the Union nationale premier, Daniel Johnson, rejected Trudeau's position on many issues. Indeed, during the subsequent election campaign Trudeau directly attacked Johnson's claim, previously voiced by the Lesage government, that Quebec was entitled to deal with foreign governments on matters that fell within provincial jurisdiction. The Union nationale organization actively supported the Conservative candidates in Quebec.[44] But even Liberal forces greeted Trudeau and his vision with great apprehension. A month before the convention most of the Liberal members of the Quebec legislature were actively campaigning against his candidacy.[45]

Over the previous few years, the Quebec Liberal Party had embraced what was anathema to Trudeau: special status for Quebec. Jean Lesage had been propounding the idea since 1965.[46] The party may have rejected René Lévesque's scheme of sovereignty-association at its 1967 convention, but, so pervasive was Quebec nationalism in the party that it had adopted an alternative scheme, defined in a lengthy report by Paul Gérin-Lajoie, that was nothing less than special status.[47]

Jean Lesage had watched Trudeau's entry into federal politics with considerable alarm. He directly protested Pearson's appointment of Trudeau as his parliamentary secretary in 1965,[48] and was offended by Trudeau's 'connerie' remark.[49] When the race began for Pearson's successor, he supported Robert Winters and despaired at the thought of Trudeau's being a candidate.[50] (Once it became clear that Trudeau was the front runner, some Quebec Liberals did come out in his support.)[51]

Speaking for Quebec

None the less, fortune favoured Trudeau, allowing him to emerge as the leading Quebec voice in the federal arena. Jean Marchand, who Pearson had presumed would be his successor, decided not to run for the leadership, in particular because his English wasn't fluent enough. Marchand did not fully share Trudeau's ideas about Quebec and its place in Canada. ('I am more in tune with Quebec nationalism than Pierre is. Of course I'm a Canadian. But in a certain sense I am more Québécois than Canadian.')[52] But, feeling that there should be a francophone candidate, he saw Trudeau as the best possibility, as did their colleague Gérard Pelletier. Indeed no other Quebec francophones did come forward.

Still the Quebec Liberals did not fall in line behind Trudeau, partly because of his views on Quebec. During the months leading up to Trudeau's formal declaration of his candidacy, Senator Maurice Lamontagne, who had played such a critical role in developing the Pearson strategy for Quebec, had persisted in making the case for special status and arguing against Trudeau's views.[53] None of the leading francophone cabinet members, other than Marchand, declared for Trudeau. The senior Quebec cabinet minister,

Maurice Sauvé, supported Paul Martin.[54] Jean-Luc Pepin, who had helped to elaborate Pearson's notions of 'co-operative federalism', came out for Mitchell Sharp, shifting to Trudeau only with great reluctance after Sharp withdrew in favour of Trudeau.[55] Léo Cadieux declared himself firmly for Paul Hellyer.[56] Jean-Pierre Côté supported Robert Winters.[57] Newly-minted cabinet member Jean Chrétien had no problem with Trudeau's vision; he had spoken against special status for Quebec.[58] But he first supported his mentor, Mitchell Sharp, before following him to Trudeau.

Nor did the Quebec caucus rally behind Trudeau. Two months before the convention, only 20 of the 56 members openly supported Trudeau. Two weeks before the convention, Trudeau's organization claimed to have the support of half the Quebec backbenchers, but one of those named then declared for Robert Winters.[59] The president of the caucus supported Paul Hellyer. According to a report prepared three days before the convention, the Quebec caucus was so badly divided that if the party as a whole had been in such shape it would have had difficulty surviving the convention.[60] In the end, apparently the majority of Quebec MPs did vote for him.[61]

Trudeau's ascension as primary federal spokesman for Quebec was further aided in July 1968 by the death of André Laurendeau, at the age of 56. One of the leading francophone intellectuals of his generation and the spiritual heir to Henri Bourassa, Laurendeau had gone to Ottawa as co-chair of the Royal Commission on Bilingualism and Biculturalism in order to represent the established French-Canadian view of dualism. As we shall see, that view pervaded the deliberations and reports of the commission as long as he presided over them. No one else in the commission, or in the federal arena, possessed Laurendeau's stature.

With Laurendeau's death, there was no one on the federal scene who could credibly dispute Trudeau's claim that his vision of Canada represented the aspirations of the Québécois, and Trudeau had no difficulty disposing of those few English Canadians who tried to do so. Thus, Trudeau's vision of Canada, however widely it may have been rejected in Quebec, was accepted as the official definition of 'what Quebec wants'.

The Trudeau Vision and English Canada

Trudeau's vision of Canada had even less relationship to the predominant English-Canadian idea of Canada than it did to that of most Quebeckers. Certainly, English Canadians had never displayed much interest in dualism, even in Trudeau's highly attenuated linguistic form. And the predominantly English-Canadian provincial governments had all acted to reduce or eliminate French language rights, apparently with the support of most of their English-Canadian majorities. Nor had English Canadians ever showed much concern over the marginal status of French in federal institutions. English Canadians may have believed in human rights, to varying degrees, but they clearly did not see language rights as one of them.

By the same token, English-Canadian political and intellectual élites were far from united in support of a constitutional bill of rights. After all, Canada had always followed the British practice of relying upon convention and common law to protect basic rights. The notion of a charter collided with the British principle of parliamentary supremacy. John Diefenbaker did succeed in securing a Canadian Bill of Rights, as a simple act of Parliament, but of course it had nothing to do with protecting language rights. Indeed, when as prime minister, Trudeau presented his proposal for a bill of rights in February 1969, most provinces either rejected it outright or sought to restrict it to political rights alone.[62]

None the less, even if Trudeau's vision of Canada had little similarity to the way most English-Canadians thought of their country, it still had something to offer. Whereas Quebec francophones were becoming more rooted than ever in their historical notion of Canada, English Canadians were becoming increasingly uneasy with theirs. The notion of Canada that was rooted in the British connection and British political traditions was being threatened by the decline of Britain and the spread of American dominance throughout the world. Indeed, a distinctly Canadian nationalism had been steadily growing, thanks in part to a series of actions by the federal state itself.

Trudeau's vision provided some content to this emerging sense of Canadian nationhood. He offered Canada a new, compelling purpose that had significance for the world as a whole. Canada would show how different groups could live peaceably in the same country. Moreover, Canadians would not simply share the same country but they would come together to create a new society. In the process, Canada, and Canadians, would assume an importance that they had never had before. As H.D. Forbes has written:

> Trudeau's vision was a *moral* vision because it involved more than just good economic planning to increase the material wealth of Canadians. . . . It appealed to their moral sense, challenging them to rise above their irrational fears and traditional prejudices in order to do something important for mankind.[63]

In short, Canada would be a different kind of nation because it would transcend conventional nationalism, and indeed emotions of any kind. Of course, such a sense of historic purpose can itself provide a powerful focus for nationalism, even if it should be in the name of a 'non-nation'. It might even support a sense of superiority to lesser countries.

Several years later, when the Canadian experiment seemed to be threatened by the unexpected election of René Lévesque's Parti Québécois, Trudeau expressed this new Canadian messianism in especially dramatic terms:

> Times, circumstances and pure will cemented us together in a unique national enterprise, and that enterprise, by flying in the face of all expectations, of all experiences, of all conventional wisdom, that enterprise provides the world with a lesson in fraternity. This extraordinary undertaking is so advanced in the way of social justice and of prosperity, that to abandon it now would be to sin against the spirit, to sin against humanity.[64]

Even if English Canadians did not come to believe that the unity of the Canadian nation had such universal significance as Trudeau wished, it was important for most of them. In these terms as well, Trudeau's vision had something to offer; namely a strategy for solving the Quebec problem. It was a strategy moreover that was far more congenial to most English Canadians than the effort to accommodate Quebec nationalism that Pearson and others had so labouriously pursued. With Trudeau's strategy accommodation was no longer necessary; in fact, it was counter-productive. Instead, unity could be achieved through official bilingualism and a constitutional charter, measures applied throughout the country as a whole. Quebec could be treated as a province just like the others, and Quebec francophones would become Canadians like everyone else.

It is not surprising that many English Canadians should have seen Trudeau as the saviour, the embodiment of the Canadian nation—the perfect example of the new Canadian. This sentiment is evoked especially well by two leading English-Canadian journalists. Peter C. Newman described Trudeau's performance at the 1968 Liberal convention:

> It's as though Trudeau is performing what Norman Mailer once described as 'the indispensable psychic act of a leader, who takes national anxieties so long buried and releases them to the surface where they belong'. . . . He seems to hold out the promise that the process of discovering Canada has not come to an end, that Expo 67 wasn't just a momentary phenomenon, that this is a young nation with vast, unexploited possibilities. He personifies the hoped-for sophistication of the perfectly bicultural Canada of tomorrow.[65]

Remembering the mood of 1968, Richard Gwyn writes:

> The 1968 election and the Centennial and Expo were together the last
> time we were wholly confident of ourselves as a country. . . . In 1968, we
> invested a part of our national psyche in Trudeau. . . . We called it, in 1968,
> Trudeau-mania. Really, it was Canada-mania.[66]

From his different vantage point, Claude Ryan commented sardonically on
the tendency of English Canada, ever since the fall of St Laurent, to look to
Quebec for a 'political messiah' who will enable Canada to progress while at
the same time avoiding discontent among French Canadians. Trudeau was
simply the latest in a long line of candidates. To that point, no one had proved
equal to the task.[67]

There is, of course, considerable irony in the possibility that English
Canadians should have seen Trudeau as saviour of the Canadian nation. In his
writings, he had gone to great pains to dissociate himself from Canadian
nationalism, just as he so passionately rejected nationalism in general.
'Manifeste pour une politique fonctionnelle', the 1964 manifesto of which
he was a primary author, had declared:

> Making nationalism the decisive criterion for policies and priorities is a
> sterile and reactionary choice. . . . Whether it be the first budget, in June
> 1963, of the Honourable Walter Gordon, the regulations of the Board of
> Broadcast Governors on Canadian content, the current intolerance of
> 'white, Anglo-Saxon Protestants', or the widespread notion that 'the State
> of Quebec' should be the economic arm of French Canada, we are dealing
> with the same problem.[68]

As for Canada, it is simply a fact of history. To break it up would be to evade
the real issues. To integrate it with the United States would be in conformity
with world trends, but would be a mistake *at the present time*:

> First of all, there is this legal and geographic fact: Canada. To try to split it
> in two . . . strikes us as an escape from real and important tasks that need to
> be done. To try to integrate it with another geographic entity also strikes us
> as a futile undertaking at present, even though, in principle, that might seem
> more in accord with the way the world is evolving.[69]

Walter Gordon recognized that he was 'not a nationalist' and hesitated to
support Trudeau for the Liberal leadership.[70] By the same token, upon
becoming prime minister, Trudeau had little patience for the concerns of
English-Canadian nationalists about the economic and cultural domination

by the United States. Walter Gordon abandoned the Liberal Party to found the Committee for an Independent Canada.[71] Of course, Trudeau's position evolved substantially during his tenure as prime minister.

At the same time, beyond offering English Canadians new hope and meaning for their country, whether as beacon to the world or a nation reunited by bilingualism, Trudeau had the more prosaic appeal of being a Quebec francophone who seemed prepared to put Quebec in its place. He may not have proclaimed that intention himself, but his vehement opposition to special status may have seemed to promise as much, especially if his plans for official bilingualism should be ignored.

Finally, the fierceness of Trudeau's opposition to Quebec nationalism may have reassured English Canadians who were troubled by the continuing acts of violence by the Front de libération du Québec. Trudeau, it seemed, could be relied upon to restore order and respect for the law in Quebec. His defiance of separatists hurling projectiles at the dignitaries' stand at the St-Jean Baptiste parade could not have come at a more opportune moment: the evening before the 1968 federal election.

Whatever the precise balance of factors at work, Pierre Trudeau's vision of Canada clearly did mobilize support among some English Canadians, both in his campaign for the Liberal leadership and in the subsequent federal election. And, unlike their Quebec counterparts, leading English-Canadian intellectuals actively supported Trudeau's candidacy from the outset. Among them was Ramsay Cook, who had left the NDP in protest over the question of 'two nations'. For Cook, Trudeau was 'straight' on Quebec.[72] Eventually 600 academics signed a petition in support of Trudeau's candidacy.[73]

Similarly, a number of rising young Ontario MPs, such as Donald Macdonald and Robert Stanbury, formed an organization to rally support for Trudeau. Later, when Mitchell Sharp withdrew from the race, he threw his support to Trudeau. Indeed, Lester Pearson favoured Trudeau as his successor and let it be known in several ways.[74]

Still, to support Trudeau was not necessarily to endorse his approach to national unity, which in fact made some of his supporters quite uneasy. To the end, Pearson had serious reservations about Trudeau.[75] He had preferred that his successor be a francophone, but his first choice had been Marchand. Even Mitchell Sharp, during his campaign for the Liberal leadership, made an effort to distinguish his position from Trudeau's, declaring that Ottawa should be flexible in its dealings with Quebec, because a confrontation between Ottawa and Quebec City would be 'disastrous' for the country's future. After withdrawing in favour of Trudeau, Sharp still said he would prefer that Trudeau be less rigid in constitutional matters, although he did not expect any major disagreements with Trudeau.[76]

Winning the 1968 Election

Turning to the general public, whether in Quebec or in English Canada, how should Trudeau's 1968 electoral victory be interpreted? Certainly, his personal appeal was a large part of the story. But how significant were his ideas on Quebec and its place in Canada? For that matter, the Liberals may have won a strong parliamentary majority, 155 of 264 seats, but they received less than half of the popular vote: 45.5 per cent.

Even in Quebec, the Liberal support was not as great as it might have seemed. Although the Liberals' victory in 56 of Quebec's 74 ridings was interpreted by some observers as proof that Trudeau's vision expressed the aspirations of francophones, it is not clear that the Liberals were supported by a majority of Quebec's francophones. Although the Liberal popular vote in Quebec was the highest of all the provinces, it was still only 53.6 per cent; and francophones in Quebec were considerably less likely than non-francophones to support the Liberals.[77]

Even then, the Liberal support may have been based as much on Trudeau's favourite-son status as on his vision of Canada. (Trudeaumania, of course, was a distinctly English-Canadian phenomenon.[78]) However receptive the PC and NDP may have been to Quebec's demands for distinct status, the leaderships of both parties were effectively English-Canadian. The PCs may have enlisted Marcel Faribault as their Quebec leader; the NDP had the highly popular Robert Cliche. But neither of them even held seats; Trudeau was already prime minister.

In any case, the 1968 electoral victory had the direct result that Trudeau's vision reigned supreme in the Liberal Party and in the federal government. The two other federal parties were still, officially, in favour of the 1960s strategy of developing openings to Quebec nationalism, but Trudeau's electoral victory took care of that too. The predominantly English-Canadian PC and NDP leaderships found their positions untenable when a Quebec francophone prime minister, who had become the effective spokesperson for Quebec at the federal level, was claiming on the basis of deep personal knowledge of Quebec that such a strategy was both unnecessary and wrongheaded. Not surprisingly, many English-Canadians voters were finding his arguments very appealing.

Indeed, during the 1968 election campaign Trudeau had been unsparing in his condemnation of the PCs and NDP for their Quebec strategies. He attacked the Progressive Conservatives for their two-nations vision of Canada, portraying the party as hostage to Quebec nationalists. Stanfield, who by this point was moderating his support of two nations, accused Trudeau of misrepresenting the PC position.[79] Speaking in Saint John, Trudeau zeroed in on Marcel Faribault and other Quebec PCs who claimed that their conception of two nations was based on a 'sociological' sense of nation. He argued that not only did this notion reject one-third of the country but that in any event it implied bi-national political institutions. He challenged Faribault and others to 'say quite frankly that they are not talking of two nations in the sociological sense or any other—two nations which can lead into the kind of political consequences of special status.' And he denounced special status as being not only unworkable but an insult to Quebeckers: 'The people of Quebec don't want special status, treatment or privilege. They don't need a wheelchair or a crutch to get along.'[80]

Trudeau's comments on the NDP's support for special status provoked NDP leader Tommy Douglas to charge that Trudeau was dividing Canada as it had not been divided for a long time. 'Anyone who talks about special status for Quebec or any negotiation is automatically called a separatist [by Trudeau].'[81]

The PCs and the NDP: Falling in Line

After the election, the PCs and the NDP soon fell in line with the new Trudeau orthodoxy. In the case of the PCs, the commitment to accommodate the demands of Quebec nationalists had in any event been qualified. Moreover, the architect of the opening, Marcel Faribault, went down to ignominious defeat. Thus, the PCs simply abandoned their strategy; no formal debate was necessary.

With the NDP things were more complicated. There, the commitment to an accommodation of Quebec nationalism was more deeply rooted. In fact, there had been pressure in the party in the late 1960s for a stronger position. Many of the members of the Quebec NDP had never been satisfied with the party's positions, which did not allow for as thorough a change in Quebec's constitutional position as they wanted. And the party had not granted their long-held wish for a formal recognition of Quebec's right to self-determination. In fact, the Quebec members had not even dared to present the proposition to the party, knowing it would be rejected.

By the late 1960s, however, pressure from Quebec was joined by radicalized forces within the English-Canadian membership, grouped around the Waffle. At the 1971 NDP convention the Waffle and the Quebec NDP combined to support a resolution calling for formal recognition of Quebec's right to self-determination. For the party leadership this was unacceptable. Though it was prepared to support renunciation of the use of force to prevent separation, it feared that the notion of a right to self-determination conveyed an openness to Quebec independence that would offend the Canadian nationalism of most English Canadians. The leadership presented an alternative resolution, 'Towards a New Canada', which, though it declared that 'The unity of this country cannot be based on force', eschewed the language of self-determination. After a prolonged and at times emotional debate, the leadership's resolution was endorsed by a vote of 853 to 423.[82]

Other sections of the leadership's resolution made it clear that not only were the leaders fiercely opposed to the position on Quebec self-determination advanced by the Waffle and the Quebec NDP, but they were now even opposed to the whole approach to the Quebec question that the party had struggled so hard to develop during the 1960s. This too, they had concluded, was beyond the limits of acceptability for most English Canadians. Thus, 'Towards a New Canada' declared:

> We have attempted to resolve these [constitutional] differences with phrases which have proven to be open to a dual interpretation, something which has created sharp difference within all political parties. These phrases, such as 'two nations', 'special status', 'equal partnership', have often proved to be obstacles to agreement rather than aids. The time has come to find precise ways of stating the deep issues in order to bring to the fullest clarity the major differences.

The resolution offered no hint as to what the 'precise ways' might be. It simply called for the NDP federal council to 'establish machinery' that would define the assumptions and procedures for 'a complete renegotiation of our constitutional arrangements'.[83] In effect, it was calling a halt to the whole effort to find an accommodation of Quebec nationalism.

In the words of Charles Taylor, a leading figure in that effort, expressions such as 'two nations' and 'special status' had become 'ping pong' words that meant different things in English Canada and Quebec, and that had come back to haunt the NDP.[84] To put it more concretely, the NDP's overtures to Quebec nationalism had not brought the expected electoral benefits in Quebec, and during the 1968 election they had become a liability in the rest of the country.[85]

The fact of the matter is that the reason 'two nations' and 'special status' had become a liability for the NDP was the new prominence of Pierre Trudeau and his message. Whereas the Quebec NDP, and Quebec in general, had been moving to a more radical position on Quebec-Canada relations, the leadership of the NDP and most of English Canada were stepping back. In both cases, the explanation is the same: when Pierre Trudeau became prime minister, the struggle to find in Canadian federalism an accommodation of the new Quebec nationalism, a struggle that had enlisted all three federal parties, had come to a full and irrevocable end.

Now firmly established in power, Trudeau and his like-minded colleagues were free to pursue their new strategy for dealing with the Quebec question. In the process, the premises on which the Pearson government had struggled to develop its approach were definitively abandoned. Rather than seek to accommodate Quebec nationalism, 'coming to terms with the Quiet Revolution' as Pearson put it in his memoirs, the Trudeau government tried to confront Quebec nationalism head on and to replace it with a new Canadian identity. By and large the federal government acted as if Quebec were simply a province like the others, and avoided policies that threatened to suggest otherwise.

We will see in the next chapter how the Trudeau government tried to apply its language policy on a pan-Canadian basis, minimizing concessions to regional differences in language use, and especially to the notion that in Quebec the francophone majority might need special attention. The following chapter will consider why the Trudeau government rejected the concept of biculturalism, so carefully elaborated by the royal commission that Pearson had established, in favour of multiculturalism. Finally, we will see how, when it came to federalism and the constitution, the Trudeau government had no patience whatsoever for the Pearson government's notions of asymmetry and particular status.

Throughout the 1960s, Trudeau had insisted that the Pearson government's policy of accommodation could only intensify the national unity problem rather than ease it. His new confrontational approach promised to resolve the issue once and for all. Yet, 30 years later the problem is more acute than ever.

PART TWO

Making a
New Canada

CHAPTER 4

Official Bilingualism:
Linguistic Equality From
Sea to Sea

The centre-piece of Pierre Trudeau's strategy for integrating Quebec francophones into a new Canadian identity was official bilingualism. The concern of the federal government with language policy did not begin when
Trudeau became prime minister. Lester Pearson's government had taken
some first steps, especially toward strengthening bilingualism in the federal
government's own operations. But Trudeau and his close colleagues acceler-
ated the pace of language reform and gave it a sharper definition, bringing it
more closely in line with Trudeau's individualist brand of liberalism and
reflecting his determination that language reform should serve to integrate
the Québécois with the whole of Canada.

During the 1960s, there was open debate about the precise directions
that language reform should take. The Royal Commission on Bilingualism
and Biculturalism in particular was highly critical of the methods the Pearson
government had adopted to strengthen French in its own operations.
Moreover, it was divided over whether language policy should be restricted
to the defence of linguistic minorities or whether it should also address the
specific needs of Quebec's francophone majority.

By the end of the 1960s, such questions were no longer debated in federal circles. In language policy, as in so many areas touching on national unity,
or Quebec's relationship with the rest of Canada, the Trudeau government
was able to establish a new orthodoxy, which neither the Progressive
Conservatives nor the New Democratic Party was prepared to challenge. In
effect, Canada's political class, and much of English-Canadian public opinion, perhaps without fully realizing it, had made an historic choice about language policy. Before long, however, it was to become evident that many
Quebec francophones, including leading federalists in the provincial arena,
had not fully subscribed to that choice.

MAKING OTTAWA BILINGUAL

A central goal of Trudeau's language reform was to place French on an equal footing with English in the federal government's own institutions. Trudeau had experienced, and been alienated by, the dominance of English and anglophones during his unhappy years at the Privy Council Office between 1949 and 1951. He had come back to Ottawa determined to change all that.

Daunting as the objective of a bilingual federal government may have been, it clearly was a *sine qua non* of any strategy to deal with the Quebec question. Even the most nationalist of Quebec federalists agreed on that. After all, André Laurendeau, who had deep family roots in Quebec's nationalist circles and was editor of *Le Devoir*, was the co-chair of a federal royal commission whose primary mandate was to establish bilingualism and biculturalism in federal institutions. Even if Quebec were to obtain special status, Ottawa would still be dealing with Quebec citizens in many areas. It needed to have the capacity to do so, and to be seen in Quebec to have that capacity.

None the less, the objective of a bilingual federal government had another special importance for Trudeau. If he was to have any hope of reaching his consuming goal of making Quebec francophones see the federal government as their *primary* government, Ottawa must become truly bilingual. Quebeckers would have to be convinced that French was fully equal to English and that francophones had finally assumed their rightful place.

This would be a very tall order. Historically, the ideal of linguistic equality in Ottawa had never been acknowledged in more than the most symbolic terms. Some parts of the federal government did have a certain bilingual public face, thanks to section 133 of the British North America Act. Both languages were used in the deliberations of Parliament and the Supreme Court. Laws, the record of parliamentary debates, and other important public documents were published in both languages. The internal operations of the government, however, were a different matter. Although francophones usually had a share of cabinet seats that approximated their proportion of the Canadian population, they had never held portfolios with important economic responsibilities: finance, trade and commerce, or labour. Instead, they tended to predominate in such positions as postmaster general, secretary of state, minister of public works, and minister of justice.[1] For that matter, cabinet meetings were conducted almost exclusively in English.

As for the federal bureaucracy, it was essentially an English-language institution controlled by anglophones, as Trudeau himself had discovered. Francophones had always been under-represented in the upper levels of the federal civil service, as indeed, they had been in the bureaucracy of the

United Canadas.[2] Confederation had done little to improve the situation. To make matters worse, after the First World War, the place of francophones had been further weakened by the preferential status of war veterans and the establishment of the Civil Service Commission, whose recruiting practices tended to be oriented toward the English-language educational systems. As a result, the francophone presence had fallen almost by half, from about 22 per cent in 1918 to 13 per cent in 1946.[3]

Moreover, most of the francophones in the civil service had to work primarily in English. The assumption was that rationality and efficiency precluded the extensive use of French.[4] Thus, the status of French as a language of work was not seen as a legitimate policy concern. In fact, the federal government had no policy on bilingualism in the public service until April 1966.

The Pearson Government

From the time it took office in 1963, the Pearson government steadily worked toward developing such a policy, alarmed as it was at the mounting challenge to national unity. In June 1963, the president of the Privy Council, Maurice Lamontagne, proclaimed the objective of 'perfect equality for the two official languages' in every department. To that end, a special cabinet committee was established, and 1975 was set as the target date for full implementation. The commission issued a directive that linguistic qualifications should appear in advertisements for all competitive positions. Finally, on 6 April 1966, Prime Minister Pearson proclaimed a general policy that would allow public servants to work in their own language and to apply 'their respective cultural values'. In effect, the government had committed itself to creating a public service that was not only bilingual but bicultural as well.[5]

The primary means the government adopted to achieve this goal was language training, which was expanded very rapidly. Starting with 42 enrolments in 1963–4, the Civil Service Commission's courses had already grown to 3,188 enrolments by 1966–7, at a cost of about $3.7 million and with 200 teachers and 100 additional staff. It was estimated that by 1971 the cost of the program would grow to $10 million yearly.[6] The government had embarked on an ambitious and expensive program.

The B&B Commission

The Royal Commission on Bilingualism and Biculturalism saw reform of the federal government's own operations as the highest of priorities. In the first volume of its report, the commission declared it was 'inescapable' that 'bilingualism becomes essential first in the institutions shared by all Canadians'.[7] However, given its own understanding of the notions of bilingualism and biculturalism, as well as its mandate to create an 'equal partnership' between English Canadians and French Canadians, the commission entertained methods and made recommendations that differed radically from the policies of the Pearson government.

The basic recommendation of the commission was to establish official bilingualism within the federal government: 'We recommend that English and French be formally declared the official languages of the Parliament of Canada, of the federal courts, of the federal government, and of the federal administration.'[8] Though it had no specific recommendations for the operations of the federal cabinet, Parliament, or the Supreme Court, it had much to say about the public service, devoting most of Book III, *The Work World* to an analysis and elaboration of recommendations.

The commission contended that within the public service equal partnership necessarily required equality between cultures. A truly 'bicultural' public service entailed 'the coexistence and collaboration of the two cultures so that both can flourish and contribute to the overall objectives of government'.[9] Equal partnership meant that francophones not only must be present at all levels but they must be in a position both to work in their own language and to express their own culture. Much more was required than individual bilingualism; indeed, individual bilingualism was quite secondary.

From this perspective the reforms of the Pearson government were both insufficient and ill-conceived: 'If we have not achieved a bicultural Public Service in Canada it is precisely because bilingualism in the Service has been individual and not institutional in character.'[10] The policy of the federal administration 'envisages the general use of language training to encourage bilingualism' so that individuals may be completely free to work in their own language. Yet, 'no other country with more than one language and culture has ever been able to place sole confidence in such a procedure.' In the case of the Canadian public service, given both the predominance of unilingual anglophones and the basic confinement of bilingualism to francophones, 'the French language cannot develop in direct competition with English, no matter how effective recruitment and language-training programmes may be.'[11]

For that matter, the commission argued that the language training programs had produced very mediocre results. Pedagogy could be improved, but without the structural changes to the public service that it proposed, 'students will only participate in a waste of time, energy, and money'.[12]

The commission derived two basic recommendations, which amounted to radical new departures in making a bilingual public service. First, for an 'active and effective francophone participation at the highest levels', appointments to positions of deputy minister, associate deputy minister, and assistant deputy minister, as well as equivalents in Crown corporations and other federal agencies, should 'be administered so as to ensure effectively balanced participation of anglophones and francophones at these levels.'[13]

Second, so that the francophone culture could indeed flourish in the public service, 'French-language units' should be designated in all federal departments, Crown corporations, and other agencies, as well as in regional offices where the francophone character of the area warranted. In those units French would be the language of work, as it would be the language of communication with the rest of the public service. Moreover, these units, which had to be *existing* units, 'must perform important and integral functions within departments and agencies—they must be essential to the overall work of the department.'[14] (There would be parallel English-language units in Quebec.) In this fashion, the public service could be made bilingual and bicultural without the enormous program of language training on which the Pearson government was embarked. In any event, language training could never produce satisfactory results without structural changes along these lines to ensure that graduates would have the opportunity to put their new linguistic skill to use.[15]

However more effective the commission's preferred approaches might have been in achieving the goal of a bilingual civil service, they violated the integrationist notion of national unity held by many English Canadians. *The Globe and Mail* declared that, rather than seeking to bring Canadians together, the commission seemed to call for a return to the two solitudes and, in doing so, tested the limits of English-Canadian support for bilingualism. The *Toronto Star* denounced the proposal for 'French ghettos' in the public service.[16]

The Trudeau Government

In any event, Trudeau had no inclination to provide the leadership that would have been necessary to implement the B&B Commission's radical new departures. Notions of balancing appointments on a linguistic basis were hardly compatible with his brand of liberalism. And the segregation of workers according to first language also ran counter to his individualism. So the federal government carefully avoided any formal system of 'balanced representation' at the top levels: instead, certain positions were defined as 'bilingual' and thus were open to all on the basis of skill in both languages.

Nor was the B&B Commission's scheme of French-language units pursued rigorously. In the early 1970s the federal government did designate, on an experimental basis, a number of entities to be French language units, but the overwhelming majority, 330 of 457, were in Quebec.[17] In Ottawa, those units accounted for only 5 per cent of the total number of positions,[18] and they tended to be units that were already operating in French rather than the result of an effort to guarantee 'equal partnership' throughout the public service as a whole.

In 1975 the Treasury Board announced that as a result of this experiment it was prepared to adopt the scheme. But in response to protests from anglophone civil servants and their union representatives, it accepted a series of qualifications that, in the opinion of the commissioner of official languages, threatened to undermine the concept.[19] And three years later, the Treasury Board was still deliberating about where to locate the units.[20] In the end, the idea largely gave way to a scheme of designating areas in which, given the wide use of both English and French, employees can choose to work in either.[21] In effect, the idea of French-language units was replaced by bilingual units.

Resistance to the idea of French-language units came in part from francophone civil servants who feared that without work experience in English their chances for mobility would be gravely handicapped. In other words, they presumed that English would continue to have pre-eminence in Ottawa no matter what reforms were introduced. But the concept also met with resistance from English Canadians, both in the public service and outside it, who found linguistic segregation to be threatening. During the early 1970s, Keith Spicer, the first commissioner of official languages, defended the concept in each of his annual reports and attacked the government for foot dragging.[22] But in his last report he passed over it in silence.[23]

To have had any chance of acceptance, the idea would have needed the vigorous leadership of the prime minister. That was not forthcoming. Instead, the Trudeau government followed the Pearson government's path of relying primarily upon language training to create a bilingual service—the approach that the B&B Commission had so firmly attacked. With the emphasis on language training, a very large number of positions were designated as bilingual. The number greatly exceeded the B&B Commission's assessment of what was necessary, given its alternative structural changes.

Mixed Success in Making Ottawa Bilingual

The public face of the federal government has changed profoundly over recent decades. Leaders of national parties are expected to be bilingual, as some leadership candidates have ruefully discovered. Indeed, bilingualism is expected of major cabinet ministers. Francophones have become much more visible in federal cabinets, assuming positions such as Finance, and Trade and Commerce from which they were absent in the past. Yet, in the public service, which was the part of the government to which the B&B Commission had devoted most of its attention, the results are more mixed, especially if measured against the commission's ideals.

The public service has become bilingual in the sense that a substantial proportion of positions formally require bilingualism: 30.3 per cent in 1995, although only 17.3 per cent of these positions required the top level of bilingualism.[24] Moreover, the proportion of francophones in the public service grew from 21.5 per cent in 1961[25] to 28.0 per cent in 1995.[26] Most important, at the management level the proportion of francophones rose to 20.6 per cent in 1980 and 22.9 per cent in 1993.[27] Thus, francophones have now secured a presence in even the upper levels of the public service that approximates their proportion of the Canadian population.[28]

There has been less progress, however, in making the public service a bilingual and bicultural institution, based upon 'equal partnership', in which francophones can work in their language and express their culture. Whereas French has become the main language of work in the federal offices in Quebec, the situation at the seat of federal power is quite a different matter. As the commissioner of official languages declared in his 1990 report, 'French still does not have its rightful place in the federal administration.' Virtually nothing had changed since a 1984 Treasury Board study of official languages in the workplace, which 'showed that French was used only approximately 30 per cent of the time in bilingual regions. The prime minister himself deplored the fact in 1985 that language of work was often pure "folklore"'.[29] In his 1994 report the commissioner lamented that 'the years come and go, but unfortunately the picture of language of work in the federal administration remains the same: it is the Sleepy Hollow of official languages.'[30]

The previous year he had reported on the results of the commission's own study, based on focus groups in Ottawa-Hull and Montreal: 'Broadly speaking, the focus groups told us that in the area of language public servants choose the path of least resistance. In Ottawa this means functioning mostly in English, in Montreal it means functioning mostly in French.'[31]

In short, without structural changes such as those proposed by the B&B Commission, the federal public service was doomed to remain a primarily English-language institution, albeit with a greatly increased number of francophones.[32] Despite the investment of enormous resources in language training, the federal public service has yet to become effectively bilingual, let alone bicultural.

MAKING CANADA BILINGUAL

The Trudeau regime's ambitions for language reform went far beyond establishing bilingualism in Ottawa, however central that objective may have been. The ultimate goal extended to the whole of Canada. Wherever they live, Canadians, as Canadians, should be able to deal with the federal government in their own language, whether it be French or English. Moreover, in important areas, such as education, they should be able to receive services in either language from provincial governments too. As a result, the very presence of francophones throughout Canada would be strengthened.

In part, this conception of linguistic equality extending throughout the country stemmed logically from Trudeau's commitment to individual rights.[33] The notion of pan-Canadian linguistic equality, however, was rooted in Trudeau's primary political goal: to defeat Quebec nationalism. If all of Canada, rather than just Quebec, was to become home to the French language, he kept insisting, then the very basis of Quebec nationalism would be undermined. Indeed, Trudeau claimed that little else was necessary to do the job: the constitutional entrenchment of language rights alone offered 'a solution to a basic issue facing Canada today'.[34]

Once language rights were entrenched, Trudeau declared in 1968, then French Canada would stretch from Maillardville in British Columbia to the Acadian community on the Atlantic Coast and: 'Once you have done that, Quebec cannot say it alone speaks for French Canadians.'[35]

Demographic Trends: The Marginalization of French

To make all of Canada home for French, so that French Canada would stretch from coast to coast would have been a tall order. Historically, French Canada had always been concentrated in Quebec, and the very presence of French in other parts of the country had been steadily receding ever since Confederation.

Only one of the four original provinces had a francophone majority. According to the 1871 census, 78 per cent of Quebec's population was of French descent;[36] French Canadians made up only 16 per cent of the population in New Brunswick,[37] 4.7 per cent in Ontario,[38] and 8.5 per cent in Nova Scotia.[39]

The addition of more provinces to Confederation did not break this pattern. When Prince Edward Island joined in 1873 it was overwhelmingly anglophone: according to the 1881 census, only 10 per cent of its population was of French descent.[40] Initially, the incorporation of western Canada had offered the promise of a new francophone base. When Manitoba became a province in 1870, English-speakers and French-speakers were about equal in numbers.[41] But by 1891, the francophones had shrunk to 7.3 per cent.[42] In 1949, the last addition, Newfoundland, only reinforced the established pattern: according to the 1951 census, barely 0.5 per cent of its population, 2,321 individuals, had French as their mother tongue.[43]

By the time Pierre Trudeau assumed office in 1968, the linguistic structure of Canada was more rooted than ever in territorial division. The marginalization of francophones in most provinces was dramatically revealed by the 1971 census, which for the first time supplemented its standard question on mother tongue with a question on the language Canadians normally used at home, a much more precise measure of the number of francophones. In New Brunswick, 31.4 per cent gave French as their home language, but the proportions were far smaller in the other provinces. The next highest, Ontario, was only 4.6 per cent, followed by 4.0 per cent for Manitoba, 3.9 per cent for Prince Edward Island, and 3.5 per cent for Nova Scotia. In the remaining provinces the proportions with French as their home language were truly infinitesimal: 1.7 per cent in Saskatchewan, 1.4 per cent in Alberta, 0.5 per cent in British Columbia, and 0.4 per cent in Newfoundland.[44] Even in 1971, then, the idea of a French-Canadian nation from sea to sea was totally unrealistic. French Canada never had stretched from coast to coast, and it certainly could not be *made* to do so.[45]

The steady decline in the French presence in most provinces had two causes. First, many provinces received large numbers of British immigrants; French immigrants were a rarity, even in Quebec. Immigrants of other origins tended to join the anglophone populations, even in Quebec, where the anglophones were economically much stronger than the francophones.

Second, the francophone minorities of most provinces lost ground through assimilation, especially as they left the relative isolation of rural communities to migrate to the major cities. In most cities, the overwhelming numerical superiority of anglophone speakers, reinforced by control of the principal economic activities, ensured that assimilationist pressures of urban life would favour English. Unlike the situation of the anglophone community of Montreal, the minority position of francophones was not offset by economic or political power. In fact, it was reinforced by economics and politics. Thus, as Table 1 shows, in every province but Quebec and New Brunswick, the majority of Canadians of French origin did not use French as their primary language at home.

And of course Canada's political institutions were themselves patterned on the assumption that French Canada was effectively concentrated in Quebec. For certain purposes federalism protected the position of francophones in Quebec, making them an electoral majority, but for the same purposes it doomed francophones elsewhere to political marginality. Nor did the terms of Confederation provide for offsetting measures.

We have also seen that historically all governments but Quebec acted as if territorial unilingualism and the provision of public services in a single language were operative principles of Confederation. In effect, they reinforced the social pressures working against French. When Manitoba was created in 1870, English and French were given equal status in the new legislature,

TABLE 1: FRANCOPHONE LINGUISTIC RETENTION RATE, 1971

	French Ethnic Origin	French Home Language	French Home Language as Proportion of French Ethnic Origin
Canada	6,180,120	5,546,025	89.7%
Newfoundland	15,410	2,295	14.9
Nova Scotia	80,215	27,220	33.9
New Brunswick	235,025	199,080	84.7
PEI	15,325	4,405	28.7
Quebec	4,759,360	4,870,105	102.3
Ontario	737,360	352,465	47.8
Manitoba	86,510	39,600	45.8
Saskatchewan	56,200	15,930	28.3
Alberta	94,665	22,700	24.0
British Columbia	96,550	11,505	11.9

Source: *Census of Canada, 1971,* vol. I, Part 3, Tables 2 and 26.

reflecting their roughly equal numbers in the new province. However, after the very rapid decline in the francophone proportion of the province's population, the Manitoba government in 1890 formally ended the official use of French in provincial institutions and abolished denominational schools, thus in effect eliminating French-language education. Similarly, in 1912 the Ontario government passed Regulation 17, which required that English be the sole language of instruction after the third year of schooling. In the early 1930s, New Brunswick revoked Regulation 32, thus precluding French-language education in most of that province.[46] The pattern of provincial policy was clear.

For its part, the federal government had done little to counter this pattern. Typically, it did not call upon provincial governments to reverse their policies, nor was it very responsive to the entreaties of French-Canadian organizations such as the Conseil de la vie française en Amérique, which called upon Ottawa to use both official languages in its publications, to favour French-language radio in Western Canada, and to project a bilingual image of the country. Ottawa even refused the Conseil's request to issue bilingual cheques throughout Canada; until 1962, it did so only in Quebec.[47] The Conseil's requests were heeded only by the Quebec government, which in effect provided funds to the Conseil and to French-language organizations in other provinces. But with the rise of the new Quebec nationalism in the 1960s, Quebec government officials downgraded this support, focusing instead upon the state of French in Quebec.[48]

Under those circumstances, the Trudeau ideal of a pan-Canadian linguistic equality could not have been more ambitious. It sought to reverse the entrenched pattern of a century of Canadian history. Both demographic trends and political forces were stacked against it.

The B&B Commission

The goal of reversing the historical trend was shared by the Royal Commission on Bilingualism and Biculturalism. But the commissioners did not all subscribe to the premises underlying Trudeau's vision of a bilingual Canada, whether his emphasis on the individual or his determination that Quebec must have precisely the same status as the other provinces. In fact, leading members of the commission, especially André Laurendeau, approached the whole question of a bilingual Canada from a very different direction. In the process, they identified issues and forces that were to frustrate severely the Trudeau government's plans for a bilingual Canada.

The commission spelled out its approach at the beginning of its first volume, both in an interpretation of its terms of reference and in an introductory chapter, 'Bilingualism of Individuals and States'. It carefully distinguished between bilingualism as a trait of individuals and as a characteristic of countries. Very few individuals are truly bilingual: 'We know that complete bilingualism—the equal command of two languages—is rare and perhaps impossible.'[49] If countries are bilingual it is because they contain groups of people for whom different languages constitute their primary means of expression. By the same token, the survival of this bilingualism depends upon the strength of these groups—'unilingual nuclei—that is, two or more groups of persons who habitually live and work in one language, resorting to the other language only to communicate with fellow citizens of that language.'[50]

It is not the responsibility of the bilingual state to propagate individual bilingualism, because 'if everyone in a bilingual state becomes completely bilingual, one of the languages is rendered superfluous',[51] and will disappear. Instead, a bilingual state must provide services to citizens in their own languages and ensure that members of the minority linguistic group are not disadvantaged. That may impose obligations upon the majority linguistic group 'to guarantee survival and equality for the minority group'.[52]

Thus, in interpreting its mandate to inquire into 'the existing state of bilingualism' in Canada, the commission declared that its first concern must be not with individual bilingualism but with the state of English and French, 'each being considered by itself' since 'the question of the life and vigour of each language must have priority. The problem of the first language must come first: it is vital; it is more essential for the human being than questions about a second language.'[53]

It was clear that in Canada the francophones were the minority group and that their relative disadvantage in Canada and isolation from francophones internationally would have to be addressed. It was also clear that this group was heavily concentrated in Quebec. Using a fateful phrase, the commission stated that it recognized 'the main elements of a distinct French-speaking society in Quebec'.[54] In fact, the commission declared: 'Quebec constitutes an environment where the aspirations and needs of four out of five francophones in Canada can be satisfied. The mere fact of this concentration leads to a spontaneous French way of life and makes that way of life easier to organize.'[55]

With that interpretation of language and its roots in Canada, how was the commission to formulate a language regime that would strengthen Canadian bilingualism? What linguistic rights should Canadians enjoy in dealing with their governments? What obligations did the ideal of Canadian bilingualism impose on Canadian governments? Do these rights and obligations apply equally to all governments, federal and provincial? Should they be the same in all parts of the country?

The commission had to choose between two competing principles, each of which had found expression in other countries. According to the 'territorial' principle, language rights vary from one part of the country to another; the rights available to citizens depend upon the region in which they live. Under the 'personality' principle, language rights are the same throughout the country.

Each principle has its advantages and, over the years, has had its fierce advocates. The personality principle attaches uniform rights to citizenship and facilitates movement across a country. It favours geographically dispersed linguistic groups: however few in number the members of a language group may be in any locality they possess the full set of language rights. The territorial principle, on the other hand, offers language groups the security that comes from effective dominance over certain regions. In effect, a language group trades minority rights in one region for majority rights in another. Simply put, personality favours minorities; territoriality favours majorities.[56]

As it happened, the commission was well aware of the choice before it and of the ways in which the principles had been applied elsewhere. It had sponsored no fewer than 10 academic studies of language regimes in other countries.[57] Moreover, in its first book of recommendations, *The Official Languages*, the commission discussed four existing regimes in some detail: Belgium, which most clearly embodied territoriality; South Africa, the clearest embodiment of personality; Switzerland, which combined personality at the federal level with territoriality at the local (canton) level; and Finland, which featured a territorially limited accommodation of a second language.

The commission recognized that the experience of other countries seemed to commend the territorial principle to Canada. Canada's linguistic make-up was much closer to that of Belgium, which had adopted the territorial model, than South Africa, the clearest example of the personality model.[58] The territorial principle also had some advantages: 'The minority language is guaranteed priority in some areas and a large majority of the total population may be served in its own language.'[59]

However, the commission rejected territoriality in favour of the personality principle, arguing that the Canadian population was too mobile for such a scheme. More important, 'it would lead to the recognition of only the majority's rights and to oppression of the official language minorities'.[60] Beyond linguistic justice, the commission saw these official-language minorities as important forces for Canadian political integration. In its *Preliminary Report*, the commission had emphasized the symbolic importance of the francophone minorities. The bond that Quebec francophones had formed with these minorities was an important force for national cohesion.[61]

At the same time, the commission felt compelled to make some important concessions to territoriality, in recognition of the demographic structure of the country: 'We take as a guiding principle the recognition of both official languages, in law and practice, *wherever the minority is numerous enough to be viable as a group*' [emphasis added].[62]

So it called upon only two provinces, New Brunswick and Ontario, to adopt the Quebec model and to 'recognize English and French as official languages and ... accept the language regimes that such recognition entails'[63]— in effect, to become officially bilingual. Other provinces were to follow suit should their official-language minority reach 10 per cent. Otherwise, they should simply allow English and French in legislative debates and offer appropriate services in French for their francophone minorities.[64] Also, a constitutional amendment would require all provinces to establish schools in both official languages.[65]

By the same token, the commission recommended that the full provision of government services by federal and provincial governments in both official languages be limited to certain parts of the country. Apparently inspired by the Finnish example, it proposed a scheme of 'bilingual districts' in which the full range of government services—federal, provincial, and municipal— would be bilingual.[66] Federal and provincial governments would have to provide bilingual services directly through the offices they maintain in these districts, as opposed to relying upon communication with offices in their capitals. And all local governments in the district would need to provide bilingual services.

Finally, when they came to address language issues in Quebec, as opposed to the rest of the country, the majority of the commissioners tried to limit their application of the personality principle. They accepted the principle of formal equality between French and English in provincial governmental institutions. This was sanctioned both by the constitution, thanks to section 133 of the BNA Act, and the long-standing practices of the Quebec government. But the economy was a different matter. For commission co-chair André Laurendeau, in particular, the status of French in Quebec's economy and society was one of the most important questions facing the commission.[67] Indeed, the commission had sponsored several studies of such matters as the ethnic patterns of ownership in the Quebec economy and differences in income between anglophones and francophones in Quebec. These studies demonstrated overwhelmingly the inferior position of French and of francophones in Quebec; their publication was to have an explosive effect in Quebec, confirming as they did the arguments of many nationalists.

Laurendeau and some of his colleagues were convinced that these imbalances must be redressed and that governments must take direct responsibility for doing so. After detailing at length the inferiority of French and francophones in the Quebec economy, the commission proposed that 'in the private sector in Quebec, governments and industry adopt the objective that French become the principal language of work at all levels.'[68]

This departure from the personality principle when it came to the private sector was not lost on one of the commissioners: Frank (F.R.) Scott, McGill law professor and pillar of the Montreal English-Canadian community. In a spirited dissenting statement Scott declared: 'It seems to me that, consciously or unconsciously, the other commission members have departed from the principles laid down in Book I of our *Report*, where we defined "equal partnership" and rejected the territorial principle as being inappropriate for determining a language policy for Canada.'[69]

In short, the commission may have opted for the personality principle but not without important qualifications. Only two provincial governments were to join Quebec and become officially bilingual. Bilingualism in local offices of federal and provincial governments and in municipalities was to be restricted to selected bilingual districts. And when it came to the Quebec economy, the majority of the commissioners were not prepared to let the personality principle stand in the way of government measures designed to favour French over English, whatever might be the resulting logical contradiction, and dissension among the commissioners.

The Trudeau Government

The commission's concessions to territoriality were lost on Pierre Trudeau. Given his starting point of individual liberalism, the purpose of language policy could only be to protect the rights of individuals rather than to protect or promote linguistic collectivities. Only the personality principle was legitimate.

The centre-piece of Trudeau's language reforms was the Official Languages Act, passed in 1969. The Act called for notices, regulations, decisions, and similar materials to be published in both official languages; required departments, agencies, and Crown corporations to provide bilingual services in Ottawa-Hull, at its headquarters, in bilingual districts, and to the travelling public anywhere in Canada where demand warranted; stipulated the role of official languages in judicial proceedings; described the procedure for creating federal bilingual districts; and outlined the office, powers, and responsibilities of the commissioner of official languages.[70]

In its effort to implement official bilingualism throughout the country, Ottawa went well beyond the terms of the Official Languages Act. The 1960s and 1970s saw a major expansion of Radio-Canada's television and radio services beyond Quebec. Through the secretary of state, financial support was given to the organizations that represented, and provided services to, the official-language minorities. Finally, Ottawa began making extensive transfer payments to provincial governments to support both the education of official-language minorities in their own language and the instruction of children in the other official language.

At the same time, the Trudeau government dispensed with the B&B Commission's two main concessions to territoriality. First, even though the Official Languages Act contained provisions for the bilingual districts that the commission had envisaged, Ottawa failed to establish them. It did create two advisory committees to recommend which districts should be designated but rejected the advice of each of them.[71]

When the essence of the Official Languages Act was constitutionalized in the new Charter of Rights and Freedoms, no provision was made for bilingual districts. Instead the right to use either language to communicate with a federal office (other than a 'head or central' office) was made dependent upon 'demand' and upon 'the nature of the office'. Clearly, these two criteria will not produce uniform results in all departments of the federal government. In any one locality, demand may be sufficiently high for one type of federal service but not another. By their nature, some offices may be able to provide bilingual services quite easily whereas others may not. When the Official Languages Act was amended in 1988, all reference to official language districts was removed.

Second, the federal government made no formal effort to implement the commission's recommendation of a concerted action to strengthen the use of French in the Quebec economy. Even when, in 1974, the Bourassa government adopted a francization program for Quebec enterprises, as part of Bill 22, Ottawa did not follow suit.

The first commissioner of official languages, Keith Spicer, did say in his 1970 report that he would support 'within the Quebec sector of the federal administration, the often expressed will to make French Quebec's essential language of official, economic and social intercourse'.[72] Indeed, there was substantial progress in making French the essential language of work in federal offices located in Quebec. Less progress was made with federal Crown corporations. Nor did the federal government formally make working-language practices a criterion in awarding contracts to private enterprises, as the Quebec government did with its francization programs.

In part, Ottawa was constrained by its commitment to official bilingualism and the welfare of linguistic minorities. But Gilles Lalande, co-secretary of the B&B Commission and deputy commissioner of official languages from 1980 to 1985, wrote in 1987 that federal officials were also concerned that measures to strengthen French in Quebec might simply encourage Quebec nationalism (as the Trudeau orthodoxy would suggest). 'That is why federal authorities so consistently shied away from publicly acknowledging the need to consolidate the status of French in Quebec.' Lalonde called upon federal officials 'to pay more attention to Quebec's desire—unequivocally expressed in three high-profile pieces of legislation (Bills 22, 63 and 101)—to make French the normal and usual language of work, education, communication, trade and commerce within its borders.'[73]

To the extent the federal government did intervene in Quebec, it strengthened the position of the anglophone minority. Until quite recently, for instance, more than half of Ottawa's spending on the teaching of French and English as first and second languages went to Quebec's anglophone minority.[74] By the same token, in 1987/8, $2,220,000, 14 per cent of the Official Languages Communities program grants, went to Quebec anglophone groups.[75] In effect, Ottawa's language policy made no distinction between Quebec and the rest of Canada. In Quebec, as elsewhere, the focus was upon linguistic *minorities*.

Within this understanding of its responsibilities, however, the Trudeau government brought very substantial resources to bear. More recent governments have largely followed the same policies. As a result, very substantial progress has been made in ensuring that federal services are available in either language throughout the country, although there is still considerable room for improvement. The commissioner of official languages reported in 1994: 'On average, service can be obtained (sometimes not without insistence) in the official language of the minority three times out of four. In some regions, it is only one time out of two.'[76] Similarly, Radio-Canada could claim by 1981 that its networks of AM radio and television reached 94.5 per cent and 92.2 per cent, respectively, of the French-speaking population outside Quebec.[77]

Moreover, through the secretary of state financial support was given to the organizations representing official-language minorities, growing (in constant dollars) from $1.9 million in 1972 to $28 million in 1990, when it entailed more than 300 associations.[78] In 1987 the secretary of state identified five broad areas of activity: representation, institutionalization, services, community participation, and human resources development. On this basis, in 1989 financial support was provided to over 500 projects.[79]

On the other hand, there was only so much that the Trudeau government could accomplish within the federal government's own jurisdictions, since the bulk of government services, including the all-important matter of education, fall within provincial jurisdiction. Thus, the federal government launched a concerted campaign to induce the *provincial* governments to adopt its vision of a bilingual Canada.

The Predominantly Anglophone Provinces: Services but Not Official Bilingualism

Official Bilingualism

The Trudeau government attempted through a variety of tactics to have provincial governments adopt its framework of official bilingualism. The terms of the ill-fated Victoria Charter, the 1971 constitutional patriation package that died for want of Quebec's approval, showed the Trudeau government's determination that all provincial governments should follow the same formula of linguistic equality. The Charter set out a series of rights, but none of them had been agreed to by *all* provinces. Either language could be used in provincial legislatures, except in the three western provinces. Provincial statutes were to be published in both languages in Ontario, Quebec, New Brunswick, and Newfoundland. French and English were to have equal status in the courts of Quebec, New Brunswick, and Newfoundland. Finally, citizens could use either language to communicate with head offices in Ontario, Quebec, New Brunswick, Prince Edward Island, and Newfoundland. Of course, Newfoundland had the smallest proportion of minority language speakers of any province. In effect, the Trudeau government simply mustered as much commitment as it could to each element of official bilingualism. A provision enabled recalcitrant provinces to 'opt in' at a later point; clearly the hope was that they would be pressured to do so.[80]

In other cases, the federal government relied upon the various francophone minority organizations, which had become heavily dependent on federal funding, to lobby their provincial governments on behalf of official bilingualism. This practice was even formalized in a secretary of state *Grants and Contributions Manual, 1988,* which governed support for official-language communities. A list of the aims of activities that the secretary of state was prepared to support financially included 'the passing and implementation of legislation recognizing the equal status of the two official languages'.[81]

The B&B Commission, it will be recalled, had called upon only two provinces to become officially bilingual: New Brunswick and Ontario. The other provincial governments were simply to allow both languages to be used in legislative debates.

In the end, only one province, New Brunswick, adopted a formal scheme of official bilingualism in which French and English have equal status.[82] The B&B Commission's recommendations were incorporated in The Official Languages Act of New Brunswick in 1969 and later in section 16(2) of The Constitution Act, 1982: 'English and French are the official languages of New Brunswick and have equality of status and equal rights and privileges as to their use in all institutions of the legislature and government of New Brunswick.' Sections 17(2) and 18(2) provide for the use of both languages in the New Brunswick legislature; section 19(2) does the same for New Brunswick courts. In addition, section 20(2) establishes the right of the residents of New Brunswick to communicate with and be served by 'any office of an institution of the legislature or government of New Brunswick in English or French'.

Although no other province has gone that far, the Ontario government has come closer than the rest.[83] In a carefully staged incremental fashion it steadily raised the formal status of French in its institutions and expanded the range of government services to its francophone minorities. Starting with authorization of French in the Ontario legislature in 1970, the province adopted a policy on French services in 1972 and created the Office of the Coordinator of French-Language Services in 1977. In 1984 the government approved the creation of a French-language TVOntario network. Finally, The French Language Services Act, passed in 1986 under the Liberal government of David Peterson, declared that 'the French language is recognized as an official language in the courts and in education',[84] consolidating measures that had been adopted under the Conservatives. In addition, the law incorporates the B&B Commission's bilingual-districts scheme, designating 22 districts in which all ministries must provide French-language services (as they must at their head offices). Non-profit corporations may be designated under the Act to have similar obligations. Under the terms of the Act, both languages may be used in legislative proceedings and are used in records of debates, and, since 1991, legislation is adopted in both languages.

None the less, Ontario has steadfastly avoided any declaration that French and English are official languages. Even the NDP government of Bob Rae failed to do so. The present Harris government is certainly not favourably disposed; during its opposition days the Harris Conservatives championed a greater territorialization of language services in Ontario.[85]

During the 1980s, the three Prairie provinces were all forced to confront the issue of official bilingualism, in light of Supreme Court decisions upholding their obligations under nineteenth-century statutes. In each case, there was clear resistance among anglophones to official status for French.

In the case of Manitoba, the resulting conflict was especially acrimonious. In 1979 the Supreme Court ruled that the province was still bound by the Manitoba Act, 1870 and that all laws passed since 1890 were unconstitutional since they had not been enacted in both official languages. The Manitoba government began translating all its statutes into French, but by 1982 it became concerned that the translation was not proceeding fast enough and began to fear that all its laws might soon be declared unconstitutional. Accordingly, Howard Pawley's government negotiated an agreement with Franco-Manitoban leaders to refrain from any court challenge on condition that English and French be declared official languages, that a specific number of statutes be translated into French, and that expanded French-language services be offered by the provincial government as well as municipalities and school boards. (All of this was to be constitutionally entrenched.)

The resulting bill provoked strong opposition among Manitoban anglophones. A final version of the legislation, released in January 1984, did not contain constitutional entrenchment and made it clear that, although English and French were to be designated as official languages of Manitoba, the province was not to be completely bilingual. None the less, the Conservative opposition stalled legislative proceedings and popular protests mushroomed. Finally, in February the government allowed the French-language rights bill to die on the order paper. In 1985 the Supreme Court confirmed that Manitoba's English-only legislation was invalid and ratified an agreement by which all pertinent statutes were to be translated by 1991.

The issue surfaced again in the late 1980s when the Conservative government of Gary Filmon introduced legislation to expand French-language services. In this case, Quebec's proclamation of Bill 178, which will be discussed later, was used as a pretext for withdrawing the bill. In 1990 a French-language-services bill was passed, but there has been no new attempt to declare French an official language.

As for Saskatchewan and Alberta, in 1988 the Supreme Court declared that they were still bound by provisions of the Northwest Territories Act, 1891, which among other things required that all statutes be enacted and printed in both languages. The court's judgement, however, gave the provincial governments the option of repealing the 1891 law and declaring all existing statutes valid even though they were enacted and printed in English only. Saskatchewan passed Bill 2, which affirmed the right to use English and French in the legislature and courts (in criminal cases), affirmed the validity (but not necessity) of enacting laws in both languages, and provided for the translation into French of statutes to be selected by cabinet.[86] For its part, Alberta passed Bill 60, which affirmed the right to use both languages in the legislature and in oral proceedings in certain courts but contained no undertaking to translate statutes nor allowed for the possibility of enacting laws in both languages.[87]

In the remaining predominantly English-speaking provinces, there apparently has been no movement towards making French an official language in government institutions.

French-Language Services

With respect to French as a language of public services as opposed to a language of government institutions, most provinces have in fact adopted reforms. That has been largely due to heavy prodding, and financial assistance, from Ottawa, in particular, extensive grants to provincial governments under the Official Languages in Education Program. In 1989/90 over $81 million was made available to the provinces for education for francophone minorities. (It should be noted that at the same time over $62 million was provided for the education of Quebec's anglophone minority.)[88]

In fact, in 1990 all the provinces had agreements with the federal government spelling out the terms of financial assistance for minority-language education; eight provinces also had agreements regarding other minority-language services.[89] In addition, under section 23 of the Charter of Rights and Freedoms, the provinces are required to provide minority-language schools. Some francophone groups have persuaded the courts to order provincial governments to comply.

As a result, all provinces now offer minority-language education; most of them provide some other French-language services as well. Although some provinces have been reluctant to allow francophone communities to manage and control French-language schools, in March 1990, the Supreme Court ruled that the provinces were in fact obliged to do so, under section 23 of the Charter. In principle, the provincial governments have been trying to comply with the decision, but their critics claim that many of them have been dragging their feet.[90]

Finally, the federal government has provided funds to provinces, largely on a cost-shared basis, to support public services to official-language minorities in areas other than education, including health care, social services, small business development, support for media, and legal services.[91]

In sum, over the last two decades the predominantly anglophone provinces have willingly or unwillingly expanded French-language services. But, with the exception of New Brunswick, they have been very reluctant to afford French an equal status with English. Even Ontario, which has moved furthest in the direction of official bilingualism, has stopped short of formally proclaiming such a regime. Nor should this resistance be surprising: it simply recognizes the demographic structure of the provinces. In Canada as a whole linguistic equality has a certain logic, given the 75/25 per cent ratio of anglophones to francophones. But among the provinces only New Brunswick approximates this. Elsewhere, the demography is simply too heavily weighted in favour of the majorities to afford any credibility to notions of linguistic equality.

Quebec Abandons Official Bilingualism

Meanwhile Quebec, whose *de facto* regime of official bilingualism had been the model for the B&B Commission and the federal government, has itself formally moved away from linguistic equality. Whereas the federal government set the protection of francophone and anglophone minorities as the goal of language policy and tried vigorously to persuade the provinces to act accordingly, the Quebec government has adopted the contradictory policy of protecting and advancing a linguistic majority. This policy has been propelled by two basic considerations.

First, the 1960s saw a new demographic vulnerability of francophones in Quebec. In the past, a high birth rate among Quebec francophones had always compensated for the tendency of immigrants to integrate with Quebec's anglophone population. But in the 1960s the francophone birth rate declined rapidly. By the late 1960s there was widespread concern among Quebec nationalists that the francophone proportion of the Quebec population would start falling from its historical level of 80 per cent. In Montreal, where most immigrants tended to settle, the historical proportion of francophones had been no more than two-thirds. If past levels of anglicization of immigrants continued, francophones might cease to be the majority. These fears were given a certain authority by the publication of demographic projections. Most notably, in 1969 the province's leading demographer, Jacques

Henripin, predicted that if current trends were to continue, by the year 2001 francophones might constitute no more than 53 per cent of Montreal's population.[92] It was not difficult to argue that if francophones lost control of Montreal, the province's metropolis, their control of the province itself might be at stake.

Second, the 1960s saw the impact of changes in the social structure of French Quebec. During the 1950s there had emerged a new francophone middle class of salaried professionals whose work consisted of creating or disseminating and applying knowledge, which they could best do in their first language, French. Often their professional mobility was blocked by the pre-eminence of English as a language of work in the upper levels of the Quebec economy. This new middle class therefore had a particular interest in the quality of French and its general status in Quebec.[93] During the 1960s, the members of this class had obtained work in the rapidly expanding provincial state and public sector, but by the end of the 1960s such positions were no longer being created at the same rate. Increasingly, then, new middle-class francophones would have to look to the private sector for managerial opportunities. Confronted with the continued predominance of English in these positions, they increasingly called upon the Quebec government to intervene so as to alter the language practices of the workplace.

These twin pressures led successive Quebec governments to define a new language regime for Quebec. The first government to do so, led by the Union nationale under Jean-Jacques Bertrand, focused mainly on the access for immigrant children to English-language schools, the primary route to anglicization. Rejecting the nationalists' demands, in 1969 the government passed Bill 63, which established the right of all parents to choose the language of instruction of their children. To do so it had to override the organized objections of a large number of francophone nationalists, including a 50,000-person demonstration before the Quebec legislative buildings. In a vain attempt to appease the nationalists, the bill contained a provision calling for the creation of a commission of inquiry, under Jean-Denis Gendron, to investigate the state of the French language in Quebec.

The Liberal government of Robert Bourassa, first elected in 1970, found itself confronted with growing francophone concern over the twin issues of access to English-language schools and French as a working language. Meanwhile, the Gendron Commission, like the B&B Commission, pursued a broad-based investigation of language issues in Quebec, with public hearings and an extensive research program. In 1972 it delivered its report. Citing the central importance of 'collective action . . . to affirm or consecrate the French fact in Quebec', the commission recommended that French alone be proclaimed the official language, while French and English would be declared 'national' languages.[94] Although it did not make any recommendations about access to English-language schools, the commission proposed measures to make French the language of internal communication in the work world as well as measures designed explicitly to increase the proportion of francophones in managerial positions.[95]

The Bourassa government responded in 1974 with its Bill 22, which made French alone the official language of Quebec and its governmental institutions; access to English-language schools would be dependent upon children demonstrating a 'sufficient knowledge' of English; and a series of measures were to be adopted to induce private firms to 'francize' their operations. In effect, a government clearly committed to Quebec's remaining part of the Canadian federation imposed a regime under which only one language would have official status in a given territory and the state would openly seek to strengthen the position of the linguistic majority, restricting minority rights in the process.

The Parti Québécois government's Bill 101, passed in 1977, simply built upon the framework established by its federalist predecessors. Access to English-language schools was restricted on the basis of the parents' mother tongue (as measured by their language of education) rather than the child's knowledge of English. That is, a parent had to have been educated in English—and in Quebec. And private enterprises were to be obliged to pursue francization programs rather than simply urged to do so. To be sure, even Bill 101 assured Quebec anglophones of rights and services that exceeded those available to any of the francophone minorities, with the possible exception of those in New Brunswick.[96]

The differences in language policy could not have been clearer. Ottawa had vigorously tried to establish a language regime inspired by the personality principle and the ideal of linguistic equality and the protection of linguistic minorities. Quebec, on the other hand, was committed to a territorially defined language regime based on the promotion of its linguistic majority, even at the expense of minority rights. During the 1980s the Bourassa government even opposed in court the demands by francophone minorities to educational services under the Charter, for fear that a victory would hamper Quebec in its dealings with its anglophone minority.

The Bourassa government had been forced to recognize that abandonment of official bilingualism and the personality principle were the almost unavoidable response to linguistic conditions in Quebec. Only on the basis of French primacy could the Quebec state seek to reverse the historical inferiority of French in the province. It is difficult within a framework of formal equality between languages to legitimize state intervention on behalf of the *majority* language, even if it may be the one that is in an inferior situation or under assimilationist pressures. Frank Scott had demonstrated this point with devastating effect in his dissent from the B&B Commission's proposals to strengthen the position of French in the Quebec work world.

Moreover, the Quebec government could not ignore the fact that for Quebec francophones the most important linguistic issue was in fact the status of French in Quebec. Jean Marchand, member of the B&B Commission before entering federal politics with Trudeau and Gérard Pelletier, confirmed this in a revealing interview in the mid-1970s:

> This is what I learned in the [B&B] commission when we went around meeting the people. We visited a small place in the Lake St John area [in Quebec]. I'd say: 'What's wrong?' And the people would say: 'The manager of the mill or whatever it was has been here for ten years—and he has never learned to say either "yes" or "no" in French. We all had to learn English.' The population in that area is 99.9 percent French.
>
> So, for me, this was much more the cause of the trouble in Quebec than the fact that there was no bilingualism, say, at the Vancouver airport. Actually, at that time, nobody was travelling by airplane, or just a few people. I think that the main source of dispute or conflict or tension or friction—call it whatever you want—was Quebec itself and the federal institutions where there was surely no equality for all practical purposes.[97]

In fact, several months before the Bourassa government introduced Bill 22, Gérard Pelletier, who had been responsible as secretary of state for implementing the federal Official Languages Act, had given a major address in which he seemed to be calling for precisely such a measure. Before the Montreal Chambre de commerce, Pelletier had called upon the Quebec government to follow the approach that Ontario had taken when introducing French-language schools:

> The provincial government [of Ontario] began by affirming that Ontario was first and foremost an English-speaking province and that all citizens, for their own good and the good of the province, should know English. After this cool and firm statement, it was also declared that this should not prevent the authorities from respecting the rights of Franco-Ontarians, nor should it prevent them, with the help of the government, from developing their own language or encouraging the study of French in the entire educational system.
>
> I strongly wish that Quebec authorities would assert Quebec's character as firmly and as forthrightly, at the same time reaffirming their intention to respect the English-speaking minority as in the past. Who could object

to this proposition which would have the advantage of being perfectly symmetrical with the stand of the neighbouring province? And who can deny the need to state as firmly and as frequently as possible the necessity of Quebec's remaining resolutely French?[98]

Yet, for Pierre Trudeau only official bilingualism would do; Bill 22's departure from that formula made it totally unacceptable. Indeed, in an address to the Quebec wing of the federal Liberal party in 1976, he branded the bill a 'political stupidity'.[99] By making French the only official language it greatly complicated the federal government's efforts to persuade the rest of the country that there are two official languages.

Trudeau did say that he would have accepted a designation of French as 'the main language', 'the language of work', or even 'the national language'. He even claimed to support 'the spirit' of Bill 22. None the less, as I have argued, it is difficult to see how, within the framework of official bilingualism, the Quebec government could have actively promoted one language, French, whether it be called 'the national language' or anything else. In particular, it would have had difficulty justifying any measures designed to make French prevail over English, as in the work world. Certainly, the Ontario model that Pelletier commended was not official bilingualism. In his own words, it was based on Ontario being 'first and foremost English-speaking'.

Not only did the Trudeau government denounce Bill 22, but the pursuit of its formula of official bilingualism at the federal level led to measures in support of Quebec's anglophone minority that have run directly counter to the Quebec government's promotion of French. For instance, under its program of financial support for minority-language community organizations, in 1987/8 Ottawa granted $1,200,000 to Alliance Québec, which has funded court challenges against Bill 101 and lobbied for changes in the bill.[100]

Indeed, when in 1988 the Mulroney government presented the draft of a revised Official Languages Act, the Quebec government strongly objected to a provision which authorized Ottawa to support organizations promoting bilingualism. Quebec City declared that support for such organizations would contradict the objectives of Bill 101. Finally, Ottawa agreed to negotiate an agreement with Quebec to ease these concerns.[101]

In sum, the Trudeau government had relatively little success in its concerted effort to secure provincial adoption of its model of official bilingualism. In fact, only one province is now officially bilingual. Others have openly resisted the notion or, in the case of Quebec, have abandoned it. Ottawa had much more success in inducing provincial governments to provide services in French to their francophone minorities. Still, provision of service beyond the minimum guaranteed under the education rights of the

Charter much depended upon Ottawa's readiness to foot the bill through transfer payments.

Continued Decline of the Francophone Minorities

The provision of federal and provincial French-language services outside Quebec has failed to achieve Trudeau's goal of creating a francophone presence from coast to coast so as to defeat Quebec's claim to speak for French Canada.

The historical pattern of assimilation among most francophone minorities has not only continued but increased. This can be seen in census data on the proportion of individuals of French mother tongue who use English more than French as their home language. In 1971 the figure (outside Quebec) was 27 per cent. In 1981 it had risen to 27.8 per cent. By 1991 it had reached 34.8 per cent.[102] To be sure, one could argue that without the language reforms the rate of assimilation would be even higher. But that is hardly an argument that the policy has succeeded.

Why was the historical assimilation of the francophone minorities not stemmed, let alone reversed? Supporters of the Trudeau government's efforts doubtlessly would insist that the responsibility lies with the provincial governments, which, as we have seen, were often less than whole-hearted in the support of their francophone minorities. However, part of the reason must also be the way the policy was conceived, with its emphasis on individual as opposed to collective rights.

In 1990 Trudeau took pride in relating how he and his colleagues succeeded in framing the language provisions of the Charter of Rights and Freedoms. They had drafted a charter in which language rights were assigned directly to individuals rather than collectivities: 'What we were seeking was for the individual himself to have the *right* to demand his choice of French or English in his relationships with the federal government, and the *right* to demand a French or English education for his children from a provincial government.'[103] One might say the same of the Official Languages Act, which inspired these provisions. Trudeau acknowledged that he avoided collective rights partly to avoid sanctioning the Quebec government's claim to represent a francophone collectivity. Yet in the process, the Trudeau government wedded itself to a vision of language reform that ignores the social context of language.

As the B&B Commission so cogently argued, for most individuals the primary purpose of a language is to enable them to function within a community. If they should choose one language over another for such matters as government services and education, they will choose the one that is shared by the community of which they are part. The right to choose one language over another in dealing with the state has little concrete meaning, however firmly it may be protected by the constitution, unless that language is part and parcel of one's daily life, both personal and public. The purpose of language policy should be to give the community in which a language is based the means to maintain itself and to develop.[104]

Even if the Trudeau government's ideal of a bilingual Canada had been more clearly geared to linguistic collectivities, it would have been faced with the fundamental problem that state intervention, however conceived, can do little to counter the powerful assimilationist forces to which most francophone minorities are exposed. Simply put, there is a normal tendency for a single language to prevail in any area. If two or more should be present, eventually one will prevail—if need be through assimilation or displacement of the others. To be sure, in rural areas distinct linguistic communities can co-exist as self-contained pockets of farms and villages. But in urban areas, the pressures for dominance by a single linguistic community are far greater as people become incorporated into common institutions, such as the workplace and the media; and, with the weaker social constraints of urban life, personal contacts and intermarriage between linguistic communities become easier.[105]

In fact, intermarriage has been a most powerful force for assimilation of francophones outside Quebec. The 1991 census showed that outside Quebec 92.8 per cent of children have French as their mother tongue if both parents are francophone, but only 13.2 per cent do if one parent is anglophone and the other francophone.[106] Indeed, in 1994 the commissioner of official languages joined with the Fédération des communautés francophones et acadienne du Canada to organize a colloquium on exogamy and strategies that might reduce assimilation.[107] It is not self-evident what these strategies might be or how they could be effective.[108]

Of the 19 metropolitan areas outside Quebec and New Brunswick, there are only two where more than 3 per cent of the residents speak only French at home: Ottawa (29.8 per cent) and Sudbury (19.6 per cent).[109] Thus, among other things, the chances of children marrying non-francophones are correspondingly high. As well, the language of work, at least in the private sector, is primarily English. So, even if children should have French as their mother tongue and should be given a complete education in French, the chances are that they will have to work in English unless they can find work in public or quasi-public institutions providing education and other services in French. And even if Radio-Canada should be available to them, the English-language media will still offer far greater diversity and appeal.

Not only are the francophone minorities under increasing attack from assimilationist pressures, but they have also been disadvantaged by declining

TABLE 2: FRENCH AS HOME LANGUAGE

	1971		1991	
	Number	**Percentage**	**Number**	**Percentage**
Canada	5,546,025	25.7	6,288,430	23.3
Newfoundland	2,295	0.4	1,340	0.2
PEI	4,405	3.9	3,050	2.4
Nova Scotia	27,220	3.5	22,260	2.5
New Brunswick	199,080	31.4	223,265	31.2
Quebec	4,870,105	80.8	5,651,795	83.0
Ontario	352,465	4.6	318,705	3.2
Manitoba	39,600	4.0	25,045	2.3
Saskatchewan	15,930	1.7	7,155	0.7
Alberta	22,700	1.4	20,180	0.8
British Columbia	11,505	0.5	14,555	0.4

Sources: *Census of Canada, 1971*, cat. 92–726, Table 26; *Census of Canada, 1981*, cat. 92–910, Table 2; *Census of Canada, 1991*, cat. 93–317, Table 1 (as reproduced in Harrison and Marmen, *Languages in Canada*, Table A.2).

fertility and the integration of immigrants with the anglophone majorities of their various provinces.[110] As Table 2 shows, the 1991 census records a decline, in all provinces but Quebec, New Brunswick, and British Columbia, in both the proportions and actual number of residents speaking French at home. In British Columbia the number of francophones has risen, but the proportion has slipped; both the number and the proportion are infinitesimal. The proportions of francophones are now below 3 per cent in all provinces but Ontario (3.2 per cent), New Brunswick (31.2 per cent) and, to be sure, Quebec (83.0 per cent). Overall, people who speak French at home make up 3.2 per cent of the Canadian population outside Quebec, down from 4.3 per cent in 1971.[111]

In Quebec, there has been a parallel decline of the anglophone minority, but for quite different reasons. There, the primary cause was out-migration to other provinces. Over the period 1966–91, about 275,000 more anglophones left Quebec for other provinces than entered Quebec from other provinces.[112] This out-migration appears to have been partly due to the movement toward French primacy in Quebec. Thus, the most substantial out-migration occurred in 1976–81, the period during which the Parti Québécois first took office and Bill 101 was declared. However, other factors were also at play: the shift in head offices from Montreal to Toronto, which was in part propelled by continental economic forces and was well under way before the upsurge of neo-nationalism in the 1960s.[113] And out-migration was offset to a certain extent by in-migration of anglophones, from Canada and elsewhere. Indeed, there has always been a fair amount of anglophone movement over the Quebec border in both directions. None the less, from 1961 to 1991, the proportion of the Quebec population with English as mother tongue fell from 13.3 per cent to 9.2 per cent.[114]

Despite the best efforts of the federal government and substantial efforts by some provincial governments, Canada has inexorably continued to be more and more segregated by language. Indeed, Quebec now contains 89.9 per cent of Canadians using French at home; the rest of Canada contains 95.9 per cent of Canadians using English at home.[115] Most demographers agree that outside Quebec a strong francophone presence is not likely to continue except in certain regions of New Brunswick and Ontario. Outside Quebec no more than 3 per cent of the population will be French-speaking by the end of this decade.[116] By the same token, even the most optimistic projections for Quebec's anglophones predict some decline in their share of the total Quebec population.

MAKING CANADIANS BILINGUAL

There was a final component in this vision of a bilingual Canada—the spread of individual bilingualism among Canadians. As we have seen, the B&B Commission did not emphasize individual bilingualism. It had declared that the health of the two linguistic communities as distinct entities, most specifically the French one, was of far greater urgency than the promotion of personal bilingualism. Book II, on education, concentrates on education for official-language minorities. The commission did propose that 'the study of the second official language should be obligatory for all students in Canadian schools'[117] but stressed that it did not presume that this would necessarily produce bilingual students:

> Our concern . . . has not been to provide the opportunity to become highly proficient in all skills of the second official language. Rather, we wanted to ensure that all children should have an introduction to the language which would make it possible for them to further develop or re-acquire the skills after leaving school. The school is the place where the capacity for bilingualism can be established.[118]

As we have seen, the commission was highly critical of the federal government's reliance upon language training and personal bilingualism as the route to establishing a bilingual public service.

None the less, within the Trudeau vision of a bilingual Canada personal bilingualism was front and centre. Trudeau would disclaim any desire that *all* Canadians should become bilingual: 'I never expect that the average Quebecer in Sainte-Tite-des-Caps will become perfectly bilingual, nor that the anglophone in Calgary or Moose Jaw must know French. What we want is that the institutions be bilingual.'[119] Yet the expansion of personal bilingualism was the key to national unity. His vision of a bilingual Canada was not that of the B&B Commission with its two distinct linguistically defined societies. As he declared in 1988: 'Bilingualism unites people; dualism divides them. Bilingualism means that you can speak to each other; duality means you can live in one language and the rest of Canada will live in another language.'[120]

For that matter, the ideal of personal bilingualism was central to Trudeau's public image, at least in English Canada. Trudeau's own example of seemingly perfect bilingualism affected how many Canadians, at least in English Canada, understood the ideal of a bilingual Canada. It was one in which Canadians would themselves embrace both languages. National unity would come by increasing the capacity of Canadians to deal with each other in both official languages. The lowering of language barriers would bring them together. This was a message that greatly appealed to many English Canadians: by becoming bilingual they could themselves take action to unite the Canadian nation. Or, if they didn't become bilingual, they could at least make certain that their children did.[121]

Here too the Trudeau government was trying to undo long-standing patterns. Historically, few Canadians have been bilingual. In 1961, only 12.2 per cent of Canadians said they could carry on a conversation in both English and French.[122] Moreover, reflecting the extent to which in all provinces but Quebec, linguistic minorities have had little economic or political power, it is French Canadians that historically have had to become bilingual. In 1961, 70 per cent of bilingual Canadians had French as their mother tongue; yet the latter group constituted only 28 per cent of the Canadian population. In effect, they had to be bilingual to deal with the linguistic majority. Hence bilingualism was spread unevenly across the country: representing 25.5 per cent of Quebec's residents and 19 per cent of New Brunswick's but less than 8 per cent of every other province's population.[123]

Promoting Individual Bilingualism

The federal government became heavily committed to promoting individual bilingualism among Canadian youth. In 1990–1 it transferred close to $82 million to the provinces to support second-language education. In addition, it provided about $11 million in bursaries for students enrolled in summer immersion courses in post-secondary institutions and about $7 million in payment to official-language monitors who assist in post-secondary language courses.[124]

Ottawa has given generous support to Canadian Parents for French, a lobby group for French immersion education. The secretary of state fully covered CPF's expenses during the first two years after its creation in 1977; in 1988–9 it was still covering 65 per cent of CPF national office's expenses. For its part CPF actively lobbied both federal and provincial governments on behalf of bilingual education. In the early 1980s it was influential in persuading Ottawa and the provinces to enter into a new multi-year agreement on funding for bilingual education.[125]

This active support of the federal government has resulted in a remarkable growth in French-language immersion classes in most major Canadian cities. The number of anglophone children registered in French-immersion programs soared from 37,835 in 1977–8 to 288,050 in 1990–1, involving 1,592 schools and constituting over 7 per cent of all anglophone students.[126] Outside Quebec, 6.8 per cent of schoolchildren were enrolled in immersion programs, as opposed to 2.1 per cent in 1980–1.[127] Primarily for this reason, bilingualism among anglophones outside Quebec rose by 78 per cent between 1961 and 1981, reaching 5 per cent. In 1991 it stood at 6.4 per cent. In the 5–19 age group, 11 per cent are now bilingual, as opposed to 3 per cent in 1971.[128] Among francophones, the level of personal bilingualism has also gone up. Among Quebec francophones, it went from 28.7 per cent in 1981 to 31.5 per cent in 1991; outside Quebec it went from 79.0 per cent to 81.1 per cent.[129]

The federal government's efforts have had a demonstrable and impressive impact in the case of personal bilingualism. No longer is bilingualism being restricted primarily to francophones; indeed, the proportion of bilinguals has increased in every province. Yet there are qualifications to this success.[130] First, one can question the meaningfulness of respondents' claims to census takers that they have a working knowledge of another language. In fact, a study of the graduates of high school immersion programs found that 90 per cent were unable to follow French-language university courses.[131]

Second, and more important, one can question the extent to which, especially outside Quebec, an acquired knowledge of French by anglophones can actually lead to greater bilingual exchange. After all, in most parts of Canada the numbers of francophones and thus the opportunities to use French are small and in rapid decline. In fact, in all provinces but New Brunswick (and Quebec), the number of anglophone children in French immersion programs is greater than the number of francophone children in French-language schools.[132] What meaningful opportunity is there, then, for immersion graduates to use their linguistic skill?

Finally, there is some indication that the influx of anglophone children into French-language schools has threatened the francophone presence in some localities:

> Informed francophones, especially in the Western provinces, have strongly criticized some types of French immersion schools. In areas where such schools are the only ones available to children of francophones, the comments are especially severe. These schools are considered instruments of Anglicization. Where anglophones attend French schools, they often represent a sizeable minority, sometimes even a majority, and the superior sociolinguistic status in the community deflects these schools from their primary purpose, which is to provide an environment for the learning of French.[133]

OFFICIAL BILINGUALISM AND SECURING NATIONAL UNITY

Taken as a whole, the results of the Trudeau campaign to implant its vision of a bilingual Canada have at best been mixed. Within its own institutions, the Trudeau government greatly enhanced the role played by francophones but failed to make the public service effectively bilingual. The predominantly English-Canadian provincial governments have expanded their services to francophone minorities but have generally balked at official bilingualism. Except for Quebec and New Brunswick, the assimilation of francophones has continued. Quebec has formally rejected official bilingualism while continuing to provide public services to its anglophone minority, which has itself declined. The federal government can point to success in its effort to expand personal bilingualism, especially among young anglophones. However, the continued decline in the number of francophones in most parts of Canada means that the enhanced bilingualism of anglophones will be of little use in their immediate communities.

Whatever success these various measures may have had in achieving their specific objectives, they must be judged against the underlying purpose of strengthening national unity. If French were to achieve equality throughout Canada, so the argument went, Quebec francophones would identify less with Quebec and more with Canada as a whole and its government in Ottawa. And as anglophone Canadians became more aware of the French fact, and perhaps even became bilingual, they would be united with francophones in a common attachment to a bilingual Canada. To what extent has this happened? And what have the consequences been for national unity?

Francophone Quebec: Bilingualism in Ottawa with Unilingualism in Quebec

It was obviously important for most Quebec francophones that the federal government become truly bilingual. As we saw, such lifelong Quebec nationalists as André Laurendeau were firmly committed to this ideal. To the extent the ideal was achieved, then, Quebec francophones were indeed likely to feel less estranged from the federal government. There were, however, real limits to these changes: in the public service francophones became much more numerous but they were not necessarily able to work in French. These limitations were reported regularly in the Quebec media. But at least for the first time the federal government was moving in the right direction. Similarly for a good number of Quebec francophones, the fate of the francophone minorities was indeed important, and changes in the way governments treated them were all to the good.

Still, however much Quebec francophones may have cared about these questions and been gratified by the steps that were taken, the most important issue for them was the status of French in Quebec, as it always had been. Moreover, in the Quebec of the 1960s and 1970s, the issue was acquiring much greater urgency than ever before. Few Quebec francophones were prepared to subordinate the status of French in Quebec to improvements in the status of French elsewhere.

The accentuated concern with the status of French in Quebec did not necessarily lead to a rejection of the Canadian federal order. But it did render very problematic a conception of Canadian federalism in which language rights are the same everywhere and in which government policy is interested primarily in the fate of linguistic *minorities*, whether francophone or anglophone.

That was the underlying flaw in the Trudeau strategy. It presumed that dissatisfaction with the status of French in Quebec could be traded off against gains elsewhere. The error of this strategy was clearly revealed in the mid-1970s when, despite demonstrable improvement in the status of French both in Ottawa and some other provinces, the federalist government of Robert Bourassa responded to public pressures by abandoning Quebec's long-standing linguistic equality with Bill 22.

In effect, Quebec francophones could support official bilingualism in Ottawa and recognition of French rights in other provinces, yet also support the primacy of French in Quebec. There was a contradiction only if one believed, as the Trudeau government did, that linguistic equality should apply throughout Canada, provincially as well as federally.

The B&B Commission had recognized that the fate of French in Canada was, in the last analysis, dependent upon its vitality in Quebec, the home of 80 per cent of Canada's francophones. That is why it had proposed that concerted governmental action be taken to strengthen the place of French in the Quebec economy. In doing so, it had entered into a certain contradiction with its general endorsement of the personality principle, but at least it was struggling to address the full reality of the French language in Canada.

In denying a central element of this reality, the Trudeau government made its linguistic agenda irrelevant to the primary concerns of most Quebec francophones. It was left to the Quebec government, whether it be in federalist or sovereigntist hands, to address the status of French in Quebec. Indeed, when Ottawa did intervene in Quebec, it was on behalf of the anglophone community. In that respect the Trudeau government's language policy was in fact antagonistic to the primary concern of most Quebec francophones. Beyond that, Ottawa's insistence on linguistic equality and official bilingualism for federal and provincial governments alike brought into question the very legitimacy of measures such as Bill 22, which had the overwhelming support of Quebec francophones. Nor did Trudeau hesitate to make the point.

The result, then, was to make the federal order seem hostile to the primary linguistic concerns of Quebec francophones. To that extent, the Trudeau strategy of language reform became a source of conflict and division rather than the instrument of reconciliation it was intended to be.

Not surprisingly, Trudeau's strategy of linguistic reform failed to make Quebec francophones any less attached to Quebec as their primary national community, let alone to see themselves first and foremost as Canadians. Even if the federal government's efforts to strengthen the use of French outside Quebec should have made Quebec francophones see the rest of Canada as more hospitable to them, they well knew that nowhere else in Canada could there be as complete and dynamic a francophone society as in Quebec. Whatever the treatment of the francophone minorities in the other provinces, Quebec was bound to remain the centre of francophone life in Canada, as it always had been. Indeed, it was bound to remain, in the B&B Commission's own words, 'a distinct society'. No matter how vigorous Ottawa's efforts on behalf of the French fact elsewhere, Quebec francophones would continue to identify with Quebec and to want the Quebec state to have the powers necessary to protect and promote the French language in Quebec. The Trudeau strategy did nothing to change that.

Anglophone Canadians: Opposing Responses

In anglophone Canada, there were two very different reactions to the Trudeau government's language reforms. Some Canadians embraced the vision of a new bilingual Canada; others bitterly resented it. Both reactions generally precluded any recognition of Quebec's distinctiveness, a basic given for most Quebec francophones; either way, the result was strong indignation when Quebec then proceeded with its own transition to primacy for French. In these ways as well, the Trudeau linguistic strategy, with its emphasis on linguistic equality at provincial as well as federal levels, did as much to impede as to promote national unity.

For some English Canadians the Trudeau reforms offered an appealing vision of Canada. The decline of the British connection and the alarm at American domination had fostered the search for a distinctively Canadian identity. Bilingualism, especially as both personified and championed by Trudeau, seemed to be an answer. Canada would become a truly bilingual nation, and Canadians would be personally enriched by the experience of bilingualism. In that they would be different from and superior to their southern neighbour; indeed, Canada could provide leadership to the rest of the world by showing how linguistic antagonisms can be overcome.

Some English Canadians were more than prepared to support Ottawa's campaign to establish official bilingualism as widely as possible at the provincial as well as federal levels. To question this endeavour was to question Canada's national identity and to oppose a fundamentally progressive cause. By the same token, if English Canadians supported equality between French and English, so it was also their national duty to become bilingual themselves, or at least to ensure that their children did. This nationalist sentiment was at least partly responsible for the dramatic popularity of French immersion programs outside Quebec. Canadian Parents for French, an organization representing parents of immersion schoolchildren and funded primarily by the federal government, became a powerful lobby for official bilingualism and the Trudeau vision of Canada.[134]

When the Quebec government abandoned linguistic equality with Bill 22 and Bill 101, these English Canadians considered it a denial of the new vision of a bilingual Canada. Moreover, Quebec appeared to be acting in bad faith. Rather than taking measures needed to correct the historical disadvantage of French in Quebec, Quebec seemed to be violating a contract it had made with English Canada by which official bilingualism would be the rule throughout the country. Finally, it seemed to be a denial of the efforts made by some English Canadians to honour this presumed contract. Having supported official status for French and expansion of French-language services in their province, and often having enrolled their children in immersion programs as well, these English Canadians were outraged to discover that Quebec francophones seemed to be so indifferent to all their well-intentioned gestures.

Similarly, English-Canadian supporters of a bilingual Canada saw no reason to accept the continuing demands of Quebec nationalists for recognition of Quebec's distinctiveness. If the whole country was officially bilingual, Quebec was no longer unique. It was no longer the home of francophones. All of Canada was now their home. In effect, all of Canada had become like Quebec.

For other Canadians, however, the Trudeau vision of a bilingual Canada was not at all appealing. First, it constituted too radical a break with their own idea of Canada. In some cases, these responses clearly were uninformed and even bigoted. For instance, in his underground best-seller, *Bilingual Today, French Tomorrow*, Lieutenant Commander J.V. Andrew claimed that the designation of bilingual positions in the federal civil services was no less than a plot 'to hand Canada over to the French-Canadian race'.[135] But the reaction was not restricted to this rather paranoid fringe. After all, 17 MPs, including a former prime minister, John Diefenbaker, refused to support the Official Languages Act in 1969. At about the same time, the eminent historian Donald Creighton declared that there was no historical basis for recognizing French outside Quebec.[136] And in 1973, J.T. Thorson, former Liberal cabinet minister and president of the Exchequer Court of Canada, was moved to write a book entitled *Wanted: A Single Canada*[137] in which he drew upon the statements of prominent Québécois to demonstrate that Ottawa's language regime did not in any event respond to the discontent of Quebec francophones.

Second, the ideal of a bilingual Canada simply contradicted the reality of Canada as many English Canadians knew it, especially in the West. After all, in a 1985 survey, only 14 per cent of anglophones outside Quebec reported hearing French daily; most said they never heard it.[138] As the late Donald Smiley noted in 1980:

> A decreasing proportion of Canadians experience duality as an important circumstance of daily life. . . . On a day-to-day and a week-to-week basis most citizens have little direct contact with members of the other linguistic community. Because of this, the resistance of most non-francophones to a view that the essential nature of their country is dualistic is understandable, even when this resistance is expressed in such ungenerous sentiments as those of people not wanting French to be forced down their throats when demonstrably no one is trying to do any such thing.[139]

The fact of the matter is that in many parts of Canada the debate about official bilingualism has been a discourse with little connection to social reality. This was shown especially clearly when francophone groups, supported financially by the federal government, used the courts to impose long-defunct constitutional provisions. For instance, when in 1988 Saskatchewan francophone leaders denounced Bill 2 and insisted on a commitment to translate *all* statutes,[140] some central Canadian politicians and opinion leaders were quick to follow suit and denounce this abandonment of Saskatchewan's francophone community. Condemning the refusal to translate all the statutes, Ontario Premier David Peterson declared, 'This puts pressure on the kinds of things that many of us believe in, in terms of nation-building, which requires respect for the minorities.'[141] Opposition Leader Bob Rae called it 'a sad day for the country when governments take away from individual rights as they have been expressed by the Supreme Court of Canada', and proclaimed that Ontario should declare itself to be officially bilingual.[142] (He failed to do so during his own term as premier.)

For its part, the B&B Commission had not called for such measures as translation of laws and bilingual records of debates in the case of such provinces as Alberta and Saskatchewan. It merely proposed the right to use either language in legislative debates. Both Saskatchewan's Bill 2, as well as Alberta's Bill 60, accorded this right.

More important, critics tended to overlook the reality of language use in present-day Saskatchewan. According to the 1991 census, in the province as a whole only 7,155 people, or 0.7 per cent of the province's population, spoke French at home.[143] Under those circumstances formal equality of French with English made little sense. And the condemnations of Saskatchewan for not agreeing to translate *all* its statutes or to begin publishing a French-language record of its legislative debates, let alone establish simultaneous translation, ignored the fact that at the time no one in the Saskatchewan legislature was fluent in French.[144] Nor was it at all clear how the perilous condition of Saskatchewan francophones would be helped by these measures.

It is not surprising that in many parts of Canada English Canadians have resisted the ideal of a bilingual Canada and the very extensive resources that were deployed to put it into effect. Nor should it be surprising that they have been angered by Quebec's insistence on making French the primary language in that province. It is as if Quebeckers, having imposed official bilingualism on the rest of Canada—at very considerable public expense—then decided not to accept it for themselves. At one point, francophones in Quebec and anglophones in other parts of Canada might in fact have been able to come to terms on territorially rooted language policy for provincial governments. However, the prominence the Trudeau government gave to official bilingualism in the early discussions of provincial language policy made that impossible.

Conclusions

The rise of discontent among Quebec francophones clearly made some measure of language reform necessary, especially in the federal government. However, the Trudeau government's implementation of language policy was driven by its ambition to implant, especially in Quebec, a new pan-Canadian identity rooted in Trudeau's individualist liberalism. This closely determined how the policy was conceived, what was acceptable, and what was not. In the process, the potential of language reform for promoting national unity was seriously compromised.

The Trudeau government's liberalism made unacceptable the B&B Commission's proposal that the federal public service have linguistically segregated units throughout the various departments and that anglophones and francophones be formally balanced at the top. Language training was more acceptable, and the emphasis was placed there, with mediocre results. This helped to ensure that, while francophones might be increasingly present in the upper levels of the public service, they had to work primarily in English.

The central importance of language reform to its national unity strategy led the Trudeau government to embrace the unattainable goal of reinforcing the francophone presence throughout Canada. In all provinces but Quebec and New Brunswick, the numbers and proportions of francophones have steadily declined. (In British Columbia the number rose but the proportion went down.) In terms of primary language, the country is more linguistically segregated than when the federal government began its efforts. That basic fact cannot be altered by the growth in the number of Canadians who have some knowledge of the other language. Nor can it ease the problems that this linguistic division poses for the Trudeau ideal of a Canada composed of individuals rather than linguistic communities.

The Trudeau government's conception of national unity resulted in a concerted campaign to persuade the provincial governments to adopt a scheme of official bilingualism that exceeded the recommendations of the B&B Commission for most provinces. It also ignored the commission's few concessions to territoriality, such as bilingual districts and support for making French the working language of Quebec. Such elements of official bilingualism as bilingual statutes were strongly resisted in most provinces since they did not square with these provinces' linguistic composition. Whereas Canada as a whole has a 75/25 per cent split between the two language groups, in most provinces the linguistic minority is far smaller. At the same time, because of the federal government's campaign for official bilingualism, most English Canadians condemned the measures that clearly were needed to strengthen the use of French in the Quebec economy and to integrate

immigrant children into francophone society and that were strongly supported by the majority of Quebec francophones.

In defence of Ottawa's approach one might argue that in the end the
regime that has emerged is probably quite reasonable: bilingualism at the federal level coupled with a diversity of regimes at the provincial level.[145]
Certainly, it is much more conditioned by territory than Trudeau or even the
B&B Commission would have wanted. However, the processes that led to this
stage were far more acrimonious than they need have been and have left a
deep residue of animosity and frustration. The potential that language reform
might have had for securing a reconciliation among Canadians, francophone
and anglophone, has been correspondingly reduced.

There is a final problem. As we shall see, the Trudeau government's language reforms did not achieve their primary purpose of persuading Quebec
francophones to abandon their demands for constitutional recognition of
Quebec's distinctiveness. Yet, it was through this promise that the Trudeau
government had persuaded many English Canadians to support the reforms,
especially for their provincial governments. After investing so much energy
and resources in an effort to make all of Canada 'bilingual', English
Canadians were even less ready to entertain Quebec's continuing demands.
In this way as well, the Trudeau government's language policy impeded
national unity rather than strengthened it.

CHAPTER 5

Multiculturalism: Reining in Duality

Beyond the status of languages, the emerging national unity strategy also had to address the status of cultures. Normally, the two are considered to be intimately related, and indeed, the established French-Canadian notion of dualism saw Canada's two languages as the direct expression of two distinct cultures.

Linguistic dualism could be made compatible with the new national unity strategy if bilingualism was cast in purely individual terms. But cultural duality was another matter. Moreover, some non-francophone Canadians had mobilized against the very concept of cultural duality. Thus, the federal government became committed to a policy that tried to combine official status for two languages with equal status for an infinite number of cultures. In other words, bilingualism was coupled with multiculturalism.

Over the years, other elements of the national unity strategy, such as bilingualism or the Charter of Rights and Freedoms, have tended to attract much more attention. Yet, in many respects the adoption of multiculturalism constituted the heart of the new vision of Canada. And rightly or wrongly many Quebec francophones have considered multiculturalism to be a direct denial of their understanding of Canada, and have vigorously rejected it.

Defining Biculturalism

The Trudeau government's policy of multiculturalism was a response to, or more precisely a reaction against, the recommendations of the Royal Commission on Bilingualism and Biculturalism.

The status of cultures in Canada was, of course, central to the B&B Commission's terms of reference. The commission was instructed to 'inquire into and report upon the existing state of bilingualism and biculturalism in Canada and to recommend what steps should be taken to develop the Canadian Confederation on the basis of an equal partnership between the two founding races.'[1]

To be sure, in an apparent recognition that some Canadians would feel excluded by this mandate, the commission was to 'tak[e] into account the contribution made by other ethnic groups to the cultural enrichment of Canada and the measures that should be taken to safeguard that contribution.' None the less, the notion of cultural dualism was front and centre. And through the reference to 'two founding races' it was presented in a way that placed it squarely within the vision of Canada that Henri Bourassa had articulated at the turn of the century and that had become the basis upon which most of French Quebec's political and intellectual classes understood Canada.

The continuity with the Bourassa tradition was no accident. As we saw, the idea of the commission had originated with André Laurendeau, who was in many respects Bourassa's spiritual heir. Dualism was fundamental to his own vision of Canada; indeed, it was only on this basis that he would have been prepared to co-chair the commission.[2] By the same token, Laurendeau was the undisputed leader of the commission's activities until his untimely death in 1968.

It is no surprise that the interpretation of the commission's terms of reference, which appears in the opening pages of the first volume of the commission's report, offers an expansive understanding of 'biculturalism'. These famous 'blue pages' were in fact written by Laurendeau himself. After surveying alternative definitions of culture, the commission defines it broadly as 'a way of being, thinking and feeling'. Culture is 'a driving force animating a significant group of individuals united by a common tongue, and sharing the same customs, habits, and experiences.'[3] Therefore, it could only be Canada as a whole, rather than individual Canadians, that was bicultural: 'Culture is to the group rather what personality is to the individual; it is rare for a person to have two personalities or two styles of living at the same time.'[4] Although cultures may not be water-tight compartments, neither should biculturalism be understood as a '*mixture* of cultures': 'each has its own existence.' Canada contained 'two dominant cultures . . . embodied in distinct societies'.[5]

The commission fully recognized the connotations of the term 'distinct societies'. For the commission, a society consisted of institutions and organizations that shared 'a rather large population' and extend over 'quite a vast territory' where that population lives as 'a homogenous group according to common standards and rules of conduct'. And the commission acknowledged that it is in precisely these terms that, in its preliminary report, it had recognized 'the main elements of a distinct French-speaking society in Quebec'. The commission took pains to note that this French-speaking society was not restricted to Quebec alone since 'elements of an autonomous society are taking shape elsewhere'. But it saw Quebec as the heart of the francophone side of Canadian duality.[6]

At the same time, while insisting that biculturalism entailed 'distinct societies' that shared a common language and culture, the commission tried to
avoid any suggestion that these might be 'closed' societies. Thus, it avoided
the concept of 'ethnicity', fearing that the term implied biological origin. To
use ethnicity as a basic organizing principle of society would be objectionable on moral, as well as practical grounds, since it 'would tend to create closed-
membership groups with newcomers condemned to remain outsiders'.[7]

Similarly, the commission strongly resisted the application of the term
'ethnic' to non-British, non-French groups, even though the term 'ethnic
groups' was placed in the terms of reference for precisely that purpose. It did,
however, recognize that if such individuals are 'to participate fully in
Canadian life', the two societies will have to welcome them and allow them
'to preserve and enrich, if they so desire, the cultural values they prize'.[8] And
the commission was clear that it was only as part of one society or the other
that these individuals could participate in Canadian life; none of the various
'ethnic' groups had a sufficiently comprehensive set of organizations and
institutions to qualify as societies.[9]

Having defined biculturalism in such broad terms, rooting it in distinct
societies, the commission was similarly bold in its definition of another term
in its mandate: 'equal partnership between the two founding peoples'. It
insisted that the equal partnership should apply not only to the two peoples,
but to their languages and cultures as well. It called for equality in the ability of individuals to obtain 'the various benefits of society' while retaining
their culture. It was careful to set the objective for individual equality as 'a
real equality of opportunity' rather than absolute equality and to recognize
that even that depends on 'the law of numbers' or sufficient demographic
strength. But the commission went on to insist that, beyond equality for individuals, equal partnership must also mean equality between communities.
Indeed, since 'language and cultures are essentially collective phenomena',
equality between language and cultures can exist only if there is equality
between the communities in which they are located.[10]

On this basis, the commission established the goal of equal participation
by anglophones and francophones in the work world, which would imply 'a
vast enlargement of the opportunities for francophones in both private and
public sectors of the economy'. It even called for political equality between
the two communities, conceiving it as a matter of 'self-determination' or 'the
extent of the control each [community] has over its government or governments'.[11] So as to make the point crystal clear, the commission spelled out
the various institutional arrangements this might entail: 'a unitary or a federal system; special status for the province in which the minority group is
concentrated; or again, for the same part of the country, the status of an asso-

ciate state; or, finally, the status of an independent state.'[12] And it insisted that for the commission to ignore the demand for autonomy that was so 'deeply entrenched in Quebec . . . would very likely mean that Quebec would refuse to listen to us.'[13] Similarly it argued that the concentration of francophones in Quebec meant that 'the place of Québécois in the French fact in Quebec in Canada will in practice have to be recognized much more than it is today.'[14]

In short, Canadian dualism was one of two 'distinct societies', historically rooted in two founding peoples that were organized on the basis of language and culture. And an equal partnership required that the two societies be politically and economically equal. This was an ambitious agenda.

The Liberal Attack on Biculturalism

The commission's agenda was difficult to square with the conception of Canada, and the strategy for national unity, that were emerging through the writings of Pierre Trudeau. Indeed, soon after the commission's creation, when it called upon Trudeau for advice as to how it should interpret its mandate, Trudeau argued for a narrowly defined focus on linguistic questions.[15] Similarly, in 1965 the publication of the commission's *Preliminary Report* was criticized severely in *Cité libre*, the liberal journal that Trudeau had co-founded in 1950. Trudeau's name does not appear among the five members of the Comité pour une politique fonctionnelle who signed the article, but reportedly he was closely involved in its writing.[16] Having decided to enter federal politics, he apparently decided it best not to sign the document. The article reveals the line of thinking that helped lead Trudeau, as prime minister, to substitute multiculturalism for biculturalism as the basis of government policy.

The Comité pour une politique fonctionnelle offered no fewer than eight critical commentaries of the commission's *Preliminary Report*, ranging from faulty methodology to weak internal logical to a failure to demonstrate the basic claim that Canada was passing through its worst crisis. For our purposes, however, the most important line of criticism (dealing with some 'confusions fondamentales') addresses the commission's interpretation of its mandate.

The comité was ready to recognize that bilingualism could be a valid objective in a modern state, as was equality between anglophones and francophones, *per se*. But the group had no patience with biculturalism and the notion of equality between citizens as members of one of two cultures. Indeed, it declared that the notion of equality between cultures 'is quite foreign to our legal thought and our political institutions. . . . And what would be the meaning in practice of a Confederation that "develops according to the principle of equality between two *cultures*"?'[17] In fact, the group was convinced that it must mean recognition of Quebec sovereignty. From their liberal perspective, equality within a given state could only be among individuals. Equality between collectivities necessarily implied separate states: 'Political science is very familiar with the idea of equality between individuals within the same state, but the idea of equality between peoples underlies the concept of national sovereignty, and it would have been interesting to see how the Commission intends to interpret its mandate without being led necessarily to propose the division of Canada into two national states.'[18]

Yet, as we have seen, there was in fact a long tradition of thought in French Quebec that did presume that peoples could be equal within the same state. The United Canadas was generally seen as a strong example: it may have been formally based on territorial units, but for many francophones it came to represent a formal equality between two peoples. The double-compact theory of Confederation first formulated by Henri Bourassa was explicitly based on the idea of formal equality between two peoples. This equality between two peoples was to be embodied in policies both of the federal government and provincial governments and in procedures for amending the constitution. Far from being alien to Canadian thought, biculturalism or equality between peoples was central to most French Canadians' understanding of Canada.

Henri Bourassa's rejection of separatism, and commitment to Canada, were beyond dispute, and the same might be said of André Laurendeau. Yet, based as it was on the premise that Canada is composed of distinct collectivities, this vision of Canada was unacceptable to Trudeau and his resolutely liberal colleagues, for it could only lead to separatism. They even argued that political science would allow no other conclusion.[19]

Upon becoming prime minister, Trudeau applied the same logic in developing policy for another category of Canadians who had always seen themselves as a distinct nationality: native peoples. In June 1969 the Trudeau government presented a White Paper that proposed nothing less than the elimination of all government arrangements that applied specifically to natives, including the Indian Act and the Department of Indian Affairs. Equality for natives was to take precisely the same form as equality for all other Canadians: 'non-discrimination' or equal status and services for natives *as individuals*.[20]

Thus, even for native peoples, equality could only mean individual equality. As Trudeau declared in 1968, natives 'should be treated more and more like Canadians'.[21] Nor was it appropriate to speak of historical aboriginal rights: 'No society can be built in historical "might-have-beens".'[22] The reasoning was precisely the same as in his analysis of French Canada. Nor did

Trudeau deny this: as in 'the case of the French in Canada . . . the way to be strong in Canada is not to be apart but to be equal to the English.'[23]

With respect to native peoples the Trudeau government was obliged to abandon its unyielding application of individualist liberalism, given the intensity of native protest. The White Paper was withdrawn. But the episode showed that the logic that had led to such a heated dismissal of biculturalism in 1965 was very much at work in the upper levels of the new Trudeau government.

Mobilization of 'Third-Force' Canadians

As it happened, during the 1960s opposition to biculturalism was also building from quite a different direction. From the moment that the B&B Commission was established, Canadians of neither British nor French descent began to argue that the bicultural vision of Canada excluded them.

As we have already noted, the 10 members of the commission did include two representatives of 'ethnic groups'. In symmetrical fashion, they were each linked with different 'dominant cultures'. A Polish Canadian, Paul Wyczynski, was a professor of French literature at the University of Ottawa; a Ukrainian Canadian, J.B. Rudnyckyj, was chair of Slavic studies at the University of Manitoba. But to some, this was simply not enough. Thus, the appointment of the B&B Commission was greeted with a complaint by John Diefenbaker, himself the first prime minister of neither British nor French descent, that 'very important ethnic groups in Canada will ask why it is they have no representation.'[24] The NDP spokesman, Harold Winch, expressed the hope that the term 'biculturalism' would not be construed so narrowly as to preclude consideration of 'the various cultures of the other countries which go to make up what we call Canadianism'.[25]

More pointed was the first Senate speech of the Ukrainian Canadian Paul Yuzyk in March 1964. Yuzyk declared that Canada had never been bicultural in the past, given both the aboriginal peoples and the ethnic pluralism of Britishers. And he cited the 1961 census figure of 30 per cent for a 'third element' to show that Canada certainly was not bicultural then. Insisting on Canada's multicultural character, he proposed that British and French be treated as 'senior partners', with full language rights, but that 'third element ethnic or cultural groups' should have the status of 'co-partners', entailing the right to have their languages and cultures offered as 'optional subjects' at all levels of education, whenever numbers warrant.[26]

Canadian Jewish leaders had also been quick to convey their unhappiness with the terms of the commission's mandate, objecting in particular to the term 'two founding races'. For that reason, the Canadian Jewish Congress did not submit a brief to the commission, while expressing in various other ways its concerns about the commission and its activities.[27]

The commission was obviously taken aback by this attack on biculturalism, especially when it started to convene formal meetings in the prairie provinces, where Ukrainian-Canadian groups, in particular, were well-prepared.[28] Indeed, the debate was joined within the commission itself, as the Ukrainian-Canadian member argued vigorously that languages other than English and French should receive recognition. The first volume of the commission's report, *The Official Languages*, which limited its recommendations to English and French, contained a lengthy dissenting statement by Rudnyckyj, who echoed Yuzyk's demand by proposing that unofficial languages should have the status of 'regional' language if they are spoken by more than 10 per cent of the population of an administrative unit. He did not, however, challenge the concept of biculturalism.[29]

The commission felt obliged to prepare a full volume entitled *The Cultural Contribution of the Other Ethnic Groups*. There it proposed a series of initiatives such as anti-discrimination measures, equal access of all immigrants to citizenship, teaching of non-official languages in public schools, elimination of restrictions on non-official languages in private and public broadcasting, and support for organizations fostering 'the arts and letters of cultural groups other than the British and French'.[30]

However, despite the claim of some observers,[31] at no point did the commission propose that the concept of biculturalism be abandoned.[32] Even without Laurendeau's guiding hand, the commission still maintained biculturalism as the basic framework for comprehending culture in Canada. Recognizing that some Canadians of non-British, non-French origin 'consider Canada to be a country that is officially bilingual but fundamentally multi-cultural', the commission responded that Canada's cultural diversity must be acknowledged, 'keeping in mind that there are *two dominant cultures*, the French and British'.[33] It insisted that 'those of other languages and cultures are more or less integrated' with anglophone and francophone communities and constitute a 'third force' only in a statistical sense.[34] By the same token, the commission declared: '[The immigrant to Canada] should know that Canada recognizes two official languages and that it possesses two predominant cultures that have produced two societies—francophone and anglophone—which form two distinct communities within an overall Canadian context.'[35] In short, the Trudeau government adopted its multiculturalism without the commission's blessings.

The federal government was undoubtedly under pressure from some non-British, non-French Canadians to substitute multiculturalism for biculturalism. Their proportion of the Canadian population had grown since the

Second World War—from 20.0 per cent in 1941 to 25.8 per cent in 1961. It had been only 12.2 per cent at the turn of the century. Moreover, this segment of the population was more urban than in the past, and thus more visible to other Canadians.[36] It was also more skilled and better educated than in the past, and thus more apt to produce leaders able to express grievances on their behalf.[37]

It is not clear, however, that the mobilization of 'third-force' groups was sufficiently broad-based to have alone induced the federal government's adoption of multiculturalism.[38] The mobilization of ethnic organizations was uneven, and heavily dominated by Ukrainian-Canadian groups.[39] Of the 55 briefs, supported by 14 ethnic groups, presented to the B&B Commission, 32 came from Ukrainian-Canadian organizations.[40] Some of the other groups actually supported the commission's positions, including the Toronto Italian-Canadian community's leaders and the Trans-Canadian Alliance of German Canadians.[41] And two years after the multiculturalism policy was announced, a survey of members of 10 'minority ethnic groups' found that most of them still were not clearly aware of the policy.[42]

Some provincial governments, presumably where ethnic organizations were especially influential, did acquiesce to the pressures. Alberta announced a multiculturalism policy in July 1971, and in September 1971, one month before Ottawa announced its policy, Ontario declared that it would convene an Ontario Heritage Conference in 1972.[43]

Ultimately, however, the adoption of multiculturalism must have been partly due to Trudeau's hostility to biculturalism. To quote Raymond Breton, himself a *Cité libre* colleague of Trudeau:

> Another incentive [for such a policy] was that multiculturalism turned out to be instrumental to the Trudeau government's political agenda. Indeed, the terms of the royal commission could be interpreted as lending support to the 'two nations' view of Canada. A policy of cultural pluralism would help to undermine a notion that was seen as dangerously consistent with the Quebec independence movement.[44]

This interpretation has also been offered by Bernard Ostry, who, as a senior civil servant, was in charge of the early implementation of the policy and worked closely with Trudeau and Pelletier.[45]

From that perspective, the importance of multiculturalism was not so much what it offered as what it excluded: biculturalism. This general attitude can be seen both in the way that Trudeau presented the policy and his relative indifference to the policy after announcing it.

Substituting Multiculturalism for Biculturalism

The new multiculturalism policy was announced by Prime Minister Trudeau in the House on 8 October 1971. In adopting multiculturalism, rather than biculturalism, the government was clear as to what it was about. Trudeau presented a document to the House outlining the government's response to the B&B Commission's Book IV. There, the difference in approach was explicit: 'The very name of the royal commission whose recommendations we now seek to implement tends to indicate that bilingualism and biculturalism are indivisible. But, biculturalism does not properly describe our society; multiculturalism is more accurate.'[46] By the same token, in his address to the House, Trudeau proclaimed, 'there are no official cultures in Canada.'[47] Through the policy, Trudeau committed the federal government to acting in four different areas:

> First, resources permitting, the government will seek to assist all Canadian cultural groups that have demonstrated a desire and effort to continue to develop a capacity to grow and contribute to Canada, and a clear need for assistance, *the small and weak groups no less than the strong and highly organized.*
>
> Second, the government will assist members of all cultural groups to overcome cultural barriers to full participation in Canadian society.
>
> Third, the government will promote creative encounters and interchange among all Canadian cultural groups in the interest of national unity.
>
> Fourth, the government will continue to assist immigrants to acquire at least one of Canada's official languages in order to become full participants in Canadian society [emphasis added].[48]

In effect, through the first principle Ottawa was committed not only to supporting actively the survival of cultures other than French and English but to assisting their development. This commitment extended to all groups that were in a position to benefit from such support, however 'small and weak' they might be.

Such a commitment did not square with Trudeau's oft-repeated insistence on the primacy of the individual and his belief that cultural groups must depend on their own resources to survive. It is not surprising, then, that his presentation of the new policy to the House of Commons dwelled primarily on the second principle: freeing the individual from barriers to opportunity:

> Such a policy should help break down discriminatory attitudes and cultural jealousies. National unity if it is to mean anything in the deeply personal sense, must be founded on confidence in one's own *individual* identity; out of this can grow respect for that of others and a willingness to share ideas, attitudes and assumptions. A vigorous policy of multiculturalism will help create this initial confidence. It can form the base of a society which is based on fair play for all.[49]

Thus, for Trudeau multiculturalism was more about freeing the individual from constraints than promoting the development of cultural groups. In fact, he ended his statement with the words '[The policy] is basically the conscious support of individual freedom of choice.'[50]

Yet the potential for conflict remained between the two goals of cultural preservation and enhancement of personal autonomy and mobility. For that matter, the goal of cultural preservation could be threatened by the third principle of promoting cross-cultural exchanges as well as the fourth principle, training immigrants in the official languages.

Development of Multiculturalism Policy

The contradiction among the goals of the new multiculturalism policy has been evident in the two stages of its implementation. The first stage focused upon preserving cultures, the second on reducing cultural and racial barriers to individual mobility.

As was to be expected, the first stage of multiculturalism was closely shaped by the groups that had so vigorously championed multiculturalism: largely white, second- and third-generation Canadians of non-British, non-French descent. For them, multiculturalism was all about the policy's first principle: helping cultural groups to continue to develop. Even more, as Breton argues, it was about asserting their status in Canadian society, relative to the Charter groups.[51]

The first minister of state for multiculturalism was Stanley Haidasz (himself a spokesperson for Polish Canadians).[52] During his tenure, several programs were established, including Canadian Identities (which focused on song and dance), Ethnic Group Liaison, Ethnic Press Analysis Service, Third Language Teaching Aids, Immigration Orientation, and Multicultural Centres. Other government agencies established such units as the Canadian Centre for Folk Culture Studies, the Ethnic Canadian Program, and the National Ethnic Archives. But most financial resources were distributed through the Multicultural Projects Grants to groups and organizations 'for such cultural activities as festivals, television programs, Saturday schools, literary clubs and art exhibits'.[53] This program in particular gave rise to the popular complaint that multiculturalism had become heavily oriented toward the Liberal Party's electoral concerns. A charge that may well have had some basis in fact,[54] it was to persist.

By the mid-1970s, a shift away from cultural preservation was already beginning. In part, this was due to public criticism, shared by a new minister of state for multiculturalism, John Munro, that through its emphasis on supporting folklore, the program was wasteful and tended to favour the better-organized groups. But it was also due to the emergence of new claimants for government programs: the leaders of racially defined groups and other 'visible minorities'.

This new kind of leadership was itself a result of a change in immigration policy, going back to the mid-1960s, that broadened eligibility beyond the white, European categories that had tended to predominate among past immigrants. For these new immigrants, preservation of their cultural distinctiveness was far less important than the need to break down racial barriers to economic opportunity and social integration. This was, of course, the second principle of Trudeau's multiculturalism policy and the one that was much more congenial to him.

The older multicultural leaders bitterly resented the change in orientation. Indeed, the national chair of the Canadian Consultative Council denounced John Munro's plans so vehemently that Munro asked him to resign.[55] None the less, by the 1980s, the program had been effectively reoriented to a focus on social issues, especially racism. In 1982, a Race Relations Unit was established and symposia were held on 'race relations and the law' and 'race relations in the media'.[56] Greater emphasis was placed on promoting intercultural understanding. And the needs of immigrant women were identified as a particular concern. In 1987 a new parliamentary standing committee on multiculturalism proclaimed that multicultural policy had indeed evolved from cultural preservation to the promotion of equality.[57]

Either way, whether the emphasis was on cultural preservation or anti-discrimination, multiculturalism did not have as central a place as language policy in the national unity strategy for countering Quebec nationalism. It may have been hoped that multiculturalism would give francophones a different understanding of Canada, but they were not to be directly affected by multiculturalism programs. In terms of francophone relations with English Canada, multiculturalism was more important for precluding biculturalism and the full recognition of duality than for anything it could provide on its own. In effect, the announcement of the policy was more important than its implementation.

Certainly, multiculturalism was not one of the prime minister's personal interests. As Manoly R. Lupul, a Ukrainian-Canadian scholar and activist, has written:

> Multiculturalism is not central to Trudeau's thinking, just as ethnicity is
> not central to his being. . . . In accepting multiculturalism as government
> policy, there is no reason to believe that he felt deeply about what he was
> doing. . . . Sheltered by his home and schooling even from Montreal's eth-
> nic diversity, Trudeau never acquired first-hand knowledge of life in a mul-
> ticultural society. . . . He is no ethnic; his bilingualism and biculturalism is
> not private and its reference point is not remote.[58]

Thus, Trudeau indeed treated multicultural policy with indifference. Whereas
he spoke regularly about bilingualism, he reportedly had nothing to say about
multiculturalism after 1971, the year he announced the policy.[59] Neither, for
that matter, did the Progressive Conservatives or the NDP show any sustained
interest in the question.[60] Beyond lack of personal commitment, the party
leaders were also aware that multiculturalism was not popular among francophones in Quebec.[61] Senior civil servants soon concluded that the program was not a priority and saw little incentive to pursue it. This was especially true of French-Canadian officials.[62]

During the Trudeau years multiculturalism was assigned to junior ministers and given small and relatively weak administrative structures. As a result,
there was little co-ordination among departments in the pursuit of multiculturalism, nor did the principal central agencies of the federal government
support the goals of the multiculturalism policy.[63] A Multiculturalism Act
was not passed until 1988, 17 years after the original announcement of the
policy, and under the Mulroney government. Official bilingualism had, of
course, been codified in law back in 1969, soon after Trudeau's assumption
of power.

This general indifference is also seen in the meagre resources assigned to
multiculturalism, especially when compared with official bilingualism. Daiva
Stasiulis has calculated that in the first year of multiculturalism, 1971/2, the
secretary of state spent over $78 million on bilingualism but only 2 per cent
of that amount, or less than $2 million, on multiculturalism. Ten years later
the gap remained: in 1981/2 close to $196 million was spent on bilingualism
but only 7 per cent of that amount, or a little over $14 million on multicul-
turalism. In 1987/8 the ratio was unchanged.[64]

MULTICULTURALISM AND NATIONAL UNITY

The question still remains, what effects did multiculturalism policy have on
the Trudeau government's fundamental goal of national unity? To what
extent did Canadians embrace the notion of a multicultural Canada? And, to
the extent they did, was the cause of national unity furthered?

Rejection in Quebec

Not surprisingly, multiculturalism was denounced in Quebec from the out-set.[65] Even public figures who were committed to Canadian federalism denounced this deviation from biculturalism and the established franco-phone understanding of Canadian dualism.[66] Indeed, the response came very quickly.

In November 1971, Quebec Premier Robert Bourassa wrote to Prime Minister Trudeau protesting the federal government's new policy. He said it contradicted the B&B Commission's mandate and the principle that had gov-erned its deliberations: 'the equality of the two founding peoples'. As well, it introduced a dubious dissociation of culture and language. Bourassa declared that, for its part, the Quebec government would not be adopting multicul-turalism in its own jurisdictions, given its responsibility to ensure the persis-tence of the French language and culture in its territory, and beyond. At the same time Bourassa pointed out that Quebec had been subsidizing ethnic groups and language training for several years and that an agreement would be needed to ensure that Ottawa's programs did not duplicate or compro-mise Quebec's.[67] The leaders of Quebec's opposition parties also denounced the new policy as an attack on Canadian duality while dismissing it as an electoral ploy.[68]

Claude Ryan, then editor of *Le Devoir*, insisted that the linking of bilin-gualism to multiculturalism was a direct contradiction of the conception of Canada that the B&B Commission presented in the 'blue pages' of Book I, 'which Trudeau claims never to have read', and which, Ryan insisted, the commission maintained throughout its Book IV. The notion of separating language and culture was dear to Trudeau's heart but had been rejected by the commission. In propounding it, Trudeau 'omits a central fact: the two official languages of Canada, far from existing in the abstract as the subject of juridical definitions, are the expression of two cultures, two peoples, two societies which give Canada its distinctive shape.'[69] And a leading Quebec sociologist, Guy Rocher, declared:

> French Canadians have struggled for generations to have bilingualism accepted—bilingualism defined not simply as the acceptance of French as an official language in Canada but recognition of French Canadians as part-ners with the English-speaking community in the country's sociological structure. By separating bilingualism from biculturalism, the Trudeau gov-ernment is betraying all the hopes French Canadians might have placed in bilingualism, as they conceived it—that is, clearly tied to its symbol and essential condition, biculturalism.[70]

Over the following years, francophone intellectual and political élites continued to reject multiculturalism as a denial of Canadian dualism.[71]

This did not, however, prevent the Quebec government from establishing programs that parallelled measures adopted by Ottawa under the rubric of multiculturalism. Indeed, as Bourassa had insisted, Quebec had already been moving in this direction before Ottawa announced its new policy, and the subsequent evolution of Quebec's programs quite closely followed that of Ottawa's, as Marie McAndrew has recently demonstrated in an unpublished paper titled, 'Multiculturalisme Canadien et interculturalisme québécois: mythes et réalités'.

Until at least the mid-1980s, the Quebec ministry of immigration and cultural communities subsidized the 'folklore' activities of various groups in the same way as did Ottawa. Indeed, under the 1981 law that created it, the ministry was explicitly charged with 'maintien des cultures d'origine'. And in Quebec schools curriculum was introduced that tended to present different cultures in the same way as multicultural programs outside Quebec. In the mid-1980s, the emphasis in Quebec's programs began to shift toward questions of racism, prejudice, and inequality, following by only a few years the reorientation of Ottawa's multiculturalism policy. As was the case with Ottawa, the reorientation was due to an increased presence of visible-minority immigrants. More recently, though, both the federal and Quebec governments have felt obliged, by backlashes among the majority population, to distance themselves somewhat from the 'cultural relativism' of their past policies.[72]

Yet, if the Quebec government adopted measures that paralleled Ottawa's, it was very careful to locate them within a different framework. The term 'multiculturalisme' was systematically eschewed in favour of 'interculturalisme' and Quebec officials insisted that their approach was fundamentally different from Ottawa's. In particular, it placed greater stress on the need of immigrants to adapt to the larger community.[73] Moreover, unlike the federal multiculturalism policy, it assumed that there is an overarching common culture.[74] Yet, many academic observers claim that at the level of concrete policy there have been few differences, other than the fact that the linguistic framework has been unilingual rather than bilingual.[75] In effect, the Quebec government tried to pursue precisely the vision that the B&B Commission had proposed of an 'open' francophone society, allowing newcomers who so wished 'to preserve and enrich . . . the cultural values they prize.'[76] But, as with the commission, there could be no concession on the basically bicultural conception of the country.

Mixed Reception Outside Quebec

Outside Quebec, the new multicultural vision of Canada was received quite differently. It was, of course, welcomed among the representatives of third-force population, largely white second- and third-generation Canadians, which had championed the policy in the first place. To be sure, leaders of these groups regularly expressed frustration with the meagre support the government actually gave to their various cultural activities. But at least the declaration by the prime minister that 'there are no official cultures in Canada' eased their fear of a secondary status that had been provoked by the notion of biculturalism.

The multicultural vision also met with support among some Canadians of British origin. Indeed, a recent survey suggests that they are more supportive than non-British, non-French Canadians.[77] Beyond defining dualism in terms that were more congenial to British Canadians by reducing it to language alone, multiculturalism offered a formula for differentiating Canada from the United States. This came at a time of growing alarm at American domination, and apprehension over the decline of the British connection, which had served so well to define a Canadian nationality in the past. Through multiculturalism and the celebration of cultural diversity, Canada could be readily distinguished from the melting pot that the United States was presumed to represent.[78]

If multiculturalism policy did help some Canadians feel better integrated into Canadian society and provided a clearer basis of Canadian identity, then it served the cause of national unity. However, it is far from clear that that has happened; in fact, cogent arguments have been made to the effect that, multiculturalism has, on the contrary, undermined national unity. With time, these arguments seem to have gathered force.[79]

First, it has been argued that multiculturalism has impeded rather than facilitated the integration of immigrants into Canadian society. In effect, there is an inevitable contradiction between the first two goals of the multiculturalism policy, namely preserving cultures and eliminating barriers to mobility. This criticism has even come from the Canadians who ostensibly benefit from the policy.

Most prominent among the critics has been the writer Neil Bissoondath, whose best-seller book, *Selling Illusions: The Cult of Multiculturalism in Canada*, argues at length that the celebration of cultural diversity has sustained divisions among Canadians and prevented its supposed beneficiaries from being fully accepted into the mainstream of Canadian life. The forms of cultural difference supported financially by federal policy amount to little more than folklore and they tend to perpetuate popular stereotypes of the ethnic group in question: 'Our approach to multiculturalism encourages the devaluation of that which it claims to wish to protect and promote. Culture becomes an object for display rather than the heart and soul of the individuals formed by it. Culture, manipulated into social and political usefulness, becomes folklore.'[80]

By the same token, a recent case study by political scientist John C. Harles has found that Laotian immigrants have been quite ambivalent about Canada's multiculturalism policy. His Laotian respondents appreciated the promise to combat possible barriers to their economic and social mobility, although they were relatively unconcerned about such obstacles. But they were quite uneasy with the goal of cultural preservation, fearing that an effort to retain a distinct Laotian cultural identity would hinder their integration into Canadian society or would simply be futile. They even expressed concern that multiculturalism might weaken the coherence of their new country.[81] Bissoondath and other critics propose that Ottawa's multiculturalism program should be substantially downgraded, if not eliminated outright, and the budget should be fully redirected from cultural preservation to battling racism through education.

As for the claim that multiculturalism can strengthen a distinctive Canadian identity, some politicians and intellectuals have begun to argue that multiculturalism has robbed Canadian identity of any real core. By this argument, if there is to be no 'official culture', then it is difficult to designate any set of values that are common to all Canadians or that characterize a Canadian community. All is lost in a cultural relativism. In the words of sociologist Reginald Bibby; 'In Canada, the time has come to address a centrally important question, both as a country and as individuals relating to each other in various spheres of life: if what we have in common is our diversity, do we really have anything in common at all?' He quotes the remark made by the political scientist Gad Horowitz in 1972 that multiculturalism is really no more than 'the masochistic celebration of Canadian nothingness'.[82]

Predictably, this critique has found great resonance among the Canadian right. Often it is a cover for simply rejecting diversity in immigration. Such is the case with William Gairdner, who laments the loss of a 'control [immigration] policy [that] was designed to ensure that the bulk of Canada's children would grow up among parents and people more or less similar to themselves, who spoke the same language and who were more or less rooted in the same Judeo-Christian religion, Graeco-Roman philosophical and legal tradition, and Anglo-European culture.'[83] Preston Manning and the Reform Party have tended to frame their attack on multiculturalism in more neoliberal terms: the state simply has no business promoting any version of culture: 'The Reform Party believes that cultural development and preservation ought to be the responsibility of individuals, groups, and, if necessary in certain cases (for example, in the case of Quebec and Canadian aboriginal peoples), of provincial and local governments. The role of the federal government should be neutral to culture just as it is toward religion.'[84]

These critiques have not been restricted to the right. Leftist intellectuals have begun to voice concerns more openly. In a recent analysis of 'English Canada', Philip Resnick dwells at length on the necessary limits to multiculturalism and the necessity for immigrants to adapt to 'an ongoing society with certain political traditions': 'English Canada is not some tabula rasa or blank sheet to be recast every time new cultural communities come along.'[85] And recently Garth Stevenson has maintained that it is a myth that multiculturalism differentiates Canada from the United States and, citing Bissoondath, argues that official multiculturalism hinders the natural integration of immigrants into the Canadian community.[86] Stevenson draws on a study by two University of Toronto sociologists, Jeffrey G. Reitz and Raymond Breton, who show that the levels of cultural retention among ethnic groups are quite similar in Canada and the United States.[87]

On the basis of a detailed analysis of the federal government's multiculturalism policy and its support for official-language minorities and women's groups, political scientist Leslie Pal argues that the funding of these groups 'fragments rather than unifies national identity'. Like programs for women and linguistic minorities, multiculturalism strengthens 'particularistic identities' and 'in-group solidarity'. Though these programs may offer up new notions of Canadian identity enshrined in such banal terms as 'unified through diversity', 'brought together by our differences', and 'the mosaic', 'the reality is a politics overdetermined by division and difference.'[88]

By the same token, on the basis of his case study of Laotian immigrants, Harles concludes that if immigrants do come to identify strongly with the Canadian political order, as his Laotian respondents obviously do, it happens *independently* of multiculturalism, at least the objective of cultural preservation. Their attachment to Canada is instead based upon rejection of their homeland, gratitude for admission to Canada, and confidence in the Canadian government.[89]

Tension between Multiculturalism and Bilingualism

To gauge the extent to which multiculturalism has strengthened national unity, we also need to assess its contradictory relationship with the main element of official bilingualism, which was the Trudeau government's national unity strategy.

By trying to link multiculturalism and bilingualism, the Trudeau government created an obvious contradiction. Although all cultures, however 'small and weak', were to be supported, only two languages were to have official status. Yet how can cultures be meaningfully supported without also supporting their languages? As a consequence, both Ottawa and many of the provincial governments have found themselves providing support for non-official languages as well.

Ottawa has long been engaged in providing financial support for instruction in non-official languages. In 1977 it introduced the Cultural Enrichment Program, to support supplementary heritage-language schools. By 1989 there were 129,000 students studying 60 languages in supplementary schools. In addition, it has established a Canadian Heritage Languages Institute in Edmonton.[90]

By the same token, the Canadian Multiculturalism Act, passed in 1988, contains in its preamble the declaration that 'whereas the Constitution of Canada and the Official Languages Act provide that English and French are the official languages of Canada and neither abrogates nor derogates from any rights or privileges acquired or enjoyed with respect to any other language' and on that basis commits the government to 'preserve and enhance the use of languages other than English and French, while strengthening the status and use of the official languages of Canada.'[91]

As for the provincial governments, most now maintain programs through which children of non-English and non-French origin can receive some training in their ancestral language. Under Ontario's 'heritage language' program, provincial funding is provided for children to receive this training either after the regular school day or during an extended school day. In most other provinces supplementary heritage-language programs are supported by federal funds alone.

To be sure, such programs of supplementary instruction in 'heritage languages' do not mean that these languages have assumed official status. After all, even Quebec, which has explicitly reserved official status to French alone, supports supplementary instruction in heritage languages, whether in the regular public schools (for about 100 hours a year) or in instruction programs maintained by ethnic groups themselves.[92] But the language of instruction in public schools remains French or, under the terms of Bill 101, English.

However, in parts of Canada where the francophone presence is marginal to begin with, such recognition of non-official languages may well place all languages other than English, including French, on the same plane. After all, in each of the four western provinces, people of French origin are outnumbered by two or three non-British groups.[93] Thus, it is not surprising that on the Prairies non-official languages have assumed the status that francophone minorities have demanded for their language: language of instruction. Since 1971, Alberta has allowed the use of non-official languages as the language of instruction in public schools. Saskatchewan has done so since 1978, and Manitoba since 1979. Now all three provincial governments are financially supporting bilingual programs in which Ukrainian or German is the language of instruction up to 100 per cent of the time in kindergarten and up to 50 per cent of the time thereafter. Alberta has other programs of instruction in English and another language—namely, Yiddish, Arabic, Polish, and Chinese.[94]

In the process the status of French is considerably diminished, becoming a language, to coin a phrase, 'like the others'. Not only has biculturalism become multiculturalism but, in the minds of some English Canadians bilingualism has become multilingualism. So it becomes all the more difficult to defend the Trudeau vision of a pan-Canadian linguistic duality in areas where francophones are outnumbered by various groups of non-British, non-French descent.

Some organizations representing francophone minorities have attacked multiculturalism for precisely this reason. In 1978 the Fédération des francophones hors du Québec declared: 'Another threat to the cultural identity and activity of francophones outside Quebec is the concept of Canada as a bilingual but multicultural country. This federal policy, which has many followers among the provincial governments, pushes us too easily and subtly to the background, to the same level as any other ethnic minority.'[95]

Finally, if multiculturalism sits uneasily with the Trudeau vision of linguistic dualism, it is positively antithetical to the established francophone notion of a comprehensive dualism entailing two distinct peoples. Given that most Quebec francophones have not abandoned that ideal and instead have been reinforced in it, then multiculturalism has indeed widened the gulf between anglophone and francophone Canadians. In the following chapters, we will see how leaders of 'multicultural' organizations were in the forefront of the opposition to even the most modest constitutional recognition of dualism, especially if it involved recognizing Quebec as the historical centre of francophone society. In that respect multiculturalism is indeed detrimental to national unity.

The impact on national unity of the Trudeau government's notion of multiculturalism has been, at best, mixed. As a vision of Canada it has been almost universally rejected in francophone Quebec. Outside Quebec, it has had a much better reception, although among the ostensible beneficiaries of multiculturalism, as among other Canadians, important critiques have emerged to the effect that it has been more detrimental than supportive of national unity. In addition, with its untenable distinction between language and culture, multiculturalism has undermined the particular status of French as an official language. Finally, it has intensified the constitutional conflict between Quebec and the rest of Canada.

Multiculturalism versus Biculturalism

If this rather negative assessment is at all valid, then the question arises as to whether the cause of national unity might in fact have been better served by adhering to the notion of biculturalism that the B&B Commission had spent so much energy developing. The ideal of biculturalism need not have precluded the emphasis on discrimination and race relations that has characterized the second stage of federal multiculturalism. In fact, such measures have been adopted by the Quebec government, acting within the framework of a francophone distinct society. But the notion of two overarching cultures might have avoided some of the fragmenting effects that Pal ascribes to multiculturalism and the promotion of official-language minorities. At the same time, by recognizing the existence of an anglophone society, biculturalism might have provided a framework in which English Canadians could have uncovered or created the sense of community that they allege multiculturalism cannot support.[96]

To be sure, biculturalism could not have eased the status concerns felt by some Canadians of neither British nor French origin. However, as things have turned out, the programs of cultural promotion and support that were first associated with multiculturalism have, in any event, fallen out of favour.

Nevertheless, official recognition of biculturalism would have greatly complicated the Trudeau government's plans on the constitutional front. By recognizing the existence of a distinct francophone society, biculturalism would have led inexorably to the question of Quebec, the centre of that society. In elaborating the concept of biculturalism in the famous 'blue pages', Laurendeau was well aware that this is where the notion led. In rejecting biculturalism, the Trudeau government made it equally clear that it had no intention of following such a path.

CHAPTER 6

Federalism and the Constitution: Entrenching the Trudeau Vision

Although central elements of Trudeau's strategy for national unity were the Official Languages Act and multiculturalism, the strategy also entailed change in the status of governments and in the constitutional framework in which they operated. After all, the Trudeau government was exceedingly ambitious in its objectives for Quebec francophones, seeking to change their political allegiances and primary identities, even their sense of nationality. Language policy was indispensable since, according to the Trudeau strategy, linguistic equality could make it possible for Quebec francophones to adopt a pan-Canadian identity. But the political order itself had to be refashioned so as to inculcate and support such an identity.

Quebec continued to be dominated by a distinctive understanding of Canada that provided clear directions as to how the Canadian political order should be organized and should function. The proper role of the federal government was to be restricted to the jurisdictions explicitly assigned to it by the BNA Act. Thus, even the Tremblay Report, not to mention the new nationalism of the 1960s, had dictated that much of Ottawa's post-war edifice of social, cultural, and economic programs had to be dismantled as an improper intrusion in provincial jurisdiction. This federal retreat did not need, however, to apply across Canada as a whole; it could be limited to Quebec. Indeed this was preferable since the second premise of the dominant francophone view of Canada was the uniqueness of Quebec as centre of Canada's francophone collectivity. This basic assumption had been a constant of francophone thought from Henri Bourassa's designation of Quebec as the 'special inheritance' of all French Canadians to the Tremblay Commission's call for Quebec to be recognized as a 'national' government to the Lesage government's schemes to grant Quebec new powers to meet its special responsibilities. It went without saying that Quebec and its government had to be party to any change in the constitutional framework. Canada was, after all, based on a compact, indeed a 'double compact' of which Quebec was a senior party.

Upon those premises Quebec nationalists had formulated demands for a fundamental reform of the Canadian political order. The Pearson government's asymmetrical arrangements with Quebec had pointed the way to a possible response to those demands, but depending, as they did, on intergovernmental agreement, there was no guarantee they would be permanent; only constitutional entrenchment could provide that. Nor did that exhaust the types of changes that might be needed. The Quebec political arena was dominated by a wide-reaching agenda of changes in federalism and the constitution that differed radically from Trudeau's agenda.

For its part, the Royal Commission on Bilingualism and Biculturalism did not give any direction as to how the constitution should be changed to accommodate these demands, though André Laurendeau clearly had wanted the commission to do so. There was no doubt in his mind that Canada's crisis could not be resolved without redefining Quebec's position in the constitution; official bilingualism alone could not do the job, however widespread it might be. The 'blue pages' of the first volume of the commission's final report, with their broad treatment of 'equal partnership' and 'biculturalism', and their emphasis on Quebec as a 'distinct society', give a clear sense of what he had in mind. But, failing to overcome resistance to his plans among other commissioners led by Frank Scott, Laurendeau agreed to postpone treatment of constitutional issues to the end of the commission's exercise, in the hope that a consensus might be reached by then.[1] With the loss of Laurendeau's leadership in 1968, that possibility disappeared.[2] The commission wound up its activities in January 1971, acknowledging in a short letter to Prime Minister Trudeau that it had not been able to come to a common position on the constitutional question. Needless to say, Trudeau was not displeased.[3]

As a result, by the 1970s there was no significant challenge in the federal arena to Trudeau's claim that his agenda of constitutional reform would satisfy the aspirations of Quebec francophones. Certainly, the opposition parties were not going to claim otherwise; we have seen how they fell into line after the 1968 election. And in the Liberal government itself, Trudeau's authority on the constitutional question was supreme. Indeed, as Mitchell Sharp recounts, the English-Canadian ministers deferred to Quebeckers on the question.[4] Dealing with Quebec and national unity was to become the preserve of Trudeau and his like-minded Quebeckers.

In the 16 years the Trudeau government held power, its handling of federal-provincial relations and the constitution fell into three distinct stages. During the first eight years, the government closely adhered to the terms of the national unity strategy that Trudeau had so clearly enunciated before assuming power. After the shock of the election of the PQ government in 1976, however, Trudeau and his closest colleagues seemed, for two or three years, to be entertaining major departures from that strategy. But with the defeat of sovereignty-association in the 1980 referendum, the government returned to the basic premises of its strategy, pursuing them with a vigour, indeed a vengeance, that was to have profound consequences for the future of the Canadian political order.

IMPLEMENTING THE NEW STRATEGY: 1968–1976

As the Trudeau government began its campaign for national unity, there was much it could accomplish without venturing into the constitutional arena. It could act by itself to modify some of the symbolic aspects of the Canadian political order and to change the status and responsibilities of the federal government, as well as those of the Quebec government. This was fortunate, since securing constitutional change was bound to be a complicated enterprise.

Making Canada Sovereign

In Trudeau's strategy, it was essential that Canada not only be sovereign, but be seen to be sovereign. Quebec francophones would not be able to think of themselves first and foremost as Canadians, rather than Québécois, unless the Canadian political community was formally defined so as to support such an identity. In the late 1940s the St Laurent government had started the process of giving form to a distinctly Canadian nationality by passing the Canadian Citizenship Act and ending appeals to the Judicial Committee of the Privy Council. The Pearson government had replaced the Red Ensign with a new Canadian flag that bore no trace of the British connection. The Trudeau government continued the process by steadily reducing the visibility of royal symbols as well as discarding the term 'Dominion' to refer to the federal government or to Canada as a whole. The federal government became no less than 'the Government of Canada', projecting a quasi-unitary image of the country. Similarly, the Trudeau government recast foreign and defence policy so as to put greater emphasis on Canada's 'national' interests, such as the protection of its territory and the promotion of national unity.[5]

The Trudeau government shrank from any effort to transform Canada formally from a monarchy to a republic, fearing that the struggle would cost more than it was worth. It was determined, however, to 'patriate' Canada's constitution, ending the symbolically embarrassing necessity of requesting the British Parliament to revise its British North America Act. But this meant contending with the provincial governments and their disparate agendas, including Quebec's, since during the early years of the Trudeau government it was presumed that patriation required the consent of all provincial governments.

Strengthening the Role of the Federal Government

According to Trudeau's analysis, Canadians would be more likely to identify with the federal government and Canada in general if they were to have a greater sense of personal connection with the federal government. This was especially the case in Quebec, where the federal government seemed to have become marginal to the lives of most francophones, thanks to the Quiet Revolution and the new profile of the Quebec state.

This strategy led to efforts in several directions. First, a new emphasis was placed on making Canadians more familiar with the many benefits the federal government was indeed providing. For instance, Ottawa embarked on a major advertising campaign. Between 1970 and 1976, the federal government increased more than fourfold its spending on advertising; from the twelfth-largest advertiser in Canada it became the largest.[6]

Second, there was an enhanced concern with the 'visibility' to Canadians of federal activities. On this basis, a much harder look was taken at shared-cost programs, through which Ottawa provided the provinces with funds to carry out their own activities while adhering to federal priorities. After all, the provinces did not usually go out of their way to tell the recipients of provincial services that funding had come in part from Ottawa. Beyond that, shared-cost programs tied the federal government to provincial activities. One response was to set limits on federal contributions to the shared-cost programs, which Ottawa started to do in 1972.[7]

Another strategy was to undertake independent federal initiatives. In effect, Ottawa tried to *make* the federal government more important in the lives of Canadians. In particular it attempted to create 'new constituencies' for itself by funding groups that represented women, consumers, environmentalists, youth, and others.[8] The Trudeau government created its own urban affairs ministry despite the provincial governments' long-standing defence of municipalities as an exclusively provincial preserve, and began offers of funds directly to municipalities.[9]

It is even possible to believe that the Trudeau government's handling of the FLQ (Front de libération du Québec) crisis, in October 1970, reflected this determination to assert the role of the federal government in Quebec.

According to one interpretation, the federal government was afraid the Quebec government might grant some of the demands of the FLQ kidnappers of British Trade Commissioner James Cross and Quebec Cabinet Minister Pierre Laporte. The Trudeau government's imposition of the War Measures Act served to place it fully in charge of the crisis. Another interpretation goes further, arguing that the War Measures Act and the stationing of Canadian soldiers in the streets of Montreal and elsewhere in Quebec were intended to intimidate not just the terrorists but all nationalists and separatists in Quebec. Whatever the merit of those arguments, they were supported both by Quebec sovereigntists and by leading federalists. In the pages of *Le Devoir*, Claude Ryan vigorously protested Ottawa's subordination of the Quebec government.[10]

Scaling Down Asymmetry

Beyond directly enhancing the role of Ottawa in Quebeckers' lives, the Trudeau government was also determined to eliminate the asymmetrical arrangements that the Quebec government had secured during the Pearson period. In some cases, as with such federally run programs as student allowances, the Quebec government replaced Ottawa as the provider of benefits, further marginalizing Ottawa in Quebec. Even in the case of shared-cost programs, which were still administered by the provincial governments, the symbolism of Quebec's ability to 'opt out' was troubling. It gave concrete form to the claim of Quebec nationalists that Quebec was a province like no other.

A reaction against asymmetrical arrangements with Quebec was already being voiced in the Finance Department in the mid-1960s and had provided Finance with part of the rationale for the changes it wished to make to fiscal arrangements. Under a new scheme of tax abatements, post-secondary education in all provinces (including Quebec) was to be financed in precisely the same fashion.

This process continued under the Trudeau government. In 1969 Ottawa announced that it was not formalizing the 'contracting out' option in the Canada Assistance Plan. Instead the arrangements remained 'transitional' and were regularly extended on that basis.[11] Quebec remained bound by the reporting obligations that went with that arrangement. Elsewhere asymmetry, even on a 'transitional' basis, simply disappeared.

Under the Established Programs Financing Act, passed in 1977 but negotiated previously, federal transfers for health and post-secondary education were no longer linked to the costs of provincial programs: instead, they would be equal to a fixed proportion of Gross National Product. In the process, Ottawa rendered moot the framework for opting out that the

Pearson government had established with its 1965 'interim arrangements'. Under that scheme, Quebec (and any other province) could opt out of a host of designated shared-cost programs. Through the 1977 arrangements the programs were collapsed into block grants that went automatically to all provinces. So while the right to opt out had been eliminated, in effect there was nothing left that Quebec, or any other province, might want to opt out of. By some readings, however, this strategy for eliminating Quebec's *de facto* special status had come with a very high price; for it undermined the federal government's capacity to influence social policy in *any* part of the country.[12] To that extent, the campaign to eliminate asymmetry ran at cross-purposes to the effort to heighten the importance of the federal government in citizens' lives.

The Constitution

In the end, though much could be accomplished by asserting federal jurisdiction and redefining fiscal relations with the provinces, the Trudeau government's national unity strategy also involved the question of the constitution. By definition, the objective of making Canada fully sovereign, in form as well as fact, required that the constitution would have to be patriated. Nor was federal action alone sufficient to accomplish Trudeau's goal of linguistic equality from sea to sea. If only to bring the provinces into line, language rights had to be constitutionally entrenched in a charter of rights. The trick was to focus constitutional revision on *these* matters.

In the 1960s, Trudeau had seen great risks in opening up the constitutional question. Just before entering federal politics in 1965, he had written, 'We must not meddle with the constitution just yet.'[13] Even after becoming justice minister he delayed addressing the question. But his hand and that of the Pearson government were forced by Ontario Premier John Robarts, who in 1967 convened an interprovincial conference grandly entitled 'Confederation of Tomorrow'.

Anxious to capture the initiative, the federal government organized a federal-provincial conference on the constitution in February 1968. There, as justice minister, Trudeau proposed a three-stage process.[14] First, there would be a discussion of the protection of human rights, of which he judged language rights to be central. Second, there would be an examination of 'the central institutions of Canadian federalism', Parliament, the Supreme Court, the federal public service, and the national capital, so as to make them more representative of 'the federal character of the country'. Only after those two stages had been completed would discussion turn to a third and final stage: the division of powers.[15]

None the less, the provinces had other ideas. Thus, the conference discussed regional development as well as language rights. And on language rights, not all provinces shared Trudeau's views of what was needed. Most important, the Quebec government insisted that the priority should in fact be the division of powers rather than language rights; nor should language rights be imposed on any province. During subsequent federal-provincial conferences, the discussion ranged over the full set of constitutional matters, including Quebec's proposals for a bi-national constitution, and on to many non-constitutional matters, such as the state of the economy, regional development, and intergovernmental issues, which were of greater concern to many of the provincial governments. Ottawa even entered into the division of powers with proposals for limits on the spending power.[16] But with the election in Quebec in April 1970 of Robert Bourassa's Liberal Party, which professed unqualified support for federalism, discussions became more intense and more focused. The result was the Victoria Charter, which emerged from a conference in Victoria in June 1971.

Despite the wide-ranging discussions that had come to dominate the constitutional meetings, the Victoria Charter adhered quite closely to the priorities outlined by Trudeau in 1968. Beyond patriation and an amending formula, the main feature of the Charter was the entrenchment of human rights—in effect, the first stage that Trudeau had identified. Included were political rights, such as freedom of expression and assembly, voting rights, and a limited set of legal rights. Also included were language rights, although, as we saw in Chapter 4, the obligations placed upon the provincial governments varied greatly among the provinces and did not extend to education rights.

On the other hand, with respect to Trudeau's second stage of constitutional discussions, the reform of central institutions, the Charter dealt only with the Supreme Court, entrenching the long-established formula that three of nine judges are from the Quebec bar, ensuring that civil law cases would be heard primarily by Quebec judges, and affording provincial consultation about appointments to the court. The Charter had relatively little to say about Trudeau's last stage of discussions, the division of powers. It eliminated the powers of reservation and disallowance, but they were already effectively defunct. Another provision dealt with income policy, adding family, youth, and occupational allowances to the constitutional category of jurisdictions that are concurrent with provincial paramountcy. Such jurisdictions are held jointly by the two levels of government, but the provinces have prior rights. The federal government would be required to advise the provinces ahead of time of any proposed legislation in these areas. But, beyond that, the provision did not spell out the implications of provincial paramountcy. It simply said that such legislation could not 'affect the operation of any law present or future of a Provincial Legislature in relation to any such matter'.

It was here that the battle was joined between Ottawa and Quebec City. In the proposals being advanced by the Quebec government, unemployment insurance and guaranteed income supplements to old age pensions would also be classified in the constitution as concurrent with provincial paramountcy. Quebec's proposal spelled out just what provincial paramountcy would entail. In the cases of family allowances, manpower training, and old-age income supplements, a provincial government could, by exercising its paramountcy, displace federal measures while being entitled to fiscal compensation from Ottawa. In the remaining instances, youth allowances and unemployment insurance, any new federal program could not affect existing or future provincial measures.[17] Conceivably, Ottawa's blanket provision about not affecting the operation of provincial laws might have met this latter condition. But it certainly could not have met the former one.

Underlying the Quebec government's proposals was its interest in establishing a comprehensive incomes policy, for which it would be responsible. Claude Castonguay, Quebec's minister of social welfare and former deputy minister of the same department, had already developed the plans for the scheme as co-chair of a provincial commission on social policy. He had been instrumental in preparing Quebec's pension fund proposals in 1964.

Quebec's proposals would have had major consequences, assuring it effective control over social policy. Still, Quebec's proposed constitutional scheme would have allowed Ottawa to play whatever role in the rest of Canada the other provincial governments accepted. In effect, Quebec was seeking a return of the kind of asymmetrical arrangement that the Pearson government had pioneered. Indeed, the terms of the proposal were largely compatible with those ad hoc arrangements.[18]

However, no matter what the possibilities might have been during the Pearson epoch, times had changed; not only was Trudeau opposed to particular status for Quebec in principle but his strategy for transforming the political allegiances of Québécois made it important for them to receive direct services and benefits from the federal government. Indeed, the federal government was planning a comprehensive guaranteed income scheme of its own.[19] As a result, Quebec's aspirations for control of social policy had to be fiercely resisted.

In the words of a leading English–Canadian scholar, Donald V. Smiley, the Victoria Charter was 'a very small constitutional package'.[20] In effect, it was limited by dictates of the Trudeau strategy. In particular, Quebec's proposals on social policy threatened the direct relations with individual

Quebeckers that the Trudeau government was anxious to maintain and reinforce. Thus, while the Charter was generally acceptable to the other provinces, it was unacceptable to Quebec. At the conference, Premier Bourassa's position was equivocal, and some participants presumed that he was in fact favourable, but upon returning to Quebec he came under considerable pressure to reject the offer.

That the Parti Québécois and sovereigntist forces should dismiss the Charter was to be expected, as was the opposition of the nationalist Société St-Jean Baptiste. However, they were also joined by the major unions and the Quebec wing of the NDP.[21] Even more significant was the opposition of prominent Quebec federalists, such as Marcel Faribault and Gabriel Loubier, the new leader of the Union nationale.[22] Even the Montreal *Gazette* saw little advantage to Quebec in agreeing to the Charter. Not only would Quebec not gain significant powers but 'an affirmative answer . . . would signify the acceptance in principle of a revised constitution that still fails to take account of the fact that Canada is, after all, a country composed of two distinct societies.'[23]

Leading the federalist opposition to the Charter was Claude Ryan, who argued that 'the Charter tends to consolidate the preponderance of the central government over the affairs of Canada and to reduce Quebec to the rank of a province like the others, without regard to its problems and priorities.' In Ryan's opinion the Charter had been opposed by such a wide variety of groups in Quebec that its acceptance by the Quebec government could be a 'tragic fraud'.[24]

There is every reason to believe that in the Quebec cabinet the Charter was opposed by such leading figures as Claude Castonguay. Apparently, at the Victoria Conference, Castonguay had insisted that Quebec be given 10 days to make its decision. It was after an all-night cabinet meeting that Bourassa finally conveyed his decision to Trudeau.[25]

Clearly, the Victoria Charter fell short of the expectations held by much of federalist opinion in Quebec, including even the Montreal *Gazette*. In particular, it did not give the Quebec government the power over social policy that leading federalists felt was necessary. Some prominent Quebeckers called on the Trudeau government to return to the bargaining table in an effort to resolve the social policy question. Trudeau made it clear, however, that the Charter had to be accepted as it was and that there was no room for further negotiation: 'If there isn't agreement, then that is the end of the matter, for now, or for a while, I hope.'[26] Given the opposition that had developed in Quebec, Bourassa had no choice but to refuse his consent. Claude Ryan concluded that in rejecting the charter Bourassa had expressed the profound convictions of the whole Quebec people.[27]

In his letter of rejection, Bourassa pointed to 'uncertainty' in the provisions dealing with income security,[28] adding, 'If this uncertainty were eliminated, our conclusion could be different.'[29] Of course, rather than poor legal draftsmanship, the real problem was disagreement over how social policy should be handled. Perhaps, through negotiation, this disagreement could have been resolved. With some movement on Ottawa's part, Bourassa's position in Quebec might have been strengthened enough that he could have accepted the Charter; that had in any event been his inclination. The other provinces might have accepted additional changes regarding social policy if that would have resolved a question in which they had little interest. Of course, there can be no certainty that movement on social policy would have done the trick; some prominent Quebeckers were also dissatisfied with the Charter's amending formula.[30] In 1973 the Trudeau government did agree to allow Quebec and any other provincial government to determine, within limits, the levels of family allowances to be given to different categories of residents. This was simply an administrative agreement, with no constitutional backing.

Whatever the possibility for resolving these questions, the Trudeau government made no further effort to get Quebec's consent on the constitutional question.[31] Nor did it take any other actions toward patriation. For three or four years, Trudeau acted as if Quebec's rejection of the Charter had in fact meant 'the end of the matter'. By 1974, however, he was beginning to suggest that patriation, even with a Charter, might be possible *without* provincial consent.[32] Finally, in a speech to the Quebec wing of the federal Liberal Party in March 1976, Trudeau threatened to proceed unilaterally with patriation, if necessary. In an uncharacteristically colloquial French, he ridiculed the intellectuals and other nationalists who might object. Nor was he charitable toward Robert Bourassa, who was frustrating his constitutional plans.[33]

Constitutional impasses notwithstanding, the Trudeau government seemed confident that its overall national unity strategy was working. Certainly, no major figure at the federal level was prepared to say otherwise: and both opposition parties were deferring totally to the Trudeau government on this question. Moreover, Trudeau and his supporters could point to the overwhelming majorities of Quebec seats that his party won in the 1972 and 1974 general elections and to the defeat of the Parti Québécois in the 1973 provincial election. In fact, Trudeau even declared, in a widely quoted statement, 'Separatism is dead.'[34]

The reality was considerably more complex. The Trudeau Liberals' popular vote in Quebec had fallen to 49 per cent in 1972, returning to 54 per cent in 1974, just slightly above the 1968 level (see Table 3).[35] Nor is it cer-

TABLE 3: FEDERAL ELECTION RESULTS, QUEBEC, 1968–1993

		Liberal	PC	NDP	Social Credit	Other
1968	vote (%)	53.6	21.4	7.5	16.4	1.1
	seats (no.)	56	4	—	14	—
1972	vote (%)	49.1	17.4	6.4	24.3	2.7
	seats (no.)	56	2	—	15	—
1974	vote (%)	54.1	21.2	6.6	17.1	1.0
	seats (no.)	60	3	—	11	—
1979	vote (%)	61.6	13.5	5.1	16.0	3.7
	seats (no.)	67	2	—	6	—
1980	vote (%)	68.2	12.6	9.1	5.9	4.2
	seats (no.)	74	1	—	—	—
1984	vote (%)	35.4	50.2	8.8	0.2	5.4
	seats (no.)	17	58	—	—	—
1988	vote (%)	30.2	52.7	13.9		3.1
	seats (no.)	12	63	—		—
					Bloc Québécois	
1993	vote (%)	33.0	13.6	1.5	49.3	2.6
	seats (no.)	19	1	—	54	1

Note: There were 74 Quebec seats from 1968 to 1979, and 75 from 1979 to 1993.
Source: As compiled by Tony J. Coulson in A. Brian Tanguay and Alain G. Gagnon, eds, *Canadian Parties in Transition*, 2nd edn (Scarborough, Ont.: Nelson, 1996), Tables B–14 to B–21.

tain that Trudeau's vision of Canada explained the support his party did receive in Quebec. At least part of it must have been due to the normal support of Quebec francophones for one of 'their own'. This 'native son' factor was demonstrated by Lemieux and Crête in their study of Quebec voting over the period 1930 to 1979: 'An anglophone leader costs the Liberal party 6 percentage points in Quebec while a francophone leader is worth, on average, an extra 2.7 percentage points.'[36]

More to the point, in Quebec, support for the Parti Québécois had risen from 23 per cent in the 1970 election to 30 per cent in 1973, although this was disguised by overwhelming Liberal majorities in the National Assembly (102 of 110 seats in 1973). The continuing impasse on the constitutional front, along with Trudeau's denunciation of the Bourassa government's position, gave added strength to the PQ's claim that Quebec's aspirations could

never be met within the federal system. In its effort to counter the PQ's growing public support, the Bourassa Liberal government felt obliged to adopt the
PQ's discourse in its own attempts to make the federal order more attractive
to Quebeckers, using such expressions as 'souveraineté culturelle' and even
referring to Quebec as 'a French state within the Canadian common market'. Such attempts to accommodate nationalist sentiments in the defence of
federalism met with little sympathy in Ottawa, where they were the occasion
for more scathing comments by Trudeau and his ministers. Yet, they were a
sign of a problem, namely that the Trudeau vision of Canada simply had little appeal to many Quebeckers.

DEALING WITH SETBACK: 1976–1980

By any reasonable standard, the election of the Parti Québécois on 15
November 1976, was a serious setback for the Trudeau government and its
national unity strategy. Although the PQ obtained only 41 per cent of the
popular vote, it had the support of a majority of francophones.[37] Votes for
the PQ were not necessarily due to support for the party's option of sovereignty-association, since the PQ had said that this would be the object of a
referendum. Indeed, surveys found that a number of PQ voters either did not
support sovereignty-association or did not understand how great a change it
would be.[38] Yet there could have been no doubt even among these voters
that the PQ stood for the vigorous promotion of Quebec as a nation and as
the first loyalty of Quebec francophones. If nothing else, the PQ's electoral
success demonstrated the failure of the federal government's campaign to
convert Quebeckers to the Trudeau vision of Canada.

Though the Trudeau government may not have read the election in precisely those terms, it did see the result as a setback. Moreover, it seems to have
been taken by surprise, and for a time appeared to be reassessing its strategy
and considering options that it would previously have dismissed out of hand.
Such was this apparent openness that some Quebec federalists were encouraged to believe that the Trudeau orthodoxy could be transcended and federalist forces could finally come together in a common cause and with a common project. The rise of such hopes explains why so many Quebec federalists
felt such a sense of betrayal when, in the early 1980s, the Trudeau government finally engineered a constitutional revision that fell fully within its
orthodoxy.

The new tone was set by Trudeau himself in a speech to the Quebec
City Chambre de commerce in January 1977, three months after the PQ election. Speaking from a text he had written himself, Trudeau began by contending that the PQ election in fact had positive aspects, notably that it would

force a choice about the future of Quebec and Canada. The referendum would make it possible, indeed necessary, at last 'to decide truly to be Canadian',[39] something that Quebeckers and indeed all Canadians had never had to do.

At the same time, implicitly recognizing that the prospect of such a choice would intensify the constitutional discussions, Trudeau declared himself open to all possibilities: 'If you want me to be flexible, I'll do it right now. I have a single condition for the constitution.'[40] His condition was the entrenchment of rights. But, even there, he departed from his long-established position by extending his notion of the rights to include *collective* rights, even *collective language rights*:

> respect for the rights of men and women, respect for human rights, and *probably respect for the collective aspect of human rights. I am thinking of language,* I am thinking of the rights of regions to exist. Beginning from this condition, we can start from zero and write a new constitution. We haven't had a new one for 110 years; we can make one. I won't shrink from any challenge [emphasis added].[41]

As to the division of powers, Trudeau remarked that the premiers naturally wanted more power for themselves but also recognized that one could say as much of the federal leaders. In the end, he insisted, these are 'politicians' quarrels'.[42] All that should really count is 'how people will be happier, better governed'[43]: 'All that I ask, as long as I am here, is to establish functionally that such and such a power should be exercised at the federal level or at the provincial level in order for the Canadian collectivity to be better off.'[44]

To be sure, in contending that Quebeckers would at last be forced to affirm their choice of being Canadian, Trudeau might be seen to have denied them the possibility of also maintaining their identity as Quebeckers, at least as a primary allegiance. None the less, his claim to be open to all manner of constitutional change, including a rethinking of the division of powers, and his explicit reference to collective linguistic rights, seemed to be a major opening—especially to Quebec federalists, who were desperately hoping that a viable 'renewed federalism' would emerge.

To spearhead the response to the new situation, Trudeau appointed Marc Lalonde to the new position of minister of federal-provincial relations in 1977. Lalonde was a long-time close associate of Trudeau's; there is every reason to believe that his actions were based on regular communication with Trudeau and were fully in keeping with Trudeau's views of what should be done. Under Lalonde's leadership, several initiatives took form, each of which departed dramatically from Trudeau's past approach.

Pepin–Robarts

In July 1977, the government established the Task Force on Canadian Unity, headed by five prominent Canadians, with a mandate, among other things, 'to advise the Government on unity issues'.[45] By reaching beyond its own confines and charging a group of high-profile Canadians with the unity question, the government seemed to be opening the door to approaches and proposals that departed from the path it had so rigorously been following.

The commissioners it appointed were virtually certain to produce just such ideas. One Quebec member, Solange Chaput-Rolland, was a well-known nationalist whose views on federalism and Canada were much closer to those of such federalists as Robert Bourassa and Claude Ryan than to those of Trudeau. One co-chair was former Ontario Premier John Robarts, whose government in 1967 had held the 'Confederation of Tomorrow' conference of which Trudeau had been so disapproving. Even more dramatic was the choice for the other co-chair: Jean-Luc Pepin, who had been closely associated with the Pearson government's notion of 'co-operative federalism' and accommodation of Quebec nationalism. Indeed, during the 1960s Pepin had come out squarely in favour of special status for Quebec and the 'two nations' idea of Canada.[46] Upon becoming prime minister, Trudeau had assigned Pepin a portfolio well removed from the national unity question: industry, trade and commerce. After being defeated in the 1972 election, Pepin had left federal politics. With Pepin's appointment, Trudeau seemed to be signalling that his own views were up for serious re-examination.

Two years later the Pepin-Robarts Commission produced a report that fully met the expectations of radical departures. Basing its view of Canada around the twin concepts of dualism and regionalism, the report broke with Trudeau's notion of an essentially linguistic dualism by placing Quebec front and centre in its conception of dualism: 'While we freely acknowledge that duality is many-sided, we would nevertheless insist that to confront the heart of the issue today is to address one main question, namely, the status of Quebec and its people in the Canada of tomorrow.'[47] It based its proposals for a renewed federalism on the premise that: 'Quebec is distinctive and should, within a viable Canada, have the powers necessary to protect and develop its distinctive character; any political solution short of this would lead to the rupture of Canada.'[48]

Presuming, as it did, that this meant that Quebec would have powers not necessarily desired by the other provinces, the commission feared that a forthrightly asymmetrical federalism would be unacceptable in the rest of Canada. Accordingly, it proposed 'to allot to all the provinces powers in the areas needed by Quebec to maintain its distinctive culture and heritage.'[49] The other provinces would not necessarily use these powers. In some cases, the powers would be declared concurrent, or shared, with provincial paramountcy; to displace Ottawa a provincial government would need to assert this paramountcy. (In effect, this was the approach embodied in the Bourassa government's proposal to the 1971 Victoria Conference.) In other cases, powers would be lodged with the provinces but could be delegated to the federal government.

To be sure, the commission did not spell out precisely which powers would need to be reassigned to the provinces. Moreover, its understanding of Quebec's distinctiveness and the powers the province therefore needed, was a fairly traditional one focused upon a 'distinctive culture and heritage'. Would that lead, for instance, to the comprehensive control of incomes policy that Quebec sought at the Victoria Conference? For that matter, another section of the report proposed measures to strengthen the free flow of goods, capital, and workers within Canada.[50] These might threaten some of the practices that the Quebec government had established during the 1960s and 1970s to exercise greater control over the Quebec economy.

None the less, the overall approach advocated by Pepin-Robarts started from the premise that Canadian federalism had to be restructured to accommodate the distinctiveness of Quebec, and that Quebec was bound to assume a role greater than the other provinces. In effect, it sought to resurrect the approach that the Pearson government had pioneered and that Trudeau had been so anxious to discard. Moreover, this approach stemmed from a conception of dualism that was centred on the Quebec question, as opposed to Trudeau's conception of a purely linguistic dualism based on the recognition of individual language rights.

In another section of its report the commission went one step further: it sought to limit any imposition of the Trudeau type of linguistic equality to the federal government. Provincial governments would subscribe to certain rights for their official-language minorities but they would be free to define the status of the languages in whatever way they thought appropriate. In fact, on this basis, the commission recommended that section 133 of the BNA Act should no longer apply to Quebec and that Manitoba should no longer be bound by the Manitoba Act of 1870. The commission even went so far as effectively to endorse Bill 101: 'We support the efforts of the Quebec provincial government and of the people of Quebec to ensure the predominance of the French language and culture in that province.'[51] The rejection of the Trudeau orthodoxy could not have been more complete.

In presenting the report to the House, Trudeau said his government accepted 'the broad lines of the Task Force's analysis' and 'endorses the basic principles which it believes should underlie the renewal of the Canadian federation'.[52] The following day he told a press conference that the report was 'dead wrong' in its language proposals.[53] He also made it clear over the next few days that he took exception to the report's emphasis on dualism and regionalism and its support for decentralization.[54] None the less, Trudeau's formal statement to the House, with its broad acceptance of the report, may have encouraged Quebec federalists to believe that the Trudeau government would look to the report for guidance.

Cullen–Couture

Beyond calling for advice on the unity question from a group of prominent Canadians that was bound to contradict the Trudeau orthodoxy, the government itself negotiated an agreement with the PQ government that seemed to signal a new willingness to recognize Quebec's claims for distinctive status. In February 1978, Ottawa and Quebec City signed a bilateral agreement on immigration, the Cullen–Couture Accord, named after the two ministers responsible.

Under Cullen–Couture, the Quebec government took effective control over the selection of a major category of immigrants to Quebec. Officials of the Quebec Immigration Department, normally based in Canadian immigration offices overseas and called 'Immigration Officers' in the agreement, were given the power to choose among candidates for the status of independent immigrants who intended to settle in Quebec. The federal involvement would be restricted to such matters as health and security. The agreement also provided for Quebec to be involved in (but not to control) the choice of other categories of immigrants, and it committed the two governments to consult on areas of common interest concerning immigration and demographic planning.

In effect, the Accord was an attempt by the federal government to accommodate Quebec's wish to maintain the province's French character by choosing its own immigrants. Claiming that historically Ottawa had made no effort to attract francophone immigrants, and that indeed the opposite had been the case, the Quebec government had established its own department of immigration in 1968.[55] No other province had involved itself directly in the selection of immigrants, at least in recent decades. Cullen–Couture was a direct response to Quebec's insistence that, given both the inability of the federal government to meet Quebec's distinctive needs and, as a consequence, the special responsibilities of the Quebec government to do so, it needed to have powers that in the rest of Canada were exercised by Ottawa. In effect, the Trudeau government seemed to be sanctioning a 'special status' for Quebec.

Indeed, the wording of the agreement departed clearly from Trudeau's established views regarding Quebec, with their emphasis on official bilingualism and linguistic equality. One passage of the agreement stated that immigration to Quebec 'should contribute to the sociocultural enrichment of Quebec, taking into account its *French character* [emphasis added].'[56] Another passage recognized that the Quebec government intended to 'take a position on the entry of foreign nationals in order to favour those who will be able to integrate rapidly into Quebec society.'[57]

To be sure, two previous agreements with the Bourassa government, one signed in 1971 and another in 1975, had already established procedures for Quebec officials to *participate* in the selection of immigrants. But only with Cullen-Couture did Quebec acquire the actual decision-making power. And the Trudeau government had granted this power to a government that had fallen into the hands of 'separatists'.

After negotiating Cullen-Couture, the federal government was concerned about this apparent recognition of a special status for Quebec and actively encouraged other provincial governments to enter into bilateral agreements on immigration. Shortly after the agreement was signed, the federal immigration minister announced that negotiations were under way with five other provinces.[58] Ultimately, five provinces did sign agreements, but they were much more limited in scope than Cullen-Couture; none of them delegated the selection process or even involved locating provincial officers in Canadian immigration offices.[59]

Cullen-Couture may also have reflected the special circumstances of immigration, which is one of the few jurisdictions that the constitution explicitly designates as concurrent, that is, both a federal and a provincial responsibility. Even there, Ottawa had the advantage of federal paramountcy. Thus, the Trudeau government may have had no intention of generalizing this approach to other jurisdictions.

However, by entering into an agreement that was specific to Quebec, explicitly geared to reinforcement of Quebec's francophone character, and creating responsibilities for Quebec that differed from the other provinces, the Trudeau government seemed to be demonstrating once again that it had recognized that a new flexible, asymmetrical approach to federalism and Quebec was needed, and that it was now prepared to pursue one. After all, the Accord had been conceived and signed by Marc Lalonde, Trudeau's alter ego.

A Time for Action

In June of 1978, the Trudeau government came forward with its own proposals for constitutional change, entitled *A Time for Action*. Compared with the three-stage approach that Trudeau had announced in the 1960s upon becoming justice minister, or with the limited scope of the ill-fated Victoria

Charter, the new proposals seemed to show a conversion to a much more comprehensive approach, covering, as they did, all areas of discussion, including the division of powers. For that reason *A Time for Action* seemed to confirm the commitment made by Trudeau the previous year, in his Chamber of Commerce speech, that he was prepared to discuss all options.

In the document, the procedure for constitutional change was to be composed of two stages. A first stage, which was restricted to federal jurisdictions, and which the federal government was prepared to pursue unilaterally if necessary, was to consist of a declaration of the Canadian federation's fundamental objectives; a reform of federal-level institutions; and a charter of rights that, at first, would apply only at the federal level. The second stage was to address the division of powers and the amending formula. Patriation, then, would not take place until the federal government and the provinces had come to terms on the matters of much more concern to them, including Quebec.

A week later, Ottawa released Bill C-60, Constitutional Amendment Bill, which was to implement phase one. The bill outlined the transformation of the Senate into a House of the Federation, half of whose members were to be appointed by Parliament and half by the provincial legislatures. It would constitutionally entrench the Supreme Court while providing for the provinces to take part in the appointment of its members (through the House of the Federation) and enlarging its membership to eleven (with four from Quebec). At the same time, it would have codified into constitutional law the basic conventions of responsible government. A charter of rights and freedoms was initially to be binding on the federal government alone; it would apply to the provincial level only after a provincial legislature had formally adopted it. Finally, the bill contained a statement of 'fundamental aims' that, though beginning with the assertion that 'the people of Canada . . . declare and affirm . . . their expectation for a future in common', also recognized Quebec's uniqueness by asserting 'a permanent national commitment to the endurance and self-fulfilment of the Canadian French-speaking society centred in but not limited to Quebec.'[60]

As it happened, Bill C-60 and Ottawa's proposed unilateral first stage were stillborn. Early in 1979, the Supreme Court pronounced Bill C-60 to be unconstitutional since such matters as the Senate and the Supreme Court came under provincial as well as federal jurisdiction. In any event, at a federal-provincial conference in the fall of 1978, Trudeau had agreed to drop the distinction between two phases of constitutional discussion. Now, one agenda was to cover all items, including the division of powers. On this basis, negotiations proceeded on a comprehensive agenda that embraced a substantial degree of decentralization of powers: restriction of the federal spending and declatory powers, and expansion of provincial jurisdiction over communications, fisheries, family law, and natural resources.

Ultimately, at a constitutional conference in February 1979, the governments failed to agree. Yet, according to one observer, this round of constitutional negotiations was the closest that the first ministers ever came during the Trudeau era to a comprehensive agreement on constitutional reform, precisely because the Trudeau government was prepared to accept decentralization as the price of provincial agreement to the resolution of the constitutional question.[61]

The openness on the part of Trudeau and his cabinet may have been the result of special circumstances, such as the Supreme Court ruling and an imminent federal election or even Trudeau's personal difficulties.[62] The fact remains, though, that here too the Trudeau government seemed to have abandoned its past approach to federalism and the Quebec question. Once again, Quebec federalists had reason to be encouraged. Although Trudeau had obviously not lost his antipathy to Quebec nationalism, apparently the shock of the PQ victory had forced him to recognize the continuing strength of Quebec nationalism and to re-examine his belief that with the right strategy Quebec nationalism could be eliminated and replaced with an allegiance to Canada.

The Quebec Referendum

The Lévesque government waited until its fourth year in office to announce the date of the referendum on Quebec sovereignty—20 May 1980. The delay seems to have been caused by tactical considerations, such as the hope that the referendum might have a better chance of winning once Trudeau had been replaced by a non-Quebecker, Joe Clark. Whatever the causes, the delay was probably a mistake, for with time the contradictions grew between the PQ's goal of sovereignty and its success in providing good government within the existing federal structure. Through such measures as Bill 101 and the Cullen-Couture Accord, some of the grievances which had fuelled popular support for sovereignty were being addressed, without sovereignty. The delay also allowed time for the Trudeau government to develop its new flexible approach to Quebec and the constitution.[63]

As far as the PQ government was concerned, the issue to be addressed in the referendum was not sovereignty *per se*, but sovereignty linked with a comprehensive economic association with the rest of Canada. That had been the party's position ever since it was founded in 1968, and it was faithfully reproduced, indeed considerably expanded, in the blueprint for sovereignty-association that the Lévesque government presented in the fall of 1979. It was called *Quebec-Canada: A New Deal* and sub-titled *The Quebec Government's*

Proposal for a New Partnership between Equals: Sovereignty-Association.[64] As these lengthy titles indicated, the government intended to present the referendum question in terms of, not rupture or 'separation', but continuity: redefining the relationship between Quebec and Canada as one of equals. In that way it hoped to tap the ideal of a dualist Canada that had so long been the basis of the francophone vision of the country.

The Lévesque government defined the purpose of the vote itself as not the actual endorsement of sovereignty-association but a mandate to the Quebec government to negotiate sovereignty-association with the federal government. Any agreement that emerged from these negotiations would have to be approved in a subsequent referendum.

These themes were developed systematically in the Lévesque government's campaign leading up to the referendum. A pamphlet sent to all voters by the Yes campaign declared: 'Sovereignty-association is . . . neither the status quo, nor separatism. It is a realistic formula that will enable genuine change without the need to overturn everything or to begin from zero' [my translation].[65] And in the National Assembly debate on the referendum question, Lévesque said, 'We say that instead of this regime . . . that everyone admits is outdated, but without casting aside a long-standing tradition of coexistence that has created a whole network of exchanges, we now owe it to ourselves to enter into a new agreement between equals, with our neighbours and partners in the rest of Canada' [my translation].[66]

By linking allegiance to Quebec with the ideal of equality with the rest of Canada, the PQ's option had a powerful appeal to the world-view of most Quebec francophones. Accordingly, the primary stratagem of the federalists became one of shifting the meaning of the referendum to more favourable ground, namely separation. For, as surveys regularly confirmed, most Quebec francophones were very apprehensive about the economic consequences of sovereignty and needed to be assured that it would be linked to an economic association. Beyond that, many francophones were not prepared to abandon the old ideal of Canada, at least a dualist one.

Given the federal government's policies over the previous 12 years, especially before the 1976 Quebec election, federalist forces could hardly lay claim to the older francophone vision of Canada, in which Quebec would have a distinct, even equal place. But they had no difficulty in addressing the presumed economic consequences of sovereignty—and they did so with a vengeance. For that matter, the PQ was implicitly admitting that the economic consequences of sovereignty could be very serious since they were linking sovereignty to an economic association. If the federalists could focus the referendum on sovereignty or separation they would be in a strong position. The key was to show that the PQ's notion of an economic association was unrealistic and sovereignty necessarily meant 'separation'.

Accordingly, federalist leaders insisted on every occasion that the rest of Canada would never accept economic association with a sovereign Quebec. To support their case, they could point to statements by provincial premiers. The four western premiers declared that they would never negotiate sovereignty-association; two premiers, Allan Blakeney of Saskatchewan and Bill Davis of Ontario, said the same thing in speeches to the Montreal Board of Trade.[67]

Without access to Canadian markets, federalist leaders proclaimed, Quebec sovereignty could only result in horrendous economic costs for Quebec through loss of exports, withdrawal of firms, cancellation of investment plans, and so on. Beyond that, a sovereign Quebec state would not have the fiscal resources to maintain the social benefits to which Québécois were accustomed. Indeed, some prominent federalists said that under sovereignty-association there would be no old-age pensions.[68]

The federalist tactic appears to have worked as a way of building support for a No vote. Surveys indicate that for most voters the issue of the referendum was not sovereignty-association, let alone renewed federalism, as the Yes forces claimed, but the dissolution of Quebec's links with the rest of Canada. For many voters this meant the loss of economic and political ties; for others, the loss was one of identity as Canadians. Whereas at various points surveys showed that close to half of Quebeckers supported the mandate for sovereignty-association sought in the referendum question, an overwhelming majority rejected sovereignty without an economic association.[69]

Federalist forces were thus able to establish ascendance well before the referendum took place. The referendum question apparently had enjoyed majority support in June of 1979. After a slump in the fall of 1979, it rebounded after the National Assembly debate on the referendum question in March 1980. During April, however, the No side took the lead, which it held until the referendum. Although the slide in the Yes vote was due partly to PQ tactical errors during April, the most important factor was the federalist campaign about dangers of 'separation'. By late April, surveys suggested that the No vote was assured of victory.[70]

After joining the debate through the Speech from the Throne in mid-April, Trudeau intervened directly with three major speeches in Quebec.[71] The first, given in Montreal on 2 May, set the tone of his campaign. A Yes vote, he said, would lead to a deadlock since, rather than a vote for separation, it would provide only a mandate to negotiate sovereignty-association. The rest of Canada had made it clear that it was not interested in such a scheme. Thus, a Yes vote would lead to the humiliation of 'the Quebec people'. Demanding to know whether, in the case of a No vote the Lévesque government was prepared to pursue a 'renewed federalism', Trudeau insisted that federalists were very much committed to such a result:

> I know no one [among those who want to stay in Canada] who doesn't want to profit from this current upheaval to renew the constitution.
>
> Mr Ryan has proposed a Beige Paper. The governments of the other provinces, from Ontario to British Columbia, have presented reports. Our government, after establishing the Pepin-Robarts Commission, has proposed a formula called *A Time for Action*, a bill called C-60 which contained, by the way, a large number of proposals for a fundamental renewal.
>
> Those, then, who want to remain Canadian are ready to change it, are ready to improve federalism.[72]

So from the outset, Trudeau linked a No vote with 'renewal' of the federal system.

In his second speech, in Quebec City, Trudeau charged the PQ with cowardice in not asking 'the real question' and in using a question 'that puts our fate in the hands of others'.[73] Joined on the stage by Jean Lesage, Trudeau evoked the courage of his francophone predecessors Wilfrid Laurier and Louis St Laurent and the greatness of Quebec premiers, including not only Jean Lesage but Maurice Duplessis, who had defended Quebeckers' rights. He insisted that 'we went to Ottawa because that is how Quebeckers have always seen their place in Canada. They saw it by being proud to be Quebeckers, fighting here [Quebec City] to defend their rights, but also affirming their rights as Canadians to send some of their best as representatives to Ottawa to affirm their place as Quebeckers within Canada.'[74]

His third speech, given in Montreal six days before the referendum, took his argument about the possibilities of 'renewed federalism' one step further. He was certain that with a No vote the changes needed would indeed take place:

> I know because I spoke to the [Liberal] MPs this morning, I know that I can make the most solemn commitment that following a No vote, we will start immediately the process of renewing the Constitution, and we will not stop until it is done. . . . We are putting ourselves on the line, we Quebec MPs, because we are telling Quebeckers to vote No, and we are saying to you in other provinces that we will not accept that you interpret a No vote as an indication that everything is fine, and everything can stay as it was before. We want change, we are putting our seats [in Parliament] on the line to have change.[75]

The referendum was, of course, a resounding victory for the No side and for Quebec remaining in the federal system. With only 40.4 per cent of the voters choosing Yes, the sovereigntists could not claim to have won a majority even of francophone voters.[76]

By some accounts, Trudeau's statement was the turning point of the referendum campaign, delivering victory to the No side.[77] But that is far from certain. Surveys had been predicting a No victory well before Trudeau intervened in the campaign. Nor do the surveys suggest any surge in No support after Trudeau's three speeches.[78]

Whatever may have been its influence on the referendum, Trudeau's pledge of change was to shape the post-referendum political climate. To be sure, he had not been precise as to the form of change that he would seek. He had endorsed no proposals nor offered any propositions of his own; he had not even indicated the general direction that the change might take. The first stage of the federal government's *A Time for Action* had been rendered moot by the Supreme Court rejection of C-60; the second stage had not been spelled out in detail. As for the Pepin-Robarts Report, Trudeau had spoken favourably of it in general, criticized some of the proposals, and then ignored it. Finally, he had avoided taking a position on a detailed outline released by the Quebec Liberal Party in late 1979, *A New Canadian Federation* (commonly known as the 'Beige Paper'). Apparently he also had asked Claude Ryan not to refer to it during the referendum campaign.[79]

None the less, during the late 1970s, Trudeau and his government seemed to show a new willingness to accommodate Quebec's distinctive needs, including the Quebec government's demands for additional powers. It was reasonable to expect that such changes would be part of the constitutional renewal that he would now try to bring about. Certainly, during the referendum campaign he had said nothing to suggest otherwise. Consequently, the Quebec federalists who wanted such changes were free to believe that they would get them.

SEIZING THE MOMENT: 1980–1985

The Constitution Act, 1982

In a speech in the House of Commons the day after the referendum, Trudeau seemed to confirm that the constitution would indeed undergo a fundamental revision along the lines of his post-1976 views and would satisfy the aspirations of Quebec. Declaring that the No vote must be interpreted as 'massive support for change within the federal framework',[80] he announced that his justice minister, Jean Chrétien, would immediately undertake a tour of the provincial governments to obtain their views on constitutional renewal.

He himself, Trudeau said, would place no conditions on constitutional discussions other than the ones he had stipulated in 1977 in his speech to the Quebec Chamber of Commerce. He outlined two conditions: 'first, that Canada continues to be a true federation' and 'that a charter of fundamental rights and freedoms be inserted in the constitution and that this charter extend to *the collective aspect of such rights as language*' [emphasis added]. Once again, then, he had professed a commitment to recognize *collective* language rights. Everything else, he insisted, was negotiable. To underline the point, he specifically referred to proposals that diverged from his own:

> The new constitution could include, if the people so wish, several provisions in our present organic laws, but it will also have to contain new elements reflecting the most innovative proposals emerging from our consultations or from the numerous analyses and considered opinions that have flowed in the last few years from the will to change of Canadians. I am referring, of course, to the many proposals made by the Canadian government since 1968, *but also to the Pepin-Robarts report*, to the policy papers issued by the governments of British Columbia, Ontario, Alberta, and by almost every province but Quebec, *to the constitutional proposals of the Liberal Party of Quebec*, many elements of which could orient the renewal of our constitutions if they were put forward by the political authorities of that province [emphasis added].[81]

But the patriated Canadian constitution that came into effect a little less than two years later falls far short of the broad range of proposals that Trudeau referred to. It contained little more than what, in 1968, Trudeau as justice minister had identified as the first stage of constitutional renewal: patriation and an amending formula coupled with a charter of rights. As for the subjects of the two subsequent stages, there is no reference to central institutions, and the only treatment of the division of powers is a section confirming provincial jurisdiction over certain natural resources. Even the limited measures of the Victoria Charter, such as elimination of the federal unilateral powers, do not appear.

Indeed, the contents are largely the same as the package Trudeau had presented in the fall of 1980 in the form of a resolution to Parliament. When he threatened to ask the British Parliament to act on the resolution, even without the consent of the provincial governments, eight provinces challenged in court his right to do so. Confronted with the Supreme Court's determination that such an action, though legal, would violate constitutional convention, the federal government had returned to negotiations with the provinces. But the outcome was not fundamentally different, faithfully reflecting, as it did, Trudeau's long-standing priorities and views.[82]

The Constitution Act, 1982, has two main parts. First, it outlines an amending formula by which some items require the unanimous consent of Parliament and all the provincial legislatures but most require only the approval of Parliament and only two-thirds of the provincial legislatures, representing 50 per cent of the population. Second, it outlines the terms of a Charter of Rights and Freedoms which, along with the standard political and legal freedoms, recognizes linguistic rights, mobility rights, and the right of individuals to equal treatment by the law despite a variety of designated characteristics. Interpretative clauses say that judicial interpretation of the constitutions must take due account of the rights of aboriginal peoples and the multicultural character of Canada. Another clause states that the 'notwithstanding clause', by which Parliament or a provincial legislature may exclude a law from application of certain parts of the Charter, cannot be applied to gender equality. Finally, other provisions call for annual first ministers' conferences, declare a commitment to equalization of Canadians' well-being and reduction of regional disparities, and affirm the existing concurrent provincial power to regulate interprovincial trade in, and impose taxes upon, nonrenewable resources, forestry products, and hydro-electrical energy.

So the package hardly embodies the openness to new ideas and approaches that Trudeau had proclaimed in his 1977 Chamber of Commerce speech and reiterated after the referendum. Nor does the package contain the recognition of *collective* language rights that he had committed himself to on both occasions. Indeed, Trudeau was later to pride himself on the fact that language rights had been recognized in exclusively individual terms: 'Language rights were assigned directly to individuals rather than collectivities'.[83]

A Response to Quebec?

It is difficult to see this document as a direct response to the ideas and proposals that had been circulating among the federalist milieu in Quebec. Certainly, it falls far short of the outline of 'renewed federalism' that the Lévesque government produced in the summer of 1980.[84]

The constitutional package also falls short of two documents that Trudeau mentioned by name in his post-referendum speech to the House and that did enjoy widespread support in Quebec: the Pepin-Robarts Report, in which prominent Quebeckers had been major collaborators, and the Beige Paper, produced by the Quebec Liberal Party and bearing the clear imprint of party leader Claude Ryan.[85] Each of them envisaged major

changes in the division of powers. In addition, both proposals contained provisions for changes in federal-level institutions.

Not only does the Constitution Act fail to enhance the powers of the
Quebec government or to reform central institutions, but under the Charter
of Rights and Freedoms the powers of the Quebec government were
reduced, directly affecting important Quebec laws. The provisions on language of education contradicted Bill 101 by requiring public education in
English to be available to all children whose parents were educated in English
anywhere in Canada, as well as to any children who have already received (or
have a sibling who has received) education in English in Canada.[86] The
mobility provision, which guarantees access to employment in other
provinces, jeopardized Quebec's law regulating its construction industry.
Moreover, neither set of provisions is subject to the 'notwithstanding
clause'.[87]

Finally, beyond the content of the Constitution Act there is, of course,
the manner in which it was brought into being. Simply put, the constitution
was patriated without the approval of the Quebec government or National
Assembly. In November 1980, 33 of the 42 members of the Liberal opposition had supported a government resolution that opposed the federal government's plans for unilateral action, called upon the Canadian Parliament
not to approve these plans since they would violate the very nature of
Canadian federalism, and warned the British Parliament against adopting any
modification to the BNA Act that did not have the consent of the provinces,
'and, in particular, of Quebec'.[88] On the day the House of Commons
approved the Trudeau government's constitutional patriation package,
Claude Ryan said he 'deeply regretted that important decisions are being
made in Ottawa without the consent of Quebec'.[89] To express their displeasure with the procedure, if not the content of patriation, Ryan and most of
the Liberal members boycotted the ceremonies.[90]

Indeed, the Quebec government appealed to the Supreme Court, arguing that such a move would be unconstitutional since the principle of duality gave Quebec a veto. In presenting the case to the court, Quebec counsel
argued that beyond a 'federal' aspect of duality, consisting of the two language
groups and their constitutional protection (in effect the notion developed
under the Trudeau regime), there is a 'Quebec' aspect, which covers

> all the circumstances that have contributed to making Quebec a distinct
> society, since the foundation of Canada and long before, and the range of
> guarantees that were made to Quebec in 1867, as a province which the Task
> Force on Canadian Unity [Pepin-Robarts] has described as 'the stronghold
> of the French-Canadian people' and the 'living heart of the French pres-

ence in North America'. These circumstances and these guarantees extend far beyond matters of language and culture alone: the protection of the British North America Act was extended to all aspects of Quebec society.[91]

In rejecting Quebec's claim, the court was upholding a previous decision of the Quebec Court of Appeals; yet the court's reasoning is far from persuasive. To reach its decision, the court imposed a standard for the existence of conventions that was far more exacting than the one it had used in a previous case.[92] Several months earlier, in ruling on the Trudeau government's plans for unilateral patriation over the opposition of eight provinces, the Supreme Court had defined a three-fold test for the existence of a convention: the past behaviour of governments; attitudes of politicians; and the existence of a supporting principle. In doing so, it was drawing on the work of leading British legal scholar, Ivor Jennings. On this basis, it had ruled that the Trudeau government had violated a convention that 'a substantial degree' of consent among provincial governments was necessary for constitutional amendments that directly affected provincial jurisdiction.

In the Quebec decision, the court interpreted the second standard, politicians' attitudes, in a much more exacting manner. In effect, only explicit statements of attitudes would do; attitudes could not be inferred from behaviour. So the court was able to argue that a Quebec veto did not exist, even though two previous attempts at constitutional revision had been abandoned when Quebec objected: the Fulton–Favreau formula of 1964 and the Victoria Charter of 1971. Critics argue that these actions (or non-actions) speak for themselves.[93] Indeed, in its previous decision the court had viewed them as significant evidence for the 'substantial degree of provincial consent' convention.[94] For that matter, the court's insistence on explicit statement of an attitude seemed to contradict the statement of Ivor Jennings that 'convention implies some form of agreement, whether expressed or implied. . . .' The court ruled that the assertion 'must be qualified'; though conventions may not be 'reduced to writing', they must at least be the object of 'utterance.'[95]

By the time the court pronounced on the matter, the Constitution Act, 1982, had already been proclaimed. The federal authorities had not felt obliged to hold up the proceedings until the court rendered its judgement; British Prime Minister Thatcher had already rejected Quebec's request that the British Parliament not act until the judgement had come down.[96] To be sure, proclamation of the Act did not end the matter since in its previous decision the court had asserted its right and responsibility to adjudicate questions of convention. But, in this case, a ruling that would have declared the new constitution to violate convention, to be in the words of Peter

Hogg 'an unconstitutional constitution',[97] would have been exceedingly awkward. Perhaps this context shaped the court's decision making. For Peter Russell, 'it was a political response to a political challenge dressed up in judicial clothing.'[98]

In any event, the court's arguments did not impress a broad range of Quebec federalists for whom constitutional patriation without the approval of the Quebec National Assembly violated their basic understanding of Canada as not only a compact among provinces but as a dualistic compact between two founding peoples. Moreover, as the Quebec counsel had argued before the Supreme Court, this sense of dualism was profoundly rooted in Quebec and its cultural distinctiveness. Revision of the constitution without Quebec's consent violated both components of a 'double compact' and was fundamentally unacceptable.

Claude Ryan, who in a recent study harks back to George C.F. Stanley's elaboration of a bicultural compact, maintains that if the court had given due regard to Stanley's arguments it could not possibly have rejected Quebec's claims to a veto.[99] Trudeau had said repeatedly that Quebec's consent was not necessary since patriation had the support of all but four of the Quebec members of the House of Commons and had a majority of votes even if the Quebec MPs' votes were combined with the National Assembly vote on a 1 December resolution;[100] Ryan called that claim 'a distortion of history'.[101]

The Trudeau government might have been on stronger ground if it had restricted itself simply to patriation and an amending formula, without a charter. There was a basic contradiction in arguing that Canada's self-respect required that the dependence on the British Parliament must be ended but using this connection to make a major change in the constitution just before patriation took place. Even then, however, there was a problem: unlike virtually all proposals for patriation, including that of the Trudeau government, the new amending formula did not grant Quebec a veto over all forms of constitutional change.[102] Especially if one presumes, as did most Quebec federalists, that Quebec had enjoyed a veto in the past, the Supreme Court's decision notwithstanding, the Trudeau package would have distressed many Quebec federalists even if it had not included a charter.

Ultimately, the question was one of the nature of Canada and Quebec's place in it. For all its efforts, the Trudeau government had not displaced the established French-Canadian view of these questions, even among leading federalists. As a result, rather than uniting the many Quebec francophones who continued to support Canadian federation, constitutional patriation served to divide them—with far-reaching consequences for all Canadians.

The Lévesque Government's Miscalculations

To a certain extent the outcome of the constitutional struggle was due to strategic errors on the part of the Lévesque government. Before the final stage of negotiations, the Lévesque government effectively abandoned Quebec's long-established demand that any patriated constitution both allow Quebec a veto over future constitutional change and give Quebec, with or without the other provinces, substantially enhanced powers. Quebec governments from Lesage to Johnson to Bertrand to Bourassa had always insisted that only under those conditions would they approve patriation. And this had been the PQ government's position in the summer of 1980.

None the less, in April 1981, Lévesque joined the seven other dissident provinces in declaring that patriation would be acceptable if it simply provided an amending formula by which (1) most matters would require approval of two-thirds of the provinces, representing 50 per cent of the population; and (2) a province would be able to opt out, with compensation, from agreement among two-thirds of the provinces to transfer any provincial powers to the federal government. Ostensibly, Quebec's pact with the other dissident provinces stemmed from fear that if the Trudeau government were to seek patriation unilaterally the package would include a charter of rights. Thus, it was better to head off such a possibility by defining a basis upon which patriation would have the consent of the provinces. It may also be that the Lévesque government was confident that Trudeau would never agree to such terms.[103] Whatever the reasoning, this move had the effect of reducing Quebec's wishes to those of the other provinces, ensuring that any constitutional revision would ignore Quebec's own long-standing needs and aspirations.

By some accounts, Lévesque made a second mistake when, during the final negotiations, he agreed to Trudeau's suggestion that the federal government's package be put to a referendum. In the process, he broke with the position that had been established with the other dissident provinces the previous April. The other premiers fiercely opposed Trudeau's referendum proposal, not the least because they feared they might lose any such contest. By seeming to break ranks with them, Lévesque ended the common front and ushered in the all-night negotiations between Ottawa and the other provinces that resulted in the compromise agreed to the next day—the basis of the Constitution Act, 1982.[104]

Whether Trudeau's referendum proposal and Lévesque's agreement to this alleged 'trap' are alone responsible for this outcome is open to debate. When the other premiers went into the final negotiations, they were obviously uncomfortable with their formal alliance with the 'separatist' PQ government; any pretext would have served their desire to be freed from it. Indeed, Lévesque may have accepted the Trudeau proposal because he was feeling a sense of estrangement from his ostensible allies.[105]

In the end, the alliance between Quebec and the other premiers was an unnatural one since it had not been based upon any recognition of Quebec's particular goals. Lévesque had simply 'signed on' to a position that already had been defined by the English-Canadian premiers. That was his mistake.

Having subscribed to this common position, the Lévesque government was in fact poorly placed to denounce the terms upon which Trudeau and the other groups had agreed. The deviation of the amending formula from the interprovincial agreement was minor: compensation for provinces that opt out of transfers of jurisdiction to the federal government would be limited to the areas of 'education and culture'.[106] The imposition of a Charter of Rights and Freedoms is, of course, a more substantial matter. But even there the direct impact on Quebec's jurisdictions had been somewhat minimized. In the case of Quebec, the provision regarding minority-language education would apply to immigrants only if the National Assembly should so decree; only application to Canadians would take effect immediately.[107] And the mobility rights would not apply as long as Quebec's unemployment rate was above the national average.[108] Most other provisions were subject to the notwithstanding clause. None the less, the Charter could still restrict Quebec's autonomy, and could provoke bitter conflicts as a consequence.

In the light of Quebec's historical demands, the primary failing of the Constitution Act, 1982, is that it neither gives Quebec a veto over constitutional change nor gives Quebec any new powers. Trudeau could correctly reply, as he was quick to do, that those goals had been abandoned by the PQ government. In the end, the PQ's strategic errors may help to explain how it was possible to revise the constitution without taking account of Quebec's long-established demands, including those of most Quebec federalists. But they do not explain *why* it happened.

A Response to English Canada?
If it is difficult to see the patriation package as a response to the predominant demands in Quebec, it is even more difficult to see it as a response to expectations and pressures in the rest of the country. Constitutional revision in general had never been a priority in English Canada. It was only the rise of constitutional discontent in Quebec that had placed it on the Canadian political agenda. With the clear-cut referendum result, many English Canadians saw no reason to pursue it any further.[109] If they felt embarrassed by the fact that the Canadian constitution was still an Act of the British

Parliament, presuming they were even aware of the fact, they were apparently quite prepared to live with it.

As for the particular constitutional project that was so dear to the Trudeau government, an entrenched bill of rights, English-Canadian opinion was divided. Most of the English-Canadian premiers were firmly opposed to the concept, which they saw as a major and ill-advised departure from Canada's political traditions. At the first ministers' conference on the constitution in September 1980, Manitoba Premier Sterling Lyon declared that 'such a transfer of legislative authority [from Parliament] to courts would amount to a constitutional revolution entailing the relinquishment of the essential principle of Parliamentary democracy, the principle of Parliamentary supremacy.' He urged his colleagues 'to retain our own heritage, and reject experiments with concepts foreign to our tradition'. The NDP premier of Saskatchewan, Allan Blakeney, put a social democratic gloss on the opposition, declaring that a charter would transfer power to the courts, giving 'an advantage to the rich' and away from legislatures, which 'were less of an advantage to the rich'.[110] The premiers' opposition to entrenchment of rights extended even to the kind of right that, for Trudeau and his colleagues, was the heart of the proposed Charter: language rights. During discussions in the summer of 1980, only four provinces were prepared to support the recognition of minority-language rights.[111]

The premiers might have been accused of being self-serving in their opposition to the Charter, concerned simply with protecting their own power. Certainly, Trudeau and others were quick to charge them with precisely that. Yet, in their arguments against the notion of a charter, the premiers were drawing upon a tradition and body of thought with deep roots in English Canada. Thus, a good number of leading English-Canadian academics voiced opposition to the Trudeau project. Donald Smiley, who himself had long opposed an entrenched charter,[112] noted in 1981 that 'there is no consensus about the matter and in legal and academic circles there is a continuing strain of anti-entrenchment argument.' In fact, he ascribed such sentiment to 'many of the more senior and respected members of the Canadian bar and bench'.[113]

None the less, there were also strong supporters of an entrenched charter. In 1960 John Diefenbaker had secured a Canadian Bill of Rights, a simple Act of Parliament that applied only to matters under Parliament's jurisdiction. For many years prominent legal scholars and civil liberties groups had been calling for an entrenched charter. Moreover, organizations representing specific categories of Canadians saw that a charter might protect or improve the position of their members.[114]

These areas of support were strongly in evidence when hearings were convened by a special parliamentary committee on the Trudeau government's constitutional resolution. Indeed, the government quickly decided to extend the televised hearings. As a result, the committee heard from a wide spectrum of groups, including native peoples, the multicultural community, women, religious groups, the disabled, gays, lesbians, business, and labour. Most of them actually argued for a stronger charter than the one being proposed.[115]

The Trudeau government was able to use these public expressions of support for a charter to challenge outright the legitimacy of the premiers' opposition. Claiming to speak for 'the people' and defining its constitutional project as nothing less than a 'people's package', the Trudeau government practised what Peter Russell has called a 'new populist constitutionalism'.[116] Indeed, the government was able to cite opinion surveys showing that a majority of Canadians supported a charter; apparently they had little knowledge of what would be in it.[117] Confronted with mobilization of support in favour of a charter, the premiers relented and agreed on condition that large sections of the Charter be subject to a notwithstanding clause.

Yet the public support that built up around the Charter does not, itself, *explain* the Trudeau government's actions. Rather than simply responding to pressures from English Canada, the Trudeau government activated these pressures by making an entrenched charter a distinct possibility.

The Trudeau government took quite a different position on other aspects of constitutional reform for which there was evidence of substantial support. First, with respect to the division of powers, most provincial governments had argued for significant modifications. Indeed, in February 1979, Trudeau had been prepared to discuss a long list of jurisdictional changes, most of them in the direction of the provinces. Yet, in the summer of 1980, he and his colleagues took quite a different position, rejecting many of the decentralizing items and adding new ones, such as eliminating provincial impediments to the economic union. At the September first ministers' conference, Trudeau summarily dismissed most of the items on a list that a coalition of premiers presented to him.[118] He had already decided to embark, alone if necessary, on a constitutional package in which there was no meaningful change to the division of powers.

Second, the provincial governments had expressed considerable interest in reform of the Senate and the Supreme Court. Some of the provincial governments had proposed that the Senate be converted to a body composed of representatives appointed by the provincial governments, modelled after the German *Bundesrat*.[119] At least one premier, Peter Lougheed of Alberta, was opposed to the concept.[120] On the other hand, there should have been no difficulty establishing a consensus on reform of the Supreme Court. This had, after all, been part of the Victoria Charter, to which all provinces but Quebec had agreed. But, unlike in the case of the Charter, the Trudeau government was not prepared to show leadership. In all likelihood, reform of central institutions fell victim to Ottawa's plans for unilateral action. The Supreme Court had already ruled, in its 1979 decision on Bill C-60, that the federal government could not unilaterally reform central institutions. Having not included this item in its agenda of unilateral action, Ottawa apparently was not prepared to see the item back on the table when it returned to negotiations with the provinces.

Clearly, the form and content of the Trudeau government's constitutional package was not a direct response to pressures from English Canada, any more than it was a direct response to the predominant pressures in Quebec. At the same time, the government was able to use the areas of English-Canadian support for one element of the package, the Charter, to mobilize opinion in favour of the project as a whole and against the opposition of provincial premiers and others.

The Trudeau government also found support for its package by tapping a concern that was shared by a good many English Canadians: the need to respond to Quebec, especially in light of the promises that had been made during the referendum debate. Here, Trudeau and his cabinet were emphatic that their package was indeed such a response. Whereas they could readily dismiss the Lévesque government's opposition as the predictable response of a 'separatist' government, the opposition of Quebec federalists, such as Claude Ryan and much of the Quebec Liberal Party, was a bit more difficult to dismiss. However, federal leaders described this position as misguided or, worse still, reflecting crypto-separatist tendencies. Or they dismissed the objection as a question of procedure rather than content. The Quebec people, Trudeau insisted, did not share the obsessions of their nationalist élite; they firmly supported the constitutional package and prized the pan-Canadian entrenchment of language rights that it offered. The argument carried some weight in English Canada. Once again, Trudeau had succeeded in interposing his own quite distinctive opinion of 'what Quebec wants', and mobilizing English-Canadian support on that basis.

Entrenching the Trudeau Vision
In short, the final result closely matched long-established priorities and the vision of Trudeau himself; it is here that we must look for the primary explanation of the Constitution Act, 1982. Finding himself back in power in early 1980 and leading the federalist forces to a resounding referendum victory four months later, Trudeau saw a historic opportunity to achieve the central objectives of his national unity strategy. He no longer had to entertain new departures and approaches as he had appeared to do in the wake of the 1976 PQ victory.

Indeed, as Trudeau prepared this new constitutional initiative he was careful to choose officials who would share the ruthlessness that he could now exercise. This excluded advisers, such as André Burelle, who had joined Trudeau in the post-1976 period, encouraged by the new openness expressed in Trudeau's 1977 Chamber of Commerce speech. It also excluded Gordon Robertson, who not only had been deputy minister of federal-provincial relations in the post-1976 period but, as clerk of the Privy Council, had been closely involved with the negotiations leading up to the Victoria Charter. Several years later, Trudeau explained in these terms his choice of Michael Kirby over Robertson:

> Let's just say that in this last stage I felt one needed almost a putsch, a *coup de force*, and Gordon was too much of a gentleman for that. It was clearly going to be rough and Gordon Robertson wasn't the man: a mandarin, concerned with the common weal, afraid of irreparable damage to the fabric of society. So I made a different choice.[121]

Having witnessed, during his stint in the Privy Council Office, the halting and heavily qualified efforts of the St Laurent government to formalize Canadian sovereignty, Trudeau was determined to resolve the matter once and for all by running the risks of unilateralism from which St Laurent had shrunk.[122] He was equally determined to achieve his long-standing objective of entrenching linguistic equality. Thus, he was adamant that any charter must contain language rights. Indeed, he declared in Quebec City in the fall of 1980 that French language rights were the whole purpose of the Charter and that the other rights had been added to avoid English-Canadian cries of 'French power'.[123] For the same reason, he rejected any qualification to the application of these rights, including the notwithstanding clause, which he finally agreed to for less important parts of the Charter.[124]

National Unity through Pan-Canadian Nationalism

The Constitution Act, 1982, can best be understood as the imposition by the Trudeau government of its *own* conception of Canada. Where it could, the government mobilized support for its initiative, inserting provisions in the Charter of Rights and Freedoms that ensured the support of specific social groups, primarily in English Canada. But where necessary, Trudeau and his colleagues were more than prepared to defy those who opposed their initiative and the conception of Canada that underlay it. This meant defying much of public opinion in Quebec, federalist as well as sovereigntist.

To defend its course of action, the Trudeau government invoked its right, as the national government, to act on behalf of the Canadian nation. Indeed, a few weeks before the referendum, Trudeau had made abundantly clear how he saw the powers and responsibilities of the 'national' government. He told the House that: 'We [the Members of Parliament] are the only group of men and women in this country who can speak for every Canadian. We are the only group, the only assembly in this country, which can speak for the whole nation, which can express the national will and the national interest'. On this basis, Trudeau declared, it was appropriate that the Fathers of Confederation gave the federal government powers, including the reservation and disallowance powers, through which it might intervene against a province that was acting 'contrary to the national interest'. After all, 'when there is a conflict of interest, not of laws, which will be judged by the courts, the citizens must be convinced that there is a national government which will speak for the national interest and will ensure that it does prevail.'[125]

Such nationalist rhetoric was, of course, very much at odds with Trudeau's 1960s writings. There, Canada was presented not as a unitary nation, but as a 'multinational federation'.[126] In fact, it was a 'pact':

> Federalism is by its very essence a compromise and a pact. It is a compromise in the sense that when national consensus on *all* things is not desirable or cannot readily obtain, the area of consensus is reduced in order that consensus on *some* things be reached. It is a pact or quasi-treaty in the sense that the terms of that compromise cannot be changed unilaterally. That is not to say that the terms are fixed forever; but only that in changing them every effort must be made not to destroy the consensus on which the federated nation rests.[127]

Yet in those writings the celebration of Canadian federalism had always been driven by a more important theme, the need to defeat nationalism, especially Quebec nationalism.[128] Federalism was less an end in itself than a means of achieving a more important goal. And, as the Trudeau government demonstrated in the early 1980s, the values of federalism could be discarded if other more promising means should become available.

The threat of unilateral patriation and the subsequent patriation without Quebec's consent were not deviations from the Trudeau vision of Canada, born of the flush of referendum victory. They followed logically from that vision and the national unity strategy that had been pursued to put it in place. During the 1970s, this vision of Canada had already been evident in the substitution of multiculturalism for biculturalism and the attempt to apply a uniform language policy across the country. It had also been seen in the concerted efforts to assert the role of Ottawa as the 'national government'.

With the 1980 referendum victory the federal government felt it could act freely,[129] and the underlying logic of its strategy was now revealed: *Quebec* nationalism was to be defeated by *Canadian* nationalism. To be sure, defenders of this approach would argue that this new Canadian nationalism was fundamentally different from Quebec nationalism. Rather than an 'ethnic nationalism' it was a 'civic nationalism', which rose above ethnicity and all other social divisions. None the less it *was* nationalism and, moreover, it was one in which the nation consists of individuals who first and foremost are Canadian. As such, this Canadian nationalism directly contradicted the vision of a federal, dualist Canada with distinct societies and multiple identities, which had been so important to generations of Quebec francophones.

The federal government's nationalism and its commitment to a unitary Canada can be seen in the way it dealt not just with the constitution but with the whole range of federal-provincial relations.[130] Thus, in November 1981 Trudeau explained why the federal government had revised its fiscal relations with the provinces so as to reserve funds for new national projects: 'We have stopped the momentum that would have turned Canada into, in everything but name only, ten countries.' The time had come, he declared, to 'reassert in our national policies that Canada is one country which must be capable of moving with unity of spirit and purpose towards shared goals. If Canada is indeed to be a nation, there must be a national will which is something more than the lowest common denominator among the desires of the provincial governments.'[131]

On this basis, the Trudeau government showed a new readiness to act unilaterally in areas where in the past it usually had sought the collaboration, even the consent, of the provinces. A striking case was the pricing of oil and gas.[132] Whereas throughout the 1970s the Trudeau government had followed a practice of negotiated bilateral agreements with the producer provinces— Alberta, Saskatchewan, and British Columbia—on 28 October 1980 Ottawa simply announced what the new prices would be. In fact, its National Energy Program entailed a number of other measures that the producing provinces saw as unwarranted intrusions into their jurisdictions and prerogatives. Similarly, in 1983 Ottawa made substantial changes and cuts to its fiscal transfers to the provinces without the usual amount of consultation.

At the same time, the Trudeau government showed a new determination to provide benefits and services directly to citizens in areas of clear provincial jurisdiction. After having agreed in 1978 to the provincial demand that it not directly fund municipalities, in 1981 it suddenly terminated the agreement and proceeded to establish new programs of direct funding of municipalities. Similarly, it altered the terms of its co-operation with provincial governments in regional development. Rather than co-fund common projects, Ottawa announced it would pursue 'parallel' projects with the provinces. By delivering projects itself, Ottawa could be more certain of receiving public credit for them. And it established its own officials in each region to formulate new projects, as well as oversee their implementation.[133]

The importance of the Quebec question to the Trudeau government is seen from the number of unilateral federal measures related to Quebec. The federal government's Bill S-31, restricting provincial ownership in transportation enterprises, was triggered by apprehension over the use the Quebec government's Caisse de dépôt et de placement, which invests pension and insurance funds, might make of its holdings in Canadian Pacific. Similarly, so as to satisfy Newfoundland's long-standing objections to the terms of its agreement with Hydro-Québec, Ottawa proposed in 1981 to expropriate a right of way through Quebec territory for transmission lines. And Ottawa twice unilaterally announced economic development projects in Quebec but not any other province.[134]

Finally, Ottawa undertook enormous advertising campaigns to ensure that citizens were aware of its activities. To quote Secretary of State Gerald Regan: 'I cannot overstate the importance of good communication by the federal government as fundamental to the survival of a strong Canada. Put starkly, unless Canadians know the worth of national government, they will not care enough to continue to have a national government.'[135] Ottawa increasingly concentrated its funds in 'advocacy' advertising in which it tried to win citizens over to its position in struggles with the provinces. Thus, the share of federal advertising funds used by the Canadian Unity Information Office rose from 4.5 per cent in 1978/9 to 25.3 per cent in 1980/1 and 21.1 per cent in 1981/2.[136]

Throughout these many measures the logic was that the key to national unity lay with the federal government's ability to rein in the provinces and assert its proper role as the 'national' government of all Canadians. Not only that, but through such measures as the National Energy Program, it would defend the national interest against the American multinationals. In the 1960s, however, Trudeau had warned against trying to secure the cohesion of a multinational federation like Canada through appeals to nationalism rather than using reason to build a consensus:

> If my premises are correct, nationalism cannot provide the answer. Even if massive investments in flags, dignity, protectionism, and Canadian content of television managed to hold the country together for a few more years, separatism would remain a recurrent phenomenon. . . . If, for instance, it is going to remain *morally wrong* for Wall Street to assume control of Canada's economy, how will it become *morally right* for Bay Street to dominate Quebec's or—for that matter—Nova Scotia's [emphasis in original]?[137]

As we shall see in the next chapter, the pan-Canadian nationalism of the final Trudeau administration did not prevent Quebec separatism from being 'a recurrent phenomenon'. Nor did it dissuade Quebec francophones from giving their primary loyalty to Quebec. Indeed such sentiments were to increase during the 1980s. The new Canadian nationalism may even have contributed to this directly, by provoking a reaction among Quebeckers. But the new Canadian nationalism engendered a recurrence of 'separatism' in a more profound sense. By reinforcing English Canadians in their resistance to *any* recognition of the continuing Quebec identity within the Canadian federation, it left Quebec sovereignty as the only alternative.

KEEPING THE REFERENDUM PROMISE?

Through the patriation of 1982 the Trudeau government attained the ultimate goal in its national unity strategy: the entrenchment of language rights from coast to coast. Yet, to secure this measure aimed at integrating Quebec francophones with the rest of the country, it had had to incur the opposition of not just sovereigntists but also a good share of federalist opinion in Quebec. Indeed, Quebec federalists were to remain badly divided for years to come. Trudeau and his defenders could reply that the final constitutional package was totally consistent with the objectives he had declared years before, as indeed it was. However, that argument has not silenced his critics.

Among many Quebec federalists there has been a lingering belief that Trudeau had in fact promised something quite different from the Constitution Act, something more in keeping with Quebec's established demands. In the one statement—his final referendum speech—in which Trudeau did make a promise, he in fact offered no specifics as to what he would try to deliver. He did not even promise to 'renew' Canadian federalism; simply to renew the *constitution*. With the Charter he certainly did do that.

Yet Trudeau must have known the context in which he made his 'promise', vague as it may have been. The very phrase 'constitutional renewal' had acquired a specific meaning in the Quebec of 1980; therefore, it was reasonable for his audience to assume that it meant, among other things, a major enhancement of the powers of the Quebec government.[138] In fact, just before making the promise, in his final speech of the referendum campaign, Trudeau had explicitly linked constitutional change with a renewal of *federalism*: 'If the answer to the referendum question is No, we have said that this No will be interpreted as a mandate to change the constitution, *to renew federalism* [emphasis added].[139]

Moreover, Trudeau's critics can argue that through previous action his government had created quite precise expectations of what a renewal of federalism would entail. It had appointed a task force of prominent Canadians, some of whom could have been expected to propose changes to Canadian federalism that would recognize Quebec's uniqueness. They did indeed make such proposals. Similarly, through Cullen-Couture, the federal government had entered into an asymmetrical arrangement that seemed to recognize Quebec's specific needs. And its own proposal, *A Time for Action*, had proposed that reform to central institutions and the division of powers be part of any constitutional change.

Defenders of the Trudeau government can respond that Trudeau and his cabinet had never actually endorsed the Pepin-Robarts proposals and had largely ignored its report. As for *A Time for Action*, it was simply a proposal that was overtaken by events. But we have seen how in his first referendum speech, when he tried to show the extent to which Canada was headed for change, Trudeau had mentioned both the Pepin-Robarts task force (claiming credit for creating it) and *A Time for Action*, along with the Quebec Liberal Party's Beige Paper. It was in terms of these proposals that he depicted the pressures for a renewed federalism. Similarly, we saw how in his speech to the Chambre de commerce in 1977 Trudeau had declared a commitment to the entrenchment of *collective* linguistic rights—a concept he had always rejected in the past.

Over the following years Trudeau argued that there could have been no misunderstanding; his position on the nature of constitutional change had always been the one he defined in the late 1960s when the process of constitutional revision began: patriation with a veto for Quebec and a charter recognizing, among other things, language rights—precisely what was in the Constitution Act.[140] Yet, these were not the notions he had evoked in the late 1970s.

In the last analysis, however, the debate over Trudeau's alleged 'betrayal' points to something more profound. Given their own understanding of Quebec and its place in Canada, a wide spectrum of Quebec federalists conceived 'constitutional renewal' in very different terms than did Trudeau. Indeed, there may have been a certain element of wishful thinking in their understanding of what the Trudeau government would do.

In short, the Constitution Act was simply out of step with Quebec opinion. It was based upon an idea of Canada that most Quebec francophones did not share, despite the best efforts of the federal government to bring them around to such an understanding. Thus, even if the Constitution Act kept the specific promise that Trudeau had made to Quebec, it could not possibly keep the larger promise of bringing Canadian unity.

CHAPTER 7

The Failure of the
Trudeau Strategy

For over 15 years Canadian politics was dominated by the Trudeau government's pursuit of a 'national unity' strategy designed to transform the way in which Quebec francophones saw Canada and themselves. The basic elements of the strategy had been spelled out in Trudeau's writings and his early pronouncements as a politician, and once he became prime minister, he rapidly mobilized the federal government to put his strategy into effect.

THE FAILURE OF THE NATIONAL UNITY STRATEGY

The strategy attempted to transform the belief in a Canadian duality held by most Quebec francophones. Rather than a compact between two communities, one anglophone and the other francophone, with the latter rooted in Quebec, Canada was to be seen as a single political community composed of individuals, of whom some spoke English, some spoke French, and a growing number spoke both. To the extent duality persisted it would apply to language alone. However, this linguistic duality would be established throughout Canada, from coast to coast. This would cause Quebec francophones to abandon their historical allegiance to Quebec and to identify first and foremost with the new Canadian political community, of which they would be an integral part.

There were several parts to the strategy. Front and centre was language reform and the drive to implant official bilingualism throughout Canada, not only in federal institutions but, to the greatest extent possible, in the provincial government as well. Coupled with the language reforms was a new approach to the status of cultures: multiculturalism or the formal equality of all cultures. Canada's political institutions were also to be transformed. The federal government was to become more important in the lives of Canadians as the 'national' government and federal-provincial relations were to be more clearly based on the equality of all provinces, Quebec included. Finally, the constitution was to be patriated and was to include a charter of rights.

These various measures were intimately linked to the goal of instilling allegiance to Canada as a single political community. The Trudeau government's language reforms were rigorously framed in terms of the rights and needs of individuals rather than collectivities and were intended to strengthen the position of the francophones throughout the country as a whole, as well as promoting individual bilingualism. Similarly, the adoption of multiculturalism was partly spurred by the desire to negate biculturalism and the cultural underpinnings of Canadian dualism.

As for constitutional reform, it was driven fundamentally by the goal of pan-Canadian bilingualism. The reason that reform had to include a charter was to entrench language rights.[1] Indeed, in the new Canadian Charter of Rights and Freedoms, the educational rights of linguistic minorities are one of the few provisions applying to the provinces that are not subject to the notwithstanding clause. That is why a charter had to be part of the patriation package, in effect inserted by the British Parliament as part of its last 'imperial' act, however much this contradicted the very logic of patriation.

With its five elements—official bilingualism, multiculturalism, strengthening of the 'national' government, uniform federalism, and a charter—the strategy provided a coherent and comprehensive plan of action. The Trudeau government pursued the strategy with a determination and concertedness that is rare in government. Trudeau and his colleagues may have had some second thoughts after the election of the PQ in 1976, but they more than made up for it in his final term in office.

In the end, the Trudeau government was remarkably successful in achieving most of its specific goals. The constitution was revised in the way Trudeau had always wanted, and without the kind of changes he did not want. The government vigorously pursued a variety of measures to assert Ottawa's role as a national government, especially during its last term in office. It eliminated much of the asymmetry of Quebec's place in federal-provincial relations. Moreover, under the new constitutional amending formula, Quebec's position was precisely the same as the other provinces. Multiculturalism was effectively established as a principle of federal politics, as well as in many provinces.

In the case of language policy, however, the results were decidedly mixed. The Trudeau government may have firmly implanted the principle of official bilingualism at the federal level, but only one provincial government, New Brunswick, followed suit. For its part, Quebec abandoned linguistic equality and adopted French as its only official language. The Charter of Rights and Freedoms obliged the provinces to provide their official-language minorities with educational services, but nothing else (with the exception of New Brunswick). More fundamentally, the francophone minorities in most provinces continued to decline in numbers. This decline seemed to have much more to do with underlying social processes than with the shortcomings of language regimes, provincial or federal. More Canadians may have acquired a knowledge of the second language, but there were fewer francophones in most parts of Canada outside Quebec and fewer anglophones within Quebec.

In short, whatever the Charter might suggest, Canada was in no way nearer the ideal of a pan-Canadian linguistic duality. More than ever, language was closely bound by territory, and Quebec was the sociological and cultural centre of Canada's francophones. The Trudeau vision of Canada was directly contradicted by a linguistic reality that, despite its best efforts, the federal government had been unable to alter.

Yet, if the specific objectives of the national unity strategy had not all been fully achieved, it was not for lack of trying. For 15 years, the energies and resources of the federal government had been systematically deployed on their behalf. What then of the fundamental objective of the strategy? Did it succeed in transforming the way in which Quebec francophones saw Canada? To that we should add a second question: what impact did the strategy have on how *other* Canadians saw their country?

THE TRUDEAU STRATEGY AND QUEBEC

Immediately after the Trudeau era, the state of political forces in Quebec might have seemed to confirm the strategy. Sovereigntist forces were in disarray, still demoralized by two successive defeats; in the 1980 referendum and the 1982 patriation. Indeed, some commentators thought that Quebec nationalism was on the way out.[2]

Even though the Parti Québécois was still in power, it was badly divided as to whether sovereignty was still an option. Shortly after the election of the Progressive Conservatives under Brian Mulroney, Lévesque had said he was ready to explore the renewal of federalism with the new government. That deviation from sovereigntism led to the spectacular resignation of leading PQ cabinet members. In September 1985, Lévesque gave up the leadership, repudiated by many of his past supporters. Now led by Pierre-Marc Johnson, who announced an ill-defined goal of 'national affirmation', the PQ was badly defeated in December 1985, winning only 38 per cent of the popular vote and 24 of 122 seats. The victorious Liberals, who were led by Trudeau's old nemesis, Robert Bourassa, proclaimed a firm commitment to Canadian federalism.

Trends at the federal level were less encouraging for the Trudeau strategy. Mulroney's victory in 1984 had in fact been due to a massive defection of Quebec voters from the Liberal party, whose share of the popular vote fell from 68.2 per cent in 1980 to 35.4 per cent in 1984. This devastating result might be attributed to Trudeau's departure; instead, it was probably more due to continuing resentment of Trudeau. His isolation of Quebec on the constitutional front clearly did much to attract political personalities to the Conservative Party and to win the support of Quebec voters for the Conservatives. Indeed, during the election campaign Mulroney had declared that if he formed the government he would try to find a basis upon which the Quebec National Assembly could consent to the constitution 'with honour and enthusiasm'.[3] Thus, many observers saw the 1984 election as a repudiation of the Trudeau vision.[4]

Such a reading is also confirmed by the apparent effect on Quebec public opinion of the various elements of Trudeau's strategy. The main element was, of course, official bilingualism. Clearly, the larger role for French and francophones in federal institutions was important to Quebec francophones, reducing their historical estrangement from the federal government. And there is little doubt that many Quebec francophones welcomed the efforts by Ottawa and, to varying degrees the provinces, to provide French-language services to francophones outside Quebec.

Nevertheless, the priority of most Quebec francophones was still the status of French *within* Quebec; few of them were ready to trade that against improvements outside Quebec. Thus, while divided over some of Bill 101's specific measures, such as the requirement that commercial signs be in French only, Quebec francophones have been strongly supportive of the bill itself.[5] For that matter, a survey taken in 1977 had found that for most Quebec francophones the status of French outside Quebec had little bearing on their attitude regarding Quebec sovereignty.[6]

As for Ottawa's formula for the status of cultures, multiculturalism, it was largely rejected in francophone Quebec. The Quebec government may have been developing programs for its 'allophone' population that paralleled many of Ottawa's multicultural programs, but Quebec's political and intellectual leaders, federalist as well as sovereigntist, firmly resisted 'multiculturalism' as a way of describing francophones' place in Canada. In cultural terms, Quebec francophones continued to see Canada as composed of two communities.[7]

Nor did the Trudeau government's efforts to redefine the relationship between Ottawa and the provinces appear to have changed Quebeckers' historical tendency to give first allegiance to the Quebec government and to see Quebec as a province 'unlike the others'. In response to a 1987 survey question offering a choice between 'a strong national government' and 'strong provincial governments and not as strong a national government', 57 per cent of Quebec respondents preferred the strong provincial government, and only 40 per cent preferred a strong national government. (Presumably support for the provincial government was even higher among the francophone respondents.) In the rest of the country, overwhelming majorities opted for a strong national government: British Columbia, 67.8 per cent; the Prairies, 64.2 per cent; Ontario, 75.4 per cent; and the Atlantic provinces, 66.9 per cent.[8]

As for the crowning element of the Trudeau strategy, the Charter of Rights and Freedoms, its reception was decidedly mixed. Opposition to the Charter did not stem from the various rights enumerated in it. An analysis of public opinion in the mid-1980s found that 'with respect to ideas about basic rights and freedoms' there were no significant differences between French Canadians and English Canadians.[9] Indeed, the Quebec National Assembly had already passed its own charter of rights, *La Charte des droits et libertés de la personne*, in 1975. In fact, mid-1980s studies suggested that Quebec francophones were just as likely as other Canadians to see the Charter of Rights and Freedoms positively, although significantly less likely to know of its existence. There is even evidence that Parti Québécois members of the National Assembly were inclined to see the Charter as a 'good thing'.[10] These various findings disprove any blanket characterization of Quebec francophones as less disposed to individual rights and more disposed to collective rights than other Canadians.[11]

None the less, there were at least three difficulties with the Charter. First, however favourable they were in principle of the various rights contained in the Charter, most Quebec francophones remained very much committed to ensuring the survival and development of a francophone society in Quebec. Potentially, the Charter might conflict with that objective.

The problem is explained well in a recent book by André Burelle, a deeply committed federalist who was closely associated with Trudeau in the late 1970s but who rejected Trudeau's post-referendum constitutional actions.[12] Burelle argues that the Charter mistakenly defines linguistic rights in purely individual terms. Yet, unlike such basic human rights as freedom of expression, which the Charter correctly treats as individual rights, linguistic rights cannot be practised on an individual basis. A language can be used only in a community. To be at all meaningful, a linguistic right has to be conceived as a collective right. The right to use a language must entail the right of a community to function in that language. And, where this requires state intervention, that should be both possible and forthcoming.

The implication of this argument for Quebec is that, given the myriad pressures favouring English, it is entirely proper for the Quebec state to adopt measures, such as Bill 101, to enable francophones to work in French and to integrate immigrants into the francophone community. In Burelle's terms, this is an exercise of Quebec francophones' collective right to be different.

From the outset, it was clear that the Charter would conflict with Bill 101. By some readings a major purpose of the Charter's guarantee of minority-language education was to invalidate the restrictions that prevented anglophone Canadians from sending their children to English schools in Quebec,[13] and the courts were indeed quick to declare unconstitutional the application of those restrictions to anglophone children born elsewhere in Canada. These specific decisions did not provoke a major public response in Quebec. Their effect was not markedly different from the terms of reciprocal agreements that the Lévesque government had proposed to the other provinces in 1978; Bill 101 contains a provision allowing for reciprocal agreements.[14] Indeed, in presenting its new proposals for Quebec's consent to the constitution, in June 1985, the Lévesque government said it was prepared to accept the application of the Charter's minority-language education provisions to Quebec in exchange for confirmation of its power over linguistic matters under provincial jurisdiction.[15] In any event, the impact of this Charter decision was not highly visible, involving relatively few children.

The public reaction was much greater in 1988, when as a result of the Charter, the 'sign law' was declared unconstitutional. This was a part of Bill 101 that affected the everyday lives of most Quebeckers. Then, the public's desire to protect the integrity of Bill 101 against the Charter was obvious.[16]

A second difficulty with the Charter of Rights and Freedoms was the pan-Canadian nationalism with which it is so intimately linked. By definition, a measure that tries to standardize rights throughout Canada as a whole, within provincial as well as federal jurisdictions, is antithetical to Quebec's claim to distinctiveness within Canada. In defining basic rights that all Canadians should enjoy, wherever they live, it reinforces the notion of Canada as the pre-eminent national community.[17]

There was, of course, a final difficulty with the Charter: the way in which it had been adopted. Here the situation was much more clear-cut. The Charter was the most important part of a package of constitutional changes that had been adopted without the consent of the Quebec National Assembly. As such, it was the result of a procedure that directly contradicted the established French-Canadian view of Canada and Quebec's place within it. On this, there was agreement among most francophones in the Quebec political arena, federalist as well as sovereigntist.

As we saw in the last chapter, all but nine of the Liberal members of the National Assembly, most of them anglophone, had joined with the PQ members in approving a resolution that rejected the Trudeau government's plan of unilateral patriation. And after the November 1991 agreement without Quebec, the National Assembly had approved a resolution condemning the agreement. Admittedly the Liberal members of the National Assembly had voted against the resolution, citing the PQ's refusal to support an amendment invoking faith in Canadian federalism; but many of them, including party leader Claude Ryan, expressed their continued rejection of patriation without Quebec's consent in other ways.[18] In the words of Quebec political scientist Gérard Bergeron: 'Agreement was . . . reached, but without the government which had enunciated principles and which was tactically excluded from the decisive nocturnal pact. How could some Quebecers not be inclined to take this exclusion personally, when matters of such importance could be decided in the absence of their representatives?'[19]

Over the years, supporters of patriation have insisted that at the time that was not the attitude of the Quebec public. If Quebeckers later were to be opposed to the move, it must be because the nationalist élites had manipulated them into such sentiments. It is true that a good number of Quebeckers, francophone as well as anglophone, apparently did not agree with the Lévesque government's refusal to sign the agreement. Immediately after the agreement, 43 per cent of Quebec francophones agreed but 33 per cent disagreed, according to the best estimate.[20] Moreover, the proportion agreeing with the government appears to have slipped over the following months.[21] None the less, a survey conducted in January 1982, found that 61 per cent of all Quebeckers felt that the accord had weakened Quebec's position within Confederation. For that matter, 51 per cent felt that Ottawa didn't understand Quebec's aspirations and 52 per cent thought it was not doing enough to promote French.[22] Trudeau himself has regularly pointed to a survey of June 1982 that showed that 49 per cent of Quebeckers agreed that 'in the long term, the 1982 Canadian constitution would be a good thing for Canada.'[23] But, as one critic has noted, the question was about *Canada's* interests as opposed to Quebec's.[24]

In any event, when it came to the heart of the matter, patriation without Quebec's consent, the position of most Quebeckers could not have been clearer. A survey on March 1982 asked Quebeckers whether they agreed or disagreed 'with the decision of the government of Canada to proceed with repatriation without the approval of the government of Quebec'; 55 per cent (61 per cent of francophones) disagreed; only 26 per cent agreed. One year before, a similar question had produced almost the same results.[25] In short, from the outset most Quebeckers rejected patriation without Quebec's approval; they were not persuaded to this position after the fact.

It is obvious that patriation without the Quebec legislature's consent was a violation of the historical understanding that Quebec francophones had held of Quebec's place in Canada. The ability of patriation and the Charter to fulfill their purposes within the national unity strategy was fatally compromised by this fact. By attacking the established French-Canadian view of Canada so directly, they simply reinforced that view.

Not surprisingly, in light of the mixed response to the different elements of the national unity strategy, the underlying objective that they were intended to serve was itself not reached. After 15 years of implementation of the strategy, Quebec francophones were by all indications no less rooted in their attachment to Quebec as their primary allegiance. In fact, surveys measuring the proportion of Quebec francophones who see themselves as 'Québécois', as opposed to 'Canadian' or 'French Canadian', grew steadily throughout that period, from 21 per cent in 1970 to 37 per cent in 1984, at the end of the Trudeau government (see Table 4). Thus, even before the new Conservative government might have acted in ways that contradicted the Trudeau strategy, identification with Quebec was already far stronger than it had been when the Trudeau government began its efforts.

It is difficult to see how the result could have been otherwise. The Trudeau strategy was attempting to displace an understanding of Canada that had been sustained by generations of Quebec's intellectual and political élites. Moreover, it was rooted in the sociological reality that francophone society was indeed centred in Quebec.

In comparison, the new vision of Canada and the appeal to Québécois' allegiances that the Trudeau government proffered could only have seemed artificial or 'constructed'. To be sure, the version of a distinctly Quebec identity that neo-nationalists began creating in the 1960s was also a 'construction'

TABLE 4: SELF-IDENTIFICATION OF QUEBEC FRANCOPHONES, 1970–1990

	French Canadian	Québécois	Canadian	Others or Not Stated
1970	44%	21%	34%	1%
1977	51	31	18	a
1984	48	37	13	1
1988	39	49	11	1
1990	28	59	9	2

aexcluded from tabulation
Source: Maurice Pinard, 'The Dramatic Reemergence of the Quebec Independence Movement', *Journal of International Affairs* 45, no. 2 (Winter 1995): Table 3.

but it was based on an underlying sense of French-Canadian nationality with deep historical roots. The Trudeau alternative had no such roots. Any attempt to link it to the Canadian nationalism of Henri Bourassa, the most clearly 'pan-Canadian' vision ever offered by a French-Canadian intellectual leader, was compromised by Trudeau's rejection of biculturalism and his dismissal of the centrality of Quebec to French Canada.

Conceivably, the Trudeau vision of Canada might have been more credible in Quebec if the language reforms that were the heart of the strategy had in fact created a Canada that was bilingual from coast to coast. But that was never a realistic goal. So there was no compelling reason for Québécois to abandon their historical assumption that francophone society was centred in Quebec.

Without any real change to the linguistic structure of Canada, the elements of the Trudeau strategy that denied Quebec's uniqueness could only be provocative. This was especially the case, of course, with the rejection of constitutional demands from Quebec, culminating in patriation without Quebec's formal consent. In that respect, the Trudeau strategy not only failed to weaken identification with Quebec, but actually strengthened it. And by preventing any possibility of additional accommodation of this identity within Canadian political institutions, the Trudeau strategy actually strengthened the appeal of Quebec sovereignty.

In the mid-1980s, these implications were not entirely evident. But, as we shall see, they soon became evident, especially as Quebec francophones were confronted with the other side to the Trudeau strategy: its profound impact on the rest of Canada.

THE TRUDEAU STRATEGY AND ENGLISH CANADA

Although the national unity strategy may have been conceived primarily for French Quebec, it fell on much more fertile ground outside Quebec. To a much greater extent than in Quebec, the strategy attracted the active support of important social forces.

First, efforts to assert the role of Ottawa, rather than the provinces as the national government of Canada had a ready-made clientele in the many social groups that had been involved in the construction of Canada's postwar welfare state. Such policies as health care may have originated with specific provinces, but they ultimately came to most Canadians through the efforts of the federal government. For English Canadians, whose sense of nationality had never been linked to their specific province and its government, the fact that these programs operated within exclusively provincial jurisdictions could not have the significance that it had for many Quebec francophones. The federal government was only assuming its proper responsibilities as the national government ensuring that all Canadians, as Canadians, enjoyed a minimal standard of living.

Second, the Trudeau government's insistence on the equality of all the provinces, including Quebec in particular, matched a growing sentiment in the Canadian west fuelled by a westward shift of the Canadian political economy.[26] In 1971 all the provinces but Quebec had agreed to the amending formula in the Victoria Charter which guaranteed vetoes for Quebec and Ontario but no other province. By the mid-1970s this was no longer acceptable. Alberta, as well as British Columbia and Saskatchewan, had a new-found interest in constitutional issues: especially in light of unfavourable Supreme Court decisions, they wanted to strengthen provincial jurisdiction over natural resources. British Columbia declared that as a fifth region it should have a veto too. Alberta proposed that *all* provinces should have a veto. The principle of equality among the provinces was reiterated at an interprovincial meeting in Edmonton. Thus, in 1981, the 'Gang of Eight' agreed on an amending formula in which for some purposes all provinces would have a veto but for other purposes no particular province would enjoy a veto. Otherwise known as 'the Vancouver formula', it was, of course, incorporated into the Constitution Act, 1982.

Third, we have seen how in 1981 the project of a Charter of Rights and Freedoms was quickly seized upon by a variety of groups, essentially outside French Quebec, as an instrument for advancing their own aspirations, whether for public policy, participation, or status. Women's groups, aboriginal leaders, multicultural groups, and official-language minorities could point to specific provisions in the Charter that recognized, if only minimally, their goals. In fact, all but the official-language minorities could claim that it was only because of the pressure they brought to bear that the provisions are there.

Moreover, these groups' vigorous support of the Charter was instrumental in forcing the English-Canadian premiers to forgo their opposition to an entrenched charter. The price of their acquiescence had been a notwithstanding clause, but within a matter of years this procedure was widely considered in English Canada to be illegitimate. In effect, the Charter had become for many English Canadians a central feature of their sense of a Canadian political nationality. In the coming years, the support for the Charter by these groups was further cemented by their success in using it to advance their objectives through litigation, often drawing upon federal funding under the Courts Challenge Program.[27] These 'Charter Canadians',[28] or less charitably the 'Court Party',[29] could be relied upon to be fierce defenders of the Charter.

The Trudeau government's policy of multiculturalism was partly a response to the demands of Canadians of neither British nor French descent, especially Ukrainian Canadians and similar categories of Canadians. Keenly frustrated with the meagre resources the Trudeau administration afforded to its multiculturalism program, these groups continued nonetheless to be enthusiastic advocates of the ideal of a multicultural Canada. By the 1980s, they had been joined by groups of non-white Canadians, who while seeking to shift the emphasis of multiculturalism from cultural preservation to the elimination of racial barriers to economic and social mobility, also championed multiculturalism as a formula for Canada. To be sure, multiculturalism had its critics in English Canada, but it also had vigorous advocates, which was not the case in French Quebec.

The status outside Quebec of the Trudeau vision's central component, official bilingualism, is perhaps more problematic. Certainly, it won the vigorous support of francophone minority groups. But English Canadians tended to be divided on the idea, at least as applied in provincial jurisdictions. Traditionally, English Canadians have not seen language rights as a human right; support for the Charter in general does not necessarily extend to support of official bilingualism. None the less, many English Canadians who did support the ideal of a bilingual Canada, proved to be determined supporters of the Trudeau ideal. A case in point is Parents for French, an organization that advocates French immersion schooling.

Not only did the separate parts of the national unity strategy each receive significant support on its own terms in English Canada, but the vision of the country they were to support had the advantage in English Canada of not having to compete with a dynamic and historical sense of nationality. The loyalty to a British nationality that many English Canadians felt during the early decades of Confederation had lost credibility with the collapse of the British Empire after the Second World War and the decline of the British connection. In a sense, then, English Canadians were in need of a new vision of their country. Moreover, in some ways, the Trudeau vision built upon the sense of a distinctly Canadian nationality that already had been emerging, thanks in part to the efforts of previous federal administrations.

So the national unity strategy was successful—but with the wrong population. As a result, it had the effect of widening the gulf between English Canadians and Quebec francophones. More specifically, it greatly strengthened English-Canadian resistance to any demands for recognition of Quebec's distinctiveness. Indeed, it left English Canadians ill-equipped even to understand Quebec's claims, which made little sense within a vision of Canada that had, in fact, been constructed to deny the uniqueness of Quebec.

Thanks to official bilingualism, French was seen as enjoying privileged status throughout Canada, robbing Quebec of any distinctiveness. To make matters worse, the expansion of French-language services outside Quebec was considered by many English Canadians to be a concession to Quebec, and a very expensive one at that. There was understandable anger when, with Bill 22 and Bill 101, the Quebec government proceeded to establish the pre-eminence of French within its own territory.

Thanks to multiculturalism, it was difficult for many English Canadians to comprehend the cultural dimension of Quebec's uniqueness since Canada was now composed of a multiplicity of cultural groups. Neither French Canada nor Quebec could have any special claim. Moreover, a myriad of groups had been organized around these other cultures, forming a vigilant defence of multiculturalism and a fierce opposition to biculturalism.

It had also become very difficult to understand the political dimension of the Quebec issue owing in large part to the Trudeau government's approach to federal-provincial relations, but also to the reconfiguration of power in English Canada toward the west. English Canadians had become firmly wedded to the idea that all provinces must have equal status.

Quebec's anger at the adoption of the Constitution Act, 1982, without its consent was doubly incomprehensible because Trudeau had persuaded many English Canadians that the substance of the changes was in fact a response to the expectations of Québécois who had voted No in the 1980 referendum. As for the notion of proceeding without Quebec's consent, the PQ government's sovereigntist commitments disqualified it in the eyes of many English Canadians from representing Québécois views about 'renewed federalism'. They were persuaded by the Trudeau government's argument that, by definition, the 'separatist' Lévesque government would never have agreed to constitutional patriation, no matter what the terms.

Each element of the Trudeau vision had been rejected by leading feder-alists in Quebec, and patriation without Quebec's consent had been opposed by most Quebec federalists, including the Quebec Liberal leader Claude Ryan. Yet in the late 1960s many English Canadians had turned to Trudeau as their guide to 'what Quebec wants'. After having apparently delivered the enormous federalist referendum victory, Trudeau's authority in English Canada was stronger than ever. In the process, the complaints of Ryan and other Quebec federalists were marginalized.

Not only did Trudeau's vision serve to render Quebec's continuing demands unintelligible to many English Canadians, but with its strong indi-vidualism it eliminated once and for all the English-Canadian support for the one approach to understanding Canada that they historically had shared with their francophone compatriots: the notion of a compact. To be sure, English-

Canadian versions of compact theory had always been centred on the provinces, as successors to the original colonies. There had never been any interest in the additional idea introduced by Henri Bourassa of a double compact; a compact between founding peoples. But at least there was the basis for a discussion, focused on the nature of the Canadian compact. With the individualism of the Trudeau vision of Canada there was no room for compacts, however defined. As English Canadians became wedded to that vision of Canada while Quebec francophones remained rooted in the notion of a compact, the very basis of discussion and debate was lost. The result could be no other than a dialogue of the deaf. All this would become evident when, in the late 1980s, Canadians debated the Meech Lake Accord, a measure designed to repair the damage of 1982.

PART THREE

Failing to
Repair the
Damage

CHAPTER 8

Bringing Quebec
into the Constitution:
Missing Two Chances

THE MEECH LAKE ACCORD

The departure of Pierre Trudeau from the political scene in the spring of 1984 opened the door to public debate about the need to repair the damage of 1982 and to obtain Quebec's consent to the constitution. Brian Mulroney's promise during the 1984 election campaign to tackle the issue appears to have contributed to his sweep of Quebec. René Lévesque rose to the challenge of defining the terms on which Quebec would sign, in the process triggering the departure of several cabinet colleagues. But since he left politics a few months later, it fell to the new Bourassa government to pick up the process. Given its clear commitment to Canadian federalism, it was much better placed to do so.

In Ontario a new premier, David Peterson, came to office in June 1985, convinced that the question had to be resolved. As long as Quebec was not a signatory to the constitution and thus not a full participant in constitutional discussions, Canada was unable to address a host of pressing issues. Fully aware of Ontario's historical role as 'broker' within Confederation, Peterson was prepared to make the case with the other premiers; indeed, two days after the election of the Bourassa government Peterson went to Montreal to meet with Bourassa.[1]

Not only were the leaders of relevant governments now committed to addressing the issue, but there appears to have been agreement among civil servants and academics concerned with intergovernmental relations that the question should be resolved. Many of the provincial officials who were veterans of the federal-provincial confrontations of the Trudeau era had never been converts to the Trudeau vision. Even among the federal mandarins there was apparently some sentiment that Quebec's absence carried real risks for the federation. The tone had been set by Gordon Robertson, the former clerk of the Privy Council and constitutional adviser whom Trudeau had passed over in his final constitutional battle. Just after the agreement of 5 November 1981 to constitutional revisions, Robertson had written, 'It would be optimistic in the extreme to think that we can avoid a new crisis on the question of separation in a very few years.'[2]

The initiative was taken by Robert Bourassa. From the outset, the 'normalizing' of Quebec's place in Canada was a priority of his government. At the swearing-in of his new government, Bourassa had broken with the PQ practice and arranged for the Canadian flag to join the Quebec flag in the National Assembly, declaring, moreover, that the flag was there to stay.[3] Then, in March 1986, the Quebec minister of intergovernmental affairs, Gil Rémillard, announced that his government was abandoning the PQ government's practice of routinely invoking the notwithstanding clause of the Charter of Rights and Freedoms when passing legislation. Arguing that acceptance of the Charter was the logical position for federalists to take, Rémillard declared, 'As for us, our principle is that we're federalists.' At the same time, he was careful to reiterate that the Constitution Act as it stood was 'unacceptable' to the Quebec government.[4]

The following May, at a special conference of academics, intergovernmental officials and interested parties, Rémillard outlined the conditions under which the Act could be acceptable to Quebec. There were five: a veto over constitutional change affecting Quebec, recognition of Quebec's status as a distinct society, limitation of the federal spending power, participation in Supreme Court nominations, and recognition of Quebec's existing powers related to immigration. In presenting these terms, Rémillard stressed that the election of his government 'signifies a new era of federal-provincial and interprovincial relations. Faithful to our federalist government, we want to guarantee Quebec its rights as a distinct society and major partner in the Canadian federation.'[5] Apparently, his presentation was well received by the audience; the five conditions he set out seemed to be 'manageable'.[6]

Collectively, the conditions were the most modest proposals for constitutional change that had come from any Quebec government in recent decades, including Bourassa's own proposals to the ill-fated Victoria Conference. In effect, they showed that the Bourassa government wanted to frame a set of proposals that might be acceptable to the rest of Canada, and thus resolve Quebec's anomalous constitutional status.[7] They also showed how little bargaining power the Bourassa government had. After the 1980 referendum, English Canadians had lost patience with the argument that Bourassa and other federalist premiers had used in the past: the need to head off the forces of Quebec sovereignty.

A tour of provincial capitals by Quebec officials found a general receptiveness to the proposals. In August, at their annual interprovincial conference, the premiers issued a communiqué announcing that their 'top constitutional priority' was to begin federal-provincial discussions, based on
Quebec's five proposals, to secure 'Quebec's full and active participation in
the Canadian federation'.[8]

The federal government watched these developments with great interest. Indeed, before running in the 1985 Quebec election, Rémillard had been
a special constitutional adviser to the Mulroney government.[9] Clearly, Prime
Minister Mulroney welcomed a potential opportunity to make good on his
election pledge to try to arrange for Quebec to accept the constitution. Such
an effort, especially if it were successful, could only consolidate the PCs' new
electoral base in Quebec.

Yet, electoral interests were not the only reason for the widespread
responsiveness to Quebec's overtures. Even if the Mulroney government's
motives could be reduced to electoral opportunism, itself a dubious proposition, Ontario premier David Peterson certainly had no reason to further the
federal Tories' electoral ambitions. Nor could he necessarily expect the
Ontario voters to reward him for his efforts. By the same token, electoral calculations would have had no significance to the intergovernmental relations
experts and officials who had welcomed Rémillard's proposals. In short, the
surge in discussions about securing Quebec's formal consent to the constitution was at least partly due to a belief among politicians and officials, outside
Quebec as well as within, that the long-term interests of the Canadian federation required that action be taken.

After further tours of provincial capitals by both Quebec officials and
federal officials, focused on the five-point proposal, Brian Mulroney wrote to
the premiers identifying what he thought could be the basis of a consensus;
his federal-provincial affairs minister, Senator Lowell Murray, sent proposals
for the outstanding issues. On this basis, the first ministers met on 30 April
at the prime minister's residence on Meech Lake. Their discussions resulted
in the Meech Lake Accord, a package of constitutional revisions incorporating all of Quebec's five proposals and adding a sixth designed to placate the
demand of Alberta Premier Getty for Senate reform. Subsequently, on 13
June 1987, the first ministers agreed to a somewhat modified revision of the
accord in legal language (generally known as the Langevin Accord).[10]

A Modest Set of Changes
Despite the many claims that the Meech Lake Accord would fundamentally
change, even destroy, Canada, it was quite limited in scope, reflecting the
modest nature of the Bourassa government's proposal which inspired it.

Some of its provisions merely formalized practices and arrangements that already existed. Even where it did introduce new departures, they were quite carefully circumscribed.

The part that was to cause the greatest controversy was, of course, the 'distinct-society clause'. A purely interpretative clause, it stated that in interpreting the constitution the courts should do so in a way that is consistent with 'the recognition that Quebec constitutes within Canada a distinct society'. Moreover, it affirmed that 'the role of the legislature and Government of Quebec is to preserve and promote the distinct identity of Quebec'.[11]

At the same time, this recognition of Quebec's uniqueness was carefully balanced by a preceding clause that referred to a Canadian linguistic duality that transcends Quebec's borders. This 'duality clause' required the constitution to be interpreted in a manner consistent with 'the recognition that the existence of French-speaking Canadians, centred in Quebec but also present elsewhere in Canada, and English-speaking Canadians, concentrated outside Quebec but also present in Quebec, constitutes a fundamental characteristic of Canada.' Parliament and all the provincial legislatures were given the responsibility for preserving this 'fundamental characteristic'.[12]

So as to ensure that the clauses would be purely interpretative, a later provision declared that they were not to diminish the powers of either the federal government or the provincial governments.[13] On this basis, it is difficult to see how the distinct-society clause could have enabled Quebec to assume any jurisdictions exclusively held by the federal government. It is more likely that the distinct-society clause might have enabled the Quebec government to maintain measures within its existing jurisdictions that otherwise violated provisions of the Charter. Even then the Quebec government would have had to persuade the courts that the measure was, under the terms of section 1 of the Charter, 'demonstrably justified in a free and democratic society'. In the opinion of a leading English-Canadian constitutional authority, Peter Hogg, the section 'should probably be seen as an affirmation of sociological facts with little legal significance'.[14]

A second area of the Accord was immigration. The Accord would have had the effect of inserting in the constitution an agreement between the federal government and Quebec patterned after the Cullen-Couture Accord.[15] In effect, it would have 'constitutionalized' the existing practice, providing Quebec with a guarantee of permanence that a simple intergovernmental agreement could not. In addition to the elements of Cullen-Couture, this constitutionalized Accord would have guaranteed Quebec a proportionate share of the total numbers for immigrants set by Ottawa each year and would have allowed Quebec to take responsibility for the integration of immigrants; Ottawa would have kept exclusive responsibility for awarding citizenship.

The Accord also called for similar agreement to be negotiated with other provincial governments. Under the constitution, it should be borne in mind, immigration is concurrent, or shared by both levels of government, but Ottawa has the power to override the provinces.

A third subject of the Accord was the federal government's use of its spending power within provincial jurisdictions.[16] If a province decided not to participate in a new cost-shared program established by Ottawa in an exclusive provincial jurisdiction, then it would have been entitled to 'reasonable compensation' by the federal government. To do so, however, it would have had to maintain a 'program or initiative' of its own that was 'compatible with the national objectives'. By implication, these objectives would be set by the federal government. At the same time, Ottawa would have remained free to establish its own spending programs in jurisdictions that are exclusively provincial.

The Accord also dealt with the Supreme Court.[17] Beyond stipulating that three of the nine justices must be members of the Quebec bar, constitutionalizing a long-standing provision of the Supreme Court Act, the Accord specified that provincial governments would be allowed to draw up lists of candidates for appointment to the court. The actual appointment would be made by the federal government, but it would be obliged to choose from such a list. In the case of the three Quebec justices, Ottawa would have been obliged to choose from a list submitted by Quebec. Otherwise, it could have chosen from whichever government's list it wished. And it can be assumed that, in the case of Quebec, if Ottawa was dissatisfied with the names submitted, it could have asked for a second list.

A similar procedure was to have been adopted for the Senate: in filling a Senate vacancy, Ottawa would choose from a list of names submitted by the government of the province in question. Like Supreme Court justices, senators would be appointed for life (to age 75, as they are now) rather than for fixed terms. The Senate arrangements were to be provisional, pending a thorough Senate reform.[18]

Finally, the Accord would have altered the amending formula so that amendments involving certain aspects of Parliament and the Supreme Court, as well as the creation of new provinces or the extension of existing ones, would require the support of all provinces. Also, 'reasonable compensation' to provinces not agreeing to transfers of jurisdiction to the federal level would no longer have been restricted to matters involving education and culture.

Not only was the Accord modest in its scope, but every element had been under discussion for years in intergovernmental circles. Indeed, some of them fell considerably short of past proposals. Constitutional recognition that Quebec formed a 'distinct society' had been proposed by the Macdonald

Commission in 1985, although as part of the constitution's preamble.[19] (The phrase itself had originated in the 1960s with the Royal Commission on Bilingualism and Biculturalism.) In an 'Open Letter to the People of Quebec' signed by Pierre Trudeau on 11 July 1980, in the midst of public debate over a preamble to the constitution, Trudeau had insisted on the existence of 'two principal linguistic and cultural communities . . . with the French community having its focus and centre of gravity in Quebec'. That phrasing was considerably stronger than that of the 'duality clause'.[20] As we saw, Bill C-60, which the Trudeau government had introduced in 1978, referred to 'the Canadian French-speaking society centred in but not limited to Quebec'.[21] (Of course, the Trudeau government had never proposed to recognize Quebec as a 'distinct society'.) The immigration provisions effectively formalized a practice established during the Trudeau era, while adding provisions regarding integration of immigrants and shares of total immigrants. The provision limiting the federal spending power fell considerably short of the proposals of the Pepin-Robarts Commission and the Beige Paper and even the Trudeau government's own 1969 proposal.[22] Provincial participation in the selection of Supreme Court justices had been an element of the Victoria Charter.[23] Under Pepin-Robarts, Quebec would have had near-equality (5 of 11) in the number of justices; under the Beige Paper it would have had equality on a special constitutional bench. The procedure for Senate appointments was quite in line with previous proposals: under Trudeau's Bill C-60, half the senators would have been named independently by provincial legislatures; under both Pepin-Robarts and the Beige Paper, members of the upper body would have been appointed wholly by provincial governments and would have acted as their delegates. As for the extension of the provincial veto of amendments, it affected only four categories of changes.

Substantial Support in Quebec

Surprisingly perhaps, given its limitations, the Accord was quite well received in French Quebec. In a survey taken just after the Langevin version had been agreed to, 61 per cent of Quebec respondents said they approved of the agreement, and only 16 per cent said they disapproved.[24] The general satisfaction extended not only to such prominent federalists as Claude Ryan, who was now a member of Bourassa's cabinet, and Solange Chaput-Rolland,[25] who had been a member of the Pepin-Robarts Commission, but even people who had played key roles in the PQ government. Louis Bernard, who had been the senior civil servant under René Lévesque, and Jean-K. Samson, who had been a constitutional adviser to Lévesque, both served on a committee of the Bourassa government charged with preparing a legal version of the Accord. Even Lévesque himself had positive things to say about the Accord, citing the progress in immigration and declaring the Accord to be 'neither very good nor catastrophic'. Ultimately, he said he could not sign it until ambiguities in the text had been resolved.[26]

One reason the Accord was well received in Quebec may have been that its significance was interpreted very broadly. In an effort to persuade Quebeckers of the significance of the Accord, Bourassa had said that Meech would 'enable us to consolidate what we already have and to make even further gains'.[27] Intergovernmental Affairs Minister Gil Rémillard said that the Accord would enable Quebec to have an enhanced presence in international relations.[28]

Yet, even without exaggeration of its concrete import, the Accord, especially its distinct-society clause, *was* very important in that it broke with the systematic rejection of Quebec's demands that had marked constitutional deliberations throughout the Trudeau era. It formally recognized the Quebec government's responsibility to protect and promote Quebec's distinctiveness, which was the essential claim of Quebec nationalists. In this, the Accord represented a clear break with the Trudeau era. In a sense, the distinct-society clause harked back to the preceding era, when Lester Pearson had tried to accommodate the new Quebec, proclaiming it to be a 'nation within a nation'. At the same time, Quebeckers could believe that agreement of all first ministers to Quebec's conditions for signing the constitution, minimal as they may have been, was an admission that the 1982 isolation of Quebec had been an error, indeed an injustice.

All this did not, of course, impress firmly committed *indépendantistes*. Jacques-Yvan Morin, a prominent member of Lévesque's cabinets, denounced the Accord as a 'trap' because it did not give Quebec any additional powers.[29] Jacques Parizeau pronounced it a major setback to Quebec's traditional demands.[30] The Société St-Jean Baptiste and the Mouvement national québécois tried to rally public opposition to the Accord. Then PQ leader Pierre-Marc Johnson called 'the Meech Lake monster' a sell-out and, on that basis, rallied the party's national council behind him.[31]

These denunciations did not seem to have much resonance with the public. For Quebec francophones who still saw themselves as members of the Canadian political community, even though their primary allegiance was to Quebec, the Meech Lake Accord and English Canada's apparent support for it meant that their vision of the country was recognized and accepted. No longer were they expected to conform to the Trudeau vision. They could be Canadians on their own terms. The Accord may have been only a minimal response to their aspirations, but it was significant none the less.

Growing Opposition in English Canada

On the other hand, however modest its terms, the Accord soon became the focus of intense opposition in English Canada. Moreover, this opposition was largely rooted in precisely the feature that had endeared it to Quebeckers: its contradiction of the Trudeau vision of Canada. At first English Canadians had tended to support the Accord. In a survey conducted on 3 and 4 June 1987, approval of the Accord ranged from 57 per cent in Atlantic Canada to 46 per cent in Ontario and 47 per cent in the West. By April 1988 however, a Gallup poll found opinion evenly split among anglophones: 26 per cent in favour, 27 per cent against, and 47 per cent undecided. By November of the following year, opinion was firmly against. In March of 1990, as time was running out for the Accord, Gallup found only 19 per cent of anglophones in favour, with 51 per cent against and 30 per cent undecided.[32] Immediately after the collapse of Meech, only 30 per cent of anglophones felt that the Accord should have been ratified; among anglophones the most popular politician was Newfoundland Premier Clyde Wells, the Accord's fiercest adversary.[33]

In part, English-Canadian opposition was due to the processes that had created the Accord—negotiations among first ministers behind closed doors. Those processes were denounced as undemocratic, and especially unacceptable when they affected the basic law of the country. Citizens had not been given the proper opportunity to express their views and participate in this revision of 'their' constitution.

The fact of the matter is that Meech had been produced through the time-honoured practices of executive federalism, just like the Constitution Act, 1982. However, the Constitution Act had imposed a different set of rules for all subsequent revisions, including Meech: resolutions had to be approved not just by Parliament but by provincial legislatures. In effect, with Meech there were public debates in 10 different provincial legislatures, often with public hearings by special committees. Yet, since the Accord had been negotiated among 11 first ministers, it would have been exceedingly difficult to modify the Accord in light of these debates.[34]

The determination of citizens and groups to express their views on Meech, usually hostile ones at that, also demonstrated another consequence of 1982. Thanks to the Charter, English Canadians had acquired a sense of 'ownership' of the constitution. No longer concerned with just the jurisdictions of governments, the constitution now defined the relationship between citizens and their governments. For many English Canadians, it was indeed the 'people's package' that the Trudeau government claimed it to be. Thus, it was all the more important that politicians should not be able to dispose of the constitution on their own.[35]

In the last analysis, however, English-Canadian opposition to Meech was an attempt to protect the Trudeau vision of Canada. As Alan Cairns asserts:

> The absence of support for the Trudeau vision of Canada among first ministers and in the leadership of the three national parties was not based on an accurate reading of the sentiments of Canadians. Pan-Canadianism, support of the Charter, belief in a leading role for the central government, and a deep uneasiness at the provincializing thrust of the Accord were generously represented, indeed probably predominant, among the groups and individuals that appeared before the Joint [Parliamentary] Committee [on the Meech Lake Accord] and in other fora outside Quebec.[36]

Several provisions of the Accord were attacked as threatening the federal government's role as the 'national' government of all Canadians. In particular, a wide variety of organizations voiced concern that the federal spending power provisions would undermine Ottawa's ability to ensure that all Canadians, as Canadians, received health and social services. It would no longer be able to enforce 'national standards' on the provinces; such new programs as a national day care system would be impossible.[37] By the same token, English-Canadian critics argued that the nomination provisions for the Senate and the Supreme Court would in effect turn control over to the provincial governments.[38]

Moreover, the debate over Meech soon became enmeshed in the struggle over the Mulroney government's proposed Canada-US Free Trade Agreement. Opponents feared that it too would undermine the ability of the federal government to maintain national social services. With the adoption of the Free Trade Agreement, the bitterness among its opponents soon extended to the Meech Lake Accord as well. The connection was, of course, encouraged by the fact that, during the 1988 federal election, the large Quebec vote for the Progressive Conservatives had ensured that free trade would come into effect. (The massive PC vote in Alberta tended to be overlooked.) Through these processes, prominent figures in the English-Canadian left came to oppose Meech.[39]

Defence of a strong 'national' government in Ottawa was a central tenet of the Trudeau vision, but was not exclusive to it. However, another line of attack on the Accord was intimately linked to the Trudeau vision: opposition to the distinct-society clause. Moreover, this clause was the most important focus of English-Canadian opposition to the Accord.

From the outset, English Canadians had been troubled by the distinct-society clause. A survey taken just after the Accord had been put in its final form, the Langevin version, found that among the specific provisions of the

Accord, the distinct-society clause was the one to receive the least support of Canadians as a whole (46 per cent); 56 per cent of Canadians outside Quebec said they disapproved of it.[40] Similarly, in their analysis of a 1988 survey, Blais and Crête found that among anglophones living outside Quebec only 28 per cent responded negatively to a simple question asking their opinion of the Accord, whereas 56 per cent responded negatively to a question that indicated that the Accord recognized Quebec's distinct character.[41]

The fact of the matter is that the distinct-society clause managed to offend each of the precepts of the Trudeau vision of Canada. For such opponents of Meech as Clyde Wells, who did not hesitate to acknowledge his intellectual debt to Trudeau,[42] the clause violated the principle of a 'true' federation: the distinct-society clause 'would not and should not create a special legislative status for one province different from that of the other nine provinces'. Indeed, he warned, no such federation is likely to survive.[43]

For champions of multiculturalism, the Accord's distinct-society and duality clauses offended their idea of Canada. The parliamentary interventions of two Liberal MPs, Charles Caccia and Sergio Marchi, included statements that the Accord constituted 'a rear-view mirror vision which may have been valid two generations ago, [an] outdated [definition of Canada] . . . primarily satisfied with only depicting our people's past and our country's history. . . . Millions of Canadians are left out who do not identify with either English or French. They have no place in the Accord, and they are outside the Constitution.'[44]

For many critics, the distinct-society clause threatened the integrity of the Charter of Rights and Freedoms. Leading English-Canadian feminists feared that the distinct-society clause might lead to a downgrading of the hard-won equality provisions of the Charter. Law professor Kathleen Mahoney wrote:

> Since 1985, women have achieved remarkable advances largely due to Charter guarantees of equality before and under the law and the right to equal protection and equal benefit of the law without discrimination. . . . I suggest that the risks to women's rights in the 1987 Constitutional Accord are not slight. Rather, it is my opinion that the Accord, if passed, will likely diminish constitutional rights that Canadian women currently enjoy.[45]

Some English-Canadian feminists even argued that the distinct-society clause might lead to the oppression of Quebec women, by facilitating repressive and discriminatory measures by the Quebec government.[46] This latter line of attack earned a stern rebuke from Quebec feminists. In testimony before the joint parliamentary committee on the Meech Lake Accord,

Francine C. McKenzie, president of the Conseil du statut de la femme du Québec, declared:

> There is no doubt that the concept [of distinct society] covers basic elements such as the aim of ensuring equality between men and women, which is already recognized in Quebec. Over the past 25 years Quebec policies have reflected this principle to such an extent that it can be said that they are an inherent part of the distinct society of Quebec. Thus it would be most odd if the recognition of this distinct society were to be seen as justifying fears of legislation undermining the rights already obtained by Quebec women as part of such society.[47]

As for the Trudeau ideal of Canadian bilingualism, groups such as Parents for French were quick to see in Meech a threat to national unity. In testimony to the joint parliamentary committee on Meech, the president of Parents for French attacked the Accord's duality clause for referring to simply the preservation of linguistic duality, unlike the distinct-society clause, which assigned the Quebec government the role of both preserving and promoting Quebec's identity:

> The limitation of the constitutional obligations on the anglophone provinces to do more than preserve the linguistic character of Canada, while recognizing Quebec as a distinct society, could eventually result in a linguistic curtain being drawn around Quebec creating not a distinct society but a ghetto, ripe for the fostering of events that might again lead towards separation. . . . Emphasis on the promotion of French outside Quebec, on the other hand, would likely result in a greater outreach to Quebec by other Canadians, francophone and non-francophone, asking her to share with them their rich cultural heritage.[48]

If in fact many English Canadians framed their opposition to the Meech Lake Accord in terms of the Trudeau vision, they of course had help from Trudeau himself.[49] After the Accord had been agreed upon at Meech Lake but before it was formalized at the Langevin session, Trudeau wrote an article virulently attacking the Accord. It was published in two major newspapers under the title 'Say Goodbye to One Canada'. This was an extraordinary act for a retired political leader.

In a polemical style that evoked Trudeau's earlier career as essayist and political activist, the article attacked each of the Accord's provisions, starting with the distinct-society and duality clauses:

> Those who never wanted a bilingual Canada—Quebec separatists and western separatists—get their wish right in the first paragraphs of the Accord, with recognition of 'the existence of French-speaking Canada . . . and English-speaking Canada'. Those Canadians who fought for a single Canada, bilingual and multicultural, can say goodbye to their dream: We are henceforth to have two Canadas, each defined in terms of its language.

Trudeau even attacked the motives and character of the Accord's federal and Quebec authors: 'The provincialist politicians, whether they sit in Ottawa or in Quebec, are also perpetual losers; they don't have the stature or the vision to dominate the Canadian state, so they need a Quebec ghetto as their lair.' In particular, he castigated that 'weakling' Mulroney for caving into the premiers' demands and putting Canada on the 'fast track' to sovereignty-association.[50]

The influence of Trudeau's diatribe on English-Canadian opinion was seen in the much tougher position that Premier Peterson of Ontario adopted during the Langevin negotiations than he had in the first round of negotiations at Meech Lake.[51] In fact, apparently without acknowledging Trudeau's influence, Peterson and Manitoba Premier Howard Pawley managed to have the phrasing modified in the duality clause that Trudeau had found particularly offensive: the terms 'English-speaking Canada' and 'French-speaking Canada' adopted at Meech Lake became 'English-speaking Canadians' and 'French-speaking Canadians'.[52] Once again, Trudeau had succeeded in redefining Canadian dualism in purely individualist terms. Beyond that, the first ministers agreed to add a provision declaring that neither the duality clause nor the distinct-society clause could derogate from 'the powers, rights or privileges' of the federal and provincial governments and legislatures.

Needless to say, Trudeau was not impressed with these modifications. He followed his newspaper article with dramatic multi-hour addresses to a joint parliamentary committee on the Meech Lake Accord and to the Senate. In the Senate presentation, where he condemned all the provisions of the Accord, he heaped particular scorn on the duality clause, even with its Langevin modifications. The problem was with the very notion of duality, however expressed. Declaring that 'duality divides groups', Trudeau then proclaimed (despite the instances we have already noted):

> We did not use the expression 'French-speaking Canadians' and 'English-speaking Canadians' in any of our constitutions. We used the concept of bilingualism. Bilingualism unites people; dualism divides them. Bilingualism means you can speak to the other; duality means you can live in one lan-

guage and the rest of Canada will live in another language, and we will all be good friends, which is what Mr Lévesque always wanted.[53]

As for the distinct-society clause, Trudeau believed that if it had any consequences at all, they would be harmful and if it did not, Quebeckers would feel they had been duped.[54] With the Meech Lake Accord and its emphasis on duality and Quebec's distinctiveness and its evisceration of the national government, 'in vain, we would have dreamt the dream of one Canada'.[55]

Whatever the specific provisions of the Accord, and Trudeau had much to say about them, the underlying problem of the Accord was the vision of Canada on which it was based. Indeed, it was the one he had worked so hard to replace. Within the Trudeau vision of Canada, the Accord could only mean the destruction of the country itself.

Thanks to such aggressive leadership, English Canadians had, by the fall of 1988, turned against the Accord.[56] Many of them were to find their views confirmed in December 1988 when the Quebec government passed Bill 178, which reinstated, in a slightly modified form, the sign law that had been declared unconstitutional by the Supreme Court. By invoking the notwithstanding clause of the Charter, the Bourassa government was able to restore the provision of Bill 101 that required commercial signs to be in French only. In doing so, Bourassa was responding to strong pressure from Quebec francophones. Francophones may have been divided about the necessity of the sign law, but with the court decision the issue had become one of the integrity of Bill 101, and the ability of the Supreme Court to superimpose the Charter upon it. Thus, the court's decision served to radicalize opinion on the sign law.[57] Under these circumstances, which directly affected an institution that was central to ensuring francophone Quebec's cultural uniqueness, neither the Charter nor the Supreme Court had any authority for many Quebec francophones. Accordingly, there was strong support among Quebec francophones for Bourassa's use of the notwithstanding clause.[58] (The fact that two Quebec courts had already determined that the sign law violated Quebec's own charter was lost in the process.)

In the rest of Canada, on the other hand, Bill 178 provoked an outpouring of opposition. In the fall of 1981, the notwithstanding clause may have been adopted in order to placate such English-Canadian leaders as Allan Blakeney, but over the intervening years, the Charter had become so deeply accepted in English Canada that the notwithstanding clause had ceased to be legitimate. Beyond that, Bill 178 was a direct attack on the ideal of a bilingual Canada that many English Canadians had adopted, and Quebec seemed to be violating a contract it had entered into with the rest of the country. Of course, this was not the first time that Québécois had made it clear that they did not feel bound to accept official bilingualism at the *provincial* level. But this manifestation was perhaps the most dramatic, involving the actual suppression of the English language and any language other than French.

Once again, Quebec seemed to be repudiating the Trudeau vision of Canada. Yet, rather than leading English-Canadian opinion to start questioning the viability of this vision, let alone the national unity strategy based on it, Bill 178 seemed instead to provoke sheer anger. The bill also provided a ready pretext for abandoning the Meech Lake Accord, on the assumption that the distinct-society clause would only facilitate greater outrages by Quebec. Manitoba Premier Gary Filmon was quick to seize the opportunity and withdraw his support from the Accord, which was already widely opposed in Manitoba.

On the other hand, whether Bill 178 actually turned English-Canadian opinion against the Accord is another matter. According to analysts Blais and Crête, a clear majority of English Canadians were already opposed to the Accord by the fall of 1988, before the episode began; the size of opposition did not significantly increase after that.[59]

In the end, of course, the Accord was not adopted. When the three-year time limit had expired, the legislatures of two provinces, Manitoba and Newfoundland, had still not approved it. This outcome was largely due to chance and personalities. Two of the original signatories to the Accord, the premiers of Manitoba and New Brunswick, were defeated before their legislatures had ratified the Accord. In the case of a third province, Newfoundland, ratification had been rescinded under the new premier, Clyde Wells. Yet, those setbacks might have been overcome. If Frank McKenna, the new premier of New Brunswick had quickly ratified the Accord, rather than delaying, pressure might have built upon the two other governments to ratify it. If Manitoba's projected ratification had not been delayed by the obstruction of one MLA, Elijah Harper, then the pressure on the remaining hold-out, Newfoundland, might have been irresistible. In short, with a somewhat different chain of events the Accord might have been saved.

Yet, even if the Accord had passed, the battle had been lost. The original purpose of the Meech Lake Accord had been to repair the damage of 1982 and 'bring Quebec back into the Canadian family'. The bitter public debate over Meech had only made matters worse. Indeed, in reaction to this debate, support for sovereignty began a marked climb five months before the Accord finally collapsed.[60] Quebeckers were led to believe that the majority of English Canadians refused to recognize Quebec as a distinct entity within Canada; the polls showing enormous opposition to 'distinct society' seemed to say as much. Rightly or wrongly, they took English-Canadian rejection of the Accord to be a rejection of Quebec.

For their part, many English Canadians were embittered by Quebec's repudiation of principles that they thought had become central to Canadian nationhood, some of which had in fact originated as ostensible concessions to Quebec. The irony is that their opposition to the Accord and to Quebec was the result of a strategy that had been presented as a way to bring the country together: the Trudeau national unity strategy. Instead, it had left English Canadians and Quebec francophones more deeply divided than ever before.

Of course, a good number of other English Canadians were opposed to Meech and its distinct-society clause from sheer animosity toward Quebec and its language rather than from any allegiance to the Trudeau vision. In at least some cases, the outrage over the suppression of English-language rights in Quebec was not matched by any particular concern with French-language rights outside Quebec. The Association for the Preservation of English Canada, for example, considered Canada to be an exclusively English-language country. The problem with Meech was not the particular way it recognized the French language, but with the very notion of recognition of French in any form. But the principled opposition of Clyde Wells and others to the Accord made it easier for these groups to express their basic animosity to Quebec and the French language.[61]

After the collapse of the Meech Lake Accord, most English Canadians remained convinced that the Accord should not have been ratified. Moreover, in a November 1990 survey, which asked who 'best represent[ed] their] view of Canada', close to 60 per cent displayed their commitment to the Trudeau vision by naming Clyde Wells, Jean Chrétien, or Trudeau himself. But among Quebec respondents, only 28 per cent chose one of the three; there is every reason to believe that among francophones the percentage was considerably smaller.[62]

For many Quebec francophones, the rejection of the Accord by English Canada was equivalent to rejection of Quebec itself. In the resulting wave of anger and humiliation, support for Quebec sovereignty soared to unprecedented heights. By November 1990, it had reached 64 per cent among Quebec residents, with only 30 per cent opposed.[63]

Canada had entered an acute crisis, far worse than any in the past. At the centre of the crisis was the difference between the anglophone and francophone idea of Canada, which, though hardly new, had never before been as clearly defined. But the two different visions of Canada were not only different, but mutually exclusive: Quebeckers persisted in an attachment to Quebec, as their prior allegiance. For many English Canadians, committed to the notion of Canada as a single political community, that was not only incomprehensible but unacceptable. After all, they had become imbued with a vision of Canada that had been designed specifically to exclude any distinctive place for Quebec. What is more, thanks to the Meech Lake debate, English Canadians and Quebec francophones were now acutely aware that their ideas of Canada were diametrically opposed.

Confronted with such an overwhelming impasse, and keenly aware of how English-Canadian opinion had rallied against domination of constitutional matters by politicians, the first reaction of the federal government and most provincial governments was simply to abandon the whole question. Instead of taking action on its own, the Mulroney government appointed a special task force, composed of prominent Canadians, with Keith Spicer as its chair, to ascertain the thoughts of citizens. After extensive public meetings, it duly reported back that the citizens were deeply frustrated with the actions of their elected leaders on constitutional questions, and indeed on most matters. In particular, it said, they were displeased with official bilingualism; the commissioners called for an independent review to clear the air. It also found citizens discontented with multiculturalism, another element of the Trudeau vision. The report proposed that funding for programs of cultural preservation be eliminated and that heritage courses be restricted to young immigrant children.[64] But the commission offered no concrete directions as to how the constitutional question should be addressed.

For its part, the Bourassa government announced that, since the rest of the country had not honoured its commitment to the Meech Lake Accord, Quebec was simply withdrawing from any further constitutional talks. In a phrase pregnant with meaning, he told the National Assembly, 'Quebec is today, and forever, a distinct society, free and capable of taking charge of its destiny and development.'[65] He obviously felt a need to assuage the public's deep anger. Finally, on 4 September 1990, the government had a bill passed creating a special committee of the National Assembly on Quebec's political and constitutional future, popularly known as the Bélanger-Campeau Commission after its co-chairs Michel Bélanger and Jean Campeau.

Soon afterward, in response to the nationalist sentiments sweeping post-Meech Quebec, the Quebec Liberal Party's constitutional committee produced a document, generally known as the Allaire Report, which called for a radical devolution of powers to Quebec. The report did not specify (presumably it was indifferent) whether a similar devolution was to take place in the rest of the country. At the same time, it was crystal-clear in its rejection of the most visible manifestation of the Trudeau vision of Canada, the Charter of Rights and Freedoms with the Supreme Court of Canada as its ultimate interpreter. The report proposed that the Supreme Court no longer have jurisdiction over Quebec: the possibility of appealing cases, including Charter cases, beyond Quebec's own courts would be eliminated outright.[66]

Moreover, Quebec's own Charter of Human Rights and Freedoms would become part of a new Quebec constitution. Finally, the report proposed that a referendum be held by the autumn of 1992 either to approve an agreement with the rest of Canada based on the proposal, if there was one, or to approve Quebec sovereignty, to be coupled with an offer to the rest of Canada of economic association.[67]

The Allaire Report represented a radical shift from the Liberal Party's 1980 Beige Paper. Reflecting the nationalist mood of the party, it was adopted at a Liberal convention as official party policy, with only slight modification.[68] Still, in an attempt to limit the damage, Bourassa closed the convention with the declaration that the party in fact has 'chosen Canada', and that 'our first choice must be to develop Quebec within Canada, in a federal structure'.[69]

Two months later, the Bélanger-Campeau Commission presented its report, which gave an overview of the constitutional impasse, outlined two options, a profoundly renewed federalism and sovereignty, and called for a referendum on sovereignty by October 1992.[70]

The Bourassa government acted on the recommendation but in a manner that gave it some of the room to manoeuvre it was so desperately seeking. In June 1991, the National Assembly passed Bill 150, which required the government to hold a referendum on sovereignty in June or October of 1992. The bill also established two special committees, one to study all issues related to Quebec sovereignty and one to evaluate whatever offers for a new constitutional arrangement might be made by the federal government. Finally, in affirming the sovereignty of the National Assembly over the wording of a referendum, it effectively reserved for the government the possibility of altering the wording of the referendum by amending the law should conditions warrant.[71]

If there was any doubt at the time, it is clear in retrospect that Robert Bourassa was, as ever, committed to Quebec's remaining within the federal system.[72] Given the state of public opinion immediately after the collapse of Meech he could have led Quebec out of Canada if he had wanted to. Yet, he certainly could not ignore the public pressure for Quebec to respond to English Canada's rejection of Meech with a referendum of its own on Quebec's future. In 1991, support for sovereignty began to fall somewhat, but a majority vote for Quebec sovereignty was still a real possibility—unless the subject of the referendum could instead be a compelling offer of a new federation. The pressure on political leaders in the rest of Canada to produce such an offer could not have been greater. Yet, even then, the 'offer' that eventually did emerge, otherwise known as the Charlottetown Accord, fell far short of expectations in Quebec, including the hopes of the Bourassa government.

THE CHARLOTTETOWN ACCORD

In the fall of 1991, more than a year after Meech collapsed, the Mulroney government took the initiative by presenting its proposals for constitutional renewal. The proposals were the subject of hearings by a joint parliamentary committee, the Beaudoin-Dobbie Committee whose report, published in March 1992, approved the government's proposals with some modifications. Unlike the Meech Lake Accord, the Mulroney proposals were highly comprehensive, covering most constitutional issues under discussion. They did not, however, really address Quebec's jurisdictional demands, and Premier Bourassa felt compelled to reject them; he even declared that the report's discussion of the division of powers, 'the key question', reflected 'an overbearing federalism'.[73]

Confronted with rejection of the Beaudoin-Dobbie Report not just in Quebec but in other quarters as well, the Mulroney government yielded to demands by provincial premiers, aboriginal leaders, and the heads of government of the two territories to be full partners in developing constitutional proposals. The ensuing 'multilateral' negotiations involved the federal government, provincial governments, territorial leaders, and leaders of the four main aboriginal groups—but not the Quebec government. The Bourassa government persisted in the attitude it had adopted after the collapse of Meech: rather than participate in any more constitutional negotiations it would wait for the leaders of the rest of the country to formulate an offer they were prepared to support.

This new round of constitutional negotiations was confronted with two competing agendas. In Quebec, the continuing resentment at the rejection of Meech by English-Canadian public opinion fuelled a sense that to offset this 'humiliation' any new constitutional package would have to go beyond Meech—it would have to be 'Meech-plus'. The Allaire Report had set the tone for these new expectations with its recommendations for a major devolution of powers to Quebec and exclusion of Quebec from the Charter and the Supreme Court. Bourassa had already denounced Beaudoin-Dobbie because it did not enhance Quebec's powers.

On the other hand, any new package had to be acceptable to the rest of Canada in a way that Meech manifestly was not. This meant addressing directly the needs and aspirations of other Canadians. Indeed, the new negotiations were widely touted as a 'Canada Round', to be distinguished from

the 'Quebec Round' that had produced Meech. Any new package also had
to be less offensive than Meech had been to the idea of Canada prevailing
outside Quebec, in other words, to the Trudeau vision. The Meech debate
had demonstrated that English Canadians were acutely sensitive to any differentiation between themselves and Quebec. It also had revealed a deep
desire for the federal government to be able to fulfill its proper responsibilities as a 'national' government.

English Canadians' attitudes regarding the constitutional question were
also shaped by a greatly heightened sympathy for the demands of aboriginal
peoples. The crisis in Oka, Quebec, in the summer of 1990, triggered by a
confrontation between Mohawks and the Quebec provincial police, had
convinced many English Canadians that any constitutional revision would
have to meet the demands of the aboriginal peoples. Indeed, a good number
of English Canadians argued that aboriginal demands were far more urgent
than Quebec's. The presence of aboriginal leaders in the new round of constitutional negotiations, for the first time in Canadian history, ensured that
aboriginal concerns would be given a favourable hearing.

Despite the complexity of negotiations involving the federal government,
nine provincial governments, two territories, and four aboriginal groups, an
agreement was in fact reached on 7 July 1992. Although the Mulroney government's original proposals may have been the starting point, there were significant modifications and departures. The fact of an agreement was a surprise
to many, not the least of whom was Prime Minister Mulroney.[74] But it was
possible precisely because the Bourassa government was absent.[75] In effect,
the 7 July agreement was English Canada's constitutional project. Indeed,
there is good reason to believe that if a referendum on the Accord had been
held in those provinces, it would have passed. By the same token, the Accord
was a highly circumscribed response to Quebec's demands.[76]

The 7 July Accord did reiterate the Meech Lake Accord's distinct-
society clause requiring that constitutional interpretation take account of
Quebec's status as a 'distinct society'. This was a *sine qua non* of any post-
Meech response to Quebec. Still, the framers of the Accord were keenly aware
of how unpopular the clause was in English Canada. The Alberta minister of
intergovernmental affairs had tried in vain to have the clause restricted to the
Accord's preamble: 'The reintroduction of these two words "distinct society"
in the proposal could have an explosive impact politically. . . . In the hands
of Mr Trudeau or someone like that, it could destroy the whole process.'[77]

Yet, if the framers of the agreement were bound to include the clause,
given expectations in Quebec, they at least could narrow its application. This
time, then, it was to apply, not to the whole constitution, as with Meech, but
only to the Charter. Beyond that, in an effort to weaken the recognition of

Quebec as a 'distinct society', they also inserted a reference to 'distinct society' in a 'Canada clause' that would 'express fundamental Canadian values'. There, 'distinct society' was to appear as one of eight different 'characteristics' that should guide the courts in interpreting the constitution. Needless to say, there was no response to the Allaire Report's demand that Quebec be excluded from the Supreme Court's jurisdiction.

As for the division of powers, the most important item on Quebec's agenda, Ottawa's prerogatives were carefully protected. By and large, any strengthening of provincial power was in areas already under provincial jurisdiction. Perhaps the clearest enhancement of provincial power was in the 'six sisters': urban affairs, tourism, recreation, housing, mining, and forestry. There, the provinces could oblige the federal government to withdraw completely. Yet, not only are these all areas of exclusive provincial jurisdiction, but they were areas in which federal activity was in any event minimal. The reservation and disallowance powers would have been eliminated, but they had long been dormant.

The Accord addressed another of Quebec's demands by giving provincial governments the right to oblige the federal government to withdraw from training and labour market development activities. However, it gave the federal government the responsibility for setting national objectives, through negotiation with the provinces, that the provinces would be bound to respect:

> There should be a constitutional provision for an ongoing federal role in the establishment of national policy objectives for the national aspects of labour market development. National labour market objectives would be established through a process which could be set out in the Constitution including the obligation for presentation to Parliament for debate.[78]

In the case of cultural affairs, another long-standing theme in Quebec's demands, the agreement called for a constitutional amendment specifying that 'provinces should have exclusive jurisdiction over cultural matters within the provinces', but it was careful to stipulate that the proposed amendment would also recognize 'the continuing responsibility of the federal government in Canadian cultural matters. The federal government should retain responsibility for national cultural institutions, including grants and contributions delivered by these institutions.'[79] To be sure, the Accord did incorporate the spending power and immigration provisions of the Meech Lake Accord, along with its amending procedure.

At the same time, the Accord of 7 July seriously addressed a number of matters that *were* on the agenda of English Canada. The Canada clause spelled out the many values that all Canadians held in common, including parlia-mentary democracy, federalism, equality of the provinces and racial, ethnic, and gender equality. It proposed a statement of principles, not enforceable in courts, that would spell out basic social services and collective bargaining rights that all Canadians should enjoy while also supporting measures to strengthen the Canadian economic union. As with Meech, the Supreme Court's authority would be entrenched, and judges would be appointed by the federal government from names submitted by the provinces. In particu-lar, the agreement addressed aboriginal concerns in an unprecedented man-ner, recognizing 'an inherent right to self-government' for aboriginal peoples and declaring aboriginal governments to be 'one of three orders of govern-ment in Canada'.

While maintaining the federal government's role as a 'national' govern-ment, the agreement also sought to address the strong grievances of, in par-ticular, western Canadians over the way the federal government functioned. The route was, of course, Senate reform. It was a matter about which the Trudeau government had been relatively indifferent. Yet, the formula for reform—equality of the provinces—was fully consistent with the Trudeau vision. Indeed, Trudeau's disciple, Clyde Wells, had joined the western pre-miers in promoting the scheme for a triple-E Senate: equal, elected, and effective. The Senate was to be composed of an equal number of elected rep-resentatives (eight) from each province, plus two from each territory and an undetermined number of aboriginal representatives. Moreover, it had a clear promise of being 'effective', since a simple majority could veto bills 'that involve[d] fundamental tax policy changes directly related to natural resources'; on most other bills, 60 per cent could force reconciliation and, if needed, a joint sitting of the House and Senate; 70 per cent could veto a bill outright.[80]

In short, the 7 July agreement was faithful to the constitutional agendas prevailing outside Quebec. It respected the clearly-stated desire of most English Canadians that the powers of the federal government not be funda-mentally weakened. It embraced the project of constitutional change that had the most support in the rest of the country: the triple-E Senate. Finally, it effectively met the demand of aboriginal peoples for self-government. At the same time, its response to Quebec's agenda went little beyond incorporating the elements of Meech; indeed, it sought to rein in Meech's recognition of Quebec's distinctiveness.

In the volatile atmosphere of post-Meech Quebec, that was not enough: only a substantial increase in the powers of the Quebec government would do. Not only did the 7 July Accord not grant such powers, but its project of a triple-E Senate would have reduced Quebec's Senate representation from

25 per cent to 10 per cent. At the same time, its provisions for aboriginal self-government led Quebec officials to fear that arrangements such as the James Bay Agreement might be endangered.

As a result, prominent Quebec federalists rejected the 7 July Accord outright. Claude Castonguay declared that the Accord reflected 'a vision which is that of anglophone Canada, based on equality of the provinces; an increased control by small provinces of central institutions and, despite appearances, a reinforcement of central power.' Since the division of powers was essentially 'unchanged', Castonguay concluded, 'In my opinion, it's a regression'.[81] The sentiment was echoed by editorial writers. Even francophone members of the Mulroney government denounced the agreement[82]. Reportedly, Bourassa had counted upon the 'multilateral' negotiations failing, and officials in the Mulroney government had been drawing up a unilateral offer that would be satisfactory for Quebec.[83] Now, he was confronted with a *fait accompli*: English Canada had decided what kind of a constitution it wanted.

Accordingly, Bourassa entered into a new round of negotiations in an effort to make the agreement satisfactory to Quebec, but, as the terms of the final agreement, the Charlottetown Accord, were to reveal, the most he could do was reduce the damage. The Accord remained devoid of any serious response to Quebec's agenda.

Instead of adding elements desired by Quebec, the main strategy for altering the 7 July Accord to accommodate Quebec was to dilute a major element of what was already there, the Senate reform so coveted by western Canada and, to a lesser extent, by the Atlantic provinces. For good measure, Quebec's (and Ontario's) representation in the House of Commons was expanded. In addition, the wording of the aboriginal self-government provisions was made satisfactory to Bourassa, if not to all members of the Quebec delegation.[84] Also, the ability of Quebec, or any other province, to veto changes to central institutions was strengthened.[85] But there was no significant expansion of the powers or general status of the Quebec government.

Unlike the Senate reform agreed to on 7 July, the Charlottetown version fell far short of the triple-E model. Representation would indeed have been 'equal', with the same number (six) of representatives from each province, plus an indeterminate number of aboriginal representatives. But it would not necessarily have been elected: to placate Premier Bourassa, provincial legislatures had the option of appointing the representatives. And, in terms of the powers it would wield, the Senate was much less likely to be 'effective'. Although the Senate could still veto, by a majority vote, bills taxing natural resources, it could no longer veto (by 70 per cent) most other measures, as in the 7 July agreement. Bills rejected in the Senate would go to joint sittings, where Senators would be outnumbered by MPs five to one. To add insult to injury, in the House, central Canadian representation was to be increased by 36 seats, from 59 per cent to 62.3 per cent.[86]

As for the division of powers, Bourassa's efforts had little effect. His main proposal, which dealt with the federal spending power, would have extended the provisions in the agreement, themselves derived from Meech, to *any* spending by Ottawa within a provincial jurisdiction, whether on a shared-cost or independent basis.[87] Presumably, it would have affected such wholly federal programs as family allowances and old age pensions. The proposal was dismissed outright by the other first ministers, most of whom energetically defended the federal spending power. Moreover, none of them had any inclination to discuss new elements at that late stage, especially after the adjustments to the Senate and House, which, ostensibly, were concessions to Quebec. In effect, the deal was set.[88] In the end, only two minor additions were made to accommodate Quebec's objections to the division of powers: a commitment to establish a general framework to guide the use of the federal spending power and a commitment to negotiate an agreement to co-ordinate and harmonize the regulation of telecommunications.[89]

In effect, Quebec had to settle for the treatment of powers already contained in the 7 July agreement. Yet, as we have seen, these were of little significance, out of deference to English Canada's wish to maintain a strong federal government. The most substantial changes, the 'six sisters', which had been drawn up by Ottawa, did not really correspond to Quebec's list. The measures regarding manpower and culture did address Quebec's concerns, but each had important qualifications that ensured a continued federal role. Beyond that, all that remained were the spending power, immigration, and amendment provisions drawn from the Meech Lake Accord,[90] plus the elimination of the long-defunct powers of reservation and disallowance.

The treatment of Quebec's status as a 'distinct society' followed the same restrictive lines as in the 7 July Accord. Quebec's 'distinct society' remained one of eight enumerated 'fundamental characteristics' of Canada. In addition, the nature of Quebec's uniqueness was narrowed by the listing of its main elements: 'Quebec constitutes within Canada a distinct society, which includes a French-speaking majority, a unique culture and a civil law tradition.'[91] In effect, the delineation was based upon a traditional conception of Quebec's distinctiveness: French-language majority, distinct culture, and the civil code; there was no reference to the distinctive economic and social institutions of contemporary Quebec. Finally, just to make certain that the Canada clause, including the 'distinct society' reference, could not directly affect the division of powers, the Charlottetown Accord adopted Meech's provision that nothing in the clause could derogate from 'the powers, rights or privileges' of Parliament and the government of Canada, or their provincial counterparts (while also referring to aboriginal governments and rights).[92]

The twin to the distinct-society clause, the 'duality clause', also was modified to make it more acceptable outside Quebec and in line with the Trudeau vision. In response to pressure from the francophone minorities, the wording was strengthened: 'Canadians and their governments are committed to the vitality and development of official language minority communities throughout Canada.'[93] Concerned about obligations to Quebec's anglophone community that might stem from this wording, Quebec insisted that in the French version 'committed' appear as *attachés* rather than the more correct *engagés*.[94]

In fact, the 7 July agreement and the Charlottetown Accord dealt with the division of powers and the status of Quebec within the same narrow limits as the federal government's constitutional proposals of October 1991 and the February 1992 report of the joint parliamentary committee (the Beaudoin-Dobbie Committee) established to assess those proposals. Premier Bourassa had denounced that package as nothing less than 'an overbearing federalism'. Six months later, despite Quebec's new participation in negotiations, nothing had changed. As Peter Russell concludes, 'The division of powers, always the centre of attention for Quebecers engaged in the renewal of federalism, basically stood as in previous drafts.'[95]

It could even be argued that Quebec's clearest 'gain', to use one of Robert Bourassa's favourite terms, was not in the division of powers, but in representation in central institutions. Under the Charlottetown Accord, representation in the House of Commons was to be increased for Quebec from 75 to 93. In addition, Quebec was to be guaranteed, in perpetuity, 25 per cent of the seats of the House. Beyond that, a majority of francophone senators in the new Senate was required on any matter that 'materially affect[ed] the French language or culture in Canada'. (To be sure, francophone senators would not necessarily come from Quebec.)

Although those changes were perhaps the most substantial of all the alterations to the 7 July agreement, representation in central institutions had not been a priority of the Quebec government. In fact, *reduced* representation might have been acceptable if traded off against enhanced powers for Quebec. The Quebec government had not even asked for the guarantee of 25 per cent seats in the House of Commons. Apparently, it was proposed by Saskatchewan Premier Roy Romanow.[96]

There were, in fact, ways in which Quebec's demand for enhanced powers could have been met without a general weakening of the federal government. But this would have meant differentiating between Quebec and the rest of Canada—a cardinal sin in the Trudeau vision. Under schemes of asymmetry, any decentralization of powers could go to Quebec alone; Ottawa would continue to perform these functions in the rest of the country. In effect, English Canada could continue to have as strong a federal government as it wished.

Asymmetrical federalism, as a basis for responding to Quebec's demands, had in fact been endorsed at the first of five public conferences organized by the federal government during the winter of 1992:

> The majority feeling about the evolution of Canadian Division of Powers appeared to be that Canada should support Québec by accepting the need for the government of that province to exercise a wider range of provincial powers, but in a constitution flexible enough to allow for the desire for citizens in other provinces for a federal government able both to maintain national standards and to address diversity and regional disparities.[97]

Indeed,

> the term [asymmetry] was used recurrently, especially (but not exclusively) when discussion turned to the implications of Quebec's possible assumption of powers that would remain in federal hands for the rest of Canada. There was a belief that diversity needs to be allowed regardless of whether asymmetry is the result.[98]

While there apparently was clear agreement on Quebec assuming an asymmetrical status, the conference report did not take a definitive position on just how that was to be accomplished and whether it was to be reserved to Quebec alone.[99] In general, the preferred mechanism for bringing about an asymmetrical status for Quebec was concurrence with provincial paramountcy, or shared jurisdiction but with a provincial option to override Ottawa.[100]

Asymmetry does raise an institutional question that Pierre Trudeau used to pursue with relish: how could Quebec MPs vote on measures that, under asymmetry, did not apply to Quebec? How could they hold cabinet portfolios that involved programs that did not function in Quebec? The problem should not be exaggerated: after all, Quebec MPs have voted on laws dealing with the Canada Pension Plan, even though Quebec has its own Quebec Pension Plan, and three Quebec MPs (Monique Bégin, Marc Lalonde, and Benoît Bouchard) have even been responsible for these programs as ministers of health and welfare. In any event, at the time, various commentators, including Tom Kent, Lester Pearson's principal adviser, were suggesting ways in which this could be handled.[101] For instance, Quebec MPs might simply not vote on such measures, which would not be considered questions of confidence.

Moreover, as some commentators pointed out, on this basis the grievances of the west against central Canadian domination would receive at least some response. Without Quebec MPs' voting, MPs from the western and Atlantic provinces would have a majority. In that case a triple-E Senate might not even be necessary.[102]

If it were, it might have been made acceptable to Quebec by coupling it with a major expansion in Quebec's powers. In fact, the documents prepared by top Quebec civil servants suggest that Senate reform might have been acceptable to Quebec if it had been accompanied by additional powers for the Quebec government:

> Owing to its distinct character, Quebec would have difficulty accepting a Senate reform in which its representation was significantly reduced. Such a reduction of Quebec's Senate representation might be justified hypothetically only by granting a particular status that would revise the division of powers to Quebec's liking.[103]

There appears to have been no serious discussion of these possibilities. Apparently Federal Constitutional Affairs Minister Joe Clark simply canvassed his fellow politicians. Once they had told him that asymmetry would be unpopular in English Canada, they did not pursue it any further.[104]

In effect, the politicians were intimidated by English Canada's attachment to the principle of equality of the provinces, which was partly a legacy of the Trudeau era. As a consequence, however, the ministers had to try to handle Quebec's demands with devices that not only had no support in Quebec but were also deeply unpopular in English Canada. Rather than a trade-off between Quebec's demands for additional powers and western Canada's demands for a triple-E Senate, the result was a package that did not meet either demand and did not give either Quebec or the western and Atlantic provinces any reason to support it.

The Referendum

Bourassa, who was determined that the referendum he was committed to would deal, not with sovereignty, but with offers of a 'renewed federalism', consented to the only terms available. On 26 August 1992 all the parties signed what became known as the Charlottetown Accord. Recognizing that

Quebec would be holding a referendum on the Accord, and facing considerable pressure in other parts of the country to hold one, the first ministers decided to hold a national referendum on 26 October 1992.

Despite the best efforts of its various authors, the Accord was resoundingly rejected both in Quebec and in the rest of the country. In Quebec, among valid votes 56.7 per cent were No (about two-thirds of the francophone voters[105]) and 43.3 per cent were Yes; in addition, 2.2 per cent of the ballots were spoiled—far more than in any other province. Outside Quebec, 54.3 per cent voted No and 45.7 per cent Yes. The proposition was approved in only Newfoundland, Prince Edward Island, New Brunswick, and Ontario (where it won by only 50.1 per cent). Once again, an attempt to revise the constitution, ostensibly designed to obtain Quebec's formal consent to the document, ended in a débâcle. Unlike Meech, however, this package was rejected in Quebec too!

The Yes forces were plagued by a good number of problems: a poorly conceived advertising campaign; disputes among the three major parties and between them and citizen activists; the failure of some political leaders to campaign as vigorously for the cause as they might have; the inability or unwillingness of many voters to ignore their antipathy toward government leaders; and so on. But the primary explanation lies with the terms of the Accord itself.[106]

From the outset, the Accord was attacked in Quebec for failing to address the essence of Quebec's demands: additional powers. Even federalists tended to think that Premier Bourassa could have done better. Jean Allaire, the author of the Quebec Liberal Party's constitutional position, denounced the Accord for not giving Quebec the additional powers it needed. He was joined in this by Mario Dumont, president of the Liberal Party youth wing. The two of them led a number of other Liberal dissidents in a 'Réseau des libéraux pour le non'.

The voters' doubts were confirmed when the transcripts of a cellular telephone conversation between two prominent Quebec officials, closely involved in the negotiations, were made public. The negotiators expressed their regret that Bourassa had 'caved in' to the English-Canadian premiers and their disbelief that he would have agreed to the Accord. One of them, who had been deputy minister for Quebec's relations with the rest of Canada, called the Accord 'a national disgrace. . . . Monsieur Bourassa should have taken a plane right away and left. What a humiliation!'[107] At the same time, survey analysis also confirms that Quebec voters were unimpressed by the provision guaranteeing 25 per cent of seats in the House of Commons.[108] According to André Blais's analysis of survey results: 'In our Quebec sample, 43 per cent said that in their view Quebec was a loser in the agreement, while only 26 per cent perceived Quebec to be a winner. Even among those opposed to sovereignty, 29 per cent had come to the conclusion that Quebec had lost. This perception had a powerful impact on the vote of non-sovereigntists.'[109] Not surprisingly, then, support for the Accord among Quebec francophones fell steadily over the course of the debate; at the outset the sides had been evenly divided.

As for the rest of Canada, a major reason for the opposition in western Canada was the limited powers of the Senate. Supporters of the Accord could argue that the reformed Senate would have great influence since the members would be elected, relatively few in number, and, given their exclusion from the cabinet, could concentrate on their Senate tasks. And in a joint sitting the Senate might prevail if it remained cohesive and the government's majority in the House were narrow. But arguments like those were far too subtle for the average voter. And Quebec's expanded representation in the House could only be all the more galling to western Canadians, given the reductions in the Senate's powers.[110]

Some survey analyses suggest that the Senate issue had little direct influence on the average western Canadian voter, as opposed to opinion leaders, although this may reflect indifference to the stripped-down reform contained in the Accord rather than indifference to the issue itself.[111] Even so, the fact remains that the Senate issue had an enormous indirect effect on the western Canadian vote since it was the deficiencies of the Accord's Senate proposal that virtually forced the Reform Party to declare itself against the Accord. Beyond that, surveys do confirm that in western Canada, and everywhere else outside Quebec, Quebec's guarantee of 25 per cent of the seats in the House of Commons was enormously unpopular.[112] More generally, in every province other than Quebec, respondents gave 'the concessions to Quebec' as the basis of their opposition far more often than any other factor.[113]

Another enormous liability of the Charlottetown Accord in English Canada was that it contained the provisions that had made Meech so unpopular in English Canada, most notably the distinct-society clause. However much it may have been limited and surrounded by a host of other 'fundamental characteristics', the distinct-society clause was still there.[114] Once again, the Trudeau vision of Canada was offended; and, once again, to make certain that all Canadians saw this, Trudeau himself intervened with a major public speech.

Beginning with an attack on the notion of collective rights, Trudeau contended that the Canada clause created a hierarchy of citizens. The distinct-society clause created 'category number one, the first and most important one', enabling the National Assembly to act on the collective rights of the francophone majority at the expense of other Quebeckers. The second category was aboriginal peoples, whose governments would be empowered to use the notwithstanding clause, thus ensuring that the clause would remain part of the Charter in perpetuity. As for the 'duality clause', he noted the weakness of the French *attachement* but declared that even the 'commitment' of the English version was meaningless. Proceeding through the rest of the Accord, he concluded with the thought that with a Yes vote Quebec's blackmail would continue and that 'this mess deserves a big No'.[115]

After Trudeau's speech, support for the Accord outside Quebec plummeted by a full 20 percentage points. Apparently many of Trudeau's English-Canadian followers had supported the Accord in the mistaken belief that he did. After they learned otherwise, they changed their minds, and by the end of the campaign they were more likely to oppose the Accord than were voters who disliked Trudeau or were indifferent to him.[116]

With such a resounding popular rejection of the Charlottetown Accord, there has been a temptation among commentators and analysts to conclude that the whole question is beyond repair and that the constitution simply cannot be revised so as to obtain Quebec's consent. Both the minimalist approach of Meech and the comprehensive approach of Charlottetown ended in disaster. The question remains, however, whether a different approach might have had a better chance. Granted that Meech was not enough to win the support of English Canada and a 'Canada Round' was necessary, might the Charlottetown Accord have been successful if in fact it had responded directly to what the different parts of Canada were demanding?

As we have seen, Quebec's wish for more powers could have been accommodated without wholesale decentralization. Such asymmetry might have been acceptable to other parts of Canada if it clearly benefited them, for example, by restricting voting by Quebec MPs, or if it had been coupled with a meaningful Senate reform. By the same token, with a real devolution of powers, Quebeckers might even have been ready to forgo the distinct-society clause. To be sure, the leaders of English Canada would have had a 'hard' sell in some parts of the country, but at least they could have pointed to concrete benefits. As it was, Quebec had entered the negotiations seeking asymmetry in powers; instead it received asymmetry in the House of Commons, which was of little consequence to Québécois but of enormous consequence—all negative—to the rest of the country.

Of course, one question that still remains: the 'Trudeau factor'. Asymmetry in powers would have evoked only too clearly the 'special status' that Trudeau had campaigned against for so long. Many English Canadians might well have agreed with him that it offended their idea of Canada just as much as did recognition of Quebec as a 'distinct society'. To that extent, the kind of accommodation that had been possible years before, under the leadership of Lester Pearson and others, may no longer have been available.

THE 1993 FEDERAL ELECTION

Like the collapse of Meech, the failure of the Charlottetown Accord left a profound mark on Canadian politics. Indeed, it closely shaped the results of the next federal election, one year later. The Liberals formed a majority government, led by Jean Chrétien, one of Trudeau's most faithful disciples. But for the first time in this century, the Liberals formed a government without a majority in Quebec, where they won only 19 of 75 seats and 33 per cent of the popular vote.

Instead, the Bloc Québécois, under Lucien Bouchard, won 54 seats and 49.3 per cent of the popular vote. It had become the party of Quebec francophones, winning the votes of about 60 per cent of them.[117] Officially committed to the goal of Quebec sovereignty, the Bloc had based its campaign on the failure of Canadian political institutions to accommodate Quebec's demands, and on Chrétien's personal involvement in both the 1982 patriation and the failure of Meech. By voting massively for the Bloc, Quebec francophones could not have demonstrated more clearly their rejection of the Trudeau vision of Canada.[118]

In the rest of Canada, the Liberals received strong support in Ontario, winning all but one seat and 53 per cent of the popular vote. They also did well in the Atlantic provinces and Manitoba. Yet, the vote in the west reflected both the continued impact of the Charlottetown débâcle and the limits to English-Canadian support for the Trudeau vision. Building upon its successful campaign against the Accord, the Reform Party won overwhelming majorities in Alberta and British Columbia. Indeed its popular vote in the country as a whole was 18.7 per cent, well ahead of both the Bloc and the Progressive Conservatives. Although it shared some elements of the Trudeau vision, such as the absolute equality of the provinces, Reform had expressed clear opposition to official bilingualism and multiculturalism. Reformers also had decidedly mixed feelings about the Charter of Rights and Freedoms.[119]

Further magnifying the impact of the Bloc's and Reform's attacks on the Trudeau vision was the functioning of the electoral system. Not only did it inflate Quebec's share of seats in the House, with the result that the Bloc formed the Official Opposition, but it discriminated heavily against the Progressive Conservatives, whose popular vote of 16 per cent was rewarded with only two seats in the House!

In short, the election had produced a Parliament that closely reflected the divisions that the Trudeau strategy had created in the country. With Jean Chrétien as prime minister, the government was deeply wedded to the Trudeau vision. The Official Opposition, on the other hand, was formally committed to sovereignty, and much of its electoral support was based on continuing resentment of Trudeau's constitutional actions in 1982. Reform, the second-largest opposition party with 52 seats, was opposed to some of the federal government's most important measures, such as multiculturalism and official bilingualism. Yet it shared with the Trudeau vision of Canada a firm commitment to the equality of the provinces and a deep opposition to any recognition of Quebec's distinctiveness. That ensured that Reform could not offer a viable alternative approach to Canadian unity.

In sum, each of the two efforts to repair the damage of constitutional patriation without Quebec's consent ended in a débâcle. In both cases, a large part of the reason was the acceptance by English Canada but continued rejection by Quebec, of the Trudeau vision of Canada that patriation had been intended to entrench.

The Meech Lake Accord may have represented the minimum conditions under which Quebec would have accepted the new constitution, but, especially with its distinct-society clause, it still violated the Trudeau vision. For that reason it was unacceptable to the overwhelming majority of English Canadians. So even if the Accord had passed, it could not have reconciled Quebec with the rest of Canada, as it was intended to do.

The Charlottetown Accord was designed to be less offensive to the Trudeau vision, attempting, for example, to rein in the scope of Quebec's distinctiveness with its distinct-society clause. But it did not give Quebec the additional powers that had become crucial in the radicalized opinion of post-Meech Quebec. Through asymmetry in government powers, the Accord might have satisfied Quebec without violating English Canadians' continued desire for a strong 'national' government. But what might have been possible in the 1960s, when the Pearson government had pioneered asymmetry, was no longer possible after the Trudeau orthodoxy had made its inroads in English Canada. Instead of applying asymmetry to federal–provincial relations, the Charlottetown Accord applied it to representation in the House of Commons, guaranteeing Quebec 25 per cent of the seats and thereby ensuring that the Accord would be rejected in much of English Canada.

In each case, Trudeau himself intervened to make it absolutely clear to Canadians just how these accords violated the conception of Canada that he had struggled so hard to put in place. And in each case English-Canadian support for the proposed accord plummeted.

Those two episodes led directly to the election in 1993 of a Liberal government that depended on English Canada for its support and an Official Opposition that was committed to sovereignty. However, the most dramatic demonstration of the failure of the Trudeau strategy for national unity was yet to come, in a new referendum on Quebec sovereignty.

CHAPTER 9

The 1995
Quebec Referendum:
Making Sovereignty
a Real Possibility

As we have seen, Quebec francophones reacted swiftly and bitterly to the collapse of the Meech Lake Accord. English Canadians' rejection of the Accord, and especially the distinct-society clause, was taken as no less than a rejection of Quebec itself. As support for Quebec sovereignty surged to unprecedented heights, pressure built on the Bourassa government to hold a referendum on Quebec sovereignty. Indeed, the Quebec Liberal Party's own constitutional committee called for such a referendum, and the party formally agreed. The Bélanger-Campeau Commission took the same position. Committed as ever to keeping Quebec in Canada, Bourassa succeeded in making the referendum focus not on sovereignty but on 'renewed federalism', thanks to the last-minute production of the Charlottetown Accord, inadequate as it may have been. To be sure, the referendum was defeated, but at least the encounter with sovereignty was avoided.

None the less, in the fall of 1994 the prospect of a vote on sovereignty re-emerged once again. This time the Quebec government itself was determined that Quebeckers should vote on sovereignty, and that they should approve it. The Parti Québécois was back in power.

A NEW REFERENDUM ON SOVEREIGNTY

Support for Sovereignty
Support for sovereignty had slipped back from its post-Meech heights, when by some measures 60 per cent or more of Quebeckers were in favour. But it still remained higher than before Meech.[1]

As one would expect, attitudes toward Quebec sovereignty are closely determined by feelings about Quebec and about Canada. An analysis of 1991 survey data[2] found that among the approximately 40 per cent of Quebec francophones who were attached primarily to Quebec, most were sovereigntists. Another third of francophones were divided in their loyalty between Quebec and Canada and were strongly federalist. This leaves a final group, about 25 per cent, which was slightly more attached to Quebec than to Canada and was equally divided between supporters of sovereignty and supporters of federalism. Many Quebeckers who are strongly attached to Quebec feel some attachment to Canada as well. But, as we have seen, the Trudeau vision of Canada requires primary attachment to Canada. To that extent, the only option left for people who identify primarily with Quebec is sovereignty.

Support for sovereignty does not seem to be much influenced by calculations of the costs and benefits of federalism; collective identity is far more important. None the less, countless studies have shown that Quebeckers who identify strongly with Quebec are much less likely to support sovereignty if they believe it would have serious economic costs. And most Quebec francophones think it would. While they believe sovereignty would strengthen the situation of the French language in Quebec, they tend to be pessimistic about the economic consequences of sovereignty, especially if there is no economic association with Canada.[3]

The Parizeau Government and Sovereignty

The first Lévesque government had sought to dispel those doubts by moving slowly to a referendum and by linking sovereignty to a comprehensive economic association with the rest of Canada. The long delay in holding the first referendum probably worked against the PQ's option. It allowed time for the federalists to organize their counter-offensive, for tensions to develop between the PQ government and party members, and so on. The delay also gave the economic and political élites outside Quebec a chance to reject the very idea of association, thus undermining the credibility of sovereignty. The Parizeau leadership was determined to avoid those mistakes. This time, a PQ government would hold a referendum within six months of assuming power and would define sovereignty simply, without extensive links with Canada.

But this bold commitment to sovereignty apparently robbed the Parti Québécois of some of its potential electoral support.[4] In the provincial election of 12 September 1994, the PQ won only 44.7 per cent of the popular vote, although that gave them 77 of the 125 seats. The Liberals, under the firmly federalist leadership of Daniel Johnson, received almost as many votes, 44.4 per cent, but only 47 seats. The bulk of the remaining votes (6.5 per cent) were won by the Action démocratique du Québec (ADQ), led by Mario

Dumont. Dumont, who was the only ADQ candidate to be elected, had left the Liberal Party in protest over Bourassa's consent to the Charlottetown Accord, but he now advocated a new Quebec–Canada partnership that fell well short of the PQ's version of sovereignty.[5]

The new Parizeau government proceeded with its declared strategy. Three months later, on 6 December 1994, it released the draft of a bill to be placed before the National Assembly. It was to come into force one year after a successful referendum unless the Assembly approved an earlier date. The draft bill began with the declaration that 'Quebec is a sovereign country'; it defined sovereignty as the exclusive power to pass laws, collect taxes, and sign agreements with other states. Other provisions of the bill affirmed that as a sovereign state Quebec would keep its existing boundaries, use the Canadian dollar as its currency, grant Quebec citizenship to all Canadian citizens living in Quebec while allowing them to retain Canadian citizenship, apply for membership in the United Nations and other international organizations, and apply existing Canadian laws in its territory unless they were repealed or amended by the National Assembly. In addition, it would adopt a new constitution that would guarantee 'the English-speaking community that its identity and institutions will be preserved' and recognize 'the right of aboriginal nations to self-government' while, in both cases, remaining 'consistent with the territorial integrity of Quebec'. The draft bill authorized the government to conclude, 'with the Government of Canada, an agreement the purpose of which is to maintain an economic association between Quebec and Canada', but it did not give any indication of the scope or terms of such an agreement.[6]

In short, under the Parizeau government's definition of sovereignty, Quebec was to assume all the powers normally held by a sovereign state. At the same time, it was not at all clear what kind of economic association Quebec would offer to the rest of Canada.

The government showed that it intended to move quickly to hold its referendum. The draft bill was to be circulated to all households in Quebec. A series of consultations were to be held in 16 regions of Quebec as well as among young people and senior citizens. The results of these consultations were to be presented to a special committee of the National Assembly, which would decide on the final version of the bill to be presented to the Assembly. These various stages were to be completed in a matter of months. By all indications, the government intended to hold the referendum in May or June of 1995, assuming it was in a position to win.

Apparently, the Parizeau government believed that by acting so resolutely and defining sovereignty so clearly it could inspire Quebeckers to have a new confidence in sovereignty and in themselves and could persuade them to forget their apprehensions over sovereignty. Surveys continued to show, however, that only about 40 per cent of Quebec residents would support sovereignty without an economic association; about 55 per cent would support sovereignty if it were combined with an economic association.[7] In a January 1995 survey, 73 per cent agreed that economic association with Canada would be essential to the success of a sovereign Quebec.[8] This public unease with sovereignty was confirmed in the various regional consultations, where most participants wanted to discuss, not the government's sovereignty plans but their grievances against the government over a whole host of routine matters.

As long as sovereignty continued to be defined as it had been by the Parizeau government, the federalist forces had the upper hand. After so many constitutional disasters, the federalists would have had difficulty promising any type of 'constitutional renewal', as Trudeau had in 1980. Nor, with the major scaling down of the federal government then under way, could they stress the concrete benefits of federalism as they had in 1980. But they could still count on mobilizing the public's fear of the economic costs of sovereignty. That tactic had been enough to ensure a federalist victory in 1980.

A Quebec–Canada Partnership

For precisely these reasons Bloc leader Lucien Bouchard tried to redefine the sovereigntist option. In early April 1995, he declared that sovereignty should be coupled with a proposal to Canada of a political partnership, inspired by the European Community.[9] Bouchard's position was strengthened several days later when the Commission nationale sur l'avenir du Québec, which was to present a final report on the public consultations, proposed that 'sovereignty should mean, for Quebec, a new beginning in a partnership with Canada which would not exclude an eventual political union'.[10] Given similar sentiments among some of his closest associates, such as Bernard Landry, Parizeau's hand was forced. On 12 June 1995 he signed an agreement with Bouchard and ADQ leader Mario Dumont by which, after a successful referendum, the Quebec government was committed to propose to Canada 'a treaty on a new economic and political Partnership'.[11]

Beyond addressing matters related to sovereignty, such as dividing federal assets and managing the common debt, the treaty 'will ensure . . . that the Partnership is capable of taking action' regarding a customs union, free flow of goods, individuals, services, and capital; monetary policy; labour mobility; and citizenship. In addition, 'nothing will prevent the two member States from reaching agreement in any other area of common interest', such as trade, international representation, defence, and environmental protection, among others.

By the same token, the treaty would 'create the joint political institutions required to administer the new Economic and Political Partnership', namely (1) a Partnership Council with decision-making power over implementation of the treaty, in which Quebec and Canada would each have a veto; (2) a Parliamentary Assembly, composed of parliamentarians appointed by the Canadian parliament (75 per cent) and the Quebec National Assembly (25 per cent), which would be limited to making recommendations; and (3) a tribunal to resolve any disputes relating to the treaty.

In effect, the agreement outlined a large number of areas in which there *might* be collaboration, without actually committing Quebec to any of them. And it called for the creation of three institutions that are commonplace in international relations. Indeed, counterparts to all three already exist between Canada and the United States. The Partnership Council and tribunal are similar to the Free Trade Commission and dispute settlement mechanism found in NAFTA. As for the parliamentary assembly, a Canada–United States Inter-Parliamentary Group has met annually since 1958.[12]

Not only was it unclear what the scope would be of any economic collaboration under the Quebec-Canada Partnership, but the agreement did not make the partnership a condition for Quebec sovereignty. The Quebec government was simply to present the proposal of partnership to Canada. The negotiations were not to continue for more than one year, unless the National Assembly decided otherwise. 'In the event that negotiations prove to be fruitless', the National Assembly would then be in a position to declare Quebec's sovereignty.[13] None the less, by outlining the potential terms of a partnership, the 12 June agreement at least gave a concrete meaning to the notion of economic association between a sovereign Quebec and Canada.

The Referendum Campaign

In September 1995 the National Assembly was presented with a modified version of the Parizeau government's original bill.[14] It was to be adopted if the Yes prevailed in the referendum. Set for 30 October 1995, the referendum was to ask the question 'Do you agree that Quebec should become sovereign, after having made a formal offer to Canada for a new Economic and Political Partnership, within the scope of the Bill respecting the Future of Quebec and of the agreement signed on 12 June 1995?'

In effect, the question made the *proposal* of partnership a condition for Quebec sovereignty, but did not require that the proposal be *accepted*. Moreover, there was no requirement, as there had been in the 1980 referendum, for the government to hold a second referendum after its negotiations with the rest of Canada. However, sovereigntist leaders insisted that, if the rest of Canada were confronted with a clear Yes vote, it would have no choice but to agree to such an arrangement.[15] On this basis, they could argue that there were no appreciable economic risks to sovereignty.

That argument seems to have reassured a certain number of voters. Indeed, that is apparently why support for a Yes vote increased over the summer of 1995.[16] After remaining stable in September, the Yes support began to climb again in late September and early October. This second increase roughly corresponded with the announcement by the Quebec government that after a successful referendum Lucien Bouchard, the architect of partnership, would head the team that would negotiate the proposal with Canada. The announcement gave further credibility to the notion that sovereignty would be coupled with an economic and political association; it also served to make Bouchard the effective leader of the Yes campaign.

Several analysts believe that Bouchard's appointment was not directly responsible for this new increase in Yes support, which apparently had begun before the announcement was made. They argue that the increase may instead have been due to especially aggressive statements by leaders in the No campaign. Claude Garcia, head of an insurance company, had told a meeting of No leaders, 'We must not just win on 30 October, we must crush them'; Laurent Beaudoin, head of Bombardier, had announced that his firm might move its factories if Quebec became sovereign.[17] There was a further surge in Yes support later when Finance Minister Paul Martin warned that up to one million jobs would be threatened by sovereignty; this represented a third of Quebec's total work force.[18]

None the less, if this argument is valid, the surges in Yes support would still be due to the impact of the partnership proposal, for which Bouchard bore the primary responsibility. It appears that once they were convinced that sovereignty would be coupled with an economic association, some Quebeckers considered the comments by Paul Martin and others as hollow threats—and were alienated by them.[19]

There can be no question that, whatever the processes involved, the sovereigntist leadership was highly effective in dispelling Quebeckers' fears about the economic consequences of sovereignty. In a survey of Quebeckers, during the last week of the campaign, half the francophone respondents believed that with sovereignty there would be *no* short-term economic costs. Moreover, 55 per cent believed that over the long term Quebec's economic state would actually improve, and of these, half believed that it would be greatly improved.[20]

Once the voters were free to base their decision on considerations other than the economic consequences, the whole dynamic of the referendum was changed. In particular, those who felt a strong identity with Quebec could act on sovereigntist arguments that allegiance to Quebec necessarily required a Yes vote. Beyond that, Lucien Bouchard could make this argument with particular effectiveness because he had left the Mulroney government and founded the Bloc Québécois in protest against proposals to weaken the recognition of Quebec's identity in the Meech Lake Accord.

The federalist forces were singularly ill-placed to respond to questions of identity. A primary identification with Quebec need not be incompatible with federalism, *per se*, but it was incompatible with the Trudeau vision of Canadian federalism that had gained ascendancy in the federal government.[21] Moreover, Prime Minister Jean Chrétien was closely associated with the Trudeau ideal. Not only that, as justice minister in the early 1980s, he had been directly involved in the events leading to patriation and a Charter without Quebec's formal consent. Indeed, during the campaign sovereigntist leaders personally attacked Chrétien, implying that he had been a 'traitor' to Quebec.[22]

For most of the campaign, the federalist forces continued to stress the economic costs of sovereignty. Despite entreaties from Quebec federalists, headed by Liberal leader Daniel Johnson, Chrétien and his cabinet refused to counter the sovereigntist appeals to Quebec identity with proposals to accommodate better that identity within the Canadian political order, whether by amending the constitution or by modifying federal-provincial relations. The federalist leaders did, however, apparently agree that their cause could only be damaged if Trudeau himself intervened; he was side-lined throughout the campaign, much to his annoyance.[23]

As the campaign entered its last week, surveys showed that the federalist strategy was not working and that support for a Yes vote had continued to grow. Confronted with the distinct possibility of defeat, the Ottawa federalists finally heeded the pleas of federalist forces in Quebec.

In a dramatic speech five days before the vote, Chrétien effectively recognized the constitutional demands of Quebec federalists. Insisting that with a No vote all means of securing change would remain open, including constitutional ones, he responded directly to the demand for a Quebec veto: 'Any change in the constitutional powers of Quebec will be made only with the consent of Quebeckers.' He even acknowledged Quebec's claim to be a 'distinct society'. During the campaign he had been listening to 'his fellow Quebeckers'

> saying that they want to see this country change and evolve towards their aspirations. They want to see Quebec recognized as a distinct society within Canada by virtue of its language, culture, and institutions. I've said it before and I'll say it again. I agree. I have supported that position in the past, I support it today and I will support it in the future, whatever the circumstances.[24]

It was not clear precisely how these commitments to a Quebec veto and recognition of a distinct society were to be met. Chrétien did not explicitly advocate placing the distinct-society clause in the constitution; at most, he was saying that he would agree to it. The fact of the matter is that despite his claim to have always supported recognition of Quebec as a distinct society, Chrétien had publicly opposed the Meech Lake Accord, in part because of its distinct-society clause.[25] But the gesture apparently shored up support for a No vote.[26]

At the same time, in making such a statement Chrétien tacitly acknowledged that the Trudeau national unity strategy had failed. Only by directly recognizing Quebec's distinctiveness could he hope to improve the chances of a No victory. Indeed, other parts of Chrétien's speech also appealed directly to Quebec nationalism and were quite out of character with his normal discourse. He even adopted a phrase he credited to Jean Lesage: 'Canada my country; Quebec my homeland'.[27]

On Friday, 27 October, a 'national unity' rally was held in downtown Montreal. At the event, which was quite compatible with the Trudeau vision, Canadians from outside Quebec joined Quebec federalists in proclaiming their attachment to Canada. It appears that the effect of the rally was to weaken the No vote because some voters were offended by what they considered an intrusion by non-Quebeckers, and because it was allegedly a violation of the Quebec law regulating spending during the referendum campaign.[28]

Quebeckers apparently made their final decision primarily on the basis of how they defined their identity. Just as in the past, support for sovereignty was greatest among those who defined themselves, first and foremost, as Quebeckers. Yet the surveys found that many Yes supporters professed a continuing attachment to Canada. A survey taken in late September found that 67 per cent of Quebeckers claimed to be 'deeply attached to Canada'; 34 per cent of those planning to vote Yes said they were attached to Canada.[29] By the same token, in a survey taken four months after the referendum, in which 54.3 per cent said they would vote Yes in a new referendum, 78.1 per cent agreed that 'we should be proud of what francophones and anglophones have accomplished together in Canada' and 85.5 per cent agreed that 'Canada is a country where it is good to live'.[30]

To be sure, some Yes voters obviously wanted total sovereignty, and nothing else. They would have voted in favour of the Parizeau government's original proposition. But most Yes voters apparently were rejecting, not Canada *per se*, but a particular idea of Canada, and a corresponding set of institutions, that denied their own conception of Quebec and its place in Canada.

The question still remains, though, as to what the Yes voters thought a Yes victory would mean. Some surveys suggest that a number of voters were confused as to the precise institutional arrangements that would come with sovereignty. In one survey, 22 per cent of respondents intending to vote Yes thought that under sovereignty Quebec would continue to be a province of Canada.[31] It also appears that some Yes voters hoped that a Yes vote would precipitate a 'renewal' of federalism by giving Quebec new bargaining power within Canada; yet they must have recognized that sovereignty was at least a possible outcome. Finally, the surveys show that most Yes voters firmly expected that sovereignty would be linked to an economic and political partnership with Canada. It is less clear what they understood such a partnership to entail. At least one study suggests that some understood partnership to be simply a free trade agreement.[32]

Yet, if some Yes voters may have been uncertain as to the precise arrangements to be created through a Yes vote, and some even hoped that the result would be a 'renewed federalism', most of them must have expected it would result in Quebec sovereignty. That was certainly the import of the two documents that the referendum question referred to—the National Assembly bill and the partnership agreement. Indeed, during the final week of the campaign Prime Minister Chrétien warned the voters that a Yes vote would lead to sovereignty. In his televised 'Address to the Nation' he declared, 'A yes vote means the destruction of the economic and political union we already enjoy.'[33]

The Vote

The turnout for the referendum was extraordinarily high—93.52 per cent of the Quebec electorate. The result was extraordinarily close—49.4 per cent voted Yes; 50.58 per cent voted No. Indeed, the No won by only 54,288 votes. Compared with the 1980 referendum, this represented a gain in the Yes vote by close to 9 percentage points on a question that constituted a mandate for sovereignty itself, with or without 'partnership', rather than for the negotiation of sovereignty-association.

Whereas the Quebec electorate as a whole was almost evenly divided, the two primary linguistic groups were not. Nearly 60 per cent of francophones voted Yes; about 95 per cent of non-francophones voted No. The proportion of francophone votes for the Yes seems to have been fairly consistent across the province. Where there were large differences among regions, they mainly reflect differences in the proportions of francophone and non-francophone voters. According to sociologist Pierre Drouilly, the francophone Yes vote was higher in eastern Montreal (66.7 per cent) and the northeastern periphery of Montreal (65.2 per cent) than in the province as a whole. West Montreal was the only section of Montreal where the francophone vote was lower (52.6 per cent) than in the province as a whole. In

Quebec City and in urban and rural areas of the rest of Quebec, the proportions of francophones voting Yes were 57.0 per cent, 59.5 per cent, and 56.9 per cent, respectively.[34]

A third component of Quebec's population, the aboriginal peoples, was largely missing from the referendum results. Three aboriginal peoples had in fact held referendums of their own several days before the Quebec government's referendum. Not surprisingly, given the long-standing opposition of aboriginal leaders to Quebec sovereignty, all three referenda massively rejected the government's proposition. The Cree voted No by 96 per cent, the Inuit by 95 per cent, and even the francophone Montagnais by 99 per cent.[35]

After the referendum, it was alleged that the official result of the government referendum was not fully accurate. Supporters of the No vote claimed that a significant number of No ballots had been improperly rejected by scrutineers who were themselves supporters of a Yes vote. However, the Quebec director of elections, Pierre-F. Côté, concluded on the basis of a special inquiry by Judge Alan Gold, that only 31 of the 22,342 referendum scrutineers appeared to have acted improperly; charges would be laid against them.[36] Some No supporters also alleged that election officials had intimidated non-francophones, who were probably No voters, and had hindered non-residents in exercising their right to vote.[37] Yes supporters countered with charges that a leading federalist organization had encouraged non-residents to declare fraudulently that they intended to return to Quebec, so that they could vote in the referendum. But even with due allowance for the allegations of the No forces, the No victory would still have been very small. Nor could the instances of impropriety alleged by the Yes forces have been responsible for the defeat of the Yes.

Another set of allegations had to do with expenditures for the 27 October rally that were not channelled through the official No organization, as required under the Quebec referendum law. Airlines had made tickets available at reduced fares, and corporations and associations provided funds to rent buses and other means of transportation. Declaring that such actions 'infringed, in a certain sense, on the democratic character of the referendum', the director of elections laid charges against 18 individuals, nine of them outside the province.[38] Still, as we have seen, the rally may have served to reduce rather than increase the No vote.

In sum, despite a number of apparent irregularities, there is every indication that a majority of legal votes went to the No side—but it was only a razor-thin majority. The result was to have a profound effect on both Quebec and English Canada. A year later, both parts of the country were still struggling with the consequences.

THE AFTERMATH

Quebec: Contradictory Processes

In Quebec, the referendum was followed by quite contradictory processes. The first was the replacement of the Parti Québécois leader. Apparently Jacques Parizeau had planned to resign if there was a No vote, but his departure was hastened by the adverse public reaction to his referendum-night speech, blaming 'money and the ethnic vote' for the defeat. His comments evoked a narrow ethnic nationalism that contradicted the PQ's official policy and was rejected by many Quebec francophones within the party, as well as outside it. Parizeau's logical successor was Lucien Bouchard, architect of the partnership commitment that had brought the sovereigntists so close to victory.

As party leader and Quebec premier, Bouchard quickly attempted to draw attention away from the sovereignty question toward issues confronting Quebec as a province within Canada. He declared a commitment to eliminate Quebec's deficit by the year 2000. In the meantime, the sovereignty question was to be put aside. The next referendum was to take place only after a provincial election, which would be called 'as late as possible' so as to allow time to address Quebec's public finances.[39] Such a stance could be justified within a sovereigntist strategy: Quebec would be better placed to assume sovereignty if its financial house was in order. It also recognized that the Quebec voters were weary of the whole question.

By concentrating on public finances, the Bouchard government ran the risk of alienating the social democratic part of its constituency—public sector workers, citizens' groups, and other social forces still committed to state intervention. The PQ's referendum success had been partly based on strong appeals to this clientele: Bouchard insisted that Quebec had no place in a Canada dominated by such neo-conservative provincial governments as those of Ontario and Alberta. By setting aside the sovereignty question, the government also ran the risk of alienating *indépendantistes* who were impatient to move on to the next stage of the struggle after having come so close to victory.

If the Bouchard government seemed determined to declare a moratorium on the sovereignty question, forces outside the Parti Québécois kept the question front and centre. First, the shock of the close referendum result produced among Quebec's anglophone and allophone population a new determination to oppose not only sovereignty, but Quebec nationalism itself. With the loss of confidence in Quebec's established federalist leadership, new leaders emerged who favoured more radical strategies. In an attempt to stave off the effects of any future referendum victory for sovereignty, some groups advocated that parts of Quebec should remain in Canada if the majority of residents wished them to. Anglophone groups also began to mobilize in favour of English-language rights, not only demanding that their rights under Bill 101 be fully respected but challenging outright the notion that Quebec should be defined as a primarily French society. The campaigns in favour of partition and English-language rights alarmed Daniel Johnson and other Quebec federalists, who were anxious to retain francophone support for federalism, but both ideas were publicly endorsed by Prime Minister Chrétien.[40] Once again, the federalists were badly divided, and at the heart of the division was the disagreement over the nature of Quebec and its francophone character.

By embracing the principle of partition, the new anglophone spokespersons were adopting a position that had long been proclaimed by Quebec's aboriginal leaders. Over the years the native leaders had invoked legal arguments to support their position that aboriginal peoples should be able to decide whether the territory they inhabit becomes part of a sovereign Quebec or remains part of Canada: most of these territories had not become part of Quebec until after Confederation, the states that had previously claimed them (Britain and France) did not have a strong argument for doing so, and the federal government has a fiduciary relationship with aboriginal peoples under the constitution.[41] Aboriginal leaders have also made moral arguments that perhaps give their claims greater weight than those of Quebec anglophones. In particular, they have argued that as First Nations they have a clearer right to self-determination than do Quebeckers. Just like the partitionist claims of Quebec anglophones, so those of aboriginal peoples have been rejected, not only by sovereigntist leaders, but also by the leader of Quebec's federalists, Daniel Johnson.[42] None the less, the combined opposition from aboriginal and anglophone groups helped to keep the question of sovereignty at the centre of public debate.

A second challenge confronted the Bouchard government's attempt to draw attention to Quebec's public finances. Economic élites inside and outside the province complained that the referendum result had created profound uncertainty among investors that could be resolved only if the Bouchard government renounced its goal of sovereignty. Indeed, during the first half of 1996, unemployment in the province increased dramatically, reaching 12.4 per cent in July.[43] There seemed to be a variety of reasons, not the least of which was the layoffs caused by the government's spending cuts. But the economic uncertainty created by the referendum result was clearly one of them.

In short, the referendum had made Quebec sovereignty a distinct possibility. As a consequence, it set forces in motion that favoured a continuing, and acrimonious, debate over the very idea of sovereignty, however keen the Quebec government was to divert discussion to other subjects. There could be no avoiding the fact that with the referendum Quebec had crossed a threshold.

Outside Quebec: Two Plans but No Effective Response

In the rest of Canada, the result of the referendum had been totally unexpected, and the shock was profound. Having long assumed that the No forces would win by a wide margin, Canadians were now confronted with the fact that the Yes side had almost won, and might well do so in a future referendum.

Moreover, most English Canadians had great difficulty understanding what could have impelled so many Quebec francophones to take such a radical step. After all, since the late 1960s the federal government had been led by Quebeckers, with a few brief exceptions. The federal government had pursued with energy, and at great expense, the national unity strategy proposed by the first of those Quebeckers, Pierre Trudeau. In particular, official bilingualism had become the norm at the federal level, transforming the face of federal institutions not only in Ottawa but throughout the country. Provincial governments had been persuaded, to varying degrees, to offer French-language services to minorities that often made up only tiny proportions of provincial populations. After all this, the Québécois were still so dissatisfied that they were prepared to leave the country!

Indeed, many English Canadians had resented such measures, which had been justified as necessary to national unity. The Reform Party had made inroads in English-Canadian public opinion with its arguments that official bilingualism, as well as multiculturalism, constituted improper uses of public resources. Arguing that the promotion of minority languages and the preservation of cultures should be private matters, Reform was calling for many of the Trudeau government's reforms to be reversed.

The fact that all these ostensible 'concessions' to Quebec had been framed in such a way as to deny Quebec's uniqueness was lost on most English Canadians. Nor could they fathom the argument that patriation with a Charter entrenching language rights was a 'humiliation' of Quebec. After all, patriation had been engineered by a Quebecker.

Beyond incomprehension as to its causes, the referendum also produced anger over its near consequences. In effect, through their Yes vote Quebeckers were threatening the survival of Canada. By declaring a desire to leave Canada, they ceased to be fellow citizens; they had become 'foreigners'. And as foreigners, they had even less claim to any further generosity or magnanimity on the part of Canadians.[44]

Perhaps an informed leadership might have been able to make this situation intelligible to English Canadians and to organize the type of response that was needed, but the Chrétien government was ill-equipped to offer such leadership. Chrétien and his cabinet were too firmly linked to the national unity strategy that had produced this state of affairs to be ready or able to persuade English Canadians to accept and recognize the claims of Quebeckers.

As political and intellectual élites outside Quebec struggled to respond to the new state of affairs, they soon settled on a 'two-plan' strategy.[45] One form of response was somehow to make Canada more attractive to Quebeckers, so as to prevent another referendum on sovereignty or at least ensure that it would be defeated. The other was to prepare for the possibility that, despite such efforts, Quebeckers might still vote for sovereignty. This meant defining negotiating positions, if indeed there was to be negotiation, and imagining the possibility of a Canada without Quebec. Given the intellectual and psychological hurdles to framing a response based on the first plan, it was perhaps inevitable that energies would tend to focus on the second.

Plan A: Making Canada More Attractive

It was quite clear what would be needed to restore Quebeckers' support for the Canadian political order. It had to be acknowledged that Quebeckers' allegiance to their province was compatible with being Canadian. And the Quebec government and legislature had to be granted both the right and the capacity to promote Quebec's uniqueness. Moreover, such changes had to be permanent; in other words, constitutional. A survey taken soon after the referendum asked whether each of four different conditions was necessary in order for Quebec to remain in the Canadian federation; each was endorsed by overwhelming majorities. At the top of the list was the transfer of powers to Quebec, with manpower and communications offered as examples (85.4 per cent agreed), followed by recognition of Quebec as a distinct society (78.0 per cent), a veto over all constitutional change (73.2 per cent), and the power to collect all taxes (63.2 per cent), an especially sweeping measure.[46] In short, an accommodation of Quebec after the referendum would require both recognition of Quebec's distinctiveness and a substantial enhancement of its powers, well exceeding the scope of Meech.

Such changes would of course not dissuade long-time *indépendantistes* from their beliefs. But they might impress the many Quebeckers who had long hoped for a renewed federalism and had been swayed by the argument of Lucien Bouchard and others that the Constitution Act, 1982, had destroyed Quebec's historical place within the Canadian federation.

Presumably, the constitution would not be changed as long as the Parti Québécois was in power; a PQ government would probably frustrate any attempt to 'renew' Canada. Yet, with Bouchard as leader of the PQ, even this was no longer certain. After all, Bouchard was himself a latecomer to sovereignty and his notion of sovereignty and the kind of relationship Quebec should have with Canada seemed much closer to René Lévesque's than to Jacques Parizeau's. Still, even if the PQ government were to reject constitutional renewal, Ottawa and the other provincial governments would have every reason to show they were committed to bringing it about. Moreover, surveys kept finding that Quebeckers still strongly preferred 'renewed federalism' to sovereignty and were very much hoping that change would be forthcoming.[47]

In short, the case for constitutional renewal could not have been stronger in the wake of the referendum. Yet there still were serious obstacles to be overcome. They may even have been made worse by the result of the referendum. As a consequence, a year after the referendum, there was still no meaningful attempt to fashion a constitutional response based on plan A.

Jean Chrétien did feel compelled to keep the promise he had made in the panic of the referendum campaign's last week. After failing to persuade enough provincial premiers to support constitutional recognition of Quebec as a 'distinct society', Chrétien resolved to deal with the matter through non-constitutional action.[48] In December the government introduced in the House of Commons a 'Resolution Respecting the Recognition of Quebec as a Distinct Society'. Under the resolution, the House recognized 'that Quebec is a distinct society within Canada'; defined Quebec's distinctiveness in the traditional terms of language, culture, and civil law; undertook 'to be guided by this reality'; and encouraged 'the legislative and executive branches of [the federal] government to take note of this recognition and be guided in their conduct accordingly'. The resolution was approved on 11 December 1995.[49]

On 29 November the government had presented a bill to the effect that the government could introduce to the House constitutional amendments in areas not requiring the approval of all provincial legislatures only if they had already been approved by Ontario, Quebec, and two or more provinces from Atlantic Canada and from Western Canada that contain 50 per cent of the population of their respective regions. In effect, the government was attempting to superimpose on the existing amending procedure the formula contained in the ill-fated Victoria Charter, thus giving a veto over all amendments to Quebec, as well as to Ontario. After howls of protest from British Columbia, the government felt obliged to depart from the Victoria formula and give a veto to British Columbia as well. After heated debates in both the House and the Senate, the bill became law on 2 February 1996.[50]

It may be argued that with those measures, the Chrétien government had kept its referendum promise, but they hadn't disposed of the grievances that had impelled it to make the promise in the first place. Under the Meech Lake Accord, as well as Charlottetown, recognition of Quebec's distinctiveness had involved a clause guiding the courts' interpretation of the constitution. The requirement that the federal government should take account of Quebec's distinctiveness in its own activities is quite a different matter. Indeed, it is not at all clear what this does entail.

The procedure governing constitutional amendments does have clearer significance. But it remains an Act of Parliament, which can be revoked or modified by future Parliaments. At the same time, some experts have argued that the measure is itself unconstitutional, since it has the effect of altering the operation of the amending formula from its original authors' intentions.[51]

In any event, with the appointment of Stéphane Dion as intergovernmental affairs minister in late January, the Chrétien government began a concerted effort to persuade English Canada to support constitutional entrenchment of a distinct-society clause.[52] But public opinion outside Quebec remained opposed to the measure,[53] and the Chrétien government still failed to get the support of enough premiers.[54]

At a conference in June 1996, the first ministers' collective inability or unreadiness to address the constitutional question led to almost farcical behaviour. The prime minister believed that he and the premiers were bound by a constitutional obligation to discuss the functioning of the amending formula adopted in 1982. Even though Premier Bouchard absented himself from this part of the proceedings, it was over in a matter of seconds. Indeed, there was some confusion as to whether it had even take place.[55] Such was the determination to avoid the constitutional question, however urgent it may have seemed in Quebec to do so. In vain had Quebec Liberal leader Daniel Johnson gone to Ottawa to persuade the English-Canadian premiers to frame a constitutional response to Quebec.

With respect to the actual conduct of federal-provincial relations, as opposed to the formal constitutional framework, the Chrétien government has taken some initiatives. In its Throne Speech of 27 February 1996, the government acknowledged that 'the referendum result gave a clear message that Quebeckers want change in the federation'. First, it undertook that any new shared-cost programs in exclusively provincial jurisdictions would be possible only with the consent of a majority of provinces and would allow provinces to opt out with compensation if they established equivalent programs. Second, it announced that it was ready to withdraw from 'such areas as labour market training, forestry, mining, and recreation'. Finally, it promised to 'work in partnership [with the provinces], focussing on such priorities as food inspection, environmental management, social housing, tourism, and freshwater fish habitat'. The first measure is in fact stronger than the spending-power provision of Meech. Moreover, withdrawal from labour market training was a major Quebec demand. The other areas listed are largely inconsequential. In any event, the undertakings concerning the spending power and labour market training remain just that: 'undertakings', which can be cancelled by future governments.[56]

In late May, the Chrétien government detailed its proposal for job training. Calling its scheme one of 'partnership', it offered to withdraw from job training within a maximum of three years while making funds available to the provincial governments for them to assume the responsibility. The federal government would negotiate the terms with each province and enter into bilateral agreements with the provinces. Bouchard called the move a 'step in the right direction' and gave his government credit for helping to produce it.[57]

The autonomy of the Quebec government has also been enhanced by the federal government's fiscal difficulties and the decline in its ability to control provincial activity through transfer payments. As such payments have become smaller, so the federal government has had to scale down the conditions attached to such transfers. Under the Canada Health and Social Transfer, funding programs for social assistance, health, and post-secondary education have been combined into a single block. Provinces are free to decide how the total funds will be divided among the three main areas. The standards of the Canada Health Act are supposed to continue to apply to the health care portion, but standards for social assistance have been lowered, and there are none for post-secondary education.[58]

The federal government's ability to maintain 'national standards' through transfers to the provinces is also threatened by the heightened aggressiveness of two 'wealthy' provinces, Alberta and Ontario, which are themselves committed to a neo-conservative reduction in the power of the state, both provincial and federal. At the interprovincial conference in August 1996, their attack on the federal government's enforcement of 'national standards' attracted the favourable attention of Lucien Bouchard.[59] However, the other premiers were far from agreeing. Many of them represented provinces that are quite dependent upon the federal government's redistribution of funds from the wealthier provinces. Indeed, although the provinces agreed to ask Ottawa to replace its enforcement of '"national standards" with a federal-provincial mechanism, they also recommended the creation of a new national child-benefit program to be administered by Ottawa'.[60]

In short, the vicissitudes of federal-provincial relations in the rest of Canada may provide opportunities for Quebec to enhance its autonomy. But, like the commitments made by the Chrétien government after the referendum, these opportunities are not guaranteed to be permanent. Nor are they necessarily in the areas that are most important to Quebec, such as culture or telecommunications. So they are not a substitute for the type of constitutional change that successive Quebec governments have asked for.

As 1996 progressed, the Chrétien government seemed to be shifting to a different strategy for the Quebec question, in effect, an updated version of the Trudeau strategy. Rather than trying to appear responsive to the concerns of Quebec nationalists, including federalists, it would instead try to persuade Quebeckers, and all Canadians, to view their country in a more positive way. In particular, the government established a Canada Information Office, with a budget of $20 million, which was designed to promote Canadian identity and hence Canadian unity—and to counter the 'lies' propagated by separatists.[61] Coupled with this initiative has been a program to make Canadian flags available to citizens free of charge. Though the program has proved much more popular than anticipated, as of August 1996 only 8.3 per cent of the requests had come from Quebec.[62]

The difficulties in framing an acceptable response to Quebec, especially in constitutional terms, were also evident in two non-governmental attempts to devise a version of plan A. On 1 May 1996, a group of 22 academics and researchers, all but three from outside Quebec, released a report entitled *Making Canada Work Better*. A few days later, the Business Council on National Issues published a set of proposals resulting from its Confederation 2000 Conferences, involving more than 100 opinion leaders. Both documents followed the same format: they discussed in turn a variety of themes applicable to Canada as a whole—redistribution of powers, with the provinces obtaining control of manpower in particular; limitation of the federal spending power; strengthening of regional representation in central institutions; and creation of a social and economic union. Only at the end did the reports turn to the question of 'duality', the term used by the Group of 22, or 'Quebec in an evolving federation', the term used by the Business Council's report.

By the same token, this treatment of Quebec or duality was heavily qualified. The Business Council's report did recommend a constitutional interpretative clause that would recognize Quebec's 'distinctive character', but rather than repeating the Meech Lake provision, it called for 'words which best describe it and are understood and accepted by Quebecers and other Canadians'.[63] It also called for an amending formula that would require Quebec's consent. Rather than including either measure as part of its six-month plan of action, the report simply said they should occur 'sooner rather than later'.[64]

The Group of 22 report saw a need for constitutional recognition of duality 'not too far down the road'. Because the Meech Lake distinct-society clause 'will be a very hard sell in the rest of the country', it proposed a variety of alternatives.[65] The clause could be reformulated to concentrate more on duality or to reflect somehow the notion that Quebec is 'culturally distinct, but fiscally equal'. In its place, Quebec, with or without the other provinces, could be given more jurisdiction over language use. Finally, Quebec could be granted a stripped-down distinct-society clause but with exclusive jurisdiction over language.[66]

Despite this pervasive apprehension among English-Canadian élites about dealing with the Quebec question, some public initiatives did succeed in addressing it in a more straightforward fashion. For instance, the CBC closeted 25 'typical' Canadians in a secluded retreat, where they proceeded to devise their own plan for a renewed Canada. Out of the exchange and confrontation between English Canadians and Quebec nationalists emerged a text that, as a statement of a general approach, succeeded better than the documents written by the élites in meeting the needs of plan A. Indeed, its description of 'the Canadian Community' evoked the vision of the B&B Commission. It updated the commission's vision by beginning with a recognition of the First Nations' 'inherent right to govern themselves', but then went on to declare:

> We believe that Canada is not only a union of provinces and territories but also a partnership of two founding peoples, two societies, two nations, English-speaking and French-speaking, which have welcomed a multitude of immigrants. . . .
>
> We believe that Canada should recognize and affirm the fact that Quebecers are a predominantly French-speaking people. Quebec is home to a culture unique in North America.[67]

Perhaps because it was produced under such unusual circumstances, the document seemed to have little influence on English-Canadian public opinion.

In sum, efforts to devise a plan A approach that would shore up Quebec's support for the federal system have at best had inconclusive results. In particular, they foundered on the task of developing a response to Quebec's constitutional concerns. The continuing influence of the Trudeau vision in

English Canada and the memory of the failures at constitutional renewal for which that vision was largely responsible, seemed to prevent élites outside Quebec, both governmental and non-governmental, from meeting the challenge that the referendum result so acutely posed. Even in the face of the virtual tie in the referendum, which made Quebec sovereignty a real possibility, English-Canadian opinion apparently could not be persuaded to adopt Meech's highly circumscribed distinct-society clause, let alone a more substantial response to Quebec.

Plan B: Preparing for Sovereignty

In striking contrast to the diffidence and caution with which élites outside Quebec attempted to devise a plan A response to the referendum was the energy with which they addressed the plan B agenda: responding to a Yes vote in a future referendum.

The Chrétien government, which was unwilling to tackle any accommodation of Quebec within the constitution, was quite prepared to defend vigorously the continuing authority of the constitution if Quebec should vote for sovereignty. Indeed, Ottawa entered into a court action to support the claim of Guy Bertrand, *indépendantiste* turned federalist, that Quebec would continue to be bound by the constitution after a Yes vote, implying in turn that Quebec could become sovereign only if the constitution should be duly amended to that effect. In doing so, Ottawa ran the risk of associating itself with other positions Bertrand was defending, such as the illegality of even holding a referendum on sovereignty. The previous year, it had not intervened regarding the authority of the constitution when Bertrand took legal action to stop the 1995 referendum.

In September 1996, after the Quebec government had decided not to contest Bertrand's action any further, the federal government decided to act on its own and submit a reference to the Supreme Court on the matter. More precisely, the court was asked to determine whether a unilateral declaration of independence by Quebec would be legal under Canadian law, whether it would be legal under international law, and finally, if it was legal under one set of laws but not the other, which one should prevail.[68]

In explaining the reasons for the reference, Justice Minister Allan Rock went to great lengths to insist that the federal government was not suggesting that Quebec could not become sovereign: 'The leading political figures of all our provinces and the Canadian public have long agreed that the country cannot be held together against the clear will of Quebecers. This government agrees with that. . . .' It was only insisting that sovereignty must be obtained under the rule of law; change should take place in an orderly process within the legal framework.[69]

Still, it is difficult to see why the reference was necessary. No serious commentator has suggested that a unilateral declaration of independence would be legal under Canadian law; and the Supreme Court is not well-placed to be adjudicating issues in international law. Beyond that, there is every reason to believe that if the Quebec government succeeded in a future referendum on sovereignty, it would try to secure sovereignty not through a unilateral declaration of independence but through an agreement with the rest of Canada, setting the terms under which Quebec becomes sovereign. The agreement could in turn be formalized through revision of the Canadian constitution. Thus, Quebec would become sovereign through a modification of the law, not in opposition to it.

Not only is this route obviously in Quebec's interests, but it was the procedure that had been outlined by the Parizeau government; the Bouchard government has said nothing to suggest that its position is different.[70] Clearly, the threat of a unilateral declaration of independence might be important in inducing the rest of Canada to negotiate in good faith. But by all indications it would be used only as a last resort: negotiations with the rest of Canada might fail to produce an agreement, or even if there was agreement, the objection of one or more provincial governments might preclude the amendment to the Canadian constitution necessary to put it into effect.[71]

However compelling the legal considerations may have been, the Chrétien government's actions clearly have had political consequences. In English Canada they have created a sense that plan A initiatives, such as constitutional accommodation, are not needed: either the pending Supreme Court ruling will frighten the Québécois into voting against sovereignty, or sovereignty simply cannot happen because it would be illegal. In Quebec, the court reference may indeed have been seen by some as an attempt at intimidation, and resented for that reason. Certainly, it has distressed the federalist leaders in Quebec, such as Daniel Johnson and Jean Charest, who publicly protested the measure and called upon the Chrétien government to concentrate on plan A. Johnson declared: 'The federal government should be concerned about exercising leadership to change Canada and to improve Canadian federalism. I would prefer that it focus its attention on other things instead of going to the Supreme Court.'[72] In fact, after the Quebec government had announced it would no longer contest Bertrand's claims, Johnson had publicly called on Ottawa to abandon the matter. Reportedly, this sentiment was shared by most Quebec members of the federal cabinet.[73] Yet, the Chrétien government clearly felt pressure from outside Quebec to respond energetically to the post-referendum situation, and it is here that it chose to act.

The federal government's actions on the legal front paralleled a series of public statements by federal politicians that emphasized the presumed costs and difficulties of Quebec sovereignty. For instance, the government took a 'hard' position about the boundaries of Quebec if it ever became sovereign. In his previous profession as university professor, the new minister of inter-governmental affairs, Stéphane Dion, had written that Quebec should not expect to keep its present boundaries; upon becoming minister, he confirmed that this was still his opinion. Chrétien quickly affirmed that that was his position as well.[74] Several days later, Indian Affairs Minister Ron Irwin said that aboriginal territory in Quebec does not belong to the province and would not belong if Quebec were to become sovereign.[75]

The prime minister has also declared that in any future referendum the threshold for a victory must be more than 50 per cent.[76] At one point, he even said that Quebec would not be 'allowed' to hold another referendum on sovereignty; it was not clear how this would be enforced.[77] The ostensible leader of federalist forces in Quebec, Daniel Johnson, dissociated himself from such opinions on partition and the threshold for a referendum victory, calling them 'totally off base'.[78]

In this climate, public debate in the media also has tended to concentrate on possible responses to a future Yes vote, as opposed to precluding such a vote through an accommodation within the federation. From the outset, prominent columnists in English Canada have called for a hard line on all the questions surrounding sovereignty[79] and a rejection of any plan A attempts to accommodate Quebec. At the same time, a spate of 'analyses' has tried to show that sovereignty would entail violence and chaos.[80]

It seems that outside Quebec much of the debate over plan B has been driven less by a desire to make contingency plans for a Yes vote in a future referendum than by an effort to prevent such a vote by making sovereignty too unattractive, or simply unattainable. As such, plan B has been highly popular outside Quebec. A November 1996 survey found that 63 per cent of Canadians outside Quebec agreed that the federal government 'should emphasize the tough conditions Quebec would have to meet if it were to leave Canada'; only 13 per cent agreed that Ottawa 'should focus on giving Quebec some of the changes it wants'.[81] However, most Quebeckers saw things differently: only 17 per cent supported an emphasis on 'tough conditions' with 45 per cent supporting a focus on changes to accommodate Quebec. By the same token, in early 1997 surveys continued to show that Quebeckers were almost evenly split on how they would vote in a future referendum.[82]

The fact remained, though, that during the first year after the referendum little progress had been made on plan A, that is, to strengthen the appeal of the Canadian political order for Quebeckers. And, as federalist leaders in Quebec said regularly, the Chrétien government's various plan B actions could not really compensate for this. If anything, they were self-defeating.

The 1995 Quebec referendum was the ultimate proof that the Trudeau national unity strategy had failed. Not only had it failed to supplant the identification with Quebec that was crucial to generating a Yes vote, but sovereigntist leaders were able to use the results of the strategy, most notably the Constitution Act, 1982, as proof to Quebeckers that their identity could not be recognized within the Canadian federation. By forcing Quebeckers to choose between Quebec and Canada, the federalist campaign had in fact made them more likely to vote Yes. A majority Yes vote was averted only by a last-minute disavowal of the Trudeau vision of Canada and the constitution.

Yet, the continued influence of the Trudeau vision in the rest of Canada, and the two constitutional débâcles it had produced, prevented English Canada from attempting to respond to the referendum result by accommodating the grievances that had produced it. Instead, energy was spent debating how the rest of Canada should respond to a new referendum with a Yes majority. In a sense, the Trudeau strategy had the perverse effect that many English Canadians could more easily imagine recognizing Quebec's distinctiveness *outside* Canada than within it.

CHAPTER 10

Conclusion:
Is Separation the
Only Answer?

THE FAILURE OF THE TRUDEAU STRATEGY

After 30 years, it is only too obvious that the Trudeau strategy has failed. In fact, rather than unifying the country, it has left Canada more deeply divided than ever before. The most dramatic demonstrations yet are the decision of 60 per cent of Quebec francophones to vote in favour of Quebec sovereignty, primarily to assert their identity as Quebeckers, and the inability of Canadian political élites since the referendum to find a way to restore Quebeckers' support to the Canadian political system.

Yet, these developments were only the most recent in a series of events. In 1990, after the collapse of the Meech Lake Accord, support for Quebec sovereignty had surged to unprecedented levels, reaching over 60 per cent of all Quebeckers. In 1993, one year after the failed attempt to resolve Quebec's constitutional status with the Charlottetown Accord, the overwhelming majority of Quebec francophones voted for the Bloc Québécois, a federal party committed to sovereignty (see Table 3 in Chapter 6). Indeed, as if to symbolize Canada's profound division, the Bloc Québécois won enough seats to form the Official Opposition.

All this had come as a shock to many English Canadians. Pierre Trudeau was supposed to have resolved Quebeckers' dissatisfaction with Canada. After all, thanks to his intervention sovereignty-association had been soundly defeated in 1980. And the patriation and revision of the constitution in 1982 had discharged the pledge with which Trudeau had won this victory. Moreover, throughout the Trudeau years the federal Liberals had always scored enormous victories in Quebec, averaging no less than 84 per cent of the Quebec seats. Thus, many English-Canadian commentators blamed Canada's present sorry state on Trudeau's successor, Brian Mulroney. He must have brought this on by aligning himself with Quebec nationalists and enabling them to propagate their myths about the 1982 patriation.[1]

On closer analysis, however, it becomes clear that the dissatisfaction of Quebec francophones with the Canadian political system had never been resolved during Trudeau's years in power—quite the opposite. The francophone No vote in 1980 was largely due to the fear of the economic consequences of separation, along with the hope that Quebec might find a new place within a 'renewed federalism'. Most Quebeckers disapproved of the 1982 patriation because the National Assembly had not given its consent. As for Trudeau's enormous seat majorities in Quebec, the popular vote told quite a different story. During the first three elections, the Liberals apparently obtained no more than half of the francophone vote; only in the last two did they have a substantial majority among francophone voters.[2] More important, it is not at all clear that those francophones who did vote Liberal were necessarily endorsing Trudeau's vision of Canada, as opposed to following the longstanding tendency of Quebeckers to prefer a party whose leader is from Quebec. By one analysis of the Liberal vote in the late 1970s, it included between 20 per cent and 30 per cent of Quebeckers who normally voted Parti Québécois provincially. The fact of the matter is that, as Lemieux and Crête argued, 'Most of the voters are nationalists. They want more power for Quebec *within* the federal system.'[3] They saw the Liberals as the most nationalist party in federal politics, thanks to its leader from Quebec. Indeed, the Liberal surge in 1979 followed a campaign in which the Liberals had used a slogan, 'Speak Up, Quebec!', which appealed directly to Quebec nationalist sentiments.[4]

Underlying the failure of the Trudeau strategy is its inability to alter the historical tendency of francophones to see themselves as a distinct collectivity, rooted primarily in Quebec. Indeed, studies show that the proportion of Quebec francophones who identify first and foremost with Quebec and call themselves Québécois grew steadily throughout the Trudeau era, from 21 per cent in 1970 to 31 per cent in 1977 to 37 per cent in 1984.[5] By 1990, the figure had reached 59 per cent.

At the same time, strong identification with Quebec did not exclude identification with Canada as well. This is clearly revealed by Table 5, which shows the results of a survey taken during the last week of the 1995 referendum campaign. Twenty-nine per cent of Quebec francophones defined themselves as 'Quebecker only'; however, as large a proportion said they were 'Quebecker first but also Canadian'. Together, these two responses represent 58.1 per cent of the respondents, about the same as the proportion of francophones that voted Yes in the referendum a week later. Another 28 per cent regarded themselves as equally Quebecker and Canadian. On the other hand,

TABLE 5: SELF-IDENTIFICATION OF QUEBEC FRANCOPHONES, 1995

Quebecker only	29.0%
Quebecker first, but also Canadian	29.1
Quebecker and Canadian equally	28.1
Canadian first, but also Quebecker	6.7
Canadian only	5.4
none of these	1.2
don't know/refuse	0.5

Administered 23–6 October 1995
Note: The question was 'Personellement vous considérez-vous: Québécois(e) seulement; Québécois(e) d'abord; Québécois(e) et Canadien(ne) à part égale; Canadien(ne) d'abord, Québécois(e) ensuite; Canadien(ne) seulement; rien de cela; ne sait pas/refus?'
Source: André Blais, Pierre Martin, and Richard Nadeau, 'Sondage omnibus référendaire', survey conducted by the polling firm Léger and Léger.

few Quebec francophones defined themselves in the terms sought through the Trudeau strategy, that is, as Canadians first. Only about 7 per cent said they were 'Canadian first, but also Quebecker' and even fewer respondents, 5.4 per cent, said they were 'Canadian only'. In short, the Trudeau strategy could not change the way in which most Quebec francophones see their country.

The Roots of Failure

In the end, the national unity strategy was defeated by the immutability of Canada's linguistic structure (see Table 6). In 1971, 87.8 per cent of all Canadians who spoke primarily French at home lived in Quebec; 93.9 per cent of all Canadians speaking primarily English lived in the rest of Canada. In 1991, the proportion of francophones in Quebec had risen to 89.9 per cent and the proportion of anglophones outside Quebec had reached 95.9 per cent.[6] In short, Canada was more segregated than ever—and Quebec francophones had more reason than ever to maintain their historical attachment to Quebec as the centre of francophone life in Canada.[7]

As we have seen, the social and economic forces favouring this increased segregation were such that even the most aggressive efforts of the federal government, with the enthusiastic support of the provincial governments, could not have reversed the trend. Certainly, entrenchment of the right to minority-language schools could not make the difference, even though the Trudeau government was willing to produce a constitutional crisis to achieve that objective.

TABLE 6: DISTRIBUTION OF ANGLOPHONES AND FRANCOPHONES, 1971 AND 1991

	Inside Quebec	Outside Quebec
English as home language		
1971	6.1%	93.9%
1991	4.7	95.9
French as home language		
1971	87.8	12.2
1991	89.9	10.5

Sources: See note 6.

It was important to Quebec francophones that the federal government acquire a bilingual face and that francophones play a more visible role within it. Yet, even if Quebec francophones might thus feel less estranged from the federal government, Quebec remained their primary base of action and, accordingly, the Quebec government their primary political institution.

Nor was it possible simply to dissolve the effects of language difference through second-language training, as in Pierre Trudeau's cry that 'bilingualism unites people; dualism divides them'. Thanks largely to the federal government's efforts, many more Canadians, especially young English Canadians, have acquired knowledge of the other official language. But for most of them, their mother tongue remains by far the more effective means of expression. Indeed, it is the primary language of the communities in which they live. The phenomenal success of immersion programs in English-Canadian schools cannot alter the fact that the only place in North America where there is a hope of maintaining all the institutions of a modern society in French is Quebec.

Yet, the whole logic of the national unity strategy depended on somehow transforming or transcending this basic social reality. Only then would it be at all possible for Quebec francophones to see themselves first and foremost as Canadians—who happen to speak French.

Without this shift in the collective identity of Quebec francophones, the various elements of the national unity strategy became irritants and provocations. The Charter of Rights and Freedoms may offer support for the francophone minorities, but in the eyes of many Quebeckers it was above all a threat to Bill 101 and the continuation of francophone life in Quebec. Multiculturalism denied the cultural dualism that has always defined the basic structure of Canada and will continue to do so. The principle of equality of the provinces is a repudiation of Quebec's centrality to francophone life. And Ottawa's claim to be a national government imposing national standards seems to deny the historical status of a distinct francophone community and the Quebec government's responsibility for it.

AN ALTERNATIVE STRATEGY

All through the last three decades an alternative strategy for Canadian unity was readily available. At its core was the recognition both of duality, understood as a relationship between societies, and of the centrality of Quebec to francophone society. Linked to the latter was an asymmetrical place for Quebec in the federal system. Finally, linguistic equality was understood in terms not of individual rights throughout the country but of zones or territories within which each language was dominant.

We saw how the first two elements of this strategy were well identified during the 1960s. Under André Laurendeau's leadership, the Royal Commission on Bilingualism and Biculturalism elaborated the notion of a bicultural Canada composed of two culturally distinct societies. Each society was to be open to Canadians of all origins. And it was inevitable that the francophone society would be based primarily in Quebec. Indeed, the Commission declared, 'The place of Québécois in the French fact in Canada will in practice have to be recognized much more than it is today.'[8] At the same time, while accepting the ideal of official bilingualism, provincially as well as federally, the commission recognized the importance of protecting and advancing the French language in Quebec.

Lester Pearson's government had pioneered new asymmetrical forms of federalism that could accommodate Quebec's particular role in Canada's dualism. Through 'contracting out' and other devices the Quebec government assumed responsibilities that in the rest of the country were held by the federal government. Usually the option was offered to all the provinces but, invariably, Quebec was the only one to take advantage of it.

In the late 1970s, the Pepin-Robarts Task Force further developed these basic notions of duality and asymmetry. Like the B&B Commission, it forthrightly asserted Quebec's central place within the Canadian duality, and, on that basis, it proposed a renewed federalism in which Quebec would have 'the powers necessary to protect and develop its distinctive character'. This necessarily meant a more asymmetrical federalism. All the provinces would be assigned the powers needed by Quebec but they would not necessarily use them.

In addition, Pepin-Robarts recognized far more fully than the B&B Commission the relationship between language and territory. It proposed that the provinces should be free to define the status of languages in the way that was best suited to their particular linguistic composition. Pepin-Robarts was fully aware that in virtually all provinces there would be one principal language. Indeed, it made a point of commending Bill 101.

Finally, in the late 1980s, the Meech Lake Accord recognized duality and Quebec's distinctiveness in the most modest of terms—interpretative clauses. And its provisions with respect to immigration and the federal spending power would have enhanced asymmetry in federal-provincial relations.

Each time, this alternative strategy was rejected in favour of the Trudeau vision of Canada.

The Alternative Strategy and English Canada

In retrospect, it might be tempting to conclude that the rejection of this 'alternative strategy' was inevitable, even without the influence of Trudeau and his vision of Canada. At the end of the day, English Canada never would have accepted duality, asymmetry, and territoriality: the social and ideological forces were too heavily weighted against them. Yet, such a view may be a case of 'reading history backwards'. It devalues the efforts of the 1960s to find an accommodation of Quebec, and it ignores the subsequent effects of the Trudeau strategy itself in producing resistance to accommodation.

There can be no question that during the 1960s English-Canadian political and intellectual élites were uneasy with the implications of duality. In adopting the rhetoric of 'two nations', the Progressive Conservatives were often careful to insist that they did not support 'associate states' or other bi-national structures. Even NDPers tried to minimize any commitment to a two-nations vision of Canada. But at least they were struggling to come to terms with the French-Canadian understanding of Canada and to incorporate it within their own vision. A dialogue had been opened, in all three federal parties; a process had been launched. With the election of Trudeau this came to an abrupt end. The English-Canadian political and intellectual élites could hardly be expected to pursue an accommodation of Quebec nationalism when Quebec's ostensible leader unremittingly denounced accommodation and was able to mobilize a fair share of English-Canadian public opinion against it as well. After all, Trudeau offered a route to a much more congenial state of affairs in which Quebeckers would be Canadians like everyone else.

Over the years Canadians of neither British nor French origin have become fierce opponents of duality. Yet this opposition was greatly reinforced by the Trudeau government's rejection of biculturalism in favour of multiculturalism, for its own reasons. As we have seen, the B&B Commission had tried to define biculturalism in a way that could accommodate Canadians of all ethnic origins. The adoption of multiculturalism by the Trudeau government put an end to such efforts.

Similarly, there has been, at least outside Quebec, the mobilization of a multitude of collective identities, from gender to race to physical disability, that are seen to supersede and deny any notion of a Canada premised on a linguistic and cultural dualism. It might be argued that they too would have precluded the alternative strategy. Yet, the Trudeau government contributed directly to the mobilization of these identities. The secretary of state provided funding to a variety of organizations, such as women's groups and ethnic organizations, as part of its effort to develop a new pan-Canadian identity. In this way, it ensured that these identities would be seen as incompatible with the older notion of Canadian duality. And the Charter of Rights and Freedoms which gave constitutional recognition to these identities, further cemented the opposition to duality and to the recognition of Quebec's distinctiveness.

These propositions are clearly demonstrated by the experience of women's groups in Canada. Historically, English-Canadian women and Quebec francophone women have looked to different states, Ottawa and Quebec City, to advance their interests. They have in fact acted dualistically. However, once English-Canadian women had mobilized around the Charter, which denied Canadian dualism and the distinctiveness of Quebec, their advancement seemed to be threatened by the desire of Quebec women to continue acting within an autonomous political arena of their own. Thus, for English-Canadian women the distinct-society clause in the Meech Lake Accord threatened their hard-won gains, leading them to oppose a measure that Quebec women considered essential.[9]

Women in English Canada and Quebec need not have become so deeply divided. What made them into antagonists was the implementation of the national unity strategy. More recently, in fact, leading feminists in English Canada and Quebec have made a concerted effort to build on their common interests, and to come to terms with Canada's dualism.

Finally, it might be argued that any English-Canadian openness to duality would eventually have been undermined by the reaction against 'élite accommodation' that now pervades Canada. Historically, such advocates of duality as Henri Bourassa did think very much in terms of a coming together of the 'natural leaders' of the two Canadian peoples. It is not too much of a stretch to think of duality as a 'conspiracy' through which élites seek to keep the 'masses' divided. This has been a theme in some English-Canadian radical writing.

Such an interpretation of duality is belied, however, by the way in which left-wing forces in Quebec have mobilized *within* the context of a Quebec nation. In the early 1960s it was francophone union leaders and leftists, including the activist Michel Chartrand, who led the campaign to have the NDP adopt a two-nations vision of Canada. If, in response to their demands, duality had been recognized, it could have strengthened popular forces in Canada. The left in English Canada and Quebec could have been working together rather than at cross-purposes.

By all indications Quebec has not experienced the growth of populist reaction against 'closed door meetings' and 'executive federalism' that has marked English Canada in recent decades. One reason for the reaction against élite accommodation in English Canada is that populist or social democratic forces have not been well represented in the federal state, which for English Canadians is the crucial one. And once again the Charter of Rights and Freedoms has been a major influence by encouraging English Canadians, for whom it has become so important, to resent any modification of 'their' constitution by élite negotiations.

The second element of the alternative strategy, asymmetry, was resisted during the 1960s by federal bureaucrats who naturally resented any weakening of their power to administer programs on a pan-Canadian basis. Yet, by all indications Pearson and his closest associates remained committed to the concept. Without the emergence of a Quebec francophone who broke with his fellow Quebeckers and attacked asymmetry, they might have been able to keep it intact.

In the 1970s, asymmetry was challenged by the growth, most notably in western Canada, of support for the principle of equality of the provinces. This new insistence on absolute equality was due partly to the new economic power of the western provinces. But it also resulted from the Trudeau government's support for the principle in its struggles with Quebec. In any event, it is not clear why equality of the provinces could not be combined with asymmetry as it was practised during the Pearson years, when such devices as contracting out were offered to all the provinces. Indeed, asymmetry could increase the representation of the western provinces in Parliament if it meant that Quebec MPs would not vote on measures that did not apply in that province. (To be sure, asymmetry in the application of the Charter would be more difficult to square with the principle of equality of the provinces.)

Finally, a language policy under which the status of languages clearly varied among the provinces, reflecting the great differences in their linguistic structures, would have been quite acceptable in English Canada; in fact, it would have been widely preferred, provided of course that it had been established at the outset. The difficulties arose when, after some provinces had already begun to respond positively to the Trudeau government's pressures for official bilingualism, Quebec made French its only official language.

In short, many of the forces working against the 'alternative strategy' were themselves greatly reinforced by the efforts of the Trudeau government. Gender, ethnicity, and race seemed antithetical to dualism partly because the Trudeau government had helped to define them that way. Rather than providing a framework within which they might have found expression, dualism was made to appear as an obstacle to their mobilization.

The Alternative Strategy and Quebec

There has always been another kind of argument against the alternative strategy, framed in terms of Quebec. Even if English Canada had been prepared to adopt it, so the argument goes, a strategy of accommodation could not have unified the country. Indeed, it might well have hastened its breakup.

One form of this argument claims that, in effect, *no* strategy would have been effective: once the idea of independence takes hold, it becomes an irresistible force and a population will settle for nothing less. None the less, in the case of Quebec, that certainly was not true in the past. The idea of a separate state has had its disciples since before the turn of the century, but a significant separatist movement did not emerge until the 1960s. Moreover, this argument underestimates the continuing attachment of Quebec francophones to Canada, even if this attachment is not in terms that all English Canadians would recognize and accept. It was evident even among some of the Quebeckers who voted for sovereignty in 1995.

Another objection to the alternative strategy is that it would have simply strengthened the drive to separation. To recognize the distinctiveness of Quebec, this argument claims, would have been to fuel the fires of separatism. Yet, the pattern over recent decades of support for Quebec sovereignty suggests otherwise. Throughout the Trudeau era, support for sovereignty grew steadily. Its greatest jump occurred, however, with the collapse of the Meech Lake Accord. That signified definitively that there would be no accommodation of Quebec's claims, even in the most minimal terms. The constitutional status quo, the product of the Trudeau strategy, is clearly unacceptable to most Quebeckers, as survey after survey has revealed. But it was only when the hope for any alternative form of polity disappeared that support for sovereignty soared.

A final form of this argument contends that a strategy of accommodation could not have worked because Quebeckers would never be satisfied. They would always ask for more. In 1971, for example, Bourassa refused at the last minute to sign the Victoria Charter, hoping to get still more powers.

Yet, in the case of the Meech Lake Accord, the Quebec National Assembly, under Robert Bourassa's leadership, had given its formal consent to a constitutional package; the problem lay with other provincial legislatures. To be sure, even after signing the constitution Quebeckers might continue to want changes. But so would other Canadians. That is in the nature of a federal system.

The fact is that underlying all these arguments is another one: it is futile to look for an accommodation with Quebec because Quebec is in the grip of an ethnic nationalism. By its very nature Quebec nationalism can never be satisfied; it is driven by irrational forces, a state-of-siege mentality, a never-ending propensity to see itself as a victim, racism and ethnocentrism, demagoguery, and so on.[10] Indeed, by one reading of Quebec nationalism it is so fundamentally illiberal that it disqualifies Quebeckers from being Canadian.[11]

Such a description of Quebec nationalism has an obvious appeal outside Quebec. It implicitly flatters non-Quebeckers, in the process glossing over the evidence that English Canadians implicitly and even explicitly distinguish between native-born and immigrant Canadians. At the same time, this view of Quebec is the logical corollary of the Trudeau vision so firmly entrenched outside Quebec. If Quebeckers reject this vision in the name of their 'nation', it must be because they reject the liberalism that it embodies. This inference, however, presumes that liberalism can take only one form, that it must be resolutely individualist and limited to questions of procedure. It cannot admit any concern with the needs of a common community. As Charles Taylor has argued, a model of society concerned with such collective goals as linguistic and cultural survival may still be liberal 'provided it is also capable of respecting diversity, especially when this concerns those who do not share its goals, and provided it can offer adequate safeguards for fundamental rights'.[12]

Still, critics of Quebec nationalism might grant this point about liberalism in general but insist that nationalism *in Quebec* is irreconcilable with any form of liberalism. It cannot respect diversity and fundamental rights because it is inherently 'ethnic': membership in the Quebec nation is reserved for those whose ancestors have been there since the days of New France. That was certainly true of the French-Canadian nationalism of the past, just as, in the rest of Canada, the idea of a British nationality or Canada as the first 'White Dominion' assumed a particular ancestry.[13] In the 1960s, however, nationalism in Quebec began the shift from this ethnic nationalism to a territorial nationalism, that considered Quebec to be the home of a society in which French is the common language of a population of many origins. This new inclusive, territorial nationalism is seen in policies of the Quebec government and in the discourse of the Parti Québécois.[14]

Obviously the transition to this new Quebec nationalism is not complete. In his referendum-night speech, Jacques Parizeau gave full expression to the older ethnic nationalism. Not only did he stigmatize non-francophones for voting No, with his line that the sovereigntists were defeated by 'money and the ethnic vote', but he insisted on referring to 'us' not as 'francophones of Quebec' but 'Québécois'.[15] Nor did he fully apologize for his comments. Yet, it is also the case that his remarks produced a storm of protest in Quebec, extending beyond the media and political commentators to the Parti Québécois itself. Indeed, such was the reaction that he had to announce the next day that he would resign as premier. After making a statement that seemed to reserve 'Québécois' for whites, Lucien Bouchard was quick to disavow any such intent and to apologize for using words that allowed such an interpretation.[16] The debate continues about what he meant at the time.

It would be naive to presume that ethnic nationalism is not a significant influence among sovereigntists. By all indications, it was crucial in the mobilization of the Yes vote among Quebec francophones. And the refusal of all but a few non-francophones to vote Yes reflected their feeling that the sovereignty project excluded them. But it would be inaccurate to claim that *all* supporters of sovereignty and the Parti Québécois reserve the term 'Québécois' (or 'Quebecker') for native francophones alone. And it clearly would be unfair to claim the same for all other francophones as well.[17]

The fact remains that virtually all francophones are committed to the development of a modern, technologically advanced society that functions first and foremost in French. As the last few decades have so clearly shown, this is really possible only in Quebec. Accordingly, most francophones are going to share in a Quebec nationalism, whether they see the nation as drawing upon people of all origins or restricted to descendants of the inhabitants of New France. Beyond recognition of this nationalism, they will want the Quebec government to have the powers that are necessary to the development of a francophone society in Quebec. This need not entail sovereignty or independence, but it does entail a vision of Canada that recognizes duality, allows asymmetry, and, at least at the levels of provincial governments, accepts the pre-eminence of French in Quebec and of English in the rest of the country. The last few decades have made that crystal clear.

It is conceivable, then, that with proper leadership English Canadians might have supported an alternative response to the Quebec question, indeed the one that the Pearson government had been developing; it is also plausible that this alternative response might have been more effective in prevent-ing the growth of support for Quebec sovereignty.

The Impact of Global Change

Undoubtedly contemporary Canada is undergoing profound changes that would have taken place no matter what strategy had been followed on the national unity front: globalization, liberalization of trade, the break-down of 'Fordist' relations—based on mass production and consumption—between capital and labour, the rise of neo-liberalism, and pressures to reduce the size and power of governments. These challenges would necessarily have reduced the resources available to the Canadian government and forced a re-exami-nation of its role in the Canadian economy and society. These processes would have tested Canada's cohesion, however solid it might have been.[18] This can be seen in many parts of the world where the desire for regional autonomy and even secession has been reinforced. As the importance and effectiveness of established states have been weakened through international processes of liberalization and integration, regional institutions and identities have become more significant. Global changes have been especially destabi-lizing for states such as Canada, in which regions with culturally distinctive populations have spawned movements for autonomy and even independ-ence. One thinks of Spain, Belgium, even Great Britain.

Such changes, though, do not *explain* the appeal of sovereignty. They are not in themselves the *reason* for sovereignty and for the rejection of the Canadian political order. The appeal of Quebec sovereignty lies above all in the affirmation of collective identity. I have argued that the continued growth in support for sovereignty over the last three decades has a lot to do with the failure of Canadian political institutions to recognize and accom-modate this identity.

Quebec neo-nationalism, and the separatist movement, emerged in the early 1960s, long before such forces as neo-liberalism and the decline of Fordist capital-labour relations had started to have their impact. They resulted largely from processes within Quebec society, notably the rise of a new middle class and organized labour. Those classes, which were themselves the product of the urbanization and industrialization that began at the turn of the century, became major social forces in francophone Quebec during the 1950s. In the 1960s, their demands for a recasting of the Quebec state bore fruit and Quebec underwent its Quiet Revolution. It is out of these processes that there arose the demands for a restructuring of Quebec's rela-tionship with the rest of Canada. In effect, during the 1960s and even the 1970s, the attack on the federal state came primarily from within Canada. At dispute was not the continued viability of the post-war Canadian models of

Keynesian state intervention and Fordist capital-labour relations, but the role that francophones should play within them.

To be sure, the case for Quebec sovereignty was clearly enhanced during the late 1980s by the reinforcement of continental economic links through the FTA and NAFTA. In effect, sovereigntists could argue that with sovereignty Quebec would continue to have access to major external markets. Thus the main argument of the federalists in the 1980 referendum—that English Canada would refuse to enter into any economic association with Quebec—lost some of its force. Moreover, Quebec's trade with the rest of Canada has been steadily decreasing, and its trade with the United States increasing.[19] Sovereigntists could even claim that the United States, in order to protect NAFTA, would prevent the rest of Canada from erecting trade barriers against Quebec. Though based upon conjecture, such arguments clearly can help the sovereigntist case.

Similarly, it can be argued that the contemporary neo-liberal attacks on state intervention have had an especially devastating effect on the Canadian government, given its high level of indebtedness. This makes it easier for sovereigntists to present the federal government as a problem, and to rebut the federalist argument that Quebeckers benefit from federalism.

Yet it is my argument that the key to understanding the present crisis is the ways in which the Trudeau strategy undermined the established francophone idea of Canada and Quebec's place in it. Trade liberalization and other forces of global change have facilitated or reinforced an ongoing process in Canada itself.

It should be noted that the Trudeau strategy is especially ill-suited to such a changed environment. After all, it is based on the premise that the Canadian state must strengthen the French presence throughout Canada, and raise the visibility and importance of the federal government, the 'national' government, in the lives of Quebeckers. Yet, the very possibility of such a role for the federal government has fallen victim to the processes of globalization and neo-liberalism.

In the end, arguments about the effects of the Trudeau strategy can only be speculative. In particular, they hinge on the kind of case I have been trying to make regarding the availability and greater effectiveness of an alternative strategy. Yet, if our case is at all plausible it raises some important possibilities.

State versus Society

My analysis points to the crucial influence that individuals can have on the course of politics and the fate of nations. Thus, it has some bearing on a continuing debate in political science between 'state-centred' and 'society-centred' interpretations of political life.[20] As the term implies, 'society-centred' theory bases the explanation of politics on the structures of society and the forces that operate there. Yet the case of Trudeau and Canada shows that in exceptional circumstances individuals, using the apparatus of the state, can have a decisive impact—if they are themselves exceptional. At the same time, the impact of this leader sprang from his ability to connect with movements and forces that were already present in society, and to mobilize them for his own purposes.

Perhaps the clearest demonstration of these processes lies with the Charter of Rights and Freedoms, the abiding goal of Trudeau's career as prime minister. For Trudeau, the Charter's central purpose was the entrenchment of language rights. Yet in 1981 a variety of groups, largely outside Quebec, quickly seized upon the idea of a charter as a way to attain a number of goals, from legal rights to gender equality to remedial action for physical handicaps.[21] It is difficult to see how, without Trudeau's deep personal determination, a charter would have been adopted, such was the opposition of most of the premiers. It is also clear, however, that without the mobilization of social forces on behalf of the project Trudeau would not have been able to prevail.

Similarly, we have seen that Trudeau had his own reasons for rejecting biculturalism, which he had made clear well before becoming prime minister. Nonetheless, it was the mobilization of 'third-force' Canadians against biculturalism that made it possible for him to replace biculturalism with multiculturalism. Finally, Trudeau's success in persuading many English Canadians to adopt his new conception of a bilingual, multicultural Canada was in large part due to English Canadians' availability for a new vision of Canada, given the weakening of the British connection.

Ironically, Trudeau was much less influential in Quebec, where his roots lay and where English Canadians assumed his authority was greatest. The explanation, just as it was in English Canada, was the ability of Trudeau and his vision to mobilize major social forces.

As we have seen, Quebec francophones have felt themselves to be members of a distinct society, rooted in Quebec. Indeed, the link between the *canadien* collectivity and Quebec was formalized in 1791, when the Constitution Act divided Lower and Upper Canada. Such was the resultant 'fit' between political institutions and social conditions that it has persisted, in one form or another, ever since, defeating one state strategy after another. Although the United Canadas had been intended to assimilate French Canadians, it was itself organized on the distinction between Canada East and Canada West. Partly for this reason, the United Canadas soon developed a highly complex system of dualism. By the same token, the leading forces behind Confederation had to abandon their dreams of a unitary state, given resistance among Quebec francophones, and adopt a federal system with Quebec as a province. Within Confederation, francophone attachment to Quebec was reinforced through recurrent conflict with anglophones. Even for such a Canadian patriot as Henri Bourassa, Quebec was 'the particular inheritance of French Canada'.

During Trudeau's term as prime minister an impressive number of Quebec francophones entered the upper ranks of the federal government. As we have seen, many of them not only occupied cabinet positions that had always been held by anglophones, but their presence as senior civil servants grew remarkably: for the first time it equalled the proportion of Quebec francophones in the Canadian population. Many of these people were intensely loyal to Trudeau and his vision of Canada. In its defence of federalism and Canada, the federal government could also count upon the support of most members of Quebec's growing francophone business class. Yet in the late 1980s, many of the same people refused to follow Trudeau in what he saw as the logical consequence of his vision: opposition to the Meech Lake Accord, in particular, the distinct-society clause. In fact, the Accord was supported publicly by many leading Quebec members of the Trudeau government: Monique Bégin, André Ouellet, Serge Joyal, Francis Fox, and Jean-Luc Pepin. And most Quebec business leaders supported the Accord, even forming a lobby group, led by Claude Castonguay, to help persuade English Canada to accept it. Clearly, their vision of Canada did not preclude recognition of Quebec's distinctiveness.

At the root of this persistent attachment to Quebec was the simple fact that francophones were concentrated in Quebec. Nothing the Trudeau government did could change that fact. Nor could it reduce the effect that this pattern had upon the political allegiances of Quebec francophones. To be sure, the federal government's efforts to persuade Quebeckers to adopt a new pan-Canadian identity were countered by the efforts of the Quebec government to promote the distinctly Québécois identity. But the Quebec government's efforts had the advantage of language and a centuries-old collective identity.

The experience of the Trudeau government is instructive for the debate between 'state-centred' and 'society-centred' interpretations of political life. In English Canada, the Trudeau government was able to mobilize social forces on behalf of its new conception of Canada; in Quebec, it was defeated by social forces. In effect, social conditions set clear limits on the influence of political leaders, and on the state more generally.

There is a final insight to be drawn. Whatever the capacity of the Trudeau strategy to mould society, whether in English Canada or in Quebec, the strategy did correspond to the world-view of a very particular stratum of society, the linguistic minorities, both in Quebec and outside Quebec, who look to the federal government to ease their relations with the linguistic majorities of their respective provinces. Trudeau's vision of a Canada in which French and English would be equal from coast to coast was the perfect response to their fears. And Trudeau, who refused to link himself exclusively with either of Canada's linguistic communities, was the perfect embodiment of this vision. Thus, it is not surprising that Montreal anglophones and francophones from outside Quebec should play disproportionately important roles in the federal government and should provide the firmest bases of electoral support for the Trudeau government.[22]

Whatever significance it might have for debates in political science, my argument has another, perhaps more important, implication—that the present impasse was not inevitable. It was the result of strategies and policies that were chosen deliberately, often with the best of intentions, and which had precisely the opposite effects of what was intended, dividing rather than unifying Canadians. In effect, we unwittingly created our present predicament.

To be sure, our present impasse also shows the extent to which institutions can become 'frozen'.[23] The 1960s were an extraordinary period when basic questions about Canada were being seriously addressed for the first time. But once the questions had been answered, with the Trudeau orthodoxy, and especially after they had been entrenched in the constitution, it became extremely difficult to open them anew. The débâcles of Meech and Charlottetown are ample testimony to that.

WHAT SHOULD WE DO NOW?

If the present crisis was not inevitable but is the result of decisions that were made, then it is possible that through a new approach and new strategies we might still be able to find our way out of the crisis. Separation is *not* inevitable.

As I have argued, an alternative to the Trudeau strategy had already been well-defined during the 1960s; it was based on duality and asymmetry. These notions were further refined in the late 1970s by the Pepin-Roberts Task Force, which also proposed greater application of the territorial principle to language regimes. This alternative strategy is the logical place to start. We need to see whether the general direction it offers can be applied to the Canada of the late 1990s.

Recognizing Differences

The basic organizing concept of the 'alternative strategy', duality, has an obvious flaw: it does not address the aboriginal question. The B&B Commission simply side-stepped the matter, saying that 'Canada's native populations' did not fall within the terms of its mandate.[24] The Pepin-Robarts Task Force did give some attention to 'the First Canadians', but the basic framework within which it sought to interpret the Canadian crisis, coupling dualism with regionalism, did not afford a clear place for aboriginal peoples. For that matter, the task force's recommendations were rather imprecise.[25] None the less, an approach that is based upon the recognition and accommodation of collectivities, even if initially understood as francophone and anglophone, has at least the potential to embrace aboriginal peoples. We saw that the Trudeau vision, with its unqualified individualism, was inherently unable even to understand the aboriginal question; the policy it produced had to be abandoned.

An attempt to conceive of Canada in terms that incorporate not only the anglophone-francophone duality but aboriginal peoples as well does not have to lead to the never-ending recognition of even smaller communities, as with such formulas as 'Community of Communities'. The notion of duality is rooted in two central features. The first is primary allegiance. Francophones, at least in Quebec, have always given their primary allegiance to a francophone society; their attachment to Canada is built upon this sense of a distinctly francophone nationality. Historically, anglophone Canadians placed themselves within a British nationality, although they now tend to identify directly with Canada. Second, the notion of duality is rooted in social structure. As the B&B Commission argued, francophones and anglophones tend to live their lives within distinct societies.

If we apply these same criteria of primary allegiances and social differentiation, then obviously aboriginal peoples emerge as members of a distinct community. There may be profound linguistic and cultural differences among aboriginal peoples in Canada, but they are transcended by the knowledge of a common origin and history.

Once these distinctions have been drawn, it becomes clear Canada cannot be thought of as a single nation. Indeed Canada contains distinct collectivities that see themselves as nations and possess the institutional and cultural distinctiveness usually implied by the term. Canada might be better understood as a 'multinational' entity. The basic premise of such a 'multinational' Canada is that nations do not have to be states in the fullest sense of the term; that is, they do not have to be *sovereign* states. Rather, their needs can be met through arrangements that give them autonomy for certain purposes—in other words, federalism. Within such a Canada, 'unity' is not achieved through the solidarity of a single nation, as in 'national unity'. Rather, it involves accommodation and consensus among the collectivities that make it up.

The first step in applying this reformulated 'alternative strategy' would be to acknowledge Canada's 'multinational' character. But what terminology should be used? The simplest way would be to designate the collectivities as 'nations'. As we have seen, Lester Pearson used the label 'nation' quite openly in his pleas for recognition of Quebec. Similarly, some present-day commentators have formulated the notion of a 'three-nation Canada'.[26] However, the term 'two nations' caused considerable unease among some English Canadians in the 1960s; 'three nations' has met with a similar response now. Thus, over the years other terms have been proposed. The B&B Commission managed to avoid the term 'nation', instead referring to 'distinct societies'. As it turned out, 'distinct society' has had an unhappy career. Widely rejected in English Canada as too big a concession, the designation of Quebec as a distinct society is seen in much of post-referendum Quebec as too little. Charles Taylor has tried to distinguish between levels of diversity within the Canadian population, reserving 'deep diversity' for francophones and aboriginals.[27] This too has provoked opposition: analysts have argued against relegating other categories of Canadians to 'lesser' levels of diversity.[28]

In fact, there is no terminology that will be acceptable to Canadians who oppose the very notion of recognizing distinct collectivities *within* Canada. Yet there is little to be gained from formulas that, in trying to avoid such opposition, afford no meaningful recognition at all. A case in point is the recent suggestion that Quebec should be designated as 'culturally distinct, but fiscally equal'.

To be effective, not only must recognition, whether of Quebec or of aboriginal peoples, be open and straightforward, but also it must have an important place in the constitution, which is the central definition of the Canadian polity. Thus, in both the Meech Lake Accord and the Charlottetown Accord, this recognition was not restricted to a preamble or 'Canada clause'. It also appeared in an interpretative clause designed to apply to the Charter of Rights and Freedoms. Such a provision would not automatically lead the courts to interpret provisions of the Charter differently when it came to Quebec or to aboriginal peoples. It would raise a consideration that the courts would need to bear in mind when, under the terms of the Charter, they determined whether a particular measure was 'demonstrably justified in a free and democratic society'.

Reorganizing Federalism

In the alternative strategy, the main formula for reorganizing our political institutions so as to better reflect a 'multinational' Canada has been asymmetry. Asymmetry would give the Quebec government the powers that follow from its responsibility for supporting and promoting Quebec's distinctiveness, without undermining the ability of the federal government to assume the responsibilities expected of it in the rest of the country. In short, it was an alternative to major devolution of functions to all provinces.

In the late 1990s the federal government is in any event devolving responsibilities to the provinces, given the weight of fiscal pressures bearing upon it. With less money to transfer to the provinces, Ottawa is less able to force the provinces to abide by 'national standards' in areas such as health care and social policy. Nor will Ottawa be able to be as active in regional economic development as in the past. It is less and less able to act as a 'national' government in any part of the country. To this extent, asymmetry loses its raison d'être.

None the less, the reason for the recent decentralization is largely financial. Thus, it does not necessarily address Quebec's particular concerns. A case in point is immigration. In recent decades the Quebec government has exercised far more power over the selection of immigrants than have the other provinces. Whereas the other provinces were prepared to leave that responsibility to Ottawa, Quebec's unique concern with a francophone society meant that it could not. By the same token, unlike the other provincial governments, Quebec could not assume that immigrants would integrate themselves with the linguistic majority. Thus, it needed to take direct responsibility for the integration of immigrants. Such considerations will continue, whatever the fiscal circumstances of Ottawa and of the provinces.

With its responsibility for promoting Canada's primary francophone society, the Quebec government is bound to take a stronger interest in support for cultural and artistic activities than will the other provinces. They can assume that their linguistic majorities will have access to the fullest range of cultural and artistic expression; Quebec cannot.

Finally, whereas many provinces are increasingly interested in assuming responsibility for job training, as part of their general concern with the strength of their economies, Quebec has an added reason: its historical determination to control education as an indispensable tool of cultural survival. In Quebec the social consensus in favour of total control of job training is correspondingly stronger than elsewhere.

In short, asymmetry in federal-provincial arrangements follows logically from asymmetry in the responsibilities of the provincial governments and in the attitudes and allegiances of the provincial electorates. Thus, it is difficult to see how Quebec's particular demand can be satisfied without some expansion of asymmetry in federal-provincial relations. Such arrangements, though, cannot be purely administrative; Quebec must have the guarantee that can be given only by the constitution.

If Quebec is to have extensive rights to 'opt out' and enter into bilateral arrangements, then the public would probably insist that all the provinces have the same rights. The most suitable constitutional device is the one favoured by Pepin-Robarts: concurrence with provincial paramountcy. So as to ensure that a provincial government was asserting paramountcy as an expression of a clear preference within the province, rather than for frivolous reasons, the constitution might require approval by a two-thirds legislative vote or a popular referendum.

Especially if asymmetry is to have constitutional sanction, the question of representation might be unavoidable. As we have seen, it has been argued that such arrangements raise the prospect of MPs voting on measures that did not apply in their province, and cabinet ministers having responsibilities that are not exercised in their province. This has not been an issue with the Canadian Pension Plan. But this criticism might acquire more force if Quebec, and perhaps other provinces, were to opt out of a large number of programs. Some commentators have proposed that, at this stage, MPs simply would not vote on measures that did not apply in their province. Indeed, such an arrangement could be formalized in the operations of Parliament. On certain days of the week Parliament would deal with matters applying to all provinces; on other days it would deal with matters that excluded Quebec, and Quebec MPs.[29] At a certain point, however, such an arrangement would in all likelihood prove impractical.[30] It would then be necessary to adopt an arrangement closer to 'confederalism', which I will turn to at the end of this chapter.

Recently, André Burelle has proposed an alternative formula for reconciling the objectives of Quebec and of the rest of Canada.[31] Drawing upon European experience, Burelle proposes federal-provincial arrangements based upon partnership and 'co-decision'. Burelle's scheme starts from the principle of subsidiarity, by which the federal government is assigned only the jurisdictions that cannot be properly assumed by the provinces. It would allow for exclusive provincial control over a wide range of areas but with the proviso that the federal government would have exclusive responsibility to pursue 'supra-provincial' functions in these areas. This would include areas of exclusive provincial jurisdiction that affect the economic and social union, such as education and health, and areas of 'double exclusive competence' where Ottawa has a clear responsibility, such as immigration, interprovincial trade, and telecommunications. This juxtaposition of provincial and federal responsibilities in the same areas would in turn require 'partnership' mechanisms for managing the interdependence of governments that would result. Within these 'partnership' mechanisms governments would jointly establish norms and objectives for a given area. Thus, standards would be set for the country as a whole through 'co-decision' rather than being defined unilaterally by Ottawa.

Burelle believes that such an arrangement would meet the objectives of most Quebeckers, at least those who are federalist. At the same time, it would avoid the different status for Quebec contained in asymmetry, as well as the institutional complications of asymmetry. But federal-provincial mechanisms of co-decision do have disadvantages of their own, especially from the point of view of English Canada. First, co-decision may not give English Canadians enough assurance that the provinces will in fact observe national standards.[32] Most English Canadians have been quite prepared to see Ottawa enforce national standards in such areas as health care. Second, the collective definition of standards through federal-provincial negotiations raises the old spectre of 'executive federalism', by which decisions are made 'behind closed doors' and then imposed on Parliament and the provincial legislatures. Indeed, the Mulroney government's original proposals for a Council of the Federation[33] was abandoned for precisely this reason. Thus, in deciding between asymmetry and a system of co-decision, it becomes a matter of weighing the advantages and disadvantages of each.

With respect to institutional arrangements to accommodate aboriginal peoples, the Charlottetown Accord pointed the way with its commitment to recognize 'the inherent right to self-government' of aboriginal peoples, who would constitute 'one of three orders of government in Canada'. The precise responsibilities of the new aboriginal governments were to be defined over a period of up to five years through negotiations among aboriginal leaders and federal and provincial governments. It was generally understood that there would be enormous variation in the powers and responsibilities of governments that make up this new third level. Not only are aboriginal peoples divided among 60 to 80 nations,[34] but the socio-economic conditions and desire for autonomy of the bands vary widely.[35] By the same token, there would be a great variation in how much authority and responsibility for aboriginal peoples remained with federal and provincial governments.[36] It is interesting that these very pronounced forms of asymmetry were not a major concern in public debate over the Charlottetown Accord. Indeed, the debate focused not on the relationship between aboriginal governments and other governments, but on the extent to which aboriginal governments were to be bound by the Charter of Rights and Freedoms. This debate extended, moreover, to aboriginal peoples themselves.[37]

Territoriality in Language Regimes

Beyond formally recognizing nationality and enhancing the autonomy of distinct institutions, a 'multinational' Canada could also be accommodated by adapting the final element of the 'alternative strategy': applying the territorial principle to language regimes. Once it was established that Canada is composed of distinct collectivities, then language could be approached in a more meaningful manner. Rather than an attribute of individuals, language would be clearly recognized as the expression of communities.

Defined on this basis, the status of languages would depend on where the linguistic communities were situated. The Pepin-Robarts Task Force pointed the way to such an arrangement with its clear distinction between federal and provincial levels. Within federal jurisdictions, English and French were to have the same status throughout the country; in provincial jurisdictions, legislatures were to be free to choose the arrangements best suited to the linguistic composition of their particular province. The provinces might be expected to provide basic services to their linguistic minorities, as Pepin-Robarts proposed. The commitment to do so might be embodied in interprovincial agreements, whether the reciprocal agreements proposed by the Lévesque government or collective agreements among all provinces. Or the provinces might decide to agree to constitutional entrenchment on an individual basis, as the Victoria Charter proposed, or collectively, as Pepin-Robarts suggested.

Services to linguistic minorities could also be conceived in terms of communities rather than individuals.[38] Not only would the recognition of minority-language rights be recognized only where there were indeed such communities, but the rights would be clearly vested in the *institutions* of those communities.[39] As various commentators have noted, we would strengthen the long-term prospects for the linguistic minorities by enabling their own institutions to provide basic educational, health, and social services. It is also clear that reinforcement of the communities' institutions is far more important than such features of official bilingualism as proclamation of laws in both languages, and the costly translation of statutes.[40]

At the same time, recognition of language rights would have to be extended beyond English and French to aboriginal languages. The same principles would prevail. Recognition would be geared to specific aboriginal communities; rights would be bestowed on the institutions of those communities.

Finally, it goes without saying that the 'national' collectivities would each have vetoes over constitutional changes that would affect their rights and prerogatives. As is the practice under the existing amending formula, these vetoes would be exercised by legislatures on their behalf. In other words, the Quebec National Assembly and the aboriginal governments would have a veto. At the same time, there is, however, no legislature for English Canada, the other presumed component of this 'multinational Canada'. The existing amending formula does, however, protect English Canada by giving a veto to all provincial legislatures on some matters and to the overwhelming major-ity on others.

In short, if the 'alternative strategy' that has been so consistently rejected over the last three decades were extended to embrace aboriginal peoples, it might still offer a way out of the present impasse, by recognizing 'national' or primary communities within Canada. To be sure, with the result of the last referendum and the consequent heightening of expectations in Quebec, the Canadian polity might have to be reorganized much more than was envis-aged in the past. Indeed, the necessary devolution of powers to Quebec might be so great as to make asymmetry untenable and instead to require some form of 'confederalism'.

Unfortunately, my analysis of English Canada's post-referendum deliber-ations suggests that it would be no easy matter to adopt this strategy. To be sure, the second element of the strategy, a reorganization of the institutions of federalism, might begin with administrative agreements among govern-ments. To a certain extent that is already happening. But the first element, recognition of Canada's multinational character, requires that the constitution be amended. The third element, a reform of language laws, also requires con-stitutional change to be meaningful. In the present circumstances it is exceedingly difficult to imagine the political conditions that might make this possible. As we have seen, the Chrétien government does not have the necessary credibility, or commitment, to persuade English-Canadian pub-lic opinion to give up the Trudeau vision of Canada, let alone the Reform Party's. Nor do enough provincial premiers seem able to rise to the challenge.

The ultimate obstacle to a 'multinational Canada' is, of course, that English Canada refuses to see itself as a distinct nationality.[41] Even in the 1960s, English-Canadian political and intellectual élites who were prepared to see Quebec (or French Canada) as a distinct entity within Canada had trouble with the idea of an English-Canadian counterpart. Now, within the Trudeau vision, in which there can be no distinct entities of any kind, the notion of an 'English-Canadian nation' is totally beyond comprehension.

If the alternative strategy is not followed in a concerted way, the essen-tial post-referendum change will be an increase in provincial autonomy of all provinces. Within some schemes, this decentralization could be very exten-sive.[42] Beyond the ongoing effects of the debt crisis and neo-liberal attacks on 'big government', decentralization could also be fuelled by the argument that it is needed as a response to Quebec. Yet decentralization alone would miss the point. It would not address the concerns about Quebec's relation-ship with Canada, as defined first and foremost in the constitution, which drove so many Quebeckers to vote Yes in the 1995 referendum.

It may well be that the Trudeau strategy and its vision of Canada are now too entrenched in Canada's institutions, and in English Canadians' understanding of Canada, to allow a major change of course. What might have been possible 20 or even 10 years ago may no longer be possible. Opportunities have been passed up and choices have been made, for better or for worse.

Beyond that, it is possible that the alternative strategy would no longer be enough to satisfy Quebec, given both the collapse of the Meech Lake Accord and the results of the 1995 referendum. Francophone anger over the rejection of the Meech Lake Accord had already led to a hardening of attitudes and a rise in support for sovereignty. Now that sovereignty has become a distinct possibility, some Quebec francophones may conclude that a more radical change to the Canadian political order would be needed. Since the referendum, relations between francophones and anglophones, both in Quebec and in Canada as a whole, have worsened. What might have seemed quite satisfactory just a few years ago may now be simply too little, too late.

Perhaps the impasse between Quebec and the rest of Canada will simply persist. Quebeckers will decide, tacitly at least, that unpalatable as the status quo may be, the costs of sovereignty are too great. Also, as it proceeds to restructure Quebec's public finances, the PQ government may alienate potential Yes voters. The broadly social-democratic coalition that is crucial to the sovereigntist movement has become increasingly unhappy with the Bouchard government's spending cuts and responsiveness to business demands. In October 1996 there were indications that the PQ government's popularity was slipping, and support for sovereignty with it,[43] although by early 1997 these trends had been reversed. In any event, under Quebec's referendum law a new referendum on Quebec sovereignty cannot be held until after the next election. Lucien Bouchard has said repeatedly he will not call that election before his government has completed the normal number of years in office. Surveys have shown that the Quebec public strongly agrees with that decision.[44] Thus, any future referendum would not take place before 1999 or 2000, at the earliest. For that matter, the Parti Québécois could well be defeated in the next election, in which case there would be no referendum at all.

A long postponement of the next referendum could dampen the ardour of *indépendantistes*. But Canada will not be united; 'national unity' will be little more than a joke. Quebec francophones and English Canadians may become even more resentful of each other's attitudes and actions. But they may be led by other concerns, such as economic insecurity, simply to put aside their unresolved differences—at least for a while.

WHAT IF IT COMES TO SOVEREIGNTY?

It is also possible that in a few years' time another Quebec referendum will produce a clear majority in favour of sovereignty. What then should English Canadians do? How should Quebeckers deal with the situation they will have created?

Our analysis of the national unity debate of the last three decades offers at least two important leads to answering these questions. First, we would need to recognize that this outcome was not inevitable. We are not naturally the worst of enemies. Nor does the result prove that one side or the other is inherently immoral or obstinate. It will have happened because of actions that were taken, or not taken, by our leaders.

Second, we would need to recognize that the Trudeau vision cannot help us deal with the concrete prospects of sovereignty. By definition, it sees the secession of Quebec in apocalyptic terms. After all, Trudeau declared in 1976 that the breakup of Canada would be nothing less than a 'sin against humanity'.[45] By this logic, secession by Quebec should be avoided at all costs. Any strategy, however risky, would be acceptable. When Trudeau spoke against the Meech Lake Accord to the Senate, he concluded with the plea, 'If it [Canada] is going to go, let it go with a bang rather than a whimper.'[46]

On the contrary, Canadians have no reason to entertain the notion that their country should end with a bang. Even within the most uncharitable opinion of Quebec society and its nationalist movement, the secession of Quebec is hardly of such moral depravity that it must be prevented at all costs. Surely, there have been enough examples elsewhere to suggest that, like Quebeckers, Canadians outside Quebec have every interest in secession's being peaceful.

Defining the Interests of Canadians outside Quebec

In fact, in the light of Canadians' clear interests one can even specify what form secession should take, if indeed it is going to happen. If economic and social instability are to be minimized, the secession should be orderly and based on 'the rule of law'. In other words, it should be done by revising the Canadian constitution so as to eliminate Quebec as a province rather than by a unilateral declaration of independence. This might be a difficult undertaking, since the consent of most or even all provincial legislatures would be needed but it is surely in Canada's interest. By the same token, so as to minimize economic uncertainty, as well as social stress, the process of secession should be quite rapid. To be sure, it can be argued that the costs of a violent, illegal, or long-drawn-out secession would be much higher for Quebec than for the rest of Canada. Yet, it is still difficult to see how Canadians outside Quebec have an interest in assuming such costs.

Canadians outside Quebec also have a clear interest in the *terms* of Quebec's secession. They have a financial interest in such questions as the share of the national debt that Quebec might assume or the division of assets. They also have a financial interest in maintaining links with Quebec that they profit from. One immediately thinks of trade relations, but there might be an advantage in co-ordinating policies in many other areas too. Finally, Canadians outside Quebec probably have an interest in Quebec's secession being on terms that will be least damaging to the coherence of a Canada without Quebec. Here, the mobility of people and goods between Ontario and the Atlantic provinces comes to mind. The wish to avoid further fragmentation of Canada probably militates in favour of a rapid, orderly secession.

As Canadians outside Quebec face the prospect of Quebec secession they would, in a way they never had before, be viewing Quebeckers as foreigners. The kinds of compromises they might make with fellow Canadians would no longer be acceptable. But that does not justify Canadians and Quebeckers treating each other as the worst of enemies either.

If this is the right way for Canadians outside Quebec to view a sovereign Quebec, several practical questions need to be addressed.[47]

Responding to a Referendum

First, how should the rest of Canada respond to a majority vote for sovereignty? Over the last few decades, a general consensus has emerged that the rest of Canada should enter into good-faith negotiations with Quebec over the terms of its withdrawal, provided the question itself is clear and the referendum conducted democratically. Lester Pearson asked, 'If it comes to secession, and the decision is democratically taken, do we accept it or fight?'[48] There might be an argument for simply ignoring the result and the expectation in Quebec that the federal government would enter into negotiations over the terms of Quebec's secession. Conceivably, the supporters of sovereignty would then lose their resolve and the Quebec government would not immediately act on its mandate. Yet, one could as easily imagine that such a response might fuel a backlash in Quebec and strengthen the hand of the Quebec government.[49] Before long, the federal government would be forced to intervene to ensure that federal laws were obeyed. So, if indeed Canadians have an interest in an orderly, peaceful secession, they should ensure that negotiations begin without undue delay.

Still, how large a majority would be necessary to trigger negotiations? It has been suggested, by Prime Minister Chrétien among others, that more than '50 per cent plus one' would be necessary. Yet a simple majority has always been the basis of decision making in Canada. Even Newfoundland's decision to join Canada was based on a majority of only 2 per cent. For that matter, in each of the last two Quebec referendums the federalist forces tacitly acknowledged that the outcome would be decided by a simple majority.[50] At the same time, a strong case can be made that Quebec should not be able to declare sovereignty until approval of sovereignty has been confirmed in a second referendum that would be held once the terms on which Quebec might become sovereign had been established through negotiations with the rest of Canada.[51]

Even if the rest of Canada decided to recognize the outcome of a Quebec referendum and enter into negotiations over the terms of Quebec's withdrawal, how should it do so? What is, in fact, 'the rest of Canada'? There is no institution that can act for the rest of Canada in any negotiations. The instrument would have to be the federal government, acting on behalf of the rest of Canada. Currently, Quebeckers occupy positions in that government that would be crucial in any such negotiations: prime minister, intergovernmental affairs minister, and finance minister. But there is nothing to prevent the Liberal Party, as the government party, from replacing these office holders with non-Quebeckers. Clearly, the nine provincial governments outside Quebec would want to be involved in the negotiations, and aboriginal leaders probably would too. But a negotiating authority could be established for this purpose.[52]

Addressing the Issues

With the logistics decided, how should negotiations proceed? Some of the items are quite straightforward. A clear case in point is the federal debt. Sovereigntist leaders have said repeatedly that Quebec would assume a share of the federal debt, but what *is* the right share? Not surprisingly, a wide range of answers have been proposed, with sovereigntists proposing much smaller shares than federalists. Yet, both sides would have a common framework for approaching the question; with a reasonable effort, negotiations could result in an agreement on a mid-point between the opposing starting positions.

A far more difficult matter is the question of aboriginal and linguistic minorities and the related question of territorial boundaries. There is every likelihood that in another referendum on Quebec sovereignty, Quebec's aboriginal peoples and anglophone community would be firmly opposed. Some of their members would demand that Quebec's boundaries be redrawn so that the territory occupied by minorities would remain in Canada.

Canadians outside Quebec undoubtedly would be concerned with the welfare of these groups. Indeed, the federal government has a fiduciary responsibility for native peoples in Quebec, as elsewhere in Canada. There is also a certain logical appeal to the argument that, if Canada is divisible, then so is Quebec.

Yet it seems very likely that if negotiations concentrated on Quebec's boundaries they would end in a stalemate. Even federalist leaders in Quebec have insisted on the 'territorial integrity' of Quebec. And although in principle, the parts of northern Quebec inhabited by the Crees and Inuit could be detached from a sovereign Quebec, it is difficult to see how the boundaries could be redrawn to accommodate all of Quebec's aboriginal and anglophone minorities.[53]

It would be far preferable to try to provide security to Quebec's minorities through reciprocal agreements between Canada and Quebec.[54] Under such agreements both Quebec and Canada would undertake to respect the rights of their minorities and provide services to their respective minorities. To provide greater security, the Quebec-Canada bodies that oversee such agreements might contain minority group leaders. In the case of linguistic minorities, the heavy concentration of francophones within a few Canadian provinces probably means that any agreement would apply to only those provinces. Conversely, in Quebec the agreement would apply only to areas of major anglophone concentration.[55]

A Canada-Quebec 'Partnership'?

Finally, beyond the terms on which Quebec becomes sovereign, what sort of relations should it maintain with Canada? During the 1995 referendum the Quebec government proposed a partnership based on the three-party agreement of the previous June. In all likelihood, a referendum question that received a majority Yes vote would make sovereignty dependent on the offer, if not acceptance, of such an arrangement. We also saw that the 1995 partnership consisted of little more than a range of possible forms of collaboration with quite conventional mechanisms to bring it about.

Where then does the interest of Canada outside Quebec lie? It is clear that relations with a sovereign Quebec could be based only on the material interests of Canada without Quebec. Quebeckers and Canadians would no longer be linked by the bonds of sentiment that have operated in the past. Indeed, many English Canadians would undoubtedly be very angry at the prospect of Quebec sovereignty and would be ready to sacrifice even their financial interests to express their outrage. Beyond that, the English-Canadian desire for democratic accountability, reflected in the reaction against 'executive federalism', would militate against giving extensive responsibilities to inter-state mechanisms. In addition, since Canada's population and economy are so much larger than Quebec's, any system of mutual vetoes would not be appealing. Finally, western Canadians would see no particular interest in arrangements that unduly benefited central Canada.

Nevertheless, it would be in Canada's interests to maintain free trade with Quebec. Indeed, that would be heavily favoured by the existence of NAFTA. There would also be a case for co-ordinating policies in a wide range of areas. On the other hand, Canadians outside Quebec would probably not see much reason to agree to the sovereigntist proposal that Quebeckers should be able to keep their Canadian citizenship. To be sure, Quebec residents would not have to be entitled to most of the benefits of Canadian citizenship, such as the right to vote in Canadian elections or to receive social benefits; these could be reserved for permanent residents of Canada. Even then, embittered at Quebec's departures, Canadians might oppose the idea. On the other hand, they might be moved by appeals from Quebeckers who were opposed to sovereignty and did not wish to lose their Canadian citizenship.

Canada without Quebec

If Quebec seceded, Canadians would have to answer a final set of questions: would they wish to maintain Canada in this abbreviated form? If so, what would need to be done? There is no doubt that, at least initially, Canadians would want Canada to remain a single country, though without Quebec.[56] Such a Canada would have considerable strengths: it would be the world's eighth-largest economy, members of its cultural community would enjoy international prominence, it would still be a leader in international rankings. Without Quebec, Canada would be more united around common political principles, largely derived from the Trudeau era, such as equality of the provinces, supremacy of the Charter, and multiculturalism. On the other hand, there would be enormous difficulties. Ontario and Atlantic Canada would be separated by foreign territory, at great psychological costs if not material ones. More important, perhaps, in Canada without Quebec, Ontario would represent one-half of the Canadian population and western Canadian suspicions would undoubtedly be aroused. The future of a Canada without Quebec is far from assured.

Is There a 'Third Way'?

It is possible that Quebec secession could be peaceful, orderly, and relatively rapid. Certainly that would be in the interests of Canadians. It is also possible that a Canada without Quebec could survive as a political entity. Initially at least, that is clearly what most Canadians would want. But all of these outcomes are not assured. It is not at all difficult to imagine far less appealing ones. As we have seen, simply organizing negotiations would be a challenge;

some of the issues to be addressed, such as the status of Quebec's minorities, could easily produce a stalemate, indeed bitter conflict. Colouring all of this would be a most unfavourable emotional climate, in which many English Canadians would be deeply angered by the very idea of Quebec secession and many Quebec francophones, having voted for sovereignty, would have little patience for the complex negotiations required for an orderly secession.

In light of the obvious difficulty in bringing about an orderly secession and the resulting hardship in both Quebec and English Canada, there could be a strong case for a third option: a radical restructuring of the Canadian political order that fell just short of sovereignty for Quebec. Indeed, such an option has been periodically advanced by English-Canadian academics, while not arousing any interest among English-Canadian political élites.[57] It has usually been labelled 'confederalism'. Although that is a misnomer, since Canada would formally still be intact, 'confederalism' does convey the fact that profound change would be involved.

With 'confederalism' most of the functions now performed by Ottawa would be transferred to Quebec and to a new federal government for Canada outside Quebec. The Canadian government would be left with little more than foreign affairs, currency, defence, and international trade. Members of the Canadian Parliament could be elected or appointed, depending on the wishes of Quebec and of Canada outside Quebec. The distribution of seats would continue to be based on population, rather than parity between Quebec and the rest of the country.

Through these changes, Quebec would not become formally sovereign, but it would no longer be simply a province. It might well become the only government that collected taxes in Quebec, but it would lose the benefits of being a province, since it would no longer receive transfer or equalization payments from Ottawa. The rest of Canada would acquire control of a government of its own and could adjust as it wished the distribution of responsibilities between that government and the provinces.

Although such an arrangement would not meet the aspirations of deeply committed sovereigntists, it might be quite appealing to many Quebec francophones who would otherwise support sovereignty. Indeed, by some readings, Lucien Bouchard would be prepared to endorse such a scheme. Nor would it be difficult to present 'confederalism' as an attenuated version of the partnership proposed by Bouchard and others.

Such a scheme might be considered undesirable by Canadians outside Quebec because it would create a new level of a government at a time when many Canadians wish to have less government in general. On the other hand, it might also have some attractions. Conceivably, with such a major devolution of powers to Quebec, the need for any formal recognition of

Quebec's distinctiveness could be avoided. Nor would Canadians be confronted with the institutional awkwardness of asymmetry. The limited number of functions remaining with the Canadian government would apply to all parts of Canada, and all MPs would vote on them. And Quebec would not be able to opt out of 'national' programs with full compensation. Indeed, there would be no federal transfer of funds to Quebec. By the same token, Canadians outside Quebec would have a government of their own.

In effect, the primary concerns of both Quebec and of the rest of Canada could be met without undergoing the obvious complications of secession by Quebec. To be sure, there would not be many shared institutions or common endeavours remaining, and collaboration would be reduced to the absolute minimum. But this might be in keeping with the deep estrangement between Quebeckers and other Canadians that has marked the referendum and its aftermath.

It remains my contention that Canada need not have come to such a juncture. The rise in support for Quebec sovereignty and consequent need to entertain 'confederal' schemes are largely the result of the rejection of the Meech Lake Accord. The Accord, which was an attempt to repair the damage caused by patriation without Quebec's consent, was itself a victim of the Trudeau vision and its influence in English Canada. These processes culminated in the 1995 referendum, which has further divided Quebec from the rest of Canada. But in light of all this, 'confederalism' might be the best available option.

Still, there are major obstacles to such an arrangement. Whatever its merits, 'confederalism' would signal the end of any vision of one Canada, whether the Trudeau version or some other one. For most English Canadians, its only appeal would be as an alternative to full sovereignty for Quebec. Thus far, the 1995 referendum has not apparently led to any general readiness to entertain such schemes. Perhaps a new referendum, with a clear majority for sovereignty, would have such an effect. But, it could also initiate quite a different dynamic with Quebeckers unwilling to settle for anything less than sovereignty and many Canadians elsewhere no longer prepared to share a country with Quebec on any terms. A determined leadership, in English Canada and in Quebec, would be needed to make 'confederalism' a real possibility.

Even now, Quebec separation is not inevitable. There are alternatives to the present impasse. The bases for an accommodation of Quebec within the Canadian polity have long existed in an alternative strategy based on constitutional recognition of duality and Quebec's place within it; asymmetry in federal-provincial relations; and territoriality in language policy. The strategy could be modified to incorporate the objectives of aboriginal peoples. If that strategy is no longer sufficient, given the results of the last referendum, a new approach, based on confederalism, could be employed. If secession should come, there is at least a chance that it could be peaceful, orderly, and fairly rapid. But none of that can happen within the Trudeau vision.

If the arguments made in this book are at all valid, they suggest some profound ironies. Pierre Trudeau, the self-declared anti-nationalist, is embraced by much of English Canada as the 'saviour' of the Canadian nation and ultimately emerges as a champion of Canadian nationalism. A strategy designed to transform the way in which Quebeckers see Canada has little effect in Quebec, but it transforms English Canada. Finally, rather than undermining the forces of Quebec separatism, the strategy strengthens them, bringing Canada to the brink of collapse.

Certainly the Trudeau vision of Canada is a compelling one, which has mobilized a large number of Canadians, primarily outside Quebec. As a result, a significant number of English Canadians now can express themselves in French, and French and francophones have assumed a much more important place in the federal government. Multiculturalism has met the status concerns of some native-born Canadians while attacking barriers to racial and ethnic equality. The Charter of Rights and Freedoms has enhanced political and legal rights and has given recognition to a wide variety of groups within Canadian society. But in light of the Trudeau strategy's original purpose of securing national unity, there can be no doubt that it has failed.

In the 1960s, Lester Pearson was derided for being weak, indecisive, and too prone to mediation and consensus building. Most of all, he was not 'straight' on Quebec. The route to Canadian unity, it was argued, lay in replacing ambiguity and contradiction with clarity and uniformity, indeed in imposing a new conception of the country. In the process, Canada would become a model to the world, resolving problems that had defeated so many others. Thirty years later, it seems clear that we would have been better served by being more modest in our ambitions and more patient with Canada's inherent complexities.

NOTES

Introduction

1   Since no single meaning is attached to the term 'Quebecker', I should specify that in this volume 'Quebecker' refers to *all* residents of Quebec, as does 'Québécois'. When referring to the French-speaking population of Quebec, I normally use the term 'Quebec francophones'.

Chapter 1

1   P.B. Waite, *The Life and Times of Confederation, 1864–1867* (Toronto: University of Toronto Press, 1962), 22.

2   Ibid.

3   Robert C. Vipond, *Liberty and Community: Canadian Federalism and the Failure of the Constitution* (Albany: State University of New York Press, 1991), 32–3.

4   Michel Brunet, *La Présence anglaise et les canadiens* (Montreal: Beauchemin, 1964), 58.

5   See ibid., 47.

6   As quoted in Peter H. Russell, *Constitutional Odyssey: Can Canadians Become a Sovereign People?*, 2nd edn (Toronto: University of Toronto Press, 1993), 13.

7   George F.C. Stanley, 'Act or Pact: Another Look at Confederation', Proceedings of the Canadian Historical Association, 1956, 5.

8   Jean-Paul Bernard, *Les Rouges* (Montreal: Presses de l'Université du Québec, 1971), 11–19.

9   Gerald M. Craig, ed., *Lord Durham's Report*, Carleton Library no. 1 (Toronto: McClelland & Stewart, 1963), 22–3.

10   Ibid., 154.

11   See William Ormsby, *The Emergence of the Federal Concept in Canada, 1839–1845* (Toronto: University of Toronto Press, 1969), 6; and Janet Ajzenstat, *The Political Thought of Lord Durham* (Montreal and Kingston: McGill-Queen's University Press, 1988).

12   Craig, *Lord Durham's Report*, 150.

13   Ormsby, *Emergence of the Federal Concept*, 123.

14   Stanley, 'Act or Pact', 7.

15   Douglas V. Verney, *Three Civilizations, Two Cultures, One State: Canada's Political Traditions* (Durham: Duke University Press, 1986), 197.

16   See the discussion of these points in ibid., 199 and in Ormsby, *Emergence of the Federal Concept*.

17   See the discussion in Donald V. Smiley, *Canada in Question*, 3rd edn (Toronto: McGraw-Hill Ryerson, 1980), 214–17.

18   Ormsby, *Emergence of the Federal Concept*, 106.

19   J.E. Hodgetts, *Pioneer Public Service* (Toronto: University of Toronto Press, 1955), 59.

20   Sir Richard Cartwright, *Reminiscences* (Toronto, 1912), 6, as quoted in Hodgetts, *Pioneer Public Service*, 59.

21   Ibid., 118–19.

22   Ormsby, *Emergence of the Federal Concept*, 124.

23   Ibid., 124–5, and Verney, *Three Civilizations*, 200–1.

24   Ormsby, *Emergence of the Federal Concept,* 120.

25   Verney, *Three Civilizations,* 200.

26   As quoted in Ramsay Cook et al., *Canada: A Modern Study* (Toronto: Clarke Irwin, 1963), 83.

27   W.L. Morton, 'The Cabinet of 1867', in Frederick W. Gibson, ed., *Cabinet Formation and Bicultural Relations*, Studies of the Royal Commission on Bilingualism and Biculturalism, no. 6 (Ottawa: Queen's Printer, 1970), 4.

28   More precisely, Quebec's House representation was set at 65; representation of the rest of the new Dominion was to be in proportion to that. There was an additional accommodation of cultural dualism: a never-enacted provision of the BNA Act for standardization of law related to property and civil rights did not apply to Quebec, with its civil code (section 94). Finally, section 98 provides that judges of the Quebec courts must be members of the Quebec bar.

29   P.B. Waite, *The Confederation Debates in the Province of Canada, 1865*, Carleton Library, no. 2 (Toronto: McClelland & Stewart, 1963), 50–1. Ramsay Cook sees this passage as an example of the general absence 'of anything that might be called "racial" thinking in the statements of the Fathers'; see Cook, *Provincial Autonomy, Minority Rights and the Compact Theory, 1867–1921*, Studies of the Royal Commission on Bilingualism and Biculturalism, no. 4 (Ottawa: Queen's Printer, 1969), 52. To be sure, later in the same statement Cartier does say that French Canadians and English Canadians would be 'placed like great families beside each other'. See *The Confederation Debates*, 51. Peter Russell sees this as evidence of dualism. See Russell, *Constitutional Odyssey*, 33.

30   Stanley B. Ryerson, *Unequal Union* (Toronto: Progress Books, 1968), chap. 18.

31   Waite, *The Confederation Debates*, 40.

32   Silver, *The French-Canadian Idea of Confederation*, 36, n. 20.

33   Stéphane Kelly, 'Les imaginaires canadiens du 19e siècle', thèse de doctorat, Département de sociologie, l'Université de Montréal, 1995, 439. Ryerson calls this 'an unconfirmed but plausible story'. See Ryerson, *Unequal Union*, 371. See also Jean-Charles Bonenfant, *La Naissance de la Confédération* (Montreal: Leméac, 1969), 18. Creighton makes no reference to such a possibility in his account of the London Conference in Donald Creighton, *The Road to Confederation* (Toronto: Macmillan, 1964), chap. 14.

34   Waite, *Life and Times of Confederation*, 109.

35   Ibid., 110.

36   Silver, *The French-Canadian Idea of Confederation*, 55.

37   Under section 133 of the British North America Act, English and French can be used in the Quebec legislature, must be used in the journals, records and statutes of the Quebec legislature, and may be used in Quebec courts. The provisions are discussed in Royal Commission on Bilingualism and Biculturalism, Book I: *The Official Languages* (Ottawa: Queen's Printer, 1967), 52–5.

38 As Silver documents, French-Canadian opinion leaders complained that the constitutional protection of Protestant schools demanded by Quebec's English Canadians would be an unacceptable restriction on their new province's autonomy. If such protection should be unavoidable, then fairness at least required that Ontario's Catholic minority should be similarly protected. See Silver, *The French-Canadian Idea of Confederation*, chap. 3.

39 *British North America Act*, s. 22 and 80.

40 The British constitutional authority K.C. Wheare took this view. See Garth Stevenson, *Unfulfilled Union*, 3rd edn (Toronto: Gage, 1989), 30.

41 *La Minerve*, 17 July 1866, as translated and quoted in Silver, *The French-Canadian Idea of Confederation*, 41.

42 *La Minerve*, 1 July 1867, as translated and quoted in Silver, *The French-Canadian Idea of Confederation*, 41.

43 The statement is by W.P.M. Kennedy, as quoted in Stanley Ryerson, *Unequal Union*, 443. See also Stevenson, *Unfulfilled Union*, 6–7.

44 Bonenfant, *La Naissance de la Confédération*, 11.

45 Waite, *Confederation Debates*, 147.

46 Waite, *Life and Times of Confederation*, 116.

47 Sir Joseph Pope, *Memoirs of the Right Honourable Sir John Alexander Macdonald* (Toronto: Musson, 1930), 339, as quoted in Donald V. Smiley, *The Canadian Political Nationality* (Toronto: Methuen, 1967), 10, n. 12. This reference is drawn from Verney, *Three Civilizations*, 231, who discusses the question at some length.

48 Morton, 'The Cabinet of 1867', 4.

49 Ibid., 5. See also the discussion in Kelly, 'Les imaginaires canadiens', 442.

50 Sir Charles Tupper, for one, recognized that French Canadians had justly felt slighted by the decision. See A. De Celles, *Cartier et son temps* (Montreal: Beauchemin, 1907), 36, as quoted in Kelly, 'Les imaginaires canadiens', 443.

51 Kelly, 'Les imaginaires canadiens', 442.

52 'It is possible to hold, therefore, that the French were in some respects under-represented in the cabinet, both in numbers and weight of portfolios'. See Morton, 'The Cabinet of 1867', 15.

53 Ibid.

54 Peter Regenstreif, 'Note on the "Alternation" of French and English Leaders in the Liberal Party of Canada', *Canadian Journal of Political Science* 2 (Mar. 1969): 118–22. The terms commonly used to refer to two leading royal commissions suggest they had anglophone and francophone co-chairs, but that was not the case. With the Rowell-Sirois Commission, Sirois was a commissioner who replaced Rowell as chair upon the latter's resignation. With the Massey-Lévesque Commission, Massey was in fact the only chair.

55 Donald V. Smiley, 'French-English Relations in Canada and Consociational Democracy', in Milton J. Esman, ed., *Ethnic Conflict in the Western World* (Ithaca: Cornell University Press, 1977), 193–6.

56 Paul-André Linteau, René Durocher, and Jean-Claude Robert, *Histoire du Québec contemporain: de la Confédération à la crise* (Montreal: Boréal, 1979), 265.

57 Jean Hamelin and Louise Beaudoin, 'Les Cabinets provinciaux, 1867–1967', in Richard Desrosiers, ed., *Le Personnel politique québécois* (Montreal: Boréal, 1972), 99.

58 Janice Staples, 'Consociationalism at Provincial Level: The Erosion of Dualism in Manitoba', in Kenneth McRae, ed., *Consociational Democracy* (Toronto: McClelland & Stewart, 1974), 288–302.

59 Cook, *Provincial Autonomy, Minority Rights and the Compact Theory*, 14.

60 Ibid., 10.

61 Robert Vipond presents compelling evidence that support for provincial rights for Ontario was an extension of a sentiment that was already present during the Confederation debates and formally endorsed by the Ontario Reform Party just before Confederation. See Robert C. Vipond, *Liberty and Community*, 33.

62 Stevenson, *Unfulfilled Union*, 76.

63 Russell, *Constitutional Odyssey*, 35–6.

64 See Vipond, *Liberty and Community*, 33.

65 Cook, *Provincial Autonomy, Minority Rights and the Compact Theory*, 41–3.

66 T.J.J. Loranger, *Letters upon the Interpretation of the Federal Constitution known as the British North America Act, (1867)* (Quebec City, 1884), 61, as quoted in Cook, *Provincial Autonomy, Minority Rights and the Compact Theory*, 30.

67 See the discussion in Cook, *Provincial Autonomy, Minority Rights and the Compact Theory*, 31; see also Stevenson, *Unfulfilled Union,* 100–1.

68 Cook, *Provincial Autonomy, Minority Rights and the Compact Theory*, 44. See also Edwin R. Black, *Divided Loyalties* (Montreal and Kingston: McGill-Queen's University Press, 1975), 151–8.

69 Silver, *The French-Canadian Idea of Confederation*, 15.

70 Ibid., 11.

71 Ibid., 23.

72 Ibid., chap. 4.

73 Ibid., 75.

74 Ibid., 169.

75 To compound matters further, upon his election in 1896 (with strong Quebec support), Wilfrid Laurier entered into an agreement with the Manitoba government that fell far short of the full restoration of French-language Catholic schools that French-Canadian nationalist leaders had been seeking.

76 Henri Bourassa, *Le Patriotisme canadien-français* (Montreal, 1902), 8, as translated and quoted in Cook, *Provincial Autonomy, Minority Rights and the Compact Theory*, 57.

77 Cook, *Provincial Autonomy, Minority Rights and the Compact Theory*, 57.

78 Stanley, 'Act or Pact', 9.

79 Ibid.

80 Ibid., 13.

81 In 1915 Bourassa insisted that the more important purpose of Confederation was to resolve conflict within the United Canadas and that it took the form of a national contract:

> La Confédération, on ne saurait trop le rappeler, fut *la résultante d'un contrat national*. Ses auteurs avaient en vue deux objets principaux: grouper les diverses colonies anglaises de l'Amérique du Nord et mettre fin aux conflits séculaires des deux races. Le second de ces objets occupa une place plus importante que le premier dans l'esprit des hommes d'État du Haut et du Bas-Canada. (Henri Bourassa, *La Langue française au Canada* [Montreal, 1915], 28, quoted in Richard Arès, *Dossier sur le pacte fédératif de 1867* [Montreal: Bellarmin, 1967], 70) (emphasis in original).

82 My translation of 'Les circonstances particulières qui ont précédé et entouré la signature du pacte fédéral.' (Ibid.)

83 Cook, *Provincial Autonomy, Minority Rights and the Compact Theory*, 62.

84 House of Commons, *Debates*, 1905, 3256, as quoted in ibid., 59.

85 Ibid.

86 Silver, *The French-Canadian Idea of Confederation*, 194.

87 Henri Bourassa, *Le Patriotisme canadien-français: ce qu'il est, ce qu'il doit être* (Montreal, 1902), as quoted in Silver, *The French-Canadian Idea of Confederation*, 194.

88 Silver, *The French-Canadian Idea of Confederation*, 194.

89 Henri Bourassa, *Pour la justice* (Montreal, 1912), as quoted in Silver, *The French-Canadian Idea of Confederation*, 205. This construction of Bourassa's argument is Silver's.

90 Henri Bourassa, *Pour la justice* (Montreal, 1912), as quoted in Silver, *The French-Canadian Idea of Confederation*, 193.

91 My translation of 'une entente plus franche et plus nette'. As Michael Oliver observed in his analysis of Bourassa's political thought, 'the plural conception of Canadian nationality was usually subordinate to the dual one.' See Michael Oliver, *The Passionate Debate* (Montreal: Véhicule, 1991), 23. Henri Bourassa, *Grande Bretagne et Canada*, 1901, as quoted in Jean Drolet, 'Henri Bourassa: une analyse de sa pensée', in Fernand Dumont et al., eds, *Idéologies au Canada français, 1900–1929* (Quebec City: Presses de l'Université Laval, 1974), 232.

92 Henri Bourassa, 'Réponse amicale à la Vérité', *Le Nationaliste*, 3 April 1904, as translated and reproduced in Joseph Levitt, ed., *Henri Bourassa on Imperialism and Bi-culturalism, 1900–1918* (Toronto: Copp Clark, 1970), 107. On Bourassa's rejection of Quebec independence, see Oliver, *Passionate Debate*, 28–30.

93 'It would be difficult to find a single English Canadian who supported the idea in the years before 1921 [the final year of study]—unless Macdonald's candidacy is accepted.' See Cook, *Provincial Autonomy, Minority Rights and the Compact Theory*, 62. See also pp. 67–9.

94 Roger Brossard, 'The Working of Confederation', *Canadian Journal of Economics and Political Science*, Aug. 1937, 355, as cited in Arès, *Dossier sur le pacte fédératif*, 84.

95 As reproduced in Quebec, *Report of the Royal Commission of Inquiry on Constitutional Problems* (Quebec City, 1956), vol. I, V.

96 Ibid., chap. 5.

97 My translation of 'Elle est devenue un thème persistant, orchestré avec diverses variations par les chefs religieux et politiques du Canada français jusqu'à l'époque contemporaine. Que les publicistes et les juristes canadiens-anglais la trouvent acceptable ou non, elle persistera comme l'un des éléments les plus tenaces de la définition que le Canadien français donne de l'histoire de son Canada'. Jean-C. Falardeau, 'Les Canadiens français et leur idéologie', in Mason Wade, ed., *Canadian Dualism* (Toronto: University of Toronto Press, 1960), 25.

98 Philip Resnick, *The Masks of Proteus* (Montreal and Kingston: McGill-Queen's University Press, 1990), 57–8, and Donald Creighton, *Canada's First Century* (Toronto: Macmillan, 1970), 277.

99 House of Commons *Debates*, I, 1944, 2, as quoted in Donald V. Smiley, *Constitutional Adaptation and Canadian Federalism Since 1945*, Documents of the Royal Commission on Bilingualism and Biculturalism, no. 4 (Ottawa: Queen's Printer, 1970), 10.

100 Smiley, *Constitutional Adaptation and Canadian Federalism*, chap. 2.

101 As quoted in Simeon and Robinson, *State, Society and the Development of Canadian Federalism*, 142. See also Joyce Zemans, 'The Essential Role of National Cultural Institutions', in Kenneth McRoberts, ed., *Beyond Quebec: Taking Stock of Canada* (Montreal and Kingston: McGill-Queen's University Press, 1995), 138–62; and Paul Litt, 'The Massey Commission, Americanization, and Canadian Nationalism', *Queen's Quarterly* 98, no. 2 (Summer 1991): 375–87. While insisting that French-Canadian reaction in general was 'remarkably sympathetic' to the commission, Litt acknowledges that French-Canadian nationalists were alarmed at the new responsibilities it proposed for the federal government. See Litt, 'The Massey Commission', n. 3. On the other hand, Michael Behiels states that only a 'small proportion of French Canadians' supported the Massey Commission and Father Lévesque's position. He details widespread opposition among French-Canadian nationalists. See Michael Behiels, *Prelude to Quebec's Quiet Revolution* (Montreal and Kingston: McGill-Queen's University Press, 1985, 206–11). So too does William D. Coleman, *The Independence Movement in Quebec, 1945–1980* (Toronto: University of Toronto Press, 1984), 70–4.

102 Claude Bissell, *Massey Report and Canadian Culture*, 1982 John Porter Memorial Lecture (Ottawa: Carleton University, 1980), 21, as quoted in Zemans, 'The Essential Role of National Cultural Institutions', 147.

103 Smiley, *Constitutional Adaptation and Canadian Federalism*, 18.

104 See the account in Russell, *Constitutional Odyssey*, 65–8.

105 Dale Thomson writes of St Laurent: 'Considered by the population as a whole, and by himself, a French-speaking Canadian, he spoke flawless English, thought in many matters like an English Canadian, and was better informed about English Canada as a whole than some of his English-speaking colleagues.' See Dale Thomson, 'The Cabinet of 1948', in Gibson, *Cabinet Formation and Bicultural Relations*, 144. St Laurent was quite able to present Canada as being 'a political partnership of two great races'. See Thomson, *Louis St Laurent:*

Canadian, 528, but he did not draw the same conclusions from this as the French-Canadian nationalists and the compact theorists.

106 Thomson, 'The Cabinet of 1948', 144.

107 My translation of 'La Confédération n'a pas été vraiment un pacte entre les provinces'. As quoted in Arès, *Dossier sur le pacte fédératif,* 92.

108 When asked whether Parliament had such a right, St Laurent simply responded that 'the principles of British freedom and British fair play' provide a surer protection of language rights than anything contained in Section 133. See Thomson, *Louis St Laurent: Canadian,* 189.

109 My translation of 'la province de Québec peut être une province comme les autres'. As quoted in Jacques Lacoursière and Claude Bouchard, *Notre histoire Québec-Canada* (Montreal: Éditions Format, 1972), 1104. See also Thomson, *Louis St Laurent: Canadian,* 378, and J.W. Pickersgill, *My Years with Louis St Laurent: A Political Memoir* (Toronto: University of Toronto Press, 1975), 256.

110 Hamelin and Beaudoin, 'Les Cabinets provinciaux', 98–9.

111 The resolution, presented by J.-N. Francoeur, precipitated a widely publicized debate in which legislators denounced English-Canadian treatment of French Canadians and Quebec while declaring their continued belief in federalism and their attachment to Canada. After this debate, the resolution was withdrawn before any vote was taken. See the account in Linteau, Durocher, and Robert, *Histoire du Québec contemporain: de la Confédération à la crise,* 583.

112 Quebec, *Rapport de la Commission royale d'enquête sur les problèmes constitutionnels,* five vols, 1956.

113 Ibid., vol. II, 72.

114 Ibid., 73.

115 Smiley, *Constitutional Adaptation and Canadian Federalism,* 72. Smiley notes that Quebec did accept federal funds in some areas including public health (including hospital construction) and public assistance.

116 Ibid.

117 On the other hand, many francophone élites were highly critical of the Duplessis government's conservative economic and social policies, and were frustrated by the extent to which Quebec's refusal of federal funds further limited the prospect that the Quebec state would intervene in Quebec's economy and society. See Michael D. Behiels, *Prelude to Quebec's Quiet Revolution* (Montreal and Kingston: McGill-Queen's University Press, 1985), and Kenneth McRoberts, *Quebec: Social Change and Political Crisis* (Toronto: McClelland & Stewart, 1993), chap. 4.

Chapter 2

1 Among other places, these processes are discussed in Kenneth McRoberts, 'La Thèse tradition-modernité: l'historique québécois', in Mikhael Elbaz et al., *Les Frontières de l'identité: modernité et postmodernisme au Québec* (Sainte-Foy: Presses de l'Université Laval, 1996), 27–45.

2 See Hubert Guindon, *Quebec Society: Tradition, Modernity, and Nationhood*

(Toronto: University of Toronto Press, 1988); William Coleman, *The Independence Movement in Quebec, 1945–1980* (Toronto: University of Toronto Press, 1984); and Kenneth McRoberts, *Quebec: Social Change and Political Crisis*, 3rd edn (Toronto: McClelland & Stewart, 1993).

3   See Michael D. Behiels, *Prelude to Quebec's Quiet Revolution* (Montreal and Kingston: McGill-Queen's University Press, 1985); and Jean-Louis Roy, *La Marche des Québécois: le temps des ruptures, 1945–1960* (Montreal: Leméac, 1976).

4   See Thomson, *Jean Lesage and the Quiet Revolution* (Toronto: Macmillan, 1984), 174–5.

5   Most observers have interpreted the Quiet Revolution in precisely these terms. See, for instance, Léon Dion, *Nationalismes et politique au Québec* (Montreal: Hurtubise HMH, 1975).

6   My translation of 'sentent qu'il y a, au Québec, un gouvernement susceptible de jouer un rôle irremplaçable dans l'épanouissement de leur identité collective, leur mode de vie, leur civilisation, leur échelle de valeurs. . . . Je crois qu'il n'y aurait pas de mal, loin de là, à reconnaître ce fait comme un des fondements du Canada de l'avenir. . . . Nous sommes déjà en voie . . . d'instituer pour le Québec un embryon de statut particulier. . . . Pour des raisons historiques et démographiques, [le gouvernement du Québec] se verrait confier, en plus de toutes les responsabilités qui doivent à notre époque normalement appartenir à un gouvernement provincial, la tâche plus particulière d'être l'instrument de l'affirmation de la communauté canadienne-française.' Address to the Canadian Club, Vancouver, BC, 24 Sept. 1965, as quoted in Gérard Boismenu, 'La Pensée constitutionnelle de Jean Lesage', in Robert Comeau, ed., *Jean Lesage et l'éveil d'une nation* (Sillery, Quebec: Presses de l'Université du Québec, 1989), 97.

7   'Cette constitution devrait, à mon sens, être conçue de telle façon que le Canada ne soit pas uniquement une fédération de dix provinces, mais une fédération de deux nations égales en droit et en fait'. Daniel Johnson, *Egalité ou indépendance* (Montreal: Éditions de l'homme, 1965), 116.

8   'On ne peut s'attendre, compte tenu des renseignements de notre histoire, à ce que les Canadiens français du Québec, qui forment 83 pour cent de la population francophone du Canada, confient la direction de leur vie sociale et culturelle à un gouvernement où leurs mandataires sont en minorité et soumis par surcroît au jeu de la responsabilité ministérielle et de la discipline de parti.' As quoted in Jean-Louis Roy, *Le Choix d'un pays: le débat constitutionnel Québec-Canada, 1960–1976* (Montreal: Leméac, 1978), 168.

9   'L'important pour les Canadiens français du Québec, ce n'est pas de pouvoir individuellement parler leur langue même dans les régions du pays où elle a très peu de chances d'être comprise; c'est de pouvoir collectivement vivre en français, travailler en français, se construire une société qui leur ressemble; c'est de pouvoir organiser leur vie communautaire en fonction de leur culture.' Ibid., 185.

10   See Michael Oliver, 'Laurendeau et Trudeau: leurs opinions sur le Canada', in Raymond Hudon and Réjean Pelletier, eds, *L'Engagement intellectuel: Mélanges en l'honneur de Léon Dion* (Sainte-Foy: Presses de l'Université Laval, 1991), 354–5.

11 Ibid.

12 From 1962 to 1965, 76 per cent were opposed and 17 per cent undecided; from 1968 to 1972 the figures were 73 per cent and 17 per cent. All these figures are drawn from a summary of survey results presented by Maurice Pinard, 'The Dramatic Reemergence of the Quebec Independence Movement', *Journal of International Affairs* 45, no. 2 (Winter 1992): 480. For that matter, support for independence grew more during the early and mid-1970s, as the Trudeau strategy was being put into effect, reaching 18 per cent in 1976, when the Parti Québécois was first elected.

13 In 1968 a new party, the Parti Québécois, absorbed the RN and RIN. However, control within the new party was in the hands of Lévesque and his colleagues from the MSA—themselves largely dissidents from the Liberal Party. The RN was a founding member, but it played a marginal role. The RIN was not even invited into the PQ; it simply disbanded. Most of its members joined the PQ but tended to be marginalized by Lévesque and his moderate colleagues. By the same token, the PQ was clearly wedded to Lévesque's conception of a sovereignty-association, as opposed to outright independence which was supported by the RN and RIN.

14 In *An Option for Quebec*, Lévesque proposed that a sovereign Quebec and Canada would remain 'associates and partners in a common enterprise'—a comprehensive association that 'would best serve our common economic interests: monetary union, common tariffs, postal union, administration of the national debt, co-ordination of policies, etc.' The collaboration could even extend to the treatment of minorities and to defence and foreign policy. René Lévesque, *An Option for Quebec* (Toronto: McClelland & Stewart, 1968), 27–9. Such an option, he insisted, cannot be described as 'separatist' (ibid., 36).

15 J.L. Granatstein, *Canada, 1957–67: The Years of Uncertainty and Innovation* (Toronto: McClelland & Stewart, 1986), chap. 8.

16 Granatstein, *Canada, 1957–67*, 45; and Philip Resnick, *The Land of Cain: Class and Nationalism in English Canada, 1945–1975* (Vancouver: New Star, 1977), 107–8.

17 Granatstein, *Canada, 1957–1967*, chap. 6.

18 Ibid.

19 Douglas LePan, 'The Old Ontario Strand in the Canada of Today', *Queen's Quarterly* 73 (1966): 487, as quoted in Resnick, *Land of Cain*, 15.

20 This point was made by Tom Kent in an interview, 20 June 1996.

21 Pepin had sketched out his conception of Canada and 'co-operative federalism' in September 1964. Among the premises of his co-operative federalism is that 'in the *socio-political* field, *the theory of two nations*, whether true or false in the eyes of history, is now recognized by the best Canadian constitutionalists and political leaders in both nations. . . . Canadian society is bi-national; the Canadian state is the result of at least a moral agreement between the two founding nations. (Address to l'Institut canadien des Affaires Publiques reproduced as Jean-Luc Pepin, 'Cooperative Federalism', *Canadian Forum*, Dec. 1964, 207, emphasis in original.)

One of the elements of cooperative federalism is 'the right of the French Canadians, "a minority not like the others", the right of Quebec, "a province not like the others", to a particular status. All we have just set forth makes possible particular status for *Quebec* within Canadian federalism if, for example, it wants to take advantage of options, "contracting out", and withdrawal from joint plans.' (Ibid., 209, emphasis in original).

On Maurice Sauvé's relationship with the Lesage government see Tom Kent, *A Public Purpose*, 278.

22 Indeed Lesage tended to deal with Pearson through Robertson and Kent, whom he found more compatible than Pearson. Kent, *A Public Purpose*, 229.

23 In March 1962 Pearson confided to a friend his 'fear and uneasiness . . . about the direction Jean Lesage feels he must go in order to cope with some of the pressures to which he is subjected.' See Granatstein, *Canada, 1957–1967*, 261.

24 Lester B. Pearson, *Mike: The Memoirs of the Right Honourable Lester B. Pearson*, eds J.A. Munro and A.I. Inglis (Toronto: University of Toronto Press, 1975), 238–9.

25 André Laurendeau, 'Pour une enquête sur le bilinguisme', *Le Devoir*, 20 Jan. 1962.

26 Royal Commission on Bilingualism and Biculturalism, *Preliminary Report* (Ottawa: Queen's Printer, 1965), 151, emphasis added. The term 'two founding races' seems to exceed the term 'les deux peuples fondateurs' used in the French-language version. According to Lamontagne, it had been substituted for 'two founding peoples' at the suggestion of Jack Pickersgill and over the heated objection of representatives of Canadian Jews but with Pearson's disclaimer that it referred to biological as opposed to ethnic characteristics. Peter Stursberg, *Lester Pearson and the Dream of Unity* (Toronto: Doubleday, 1978), 141.

27 B&B Commission, *Preliminary Report*, 151.

28 This contrasts dramatically with, for instance, the Citizens' Forum on Canada's Future (better known as the Spicer Committee), which the Mulroney government created in 1990. Among the 12 original members of the Citizens' Forum, there were only three francophones, all from Quebec. Six of the nine original anglophones appear to be of British origin. (Based on biographies in 'Cross-Canada Checkup', *Maclean's*, 12 Nov. 1990, 18–19.)

29 This structural dualism and secondary status of non-Charter-group Canadians was denounced in various places, including the House, where John Diefenbaker and an NDP member from BC, Harold Winch, criticized it in commenting on Pearson's announcement of the commission. See *Debates of the House of Commons*, 1st session, 26th Parliament, 1963, 2441, 2443. In his memoirs, Pearson acknowledged the validity of this criticism. See Pearson, *Mike*, 240.

30 Both of these statements are quoted in Peter C. Newman, *The Distemper of Our Times* (Toronto: McClelland & Stewart, 1968), 320.

31 The Murray Bay statement was quoted, with disapproval, four years later by Eric Neilsen. See *Debates of the House of Commons*, 1967, 118. On the other statement see Stursberg, *Lester Pearson*, 197–8.

32 Pearson, *Mike*, 239. To be sure, Pearson preferred the term 'co-operative feder-

alism' over 'special status' and saw institutional limits to the granting of a different role for Quebec. See the testimony of Pearson's adviser, Tom Kent, in Stursberg, *Lester Pearson*, 203, and Kent, *A Public Purpose*, 266–72.

33 Interview with Tom Kent, 20 June 1996.

34 Kent, *A Public Purpose*, 296. In addition, the agreement even contained the statement: 'The government of Quebec has expressed its firm belief that the wishes of all Canadians can be best fulfilled within a federal structure, and its resolute determination that the rights of the provinces should be exercised not to the disruption but to the enhancement of the unity of Canada.' See ibid.

35 Ibid.

36 See Donald V. Smiley, *Constitutional Adaptation and Canadian Federalism since 1945*, Document no. 4, Royal Commission on Bilingualism and Biculturalism (Ottawa: Queen's Printer), chap. 6; and Kenneth McRoberts, 'Unilateralism, Bilateralism and Multilateralism: Approaches to Canadian Federalism', in Richard Simeon, ed., *Intergovernmental Relations*, Collected Research Studies of the Royal Commission on the Economic Union and Development Prospects for Canada, vol. 63 (Toronto: University of Toronto Press, 1985), 83–6.

37 See Richard Simeon, *Federal-Provincial Diplomacy: The Making of Recent Policy in Canada* (Toronto: University of Toronto Press, 1972), chap. 3.

38 Stursberg, *Lester Pearson*, 197.

39 As quoted in Simeon, *Federal-Provincial Diplomacy*, 59.

40 Canada, *Debates of the House of Commons*, 2nd session, 26th Parliament, vol. II, 20 Apr. 1964, 2334–8.

41 See the testimonies in Stursberg, *Lester Pearson*, 189–97.

42 Ibid., 197.

43 Yves Vaillancourt, 'Le Régime d'assistance publique du Canada: perspective québécoise', thèse de doctorat en science politique, l'Université de Montréal, 1992, 181–218. See also Simeon, *Federal-Provincial Diplomacy*, 66–8; and Thomson, *Jean Lesage and the Quiet Revolution*, 401–4.

44 Mitchell Sharp, *Which Reminds Me . . . A Memoir* (Toronto: University of Toronto Press, 1994), 134–9.

45 Ibid., 137–9. Sharp maintains that his concern about Quebec MPs voting on bills, such as the Canada Pension Plan, that did not apply in their province was shared by 'many of [his] colleagues' (p. 139).

46 This interpretation was offered by Tom Kent, 20 June 1996, and confirmed by Gordon Robertson, 22 Aug. 1996.

47 Simeon, *Federal-Provincial Diplomacy*, 76.

48 Clarkson and McCall say that in early 1966 'Lesage knew Trudeau's views were bolstered by enthusiastic allies in the PMO. Tom Kent, Pearson's policy adviser, and Gordon Robertson, his clerk of the Privy Council—as well as the new minister of finance, Mitchell Sharp—had insisted that Pearson summon up the courage to resist the apparently insatiable government of Quebec by rebuffing demands that the province be allowed to opt out of further federal programs, as it had with the Canada Pension Plan in 1964.' See Clarkson and McCall, *Trudeau*

and Our Times, 100. But, although that describes accurately the views of the finance minister, Mitchell Sharp, and his deputy minister, Al Johnson, it apparently does not fully reflect the views that Kent and Robertson held at the time (interviews with Tom Kent, 20 June 1996, and Gordon Robertson, 22 Aug. 1996). Kent, who had in any event left the PMO by that point, offers a strong defence of the Pearson government's dealings with Quebec in his book, *A Public Purpose*: 'I think it can now be said to be proven that the country is better served by Pearson-style diplomacy in federal-provincial relations than by Trudeau-style confrontation.' See Kent, *A Public Purpose*, 414.

49   Interview with Tom Kent, 20 June 1996.

50   Anthony G.S. Careless, *Initiative and Response* (Montreal and Kingston: McGill-Queen's University Press, 1977), 68.

51   Johnson to Bryce, 12 Jan. 1966, as quoted in Vaillancourt, 'Le Régime d'assistance publique', 184.

52   Interview with Gordon Robertson, 22 Aug. 1996.

53   My reading differs from that of Vaillancourt, who, on the basis of his analysis of Ottawa-Quebec City dealings over social policy and of Finance's success in undermining contracting out, concludes that Pearson and Robertson had turned against asymmetrical federalism *per se*. See Yves Vaillancourt, 'Quebec and the Federal Government: The Struggle Over Opting Out', in Dan Glenday and Ann Duffy, eds, *Canadian Society: Understanding and Surviving in the 1990s*, note 22. John English believes that through 1965 federal officials, including Pearson, thought their approach to Quebec was the right one, that it was not a sign of weakness, and that they were not making undue concessions. (English himself describes the approach as 'appeasement'.) Lesage's rejection of the Fulton-Favreau formula in 1966 did, however, suggest the policy had been unsuccessful and led to a more negative retrospective view of it. See John English, *The Life of Lester Pearson*, vol. 2, *The Worldly Years* (Toronto: Knopf, 1992), 303.

54   Peter C. Newman suggests that Trudeau used his position as parliamentary secretary to Pearson to persuade Pearson to change his strategy: 'The prime minister had appointed Trudeau his parliamentary assistant on January 9, 1966, at a time when he was coming around to the view that his own policy of co-operative federalism should be abandoned for a tougher, more defensible approach. During long evenings of discussion in the privacy of the study at 24 Sussex Drive, Trudeau provided the prime minister not just with a rationale for a practical new concept of Canadian federalism but with perceptive insights into Quebec society.' See Newman, *Distemper of Our Times*, 442. See also p. 325.

55   Interviews with Tom Kent, 20 June 1996, and Gordon Robertson, 22 Aug. 1996. Writing in the summer of 1967, Donald Smiley noted, 'the Honourable Jean Marchand has not, so far as I can discover, addressed himself directly to the constitutional question.' See Smiley, *Constitutional Adaptation and Canadian Federalism*, 135. By the same token, Peacock notes that when Trudeau joined the cabinet and began to argue for a direct confrontation with Quebec nationalism,

virtually all his fellow ministers apparently resisted his arguments. See Peacock, *Journey to Power*, 210.

56   Peacock, *Journey to Power*, 122. Though trying to show that Pearson was moving toward Trudeau's position, Peacock acknowledges that 'Pearson was never entirely convinced that the uncompromising one nation–two languages approach was right.' See ibid., 121. Indeed, in a speech to be read on his behalf in Banff, shortly before the Montreal speech, Pearson refused to incorporate passages that explicitly rejected special status. See ibid.

57   Gordon Robertson, 22 Aug. 1996.

58   Kent, *A Public Purpose*, 414; and Peacock, *Journey to Power*, 212.

59   In his memoirs, Diefenbaker takes great pride in Vanier's appointment, claiming it to have been entirely his own idea. See John G. Diefenbaker, *One Canada*, vol. 2: *The Years of Achievement, 1957–1962* (Toronto: Macmillan, 1976), 60–1. But Pierre Sévigny claims that it was his idea. See Peter Stursberg, *Diefenbaker: Leadership Gained, 1956–62* (Toronto: University of Toronto Press, 1975), 199.

60   In his memoirs, Diefenbaker cites this agreement as a major achievement, while refusing to recognize the principle of exclusive provincial jurisdiction over education. See Diefenbaker, *One Canada*, vol. 2, 291.

61   Ibid., 255. See also Peter C. Newman, *Renegade in Power: The Diefenbaker Years* (Toronto: McClelland & Stewart, 1963), 282–3.

62   André Lamoureux, *Le NPD et le Québec, 1958–1985* (Montreal: Les Éditions du Parc, 1985), 40.

63   See the comments of Quebec Conservatives in Stursberg, *Diefenbaker*, chap. 12.

64   Marc La Terreur, *Les Tribulations des conservateurs au Québec de Bennett à Diefenbaker* (Quebec City: Presses de l'Université Laval, 1973); André Lamoureux, *Le NPD et le Québec, 1958–1985* (Montreal: Les Éditions du Parc, 1985), 38; and Newman, *Renegade in Power*, chap. 20.

65   Newman, *Distemper of Our Times*, 120.

66   The discussion draws in part on Dalton Camp, 'Reflections on the Montmorency Conference', *Queen's Quarterly* 76, no. 2 (Summer 1968): 185–99. See also the account of the Progressive Conservative debates over 'two nations' in Edwin R. Black, *Divided Loyalties* (Montreal and Kingston: McGill-Queen's University Press, 1975), 201–8.

67   *Report on the Montmorency Conference, Courville, Quebec, August 7–10, 1967*, prepared by the Progressive Conservative Policy Advisory Conference of the Centennial Convention, undated, 98.

68   Ibid., 102–3.

69   Ibid., 104.

70   Camp, 'Reflections', 199.

71   Frank Howard, 'Davis Assures Quebec Areas of Agreement Remain Ontario's Goal', *Globe and Mail*, 8 Aug. 1967.

72   *Report on the Montmorency Conference*, 104–5.

73   Martin Sullivan, *Mandate '68* (Toronto: Doubleday, 1968), 183.

74   Anthony Westell, 'Diefenbaker Won't Continue; Tories Back 2-Nation Plan', *Globe and Mail*, 8 Sept. 1967.

75   Michael Vineberg, 'The Progressive Conservative Leadership Convention of 1967', M.A. thesis, Dept. of Economics and Political Science, McGill University, Aug. 1968, 110.

76   Sullivan, *Mandate '68*, 198.

77   See the accounts in *The Globe and Mail*, 9 Sept. 1967. Stanfield apparently was not as clearcut in his speech, but he had already closely associated himself with the 'two-nations' theme. Some speakers did insist that they would not support 'two nations' if it were to imply separate states. Michael Starr was the only candidate to reject 'two nations' explicitly.

78   Sullivan, *Mandate '68*, 177. By the same token, he approved the Canada/Quebec Pension Plan arrangement, saying that opting out 'didn't bother [him] as long as it was available to all'. See Stursberg, *Lester Pearson*, 200. At the same time, like most English-Canadian politicians, Stanfield eschewed the term 'special status'. See Sullivan, *Mandate '68*, 177; and 'Stanfield: gare aux mots', *Le Devoir*, 1 Sept. 1967.

79   Peacock, *Journey to Power*, 81.

80   Claude Ryan, 'Le Congrès conservateur de Toronto', *Le Devoir*, 7 Sept. 1967.

81   On F.R. Scott and his vision of Quebec and Canada see Guy Laforest, *Trudeau et la fin d'un rêve canadien* (Sillery, Quebec: Septentrion, 1992), chap. 3.

82   This account of the convention draws primarily upon Lamoureux, *Le NPD et le Québec*, 85–129. The efforts of the NDP to address the Quebec question are traced in detail in Peter Graefe, 'From Coherence to Confusion: The CCF–NDP Confronts Federalism', major research paper, M.A. Program in Political Science, York University, Sept. 1996.

83   Lamoureux, *Le NPD et le Québec*, 114, my translation.

84   My translation of 'Le Nouveau Parti proclame formellement sa foi dans un régime fédéral, le seul qui puisse assurer l'épanouissement conjoint des deux nations qui se sont associées primitivement en vue de former la société canadienne, ainsi que l'épanouissement des autres groupes ethniques au Canada'. See ibid., 116. Lamoureux argues that even this modification fell far short of the full recognition of Quebec's nationhood that the Quebec caucus had wanted and that it reflected the leadership's refusal to recognize Quebec's right to self-determination (117, 126).

85   Indeed, party members did not agree on the significance of the wording. Michael Oliver, who was a prominent member of the party at the time, insists that the party did not formally endorse the two-nations formula. Though the program acknowledged that French Canadians might regard themselves as constituting a 'nation', it did not claim that English Canadians saw themselves as a nation. (Private communication, 9 June 1996.)

86   Morton, *NDP*, 59.

87   Lamoureux, *Le NPD et le Québec*, 148.

88   Morton, *NDP*, 61.

89   House of Commons, *Record of Debates*, 1st session, 27th Parliament, vol. 1, 28 Jan. 1966, 411.

90   Morton, *The New Democrats*, 77. *Canadian Dimension* maintained that the resolution fell far short of the type of special status that it had been regularly advocating:

> The NDP repeated its support for 'special status' for Quebec, though this now appears to have taken on a new meaning: Quebec would retain all of its present programs (whether it would take over some federal ones is not specified in the resolution), but the other provinces could, if they wanted to, transfer some of their programs to Ottawa. . . . Fearing to antagonize one side or the other, the framers of this policy have deliberately shorn the concept of 'special status' of any substance. It is doubtful whether anyone will be fooled by a slogan without content.

See 'The NDP Federal Convention—1967', *Canadian Dimension*, Sept.–Oct. 1967, 4.

91   *Canadian Annual Review*, 1968, 60.

92   Ibid., 35.

93   Richard Simeon and Ian Robinson, *State, Society and the Development of Canadian Federalism*, 109.

94   In Whitehorn's presentation of results from three different conventions, it appears that this figure applies to 1971 as opposed to 1979. In 1981, support had slipped to 46.2 per cent. The results of another question are clearly identified with 1971: 66.6 per cent agreed 'to provide some special recognition for Quebec "within Confederation"'. See Alan Whitehorn, *Canadian Socialism: Essays on the CCF-NDP* (Toronto: Oxford University Press, 1992), 126.

95   On Scott and Trudeau see Christina McCall and Stephen Clarkson, *Trudeau and Our Times*, vol. 2, *The Heroic Delusion* (Toronto: McClelland & Stewart, 1994), 85; and Stephen Clarkson and Christina McCall, *Trudeau and Our Times*, vol. 1, *The Magnificent Obsession* (Toronto: McClelland & Stewart, 1990), 89.

96   Desmond Morton, *The New Democrats, 1961–1986: The Politics of Change* (Copp Clark Pitman, 1986), 77–8. See also Lamoureux, *Le NPD et le Québec*. Forsey's opposition is elaborated in his 'Canada: Two Nations or One?' *Canadian Journal of Economics and Political Science* 28, no. 4 (Nov. 1962).

97   Resnick argues that the idea first appeared 'in the student movement in the middle and late 1960s, which here, as on the issue of anti-imperialism, played a seminal role.' See Resnick, *Land of Cain*, 192. He notes, 'The Canadian Union of Students and the Union générale des étudiants du Québec began to put into practice the theory of two separate nations—English Canada and Quebec' (193).

98   Gad Horowitz, 'The Future of English Canada', *Canadian Dimension*, July–Aug. 1965, 12.

99   See, for instance, George Grant, *Lament for a Nation* (Toronto: McClelland & Stewart, 1965); Kari Levitt, *Silent Surrender* (Toronto: Macmillan, 1970); and Ian

Lumsden, ed., *Close the 49th Parallel* (Toronto: University of Toronto Press, 1970).

100 Resnick, *Land of Cain*, 167–78, 201.

101 'For an Independent Socialist Canada', *Canadian Dimension*, Aug.–Sept. 1969, 9.

102 Anthony Westell, *Paradox: Trudeau as Prime Minister* (Scarborough, Ont.: Prentice-Hall, 1972), 7.

Chapter 3

1   These qualities are well captured in Michel Vastel's description of Trudeau's mindset during the 1950s:

> S'il refuse, avec un acharnement qui frise l'obsession, toute frontière qui, même en pointillés, séparerait les deux nations, c'est que Trudeau appartient à l'une et à l'autre, et même à plus encore. . . .
>
> Canadien français de naissance, de langue 'maternelle' anglaise, avec un brin d'Écossais dans les manières, 'citoyen du monde' en plus, Trudeau refuse toutes les 'boîtes', et pas seulement la québécoise. Au fond, Trudeau ne sait pas trop ce qu'il est, de crainte d'en avoir honte peut-être.

See Michel Vastel, *Trudeau: le Québécois* (Montreal: Éditions de l'homme, 1989), 101.

> With a fervour that bordered on the obsessive, Trudeau refused to recognize any frontier, even a dotted line, separating Canada's two nations—perhaps because he belonged to both of them.
>
> French Canadian by birth and mother tongue, English with a touch of Scots in his upbringing, 'citizen of the world' on top of that, Trudeau refused to be identified, not just with the 'Québécois', but with any group. Deep down, Trudeau wasn't too sure who he was, for fear, perhaps, of being ashamed.

See Michel Vastel, *The Outsider*, trans. Hubert Bauch (Toronto: Macmillan, 1990), 76.

2   Christina McCall and Stephen Clarkson, *Trudeau and Our Times*, vol. 2, *The Heroic Delusion* (Toronto: McClelland & Stewart, 1994), 32.

3   Stephen Clarkson and Christina McCall, *Trudeau and Our Times*, vol. 1, *The Magnificent Obsession* (Toronto: McClelland & Stewart, 1990), 38.

4   To quote Michel Vastel: 'Aussitôt après la mort de son père, Pierre Trudeau emprunte le nom de sa mère et se met à parler comme un Français de France. Veut-il ainsi se détacher des racines québécoises que Charles-Émile Trudeau lui a laissées, et se greffer sur la branche anglo-saxonne que lui tend Grace *Elliott*?' See Vastel, *Trudeau*, 32. 'Shortly after the death of his father, Trudeau took his mother's name and began speaking like a native of France. Could it be that he did so to reject his father's French-Canadian roots and tie himself more closely to the Anglo-Saxon heritage of his mother, Grace *Elliott*?' See Vastel, *The Outsider*, 18. McCall and Clarkson note that the whole family began to sign

its name that way and that the children were given elocution lessons in both French and English. See McCall and Clarkson, *Trudeau and Our Times*, 31–2.

5   McCall and Clarkson, *Trudeau and Our Times*, 42–8.

6   As Vastel notes, 'L'admiration que [Trudeau] porte désormais aux philosophes britanniques et aux économistes américains renforce encore, comme s'il en était besoin, le mépris qu'il porte aux élites canadiennes-françaises de l'époque.' See Vastel, *Trudeau*, 64. 'His great admiration for British philosophers and American economists reinforced (as if reinforcement were necessary) his disdain for the French-Canadian élites of the day.' See Vastel, *The Outsider*, 44. McCall and Clarkson claim that Trudeau's analysis 'of Quebec's reactionary and dysfunctional nationalism' was 'derived in large part from [Frank] Scott's [analysis]'. See McCall and Clarkson, *Trudeau and Our Times*, 70.

7   Clarkson and McCall, *Trudeau and Our Times*, 55; ibid., 57–66; and Vastel, *Trudeau*, 79.

8   Clarkson and McCall, *Trudeau and Our Times*, 59.

9   Pierre Elliott Trudeau, *Federalism and the French Canadians* (Toronto: Macmillan, 1968), 106–7.

10   Ibid., 171.

11   My translation of 'De la sorte, la doctrine sociale de l'Église, qui en d'autres pays ouvrait la voie large à la démocratisation des peuples, à l'émancipation des travailleurs et au progrès social, était invoquée au Canada français à l'appui de l'autoritarianisme et de la xénophobie. Et, ce qui est plus grave, notre doctrine nous mettait dans l'impossibilité de résoudre nos problèmes. Car, du côté négatif, elle rejetait toute solution qui pût réussir chez nos 'ennemis': les Anglais, protestants, matérialistes, etc.' Pierre Elliott Trudeau, ed., *La Grève de l'amiante* (Montreal: Éditions du jour, 1970), 21.

12   Trudeau, *Federalism and the French Canadians*, 157.

13   To quote Michael Oliver: 'Trudeau loathes, and has loathed since very early days in school, the S-nationalism [sociological nation] of French Canada. He did not believe it is possible to purge that kind of nationalism of the elements he most disliked—intolerance, narrowness, chauvinism.' Oliver's translation of 'Trudeau déteste, et a toujours détesté depuis ses premières années à l'école, le nationalisme du Canada français. Il ne pensait pas qu'il fût possible de débarasser cette sorte de nationalisme des éléments qu'il haissait le plus—intolérance, étroitesse d'esprit, chauvinisme.' See Michael Oliver, 'Laurendeau et Trudeau: leurs opinions sur le Canada' in Raymond Hudon and Réjean Pelletier, eds, *L'Engagement intellectuel: Mélanges en l'honneur de Léon Dion* (Sainte-Foy: Presses de l'Université Laval, 1991), 351.

14   Trudeau, *Federalism and the French Canadians*, 204–12.

15   Gérard Bergeron, *Notre Miroir à deux faces* (Montreal: Québec/Amérique, 1985), 84.

16   Trudeau, *Federalism and the French Canadians*, 188. For a critique of this position see Oliver, 'Laurendeau et Trudeau', 359.

17 Michel Vastel, *Trudeau: le Québécois* (Montreal: Éditions de l'homme, 1989), 138.

18 André Laurendeau, *The Diary of André Laurendeau* (Toronto: Lorimer, 1991), 154.

19 Reg Whitaker, 'Reason, Passion and Interest: Pierre Trudeau's Eternal Liberal Triangle', in *A Sovereign Idea* (Montreal and Kingston: McGill-Queen's University Press, 1992), 137.

20 Henry David Rempel, 'The Practice and Theory of the Fragile State: Trudeau's Conception of Authority', *Journal of Canadian Studies* 10, no. 4 (Nov. 1975): 24–38.

21 Whitaker, 'Reason, Passion and Interest', 143.

22 Speech made by Pierre Trudeau at Sudbury, Ont., 5 June 1968, as quoted by Robert Vipond, 'Citizenship and the Charter of Rights: Two Sides of Pierre Trudeau', *International Journal of Canadian Studies*, no. 14 (Fall 1996). Vipond argues that English Canadians have never accepted Trudeau's contention that individual rights should include language rights.

23 The proposal was contained in his submission to the Tremblay Commission. See Trudeau, *Federalism and the French Canadians*, 53.

24 Ibid., 55. See also Peter C. Newman, *The Distemper of Our Times* (Toronto: McClelland & Stewart, 1968), 330.

25 Trudeau, *Federalism and the French Canadians*, 55–6.

26 Ibid., 191 (emphasis in original).

27 Trudeau, *Federalism and the French Canadians*, 192.

28 Wayne Norman, 'The Ideology of Shared Values: A Myopic Vision of Unity in the Multi-nation State', in Joseph H. Carens, ed., *Is Quebec Nationalism Just? Perspectives from Anglophone Canada* (Montreal and Kingston: McGill-Queen's University Press, 1995), 152–5.

29 Whitaker, 'Reason, Passion and Interest', 154.

30 'De son propre schéma personnel il aura fait l'extrapolation naturelle du modèle idéal du citoyen canadien.' See Bergeron, *Notre Miroir à deux faces*, 82.

31 Anthony Westell, 'If Canada doesn't want bilingualism, I want out', *Toronto Star*, 8 Feb. 1969.

32 Ramsay Cook, *The Maple Leaf Forever* (Toronto: Macmillan, 1971), 80.

33 Clarkson and McCall, *Trudeau and Our Times*, 84.

34 In Trudeau, *Federalism and the French Canadians*, Trudeau makes a passing reference to Bourassa's relations with the Church hierarchy (p. 109); credits the federal Liberal party with preventing the rise of a federal nationalist party under Bourassa's leadership (p. 119); acknowledges that Bourassa 'humanized' the Canadian multi-national state (p. 165); and observes that, like Laurendeau, Bourassa was a target of separatists (p. 172). On the other hand, many years later, in his campaign against the Meech Lake Accord, he started both his newspaper article and his address to the joint parliamentary committee by quoting Bourassa on the need for Canadian patriotism. See Pierre Elliott Trudeau, '"Say Goodbye to the Dream" of One Canada', *Toronto Star,* 27 May 1987, and Special Joint

Committee of the Senate and the House of Commons on the 1987 Constitutional Accord, *Minutes of Proceedings and Evidence*, 2nd session, 33rd Parliament, Issue no. 14, 27 Aug. 1987, 116.

35 Trudeau, *Federalism and the French Canadians*, 31.

36 Peter C. Newman, 'Now There's a Third Viewpoint in the French-English Dialogue', *Toronto Star*, 2 Apr. 1966.

37 Don Peacock, *Journey to Power: The Story of a Canadian Election* (Toronto: Ryerson, 1968), 160.

38 See Vastel, *Trudeau*, 157, and Clarkson and McCall, *Trudeau and Our Times*, 106.

39 Speech to Quebec Liberal Convention, 28 Jan. 1968, reported in *Ottawa Citizen*, 29 Jan. 1968, as quoted in George Radawanski, *Trudeau* (Scarborough, Ont.: Macmillan—NAL 1978), 286.

40 Jeremy Webber, *Reimagining Canada* (Montreal and Kingston: McGill-Queen's University Press, 1994), 60.

41 Peacock, *Journey to Power*, 277 and 294.

42 Claude Ryan, 'Le choix du 25 juin', *Le Devoir*, 19 June 1968.

43 As quoted in Peacock, *Journey to Power*, 251.

44 Paul Gros d'Aillon, *Daniel Johnson: l'égalité avant l'indépendance* (Montreal: Stanké, 1979), 208–11; and Peacock, *Journey to Power*, 355–8.

45 Peacock, *Journey to Power*, 262.

46 Gérard Boismenu, 'La Pensée constitutionnelle de Jean Lesage', in Robert Comeau, ed., *Jean Lesage et l'éveil d'une nation* (Sillery, Quebec: Presses de l'Université du Québec, 1989), 96–104.

47 Richard Daignault, *Lesage* (Quebec City: Libre expression, 1981), 250–2. See also Roy, *Le Choix d'un pays*, 84.

48 Clarkson and McCall, *Trudeau and Our Times*, 99.

49 Dale Thomson, *Jean Lesage and the Quiet Revolution*, 363, and Westell, *Paradox: Trudeau as Prime Minister*.

50 Richard Daignault, *Lesage* (Quebec City: Libre expression, 1981), 252. See also André Patry, 'Témoignage', in Comeau, ed., *Jean Lesage et l'éveil d'une nation*, 138; and Thomson, *Jean Lesage and the Quiet Revolution*, 458.

51 Peacock, *Journey to Power*, 371.

52 'Je suis plus sensibilisé que Pierre au nationalisme québécois. Bien sûr, je suis canadien. Mais, d'une certain façon, je suis plus québécois que canadien.' As quoted in Bergeron, *Notre Miroir à deux faces*, 98, n. 73.

53 Donald Peacock, *Journey to Power*, 161–6, 195–201. Finally, a few days before the convention, Lamontagne declared for Trudeau, saying he shared Trudeau's opposition to the 'extreme' form of special status favoured by Ryan. See 'Le sénateur Lamontagne appuie Trudeau dont il dit partager "en gros" les positions constitutionnelles', *Le Devoir*, 29 Mar 1968.

54 Vastel, *Trudeau*, 168. Sullivan believes that support would have been much greater if Jean Marchand, the caucus leader, had acted more effectively. See Martin Sullivan, *Mandate '68* (Toronto: Doubleday, 1968), 305.

55 Correspondence from Jeffrey Simpson, Sept. 1995.
56 Cadieux said that Trudeau would not be his second choice either. See 'Léo Cadieux donne son appui à Paul Hellyer', *Le Devoir*, 14 Mar. 1968.
57 Ibid.
58 See Smiley, *Constitutional Adaptation and Canadian Federalism*, 135.
59 'Trudeau est assuré de l'appui de 23 députés du Québec', *Le Devoir*, 20 Mar. 1968; and 'Isabelle appuie plutôt Winters; Lessard, Hellyer', *Le Devoir*, 28 Mar. 1968.
60 'La course au leadership accentue les divisions dans le caucus du Québec', *Le Devoir*, 11 Apr. 1968.
61 Sullivan, *Mandate '68*, 317–19, 340.
62 Donald V. Smiley, 'The Case against the Canadian Charter of Human Rights', *Canadian Journal of Political Science* 2, no. 3 (Sept. 1969): 278.
63 H.D. Forbes, 'Trudeau's Moral Vision', in A. A. Peacock, ed., *Rethinking the Constitution* (Toronto: Oxford University Press, 1996), 34 (emphasis in original).
64 John Robert Colombo, *Colombo's All-Time Great Canadian Quotations* (Toronto: Stoddart, 1994), 220. In 1977 he told the American Congress that the breakup of Canada would be nothing less than 'a crime against humanism'. See 'Trudeau: Unity in Canada Won't Be Fractured', *Globe and Mail*, 23 Feb. 1977.
65 Newman, *Distemper of Our Times*, 461.
66 Richard Gwyn, *The Northern Magus* (Toronto: McClelland & Stewart, 1980), 71.
67 Claude Ryan, 'Vieille tentation du Canada anglais', *Le Devoir*, 1 Feb. 1968.
68 'Faire du nationalisme la règle décidante des politiques et des priorités est un choix stérile et rétrograde. . . . Qu'il s'agisse du premier budget, en juin 1963, de l'honorable Walter Gordon, des règlements du Bureau des gouverneurs de la radio-diffusion sur le contenu canadien des programmes, de l'intolérance courante chez les "White Anglo-Saxon Protestants", ou de la notion répandue selon laquelle "l'État du Québec" serait l'arme économique du Canada français, on est en face du même problème.' See Albert Bréton et al., 'Manifeste pour une politique fonctionnelle', *Cité libre*, May 1964, 16. In fact, they were quite explicit in their rejection of English-Canadian concern with American domination: 'Nous ne sommes pas plus émus par les clameurs de certains milieux anglophones devant l'achat d'entreprises canadiennes par des intérêts financiers américains, que par l'adoption par la province de Québec de politiques économiques basées sur le slogan de "Maîtres chez nous".' ('We are no more moved by the complaints from some anglophone circles about the purchase of Canadian companies by American financial interests than by Quebec's adoption of economic policies based on the slogan "Masters in our house".')
69 'Il y a d'abord ce fait juridique et géographique: le Canada. . . . Vouloir le scinder . . . nous apparaît comme une véritable évasion en face des tâches réelles et importantes à accomplir. Vouloir l'intégrer à une autre entité géographique nous apparaît également comme une tâche futile à l'heure actuelle, même si un tel développement peut, en principe, sembler plus conforme à l'évolution du monde.' Ibid., 17.
70 The quotation is from Vastel, *Trudeau*, 164. Vastel says that Gordon refused to

support Trudeau. Sullivan, on the other hand, says he did (Sullivan, *Mandate '68*, 320), as do McCall and Clarkson, *Trudeau and Our Times*, 87 and 453.

71 McCall and Clarkson, *Trudeau and Our Times*, 97–102.

72 J.L. Granatstein, *Canada 1957–1967* (Toronto: McClelland & Stewart, 1986), 362.

73 Newman, *The Distemper of Our Times*, 446.

74 John English, *The Life of Lester Pearson*, vol. 2 (Toronto: Knopf, 1992), 384.

75 Ibid.

76 Claude Lemelin, 'Sharp: Ottawa devra faire preuve de souplesse sur la question constitutionnelle', *Le Devoir*, 23 Mar. 1968.

77 John Meisel, *Working Papers on Canadian Politics* (Montreal and Kingston: McGill-Queen's University Press, 1972), 34–6. By my calculations, if non-francophones (who represented about 18 per cent of the electorate), voted 75 per cent in favour of the Liberals, the francophone Liberal vote would have been about 49 per cent.

78 This is confirmed by the various anecdotes and editorial statements which Peacock offers to document Trudeaumania. They are all drawn from outside Quebec. See Peacock, *Journey to Power*, 257–60.

79 Ibid., 356.

80 Anthony Westell, 'PM Challenges Quebec Tories on Two Nations', *Globe and Mail*, 21 June 1968.

81 Ronald Lebel, 'PM Creating Great Division', *Globe and Mail*, 21 June 1968.

82 See Lamoureux, *Le NPD et le Québec*, 151–5, and Morton, *NDP*, 126–7.

83 'Towards a New Canada: A New Canadian Constitution', in *New Democratic Policies, 1961–1976* (Ottawa: New Democratic Party, 1976), 92.

84 Desmond Morton, 'The NDP and Quebec: A Sad Tale of Unrequited Love', *Saturday Night*, June 1972, 18.

85 Morton notes, 'For the first time, NDP candidates began to be confronted with the [Quebec] issue in the rest of Canada.' See Morton, *NDP*, 83.

Chapter 4

1 Frederick W. Gibson, ed., *Cabinet Formation and Bicultural Relations*, Studies of the Royal Commission on Bilingualism and Biculturalism, no. 6 (Ottawa: Queen's Printer, 1970), 165.

2 In 1863, French Canadians had held only about 35 per cent of positions on the headquarters staff of the United Canadas, 'and these were obviously employed on less important tasks, for they received less that 20 percent of the total payroll.' See Hodgetts, *Pioneer Public Service*, 57.

3 Royal Commission on Bilingualism and Biculturalism [hereinafter: B&B Commission], Book III: *The Work World*, 101.

4 Ibid., 111.

5 This account is drawn from B&B Commission, Book III: *The Work World*, 114–16. At the same time, the commission notes that the commitment to 'biculturalism' was not clearly defined and apparently did not entail creating culturally distinct environments.

6 Ibid., 162–3.

7   The commission declared: 'No other part of the commission's terms of refer-
     ence appears to us to be more urgent. If we wish "to develop the Canadian
     Confederation on the basis of an equal partnership" between the two founding
     peoples, bilingualism becomes essential first in the institutions shared by all
     Canadians. This conclusion is inescapable.' See B&B Commission, Book I, *The
     Official Languages* (Ottawa: Queen's Printer, 1967), 91.
8   Ibid., 91.
9   B&B Commission, Book III: *The Work World*, 263.
10   Ibid., 264.
11   Ibid.
12   Ibid., 178.
13   Ibid., 272.
14   Ibid., 265–6.
15   Ibid., 291.
16   'Back to the Solitudes', *Globe and Mail*, 18 Dec. 1969 and *Toronto Star*, 19 Dec.
     1969. In the House, Opposition Leader Robert Stanfield called on Prime
     Minister Trudeau to disown the French-language units proposal which 'denie[d]
     any concept of effective bilingualism'. *Globe and Mail*, 19 Dec. 1969. Outside the
     House he derided the creation of a 'multitude of solitudes', *Toronto Star*, 19 Dec.
     1969.
17   Commissioner of Official Languages, *Second Annual Report, 1971–72* (Ottawa:
     Information Canada, 1973), 22.
18   Commissioner of Official Languages, *Third Annual Report, 1972–73* (Ottawa:
     Information Canada, 1974), 27.
19   Commissioner of Official Languages, *Fifth Annual Report, 1975* (Ottawa:
     Information Canada, 1976), 15.
20   Commissioner of Official Languages, *Annual Report 1978* (Ottawa: Supply and
     Services, 1979), 22.
21   D'Iberville Fortier, 'Breaking Old Habits', *Language and Society*, no. 24 (Fall
     1988): 12. On the French-language units see Scott Reid, *Lament for a Notion*
     (Vancouver: Arsenal Pulp Press, 1993), chap. 8.
22   See Commissioner of Official Languages, *First Annual Report, 1970–71* (Ottawa:
     Information Canada, 1971), 91; idem., *Second Annual Report, 1971–72*, 23–24;
     idem., *Third Annual Report, 1972–73*, 30; idem., *Fourth Annual Report, 1973–74*,
     17; idem., *Fifth Annual Report, 1975*, 15–16. Many years later, Spicer acknowl-
     edged that the statutory basis for language of work, in the Official Languages
     Act, was 'the Act's absolutely vague Section 2 which spoke only of "equal sta-
     tus, rights and privileges"'. Following Stephen Lewis's advice, he decided to
     'bluff' the idea of language of work into the provision. See Keith Spicer, 'How
     the Linguistic World Looked in 1970', *Languages and Society*, Summer 1989,
     R–12.
23   Commissioner of Official Languages, *Sixth Annual Report, 1976* (Ottawa: Supply
     and Services, 1977).

24 Commissioner of Official Languages, *Annual Report, 1995* (Ottawa: Supply and Services, 1996), Tables III.9 and III.11.

25 B&B Commission, Book III, *The Work World*, Table 49.

26 Ibid., Table III.3.

27 Commissioner of Official Languages, *Annual Report, 1993* (Ottawa: Supply and Services Canada, 1994), Table III.7. Different measures give very different estimates for francophone participation in senior levels in the 1960s. On the basis of income ($10,000 or more) the figure was 11 per cent in 1965, whereas the proportion in 'management' positions in the same year was 19.9 per cent. See B&B Commission, Book III, *The Work World*, Fig. 9 and Table 50. Presumably the 1960s measure of 'management' is not equivalent to that of the 1980s and 1990s.

28 See Sarra-Bournet's analysis of a sample of senior civil servants. His data even suggest that francophones are over-represented, although this over-representation is restricted to francophones from outside Quebec. See Michel Sarra-Bournet, '"French Power, Québec Power": La place des francophones québécois à Ottawa', in François Rocher, ed., *Bilan québécois du fédéralisme canadien* (Montreal: VLB, 1992), 220.

29 Commissioner of Official Languages, *Annual Report, 1990* (Ottawa: Supply and Services, 1991), x.

30 Idem., *Annual Report, 1994* (Ottawa: Supply and Services, 1995), 7.

31 Idem., *Annual Report, 1993*, 14.

32 See the discussion in Sarra-Bournet, 'French Power, Québec Power', 216–17.

33 Richard Gwyn quotes one of Trudeau's senior francophone ministers: 'Bilingualism, for him, was far more than just something that was essential to the survival of French Canadians. For him, it was a *human right*, no different from freedom of speech, or freedom of religion. He would no more have compromised on it than he would have compromised on any basic human right [emphasis in original]. See Gwyn, *The Northern Magus*, 59.

34 Trudeau, *Federalism and the French Canadians*, 56.

35 Speech to Quebec Liberal Convention, 28 Jan. 1968, reported in *Ottawa Citizen*, 29 Jan. 1968, as quoted in George Radawanski, *Trudeau* (Scarborough: Macmillan—NAL, 1978), 286.

36 Richard J. Joy, *Languages in Conflict* (Toronto: McClelland & Stewart, 1972), 91.

37 Richard J. Joy, *Canada's Official Languages: The Progress of Bilingualism* (Toronto: University of Toronto Press, 1992), 71.

38 Ibid., 93.

39 Joy, *Languages in Conflict*, 77.

40 Ibid., 78.

41 Joy, *Canada's Official Languages*, 106.

42 Ibid., 107.

43 Ibid., 69.

44 Calculated from *Census of Canada, 1971*, vol. I, part 3 (cat. no. 92–726).

45 In fact, this bleak prognosis had already been clearly established in 1967 by

Richard J. Joy in his *Languages in Conflict*. Originally published by the author himself, the book was published in 1972 by McClelland & Stewart.

46 See Donald J. Savoie, *The Politics of Language* (Kingston: Institute of Intergovernmental Relations, Queen's University, 1991), 7.

47 Marcel Martel, 'Les Relations entre le Québec et les francophones de l'Ontario: De la survivance aux *Dead Ducks*, 1937–1969', Ph.D. dissertation, History Department, York University, 1994, 125–8.

48 Ibid., 105, and chap. 4.

49 B&B Commission, *General Introduction*, xxviii.

50 B&B Commission, Book I, *The Official Languages*, 12.

51 Ibid.

52 Ibid., 14.

53 B&B Commission, *General Introduction*, xxviii.

54 Ibid., xxxiii.

55 Ibid., xlvii.

56 Discussions of the two principles and their relative advantages appear in Kenneth D. McRae, 'The Principle of Territoriality and the Principle of Personality in Multilingual States', *International Journal of the Sociology of Language* 4 (1975): 35–45; André Donneur, 'La Solution territoriale au problème du multilinguisme,' in Jean-Guy Savard and Richard Vigneault, eds, *Les États multilingues: problèmes et solutions* (Quebec City: Presses de l'Université Laval, 1975); Jean A. Laponce, *Languages and Their Territories* (Toronto: University of Toronto Press, 1987); and J.A. Laponce, 'Reducing the Tensions Resulting from Language Contacts: Personal or Territorial Solutions?' in Daniel Bonin, ed., *Towards Reconciliation? The Language Issue in Canada in the 1990s* (Kingston: Institute of Intergovernmental Relations, Queen's University, 1992), 125–39.

57 The studies dealt with Belgium, Switzerland, South Africa, and Finland. See B&B Commission, Book I, *The Official Languages*, 210–11.

58 Of course, South Africa's claim to a 'liberal' language regime was based only on its treatment of *white* languages, a point that the commission merely acknowledged in a footnote (ibid., 80). Two traits distinguished South Africa from the territorially based Belgium and Switzerland: the proportion of the population that can speak the official languages and the territorial concentration of the languages. By its own evidence, Canada fell far short. Whereas 66 per cent of South African whites claimed to be bilingual, only 12 per cent of Canadians made this claim. The official-language minorities of the South African provinces represented proportions ranging from 23 per cent to 39 per cent. In 9 of the 10 Canadian provinces, they constituted less than 14 per cent. On this basis, the commission concluded that Canada would have difficulty pursuing 'a policy of the South African type, where a full range of governmental and educational services is provided in both official languages in all provinces of the country' (ibid., 84).

59 Ibid., 83.

60 Ibid., 86. By the commission's calculations, these 'official-language minorities'

amounted to 'about 700,000 Canadians in Quebec whose mother tongue is English and some 850,000 scattered throughout the rest of the country whose mother tongue is French' (ibid., 87).

61 'If, therefore, French-speaking Quebecers should decide to dissociate themselves from the fate of the French minorities, and particularly if they should adopt this attitude because they felt English-speaking Canada was not giving the minorities a chance to live, separatist tendencies might then be that much more encouraged.' See B&B Commission, *Preliminary Report,* 119.

62 B&B Commission, Book I, *The Official Languages,* 86.

63 Ibid., 97.

64 Ibid., 97–9.

65 Ibid., 147–9.

66 Ibid., 105–17.

67 According to B&B Commission co-secretary Neil M. Morrison, Laurendeau had very much wanted the first volume of the report to be devoted to the status of French in the work world rather than, as it turned out, the status of French outside Quebec, and lamented the fact that the volume 'does nothing for Quebec'. See N.M. Morrison, 'Bilingualism and Biculturalism', *Language and Society,* (Summer 1989), R–8.

68 B&B Commission, Book III, *The Work World,* 559.

69 Ibid., 565. Scott noted that for Ontario and New Brunswick the commission had proposed that task forces be created to determine what measures were necessary to put French on the same basis as English as a language of work. However, in the case of Quebec, the commission set out rigid guidelines for such a task force: 'So the principles differ depending on the provincial boundaries. This is a virtual acceptance of the territorial principle. My idea of "equal partnership" is that it operates in similar fashion across Canada, "wherever the minority is numerous enough to be viable as a group".' (ibid).

70 Official Languages Act, 1st session, 28th Parliament, C-120.

71 The fate of the bilingual-districts scheme is discussed in Kenneth D. McRae, 'Bilingual Language Districts in Finland and Canada: Adventures in the Transplanting of an Institution', *Canadian Public Policy* 4, no. 3 (Summer 1978): 331–51; Kenneth McRoberts, 'Making Canada Bilingual: Illusions and Delusions of Federal Language Policy', in David Shugarman and Reg Whitaker, eds, *Federalism and the Political Community* (Peterborough, Ont.: Broadview, 1989), 141–7; and Reid, *Lament for a Notion,* chap. 6.

72 Commissioner of Official Languages, *First Annual Report, 1970–71,* 4.

73 Gilles Lalonde, 'Back to the B and B', *Language and Society,* no. 19 (Apr. 1987): 24. Lalonde did not himself refer to the 'Trudeau orthodoxy'.

74 Léon Dion, 'The Impact of Demolinguistic Trends', 66. Between 1970 and 1978 the percentage was 58 per cent. See Fédération des francophones hors Québec, *À la recherche du milliard* (Ottawa: 1981), as cited in Wilfrid B. Denis, 'The Politics of Language', in Peter S. Li, ed., *Race and Ethnic Relations in Canada* (Toronto: Oxford University Press, 1990), 170. In the face of complaints from outside

Quebec, the situation was altered somewhat. In 1989, of a total $225.7 million granted to the provinces and territories, 28 per cent went to the education of Quebec anglophones, 35.8 per cent for francophones outside Quebec, and 29.6 per cent to anglophones outside Canada. See Secretary of State, *Annual Report to Parliament, 1989–90*, Fig. 4, p. 45. See also the discussion in Denis, 'The Politics of Language', 171. Instances such as this would seem to refute Scott Reid's contention that the federal government's language policy is 'asymmetrical', that is, favouring French and francophones over English and anglophones. See Reid, *Lament for a Notion*, 63. See also the critique in C. Michael MacMillan, 'Contemporary Challenges to National Language Policy: The Territorial Imperative', paper presented to the Canadian Political Science Association, 1996, 10–12.

75 Pal, *Interests of State*, Table 7.5.

76 Commissioner of Official Languages, *Annual Report, 1994*, 7.

77 Société Radio-Canada, *Une décennie 1970–1980*, Services français de la planification du rayonnement, Oct. 1981, 14–15, as cited in Richard Chevrier, *Français au Canada: situation à l'extérieur du Québec* (Montreal: Conseil de la langue française, 1983), 19. To be sure, as Chevrier notes, francophone groups regularly complain about poor quality of reception and insufficient local production.

78 The 1971 figure comes from Denis, 'Politics of Language', 157. The 1987 figures come from Secretary of State, *Annual Report, 1989–90*, Appendix L.

79 Secretary of State, *Annual Report, 1989–90*, 73–81.

80 Simeon, *Federal-Provincial Diplomacy*, 118, and Smiley, *Canada in Question*, 76. The federal government was to publish statutes in both languages if a province should fail to do so.

81 Pal, *Interests of State*, 134.

82 See the review of linguistic reforms among the provinces in Donald J. Savoie, *The Politics of Language*, 7–15. Also for New Brunswick see Don Desserud, 'The Exercise of Community Rights in the Liberal-Federal State: Language Rights and New Brunswick's Bill 88', unpublished paper.

83 Don Stevenson, former co-ordinator of French-language services for the Ontario government, contends that with Bill 8 Ontario has for all intents and purposes become officially bilingual. See Don Stevenson, 'What Is an Official Language?', unpublished paper. To be sure, the formal declaration that English and French are official languages, as in New Brunswick, could be politically controversial, making this last step a very substantial one.

84 *French Language Services Act*, 2nd session, 33rd Parliament, Bill 8.

85 In his campaign for the Ontario PC leadership, Mike Harris had declared, 'The people of Quebec and the people of Ontario say no [to official bilingualism]. We are English. We will provide French-language services, as was our commitment.' See Derek Ferguson, 'Tory Blames Bilingualism for Backlash', *Toronto Star*, 26 Mar., 1990.

86 Bill 2 does not require that records of legislative debates be kept in both lan-

guages; it left this matter for the legislative assembly to resolve. Also, the right to use French in courts is restricted to criminal cases.

87 The 1988 court decision followed upon (but was unrelated to) a dispute over the right to use French in the Alberta legislature. A francophone legislator had demanded the right to do so, invoking the *Northwest Territories Act*, but his request was denied by the Speaker. Yet in the Saskatchewan legislature the occasional use of French (by non-francophones) had apparently not been challenged. The Alberta dispute is recounted in Timothy J. Christian, 'L'Affaire Piquette', in David Schneiderman, ed., *Language and the State* (Cowansville: Yvon Blais, 1991), 107–21.

88 Secretary of State, *Annual Report to Parliament, 1989–1990: Official Languages*, Appendix J.

89 Ibid., Appendix G.

90 See the review of provincial responses to the Mahé decision in Commissioner of Official Languages, *Annual Report, 1990*, 211–14. See also Daniel Bonin, ed., *Towards Reconciliation? The Language Issue in Canada in the 1990s* (Kingston: Institute of Intergovernmental Relations, Queen's University, 1992), 6.

91 See the account in Secretary of State, *Annual Report to Parliament, 1989–1990: Official Languages*, 73–82.

92 To be precise, Henripin and two colleagues predicted that francophones would be between 52.7 per cent and 60.0 per cent of Montreal's population and between 71.6 per cent and 79.2 per cent of Quebec's. See Hubert Charbonneau, Jacques Henripin, and Jacques Legaré, 'L'Avenir démographique des francophones au Québec et à Montréal en l'absence de politiques adéquates,' *Revue de géographie de Montréal* 24 (1974): 199–202. Henripin has recently acknowledged that the estimate was erroneous owing to incomplete data. Indeed, the francophone proportion increased rather than decreased, because of an unexpectedly large out-migration of anglophones. See Jacques Henripin, 'Population Trends and Policies in Quebec', in Alain Gagnon, ed., *Quebec: State and Society*, 2nd edn (Scarborough, Ont.: Nelson, 1993), 315.

93 These changes in French Quebec are detailed in McRoberts, *Quebec: Social Change and Political Crisis*, chaps. 4 and 5.

94 Rapport de la commission d'enquête sur la situation de la langue française et sur les droits linguistiques au Québec, vol. 2, *Les Droits linguistiques* (Quebec City, Dec. 1972), 67–8 (my translation).

95 Rapport de la commission d'enquête, vol. 1, *La Langue de travail*.

96 Savoie, *The Politics of Language*, 16.

97 As quoted in Peter Stursberg, *Lester Pearson and the Dream of Unity* (Toronto: Doubleday, 1978), 146.

98 'The Cultural Anguish of Quebec', notes for a speech by Gérard Pelletier to la Chambre de commerce de Montréal, 19 Feb., 1974, 7. This was the English version of the speaking notes; in all likelihood the address was given primarily in French.

99 'Je n'en ai pas contre l'esprit de la loi mais contre la lettre, en certain endroits. . . . Une de mes critiques les plus fortes n'est même pas source d'injustice, c'est ce

que j'appelle de la stupidité politique. . . . Si on avait dit la principale langue ou la langue de travail, la langue nationale. . . . Cela aurait grandement facilité les choses aux libéraux de reste du pays, à qui nous disons qu'il y a deux langues officielles, le français et l'anglais.' 'I have nothing against the spirit of the law but against the letter, in certain places. . . . One of my strongest citicisms is not even in terms of injustice but what I call political stupidity. . . . If they had said principal language or language of work, national language . . . that would have greatly helped things for Liberals in the rest of the country, to whom we are saying that there are two languages, French and English.' 'Le discours de M. Trudeau: Il faut qu'on se parle dans le blanc des yeux', *La Presse*, 8 Mar. 1976. Also see Pierre Elliott Trudeau, *Memoirs* (Toronto: McClelland & Stewart, 1993), 234, where he laments the fact that Bill 22 came at a time when 'we had managed at Victoria to get the provinces to accept a measure of official bilingualism even at the provincial level'.

100 Léon Dion, 'The Impact of Demolinguistic Trends on Canadian Institutions', in *Demolinguistic Trends and the Evolution of Canadian Institutions*, special issue of *Canadian Issues* of the Association of Canadian Studies, 1989, 67.

101 Bernard Descôteaux, 'Ottawa négociera avec le Québec sur la loi des langues', *Le Devoir*, 8 June 1988, and Bernard Descôteaux, 'Ottawa et Québec s'entendent sur les langues officielles', *Le Devoir*, 18 Aug. 1988.

102 Calculated from Brian R. Harrison and Louise Marmen, *Languages in Canada* (Scarborough, Ont.: Prentice-Hall; published jointly with Statistics Canada, 1994), Tables A.1 and A.2.

103 Pierre Elliott Trudeau, 'The Values of a Just Society', in Thomas S. Axworthy and Pierre Elliott Trudeau, eds, *Towards a Just Society* (Markham: Viking, 1990), 368.

104 André Burelle, *Le Mal canadien* (Montreal: Fides, 1995), 73.

105 Under quite special circumstances, it may still be possible for two linguistic communities to persist in an urban area. Montreal comes to mind. Historically, Montreal has supported two large communities, but each was part of a larger linguistic community from which it could draw its strength. Within Quebec itself, the francophone community may have been overwhelmingly dominant in numbers, but Montreal anglophones were, of course, linked to the essentially anglophone society outside the province. Moreover, the Montreal anglophone community drew economic strength from that link, which solidified its place in Montreal and even allowed it to impose English as the main language of the upper levels of Montreal's economic institutions. In effect, Montreal was at the intersection of two linguistic communities and was itself divided between them.

106 Harrison and Marmen, *Languages in Canada*, Table 5.4.

107 Commissioner of Official Languages, *Annual Report, 1994*, 79.

108 On the basis of a careful analysis of data from the 1986 census, Réjean Lachapelle has argued that the rate of anglicization of children in mixed marriages has decreased in recent decades. He traces this to the higher status of French. None the less, in Canada outside Quebec anglicization still stands at 32.4 per cent in the youngest cohort. See Réjean Lachapelle, 'Demography and

Official Languages in Canada', in Daniel Bonin, ed., *Towards Reconciliation? The Language Issue in Canada in the 1990s* (Kingston, Ont.: Institute of Intergovernmental Relations, Queen's University, 1992), 86–9.

109 Calculated from Statistics Canada, *Home Language and Mother Tongue, 1991,* Table 3, cat. no. 93–317. Data were not provided for Ottawa without Hull.

110 Harrison and Marmen, *Languages in Canada,* 52–4.

111 Ibid., Table A.2.

112 Ibid., Table 5.3.

113 Alain G. Gagnon and Mary Beth Montcalm, *Quebec: Beyond the Quiet Revolution* (Scarborough, Ont.: Nelson, 1990), 6; and Kenneth McRoberts, 'The Sources of Neo-Nationalism in Quebec', *Ethnic and Racial Studies,* 7, no. 1 (Jan. 1984): 55–85.

114 Harrison and Marmen, *Languages in Canada,* Table A.1.

115 Calculated from ibid., Table A.2. See also the data in Reid, *Lament for a Notion,* chap. 4.

116 Réjean Lachapelle and Jacques Henripin, *La Situation démolinguistique au Canada: Évolution passée et prospectives* (Montreal: Institut de recherches politiques, 1980, Table 8.2). To be precise, they produce four percentages (based upon different economic and linguistic conditions) ranging from 2.2 per cent to 3.5 per cent. Their prediction of 3.2 per cent is supported by Marc Termote, 'L'Évolution démolinguistique du Québec et du Canada', in Commission sur l'avenir politique et constitutionnel du Québec, *Éléments d'analyse institutionnelle, juridique et démolinguistique pertinents à la révision du statut politique et constitutionnel du Québec,* Document de travail, numéro 2 (n.p., 1991), 266.

117 B&B Commission, Book II: *Education,* 302.

118 Ibid., 266.

119 Radawanski, *Trudeau,* 287.

120 *Debates of the Senate,* 2nd session, 33rd Parliament, vol. 132, 30 March 1988, 2993.

121 This English-Canadian attitude was seen in representations made to the B&B Commission during its cross-country hearings. In its *Preliminary Report* the commission noted that English Canadians in such cities as London, Ontario, tended to concentrate on strategies for increased personal bilingualism, whereas francophones in such places as Sherbrooke and Trois-Rivières expressed their discontent with the subordinate positions of the French language and of francophones in the economy and society of Quebec, making few references to the francophone minorities. See B&B Commission, *Preliminary Report,* 39.

122 Joy, *Canada's Official Languages,* 121.

123 B&B Commission, Book I, *The Official Languages* (Ottawa: Queen's Printer, 1967), 38.

124 Secretary of State, *Annual Report, 1990–91: Official Languages,* Appendix K.

125 Pal, *Interests of State,* 166–71.

126 Commissioner of Official Languages, *Annual Report, 1990,* Table D.1 and p. 272.

127 Harrison and Marmen, *Languages in Canada,* Table 4.6.

128 Harrison and Marmen, *Languages in Canada*, Table 4.4; and Commissioner of Official Languages, *Annual Report, 1992*, 16.

129 Harrison and Marmen, *Languages in Canada*, Table 4.4.

130 See the penetrating analysis of immersion programs in Eric Waddell, 'Some Thoughts on the Implications of French Immersion for English Canada', in David Schneiderman, ed., *Language and the State: The Law and Politics of Identity* (Cowansville, Que.: Yvon Blais, 1991), 423–32.

131 Arthur Leblanc, *Bilingual Education: A Challenge for Canadian Universities in the '90s* (Winnipeg: Continuing Education Division, University of Manitoba, 1986), 52, as cited in Eric Waddell, 'Implications of French Immersion', 427. See the discussion of the success of immersion French in *Language and Society*, no. 12 (1984): 44–60. Whereas in two articles education specialists are largely positive, in the third article Université de Montréal linguist and education professor Gilles Bibeau contends that the results of 20 years' experience suggest that 'pure' immersion is 'dépassé', since 'it has not enabled children to become as bilingual as was hoped.' He recommends simpler approaches that could be integrated with the education of most children. Gilles Bibeau, 'No Easy Road to Bilingualism', *Language and Society*, no. 12 (1984): 47. A critical evaluation is also offered by Marie-Claude Mosimann-Barbier, *Immersion et bilinguisme en Ontario* (Rouen: l'Université de Rouen, 1992).

132 In 1989–90, there were 241,095 children in French immersion programs outside Quebec but only 155,455 children in French-language schools outside Quebec. Secretary of State, *Annual Report, 1990–91: Official Languages*, Appendix I. See also the discussion in Eric Waddell, 'Implications of French Immersion', 425.

133 Léon Dion, 'The Impact of Demolinguistic Trends', 60.

134 Pal, *Interests of State*, 166–71.

135 J.B. Andrew, *Bilingual Today, French Tomorrow: Trudeau's Master Plan and How It Can Be Stopped* (Richmond Hill: BMG, 1977), 11.

136 Donald Creighton, 'The Myth of Biculturalism,' in Donald Creighton, *Towards the Discovery of Canada* (Toronto: Macmillan, 1972), 256–70.

137 J.T. Thorson, *Wanted: A Single Canada* (Toronto: McClelland & Stewart, 1973), 149.

138 1985 Canadian Facts survey cited in Michael O'Keefe, *An Analysis of Attitudes towards Official Languages Policy among Anglophones* (Ottawa: Office of the Commissioner of Official Languages, Policy Analysis Branch, Oct. 1990), 8.

139 Donald Smiley, 'Reflections on Cultural Nationhood and Political Community in Canada', in R. Kenneth Carty and Peter Ward, eds, *Entering the Eighties: Canada in Crisis* (Toronto: Oxford University Press, 1980), 33.

140 'Francophones Urge PM to Protect Their Rights', *Globe and Mail*, 5 Apr. 1988. When the Supreme Court reached a similar decision in Manitoba, francophone groups there instead tried to negotiate a package of French-language services in substitution for the translation of statutes.

141 'Peterson Disappointed by Decision on New Act', *Globe and Mail*, 6 Apr. 1988.

142 Ibid.

143 Harrison and Marmen, *Languages in Canada*, Table A.2.

144 Robert Andrew, the Saskatchewan justice minister, was reported to have said that none of the MLAs was functionally bilingual (*Globe and Mail*, 5 Apr. 1988). I have found no evidence to the contrary. In examining the record of Saskatchewan legislative debates between 28 Mar. 1988 and 28 June 1988 (which straddles the introduction and debate of Bill 2) I found no objection by the Opposition Party to Andrew's statement. The record did contain three instances of French-language paragraphs in what appeared to be prepared statements. Two of them were by members of Mr Andrew's party. The third was the first three sentences of a statement by Roy Romanow calling attention to the presence in the gallery of students from a French-language school in Saskatoon. For that matter, the whole debate over Bill 2 took place entirely in English.

145 MacMillan, 'Contemporary Challenges to National Language Policy'.

Chapter 5

1 Royal Commission on Bilingualism and Biculturalism [hereinafter: B&B Commission], *Preliminary Report* (Ottawa: Queen's Printer, 1965), Appendix I.

2 Laurendeau had proposed the commission in 'Pour une enquête sur le bilinguisme', *Le Devoir*, 20 Jan. 1962. To be sure, as the Comité pour une politique fonctionnelle (see below) was to emphasize, Laurendeau's article had not mentioned biculturalism, referring only to bilingualism. Yet, as the 'blue pages' attest, there can be no doubt that biculturalism was a central concept for Laurendeau. According to Donald Horton, it was after conversations with Laurendeau that Maurice Lamontagne proposed making biculturalism part of the projected commission's mandate. See Donald J. Horton, *André Laurendeau: French-Canadian Nationalist, 1912–1968* (Toronto: Oxford University Press, 1992), 250. Claude Ryan insists that Laurendeau would not have agreed to co-chair a commission devoted to language rights without considering the political context. See Claude Ryan, 'Il a soulevé les vraies questions et refuté les réponses toutes faites', in Robert Comeau and Lucille Beaudry, eds, *André Laurendeau: Un intellectuel d'ici* (Montreal: Presses de l'Université du Québec, 1990), 279.

3 B&B Commission, Book I, *General Introduction* (Ottawa: Queen's Printer, 1967), xxxi.

4 Ibid.

5 Ibid., xxxiii.

6 Ibid., xxxiii.

7 Ibid., xxiii.

8 Ibid., xxv.

9 See the analysis of the commission's views in Michael Oliver, 'The Impact of the Royal Commission on Bilingualism and Biculturalism on Constitutional Theory and Practice', *International Journal of Canadian Studies* 7–8 (Spring–Fall 1993): 320.

10 B&B Commission, Book I, *General Introduction*, xxxix–xliii.

11   Ibid., xlv.

12   Ibid.

13   Ibid.

14   Ibid., xlvi.

15   Michael Oliver, 'Laurendeau et Trudeau: leurs opinions sur le Canada', in Raymond Hudon and Réjean Pelletier, eds, *L'Engagement intellectuel: Mélanges en l'honneur de Léon Dion* (Sainte-Foy: Presses de l'Université Laval, 1991), 341.

16   Le Comité pour une politique fonctionnelle, 'Bizarre algèbre', *Cité libre* 15, no. 82 (Dec. 1965): 13–20. The signatories were Albert Bréton, Claude Bruneau, Yvon Gauthier, Marc Lalonde, and Maurice Pinard. Trudeau had been officially a member of the group (see Clarkson and McCall, *Trudeau and Our Times*, vol. 1, 410) and as such had signed the group's 'Manifeste pour une politique fonctionnelle' published in *Cité libre* in May 1964. Michael Oliver says that Jean Marchand persuaded Trudeau not to sign the document and that Trudeau later acknowledged to Laurendeau his 'paternité partielle' of the article. (See Oliver, 'Laurendeau et Trudeau', 342). Interestingly, another member of the committee, Raymond Breton, did not sign the 1965 document. Later a sociologist at the University of Toronto, Breton was to become a leader in the study of francophone minorities and multiculturalism.

17   My translation of 'Le moins qu'on puisse dire de cette idée c'est qu'elle est passablement étrangère à notre pensée juridique et à nos formes politiques. . . . Et que signifierait en pratique une Confédération qui "se développe d'après le principe de l'égalité entre les deux *cultures*"?' (Comité, 'Bizarre algèbre', 14.)

18   My translation of 'La science politique connaît bien l'idée d'égalité entre les individus à l'intérieur d'un même État; mais l'idée d'égalité entre les peuples est à la base même du concept de souveraineté nationale, et on aurait aimé savoir comment la Commission entend interpréter son mandat, sans être amenée nécessairement à préconiser la division du Canada en deux États nationaux.' (Ibid.)

19   To buttress their point they quote statements by Max Weber and Robert McIvor suggesting that normally a nation secures its own state. Yet this was a partial and considerably outdated view of social science. For instance, at about the same time political scientists were beginning to write about the 'consociational democracy' of smaller Western European democracies that showed how, through mutual vetoes and other devices, representatives of different cultures can enjoy equality within the institutions of a common state, and the state itself can be highly stable. See Robert A. Dahl, ed., *Political Oppositions in Western Democracies* (New Haven: Yale University Press, 1966); and Arend Lijphart, *The Politics of Accommodation: Pluralism and Democracy in the Netherlands* (Berkeley: University of California Press, 1968).

20   Sally M. Weaver, *Making Canadian Indian Policy: The Hidden Agenda 1968–1970* (Toronto: University of Toronto Press, 1981), 166–8.

21   Ibid., 54.

22   Ibid., 55.

23   Ibid., 185.

24   House of Commons, *Debates*, 22 July 1963, 2440.

25   Ibid., 2443.

26   Senate, *Debates*, 3 Mar. 1964, 51–8. Yuzyk's insistence on multiculturalism did not prevent him from ending his speech with the observation that 'fundamentally we are a Christian . . . nation.' (58).

27   John Jaworsky, 'A Case Study of the Canadian Federal Government's Multiculturalism Policy', M.A. thesis, Political Science Dept., Carleton University, Sept. 1979, 49. See also Peter Stursberg, *Lester Pearson and the Dream of Unity* (Toronto: Doubleday, 1978), 141.

28   Jaworsky, 'Federal Government's Multiculturalism Policy', 50. See also Horton, *André Laurendeau*, 225.

29   B&B Commission, Book I, *The Official Languages*, 155–69.

30   B&B Commission, Book IV, *The Cultural Contribution of the Other Ethnic Groups* (Ottawa: Queen's Printer, 1970), 228–30.

31   Kallen, 'Multiculturalism', 53; and Gwyn, *The Northern Magus*, 231.

32   A member of the commission, Paul Lacoste, declared, 'Tout en étant très ouvert aux diverses cultures, il [Laurendeau] rejetait énergiquement la conception d'un Canada bilingue mais multiculturel.' See Paul Lacoste, 'André Laurendeau et la Commission sur le bilinguisme et la biculturalisme', in R. Comeau and L. Beaudry, eds, *André Laurendeau*, 209.

33   B&B Commission, Book IV, *The Cultural Contribution*, 13 (emphasis added). However, Breton does present the federal government's multiculturalism policy as a response to the commission's Book IV. See Breton, 'Multiculturalism and Canadian Nation-Building', 49.

34   B&B Commission, Book IV, *The Cultural Contribution*, 10.

35   Ibid., 4.

36   These data are taken from Breton, 'Multiculturalism and Canadian Nation-Building,' 34–5.

37   Bruno Ramirez and Sylvie Taschereau, 'Les Minorités: le multiculturalisme appliqué', in Yves Bélanger, Dorval Brunelle et al., *L'Ère des libéraux: le pouvoir fédéral de 1963 à 1984* (Sillery, Quebec: Presses de l'Université du Québec, 1988), 386.

38   This is the conclusion of Jaworsky, who cites 'notable lack of effective coordination among representatives' of ethnic groups and 'difficulty in demonstrating grass roots support'. See Jaworsky, 'Federal Government's Multiculturalism Policy', 56.

39   Evelyn Kallen, 'Multiculturalism: Ideology, Policy and Reality', *Journal of Canadian Studies* 17, no. 1 (Spring 1982), 55; and Jaworsky, 'Federal Government's Multiculturalism Policy', 53.

40   Jaworsky, 'Federal Government's Multiculturalism Policy', 55.

41   Ibid., 50–1.

42   Raymond Breton, 'Multiculturalism and Nation-Building', in Alan Cairns and Cynthia Williams, eds, *The Politics of Gender, Ethnicity and Language in Canada*,

Collected Research Studies of the Royal Commission on the Economic Union and Development Prospects for Canada, vol. 34 (Toronto: University of Toronto Press, 1986), 45–6.

43   Breton, 'Multiculturalism and Canadian Nation-Building', 47.

44   Ibid. Soon after the announcement of the policy, Ralph Heintzman offered a similar interpretation in 'In the Bosom of a Single State', *Journal of Canadian Studies*, 6, no. 4 (Nov. 1971), 63. Recently, Garth Stevenson has written: 'As concept and symbol, multiculturalism may serve a number of purposes. For Trudeau, its primary purpose was to undermine and destroy the older ideological symbol of "deux nations".' Stevenson says that the very term 'multiculturalism' was 'invented by Prime Minister Trudeau'. See Garth Stevenson, 'Multiculturalism: As Canadian as Apple Pie', *Inroads*, no. 4 (1995): 74.

45   This is reported by Jaworsky on the basis of an interview with Ostry. In addition, Ostry recounted, Trudeau and Pelletier thought that multiculturalism might ease some of the opposition to official bilingualism. See Jaworsky, 'Federal Government's Multiculturalism Policy', 59.

46   House of Commons, *Debates*, 8 Oct. 1971, 8581.

47   Ibid., 8546.

48   Ibid.

49   Ibid., 8545.

50   Ibid. Kallen notes that Trudeau's policy did not hold 'the ideal model of cultural pluralism which assumes that every individual and group desires to maintain a distinctive ethnic identity and heritage' since it 'gives recognition to the fact that some people will, inevitably, find greater human affinities *outside* their ethnic group than within it'. See Kallen, 'Multiculturalism', 53 [emphasis in original].

51   Breton, 'Multiculturalism and Canadian Nation-Building', 49.

52   The following account draws heavily from Pal, *Interests of State*, 136–40, and Breton, 'Multiculturalism and Canadian Nation-Building', 51–3.

53   Breton, 'Multiculturalism and Canadian Nation-Building', 52.

54   Pal, *Interests of State*, 136, and Jaworsky, 'Federal Government's Multiculturalism Policy', 56.

55   Pal, *Interests of State*, 137.

56   Breton, 'Multiculturalism and Canadian Nation-Building', 57.

57   Pal, *Interests of State*, 138–9.

58   Manoly R. Lupul, 'The Political Implementation of Multiculturalism', *Journal of Canadian Studies* 17, no. 1 (Spring 1982): 96–7.

59   Ibid., 98. Jaworsky comments: 'Initially Trudeau and his advisors may have had an intellectual interest in the multiculturalism policy, hoping that it would provide a constructive alternative to the potentially divisive dichotomy posed by a policy of bilingualism and biculturalism. It appears, however, that they soon lost interest in the policy.' See Jaworsky, 'Federal Government's Multiculturalism Policy', 122.

60   Jaworsky, 'Federal Government's Multiculturalism Policy', 122–3.

61   Ibid., 122.

62   Ibid., 124.

63 Ibid., 95–6.

64 Daiva K. Stasiulis, 'The Symbolic Mosaic Reaffirmed: Multiculturalism Policy', in Katherine A. Graham, ed., *How Ottawa Spends, 1988–89* (Ottawa: Carleton University Press, 1988), 95.

65 Ramirez and Taschereau, 'Les Minorités', 391.

66 Jaworsky, 'Federal Government's Multiculturalism Policy', 82–87.

67 The text of Bourassa's statement is reproduced in *Le Devoir*, 17 (Nov. 1971), 2.

68 Jaworsky, 'Federal Government's Multiculturalism Policy', 84.

69 Claude Ryan, 'L'Aide aux groupes ethniques exige-t-elle l'abandon du biculturalisme?' *Le Devoir*, 9 Oct. 1971.

70 Guy Rocher, 'Multiculturalism: The Doubts of a Francophone', in *Multiculturalism as State Policy: Conference Report*, Second Canadian Conference on Multiculturalism, Canadian Consultative Council on Multiculturalism, ed. (Ottawa: Dept. of Supply and Services, 1976), 52.

71 See, for instance, Christian Dufour, *A Canadian Challenge/Le Défis québécois* (Lantzville, BC, and Halifax, NS: Oolichan Books and IRPP, 1990), 79, and Louis Balthazar, 'Pour un multiculturalisme québécois', *Action nationale* 79 (Oct. 1989), 942–53.

72 This account is drawn primarily from Marie McAndrew, 'Multiculturalisme canadien et interculturalisme québécois: mythes et réalités', unpublished paper. See also Danielle Juteau, 'The Canadian Experiment: Multiculturalism as Ideology and Policy', paper presented to Conference on Cultural Diversity in Europe, Berlin, 1990; Danielle Juteau, Marie McAndrew, and Linda Pietrantonio, 'Multiculturalism à la Canadian and Intégration à la Québécoise: Transcending Their Limits', unpublished paper.

73 The official discourse is examined in François Rocher, 'Is a Neo-Jacobin Vision of the "Canadian Nation" Compatible with Democracy?' *McGill Études sur le Québec*, Mar. 1996, 7.

74 Juteau, McAndrew, and Pietrantonio, 'Multiculturalism à la Canadian', 11.

75 Juteau, 'The Canadian Experiment', 13; McAndrew, 'Multiculturalisme canadien et interculturalisme québécois', 13. By the same token, Juteau and McAndrew insist, on the basis of scientific research, that francophones are no more xenophobic than anglophones. See Danielle Juteau and Marie McAndrew, 'Projet national, immigration et intégration dans un Québec souverain', *Sociologie et sociétés* 24, no. 2 (Autumn 1992): 176.

76 B&B Commission, *General Introduction*, xxv.

77 Jeffrey G. Reitz and Raymond Breton, *The Illusion of Difference: Realities of Ethnicity in Canada and the United States* (Toronto: C.D. Howe Institute, 1994), 31.

78 Breton, 'Multiculturalism and Canadian Nation-Building', 50.

79 See the analysis of the opposition to, and defence of, multiculturalism policy in Yasmeen Abu-Labon and Daiva Stasiulis, 'Ethnic Pluralism under Siege: Popular and Partisan Opposition to Multiculturalism', *Canadian Public Policy* 18, no. 4: 365–86.

80 Neil Bissoondath, *Selling Illusions: The Cult of Multiculturalism in Canada*

(Toronto: Penguin, 1994), 88. See also Richard Ogmundson, 'On the Right to Be Canadian', in Stella Hryniuk, ed., *Twenty Years of Multiculturalism: Successes and Failures* (Winnipeg: St John's College Press, 1992), 45–55.

81 John C. Harles, 'Integration *before* Assimilation: Immigration, Multiculturalism and the Canadian Polity', unpublished paper, 19–23.

82 Reginald W. Bibby, *Mosaic Madness* (Toronto: Stoddart, 1990), 91.

83 William D. Gairdner, *The Trouble with Canada* (Toronto: Stoddart, 1990), 406.

84 Preston Manning, *The New Canada* (Toronto: Macmillan, 1992), 317.

85 Philip Resnick, *Thinking English Canada* (Toronto: Stoddart, 1994), 73.

86 Stevenson, 'Multiculturalism', 87.

87 Reitz and Breton, *The Illusion of Difference*, chap. 3.

88 Pal, *Interests of State*, 256–7.

89 Harles, 'Integration *before* Assimilation', 7–14.

90 These data are drawn from Jim Cummins and Marcel Danesi, *Heritage Languages: The Development and Denial of Canada's Linguistic Resources* (Toronto: Our Schools/Our Selves Foundation, 1990), 26.

91 *Canadian Multiculturalism Act*, 2nd session, 33rd Parliament, C–93.

92 Cummins and Danesi, *Heritage Languages*, 31–3. In addition, 'there are close to 30 full-time ethnic schools (mainly Jewish but also Greek and Armenian) which are subsidized for approximately 80 per cent of their operating costs by the provincial government' (30).

93 Among 'single' ethnic origins, French is outnumbered by German and Ukrainian in Manitoba, Alberta, and (along with aboriginal) in Saskatchewan, and by German, Chinese, and South Asian in British Columbia. See Pamela M. White, *Ethnic Diversity in Canada*, 1986 Census of Canada, cat. no. 98–132, Table 1.

94 This discussion of provincial programs is drawn from Cummins and Danesi, *Heritage Languages*, 33–49.

95 The Federation of Francophones outside Quebec, *The Heirs of Lord Durham: Manifesto of a Vanishing People* (Toronto: Burns and MacEachern, 1978), 65, as quoted in Jaworsky, 'Federal Government's Multiculturalism Policy', 86.

96 Resnick, *Thinking English Canada*, chap. 7. Harles is dubious about the integrative possibilities of dualism, citing the historical rivalry between the two entities and the fact that the sense of cultural cohesiveness is stronger in Quebec than in English Canada. See John C. Harles, 'Making a Virtue of Necessity: National Integration and Multiculturalism in Canada', unpublished paper, 9–13. Yet it still might have had greater potential than multiculturalism, which Harles alleges is quite unsupportive of political integration.

Chapter 6

1 On the debate between Scott and Laurendeau at the commission see Guy Laforest, *Trudeau et la fin d'un rêve canadien* (Sillery, Quebec: Septentrion, 1992), 96–104.

2 Paul Lacoste, 'André Laurendeau et la Commission sur le bilinguisme et le biculturalisme', in Robert Comeau and Lucille Beaudry, eds, *André Laurendeau: Un intellectuel d'ici* (Sillery, Quebec: Presses de l'Université du Québec, 1990), 207–13.

3   J.-P. Proulx, 'L'Histoire d'un échec qui combla d'aise Pierre-Elliott Trudeau,' *Le Devoir*, 5 Nov. 1988.

4   Mitchell Sharp relates:

> It wasn't that we were excluded from Liberal Party politics in Quebec. Rather, we realized that Quebeckers had to decide among themselves whether to stay or to leave and that our main contribution as English-speaking ministers was to give reality to Trudeau's contention that French-speaking Canadians from Quebec could play their full and appropriate part in the Government of Canada.

See Mitchell Sharp, *Which Reminds Me . . . A Memoir* (Toronto: University of Toronto Press, 1994), 170.

5   Bruce Thordarson, *Trudeau and Foreign Policy* (Toronto: Oxford University Press, 1972).

6   Calculated from W.T. Stanbury, Gerald J. Gorn, and Charles B. Weinberg, 'Federal Advertising Expenditures', in G. Bruce Doern, ed., *How Ottawa Spends: The Liberals, the Opposition and Federal Priorities, 1983* (Toronto: Lorimer, 1983), Table 6.2.

7   Richard Simeon and Ian Robinson, *State, Society and the Development of Canadian Federalism*, Collected Research Studies of the Royal Commission on the Economic Union and Development Prospects for Canada, vol. 71 (Toronto: University of Toronto Press, 1990), 287.

8   The term 'new constituencies' appears in Donald V. Smiley, *Canada in Question*, 3rd edn (Toronto: McGraw-Hill Ryerson, 1980), 110. See also Leslie A. Pal, *Interests of State* (Montreal and Kingston: McGill-Queen's University Press, 1993), chap. 5.

9   Anthony G.S. Careless, *Initiative and Response* (Montreal and Kingston: McGill-Queen's University Press, 1977), 196.

10 Ryan's arguments can be found in Claude Ryan, 'Les Mesures de guerre: trois questions', *Le Devoir*, 17 October 1970. Trudeau continues to insist that the initiative regarding the War Measures Act came from the Quebec government, as well as the city of Montreal, and that he had no alternative but to do as they wished. See Pierre Elliott Trudeau, *Memoirs* (Toronto: McClelland & Stewart, 1993), 142. However, others have claimed that this request was in fact orchestrated by Ottawa. See the discussion of this scenario, among others, in Marc Laurendeau, *Les Québécois violents* (Montreal: Boréal, 1974), 145–52. The contention that the extraordinary police powers were not necessary for the apprehension of the FLQ kidnappers appears in Ron Haggart and Aubrey E. Golden, *Rumours of War* (Toronto: New Press, 1971), 251–5. The argument that the imposition of the War Measures Act was part of an effort to intimidate Quebec nationalists and separatists in general is given credence in Reg Whitaker, 'Apprehended Insurrection? RCMP Intelligence and the October Crisis', *Queen's Quarterly*, 100, no. 2 (Summer 1993): 401–5. See also Richard Gwyn, *The Northern Magus* (Toronto: McClelland & Stewart, 1980), 129–34. A critique of the Trudeau government's actions, claiming that they were an improper asser-

tion of the federal government's authority, is made in Denis Smith, *Bleeding Hearts . . . Bleeding Country* (Edmonton: Hurtig, 1971).

11 Yves Vaillancourt, 'Le Régime d'assistance publique du Canada: perspective québécoise', thèse de doctorat en science politique, l'Université de Montréal, 1992, 239.

12 Simeon and Robinson, *State, Society and the Development of Canadian Federalism*, 201.

13 Pierre Elliott Trudeau, *Federalism and the French Canadians* (Toronto: Macmillan, 1968), 43.

14 The processes of constitutional discussions leading up to the Victoria Charter are recounted in Richard Simeon, *Federal-Provincial Diplomacy* (Toronto: University of Toronto Press, 1972), chap. 5; and Smiley, *Canada in Question*, chap. 3.

15 Smiley, *Canada in Question*, 42–3.

16 Pierre Elliott Trudeau, *Federal-Provincial Grants and the Spending Power of Parliament* (Ottawa: Queen's Printer, 1969), 38–48. The scheme is discussed in Smiley, *Canada in Question*, 86. As Smiley notes, under these schemes the citizens of a non-participating province rather than the government itself would be compensated by Ottawa.

17 This discussion draws upon Simeon, *Federal-Provincial Diplomacy*, 116.

18 Arguably, two of the areas from which a provincial government might have been able to displace federal intervention, with compensation, namely, income supplements to the aged and manpower training, fell within the terms of the Pearson government's 1965 interim arrangements for contracting out. By the same token, youth allowances had been covered under a separate agreement of the Pearson government's that allowed contracting out. As for the federal government's unemployment insurance program, it presumably would have been protected by the proposal's reference to 'new' federal programs. This leaves family allowances as the only program not falling under the Pearson government's contracting-out framework that would have been endangered by Quebec's proposal. This is based on Quebec's offer as reproduced in *Le Devoir*, 19 June 1971.

19 *Working Paper on Social Security for Canadians* (Ottawa: Information Canada, April 1973).

20 Smiley, *Canada in Question*, 77.

21 Simeon, *Federal-Provincial Diplomacy*, 120–1.

22 Claude Ryan, 'Le Dilemme de M. Bourassa', *Le Devoir*, 22 June 1971.

23 'If Quebec Says No to Victoria Charter', Montreal *Gazette*, 19 June 1971.

24 Ryan, 'Le Dilemme de M. Bourassa'.

25 Peter H. Russell, *Constitutional Odyssey*, 2nd edn (Toronto: University of Toronto Press, 1993), 90.

26 Stanley McDowell, 'Governments All Water Down Aims to Create Basis of New Constitution', *Globe and Mail*, 18 June 1971, as quoted in Simeon, *Federal-Provincial Diplomacy*, 121.

27   *Le Devoir*, 25 June 1971, as paraphrased in Simeon, *Federal-Provincial Diplomacy*, 121.
28   Smiley, *Canada in Question*, 78.
29   Ibid.
30   Ibid.
31   In 1973, responding to objections from the Quebec government, Ottawa did agree to allow provincial governments to determine, within limits, the levels of family allowance benefits to be granted to their residents. Only one other province, Alberta, subsequently took advantage of this opportunity. See Donald V. Smiley, *The Federal Condition in Canada* (Toronto: McGraw-Hill Ryerson, 1987), 237; and Garth Stevenson, *Unfulfilled Union*, 3rd edn (Toronto: Gage, 1989), 169.
32   David Milne, *The Canadian Constitution* (Toronto: Lorimer, 1991), 60.
33   Marcel Pepin, 'Si Québec ne collabore pas, Trudeau rapatriera tout seul la constitution', *La Presse*, 6 Mar. 1976. In an editorial, Claude Ryan suggested that Trudeau was driven by 'a hunger for power that is totally incompatible with the spirit of federalism' ('un desir de puissance qui n'a rien de commun avec l'esprit fédéral'). See Claude Ryan, 'Le Rêve vain de M. Trudeau', *Le Devoir*, 8 Mar. 1976.
34   'Le séparatisme est mort, pense Trudeau', *Le Devoir*, 11 May 1976. He based his claim on the fact that the PQ had linked sovereignty to a referendum rather than to the mere election of the party.
35   Assuming that Liberal support in Quebec was higher among anglophones than francophones, Trudeau and the Liberals still would not have received a clear majority vote among francophones.
36   Vincent Lemieux and Jean Crête, 'Quebec', in Howard R. Penniman, ed., *Canada at the Polls, 1979 and 1980* (Washington, DC: American Enterprise Institute for Public Policy Research, 1981), 222.
37   This is demonstrated by data summarized in Kenneth McRoberts, *Quebec: Social Change and Political Crisis*, 3rd edn (Toronto: McClelland & Stewart, 1993), 327.
38   Ibid., 329.
39   My translation of 'de choisir vraiment d'être Canadiens', *Pierre Elliott Trudeau à la Chambre de commerce de Québec, 28 janvier 1977* ([Montreal]: *La Presse*, 1977), 12.
40   My translation of 'Si vous voulez que je me montre souple, je vais le faire tout de suite. Dans la constitution, à mon avis, il y a seulement un préalable.' (ibid., 33).
41   My translation of

>   le respect des droits de l'homme et de la femme, le respect des droits humains, puis probablement le respect de l'aspect collectif de ces droits humains. Je pense à la langue, je pense aux droits des régions d'exister. A partir de ce préalable, on peut faire table rase, écrire une nouvelle constitution. Ça fait cent dix ans qu'on n'en a pas eu de nouvelle: on peut en faire une. Je ne refuse aucun défi! (ibid., 33).

42 My translation of 'des chicanes de politiciens' (ibid., 34).

43 'comment le peuple sera plus heureux, mieux gouverné' (ibid.).

44 My translation of 'Tout ce que je demanderai, tant que je serai là, c'est d'établir fonctionnellement que tel ou tel niveau de pouvoir, par exemple, doit s'exercer au fédéral ou au provincial pour que la collectivité canadienne s'en trouve mieux.'

45 The Task Force on Canadian Unity, *A Future Together: Observations and Recommendations* (Hull: Dept. of Supply and Services, 1979), 141. The Pepin-Robarts Task Force is discussed in David R. Cameron, 'Not Spicer and Not the B&B: Reflections of an Insider on the Workings of the Pepin-Robarts Task Force on Canadian Unity', *International Journal of Canadian Studies* 7–8 (Spring–Fall 1993): 331–45; and David M. Thomas, 'The Second Time Around: Pepin-Robarts Then and Now', paper presented to the Association for Canadian Studies in the United States, Seattle, 18–19 November 1995.

46 See chap. 2, note 21.

47 Task Force on Canadian Unity, *A FutureTogether*, 23.

48 Ibid., 87.

49 Ibid.

50 Ibid., 71.

51 Ibid., 51.

52 Canada, House of Commons, *Debates*, 4th session, 30th Parliament, 25 Jan. 1979, 2552.

53 Thomas, 'The Second Time Around', 40.

54 Cameron, 'Not Spicer and Not the B&B', 342.

55 See the account in Martin Pâquet, 'Le Fleuve et la cité: Représentations de l'immigration et esquisses d'une action de l'État québécois, 1945–1968', Ph.D. dissertation, History Department, l'Université Laval, Oct. 1994.

56 My translation of 'doit contribuer à l'enrichissement socioculturel du Québec compte tenu de sa spécificité française'. See Quebec, Ministère de l'Immigration, *Accord entre le gouvernement du Canada et le gouvernement du Québec portant sur la collaboration en matière d'immigration et sur la sélection des ressortissants étrangers qui souhaitent s'établir au Québec à titre permanent ou temporaire* (Montreal, 1978).

57 'entend se prononcer sur la venue des ressortissants étrangers de manière à sélectionner ceux qui pourront s'intégrer rapidement à la société québécoise' (ibid.).

58 As reported in *Canadian Annual Review, 1978* (Toronto: University of Toronto Press, 1980), 79.

59 These agreements are summarized in Kenneth McRoberts, 'Unilateralism, Bilateralism and Multilateralism: Approaches to Canadian Federalism', in Richard Simeon, ed., *Intergovernmental Relations*, Collected Research Studies of the Royal Commission on the Economic Union and Development Prospects for Canada, vol. 63 (Toronto: University of Toronto Press, 1985), 90.

60 The latter phrase, it might be noted, was very similar to the 'duality clause' of the Meech Lake Accord that Trudeau was to criticize so severely 10 years later. Peter Russell notes that, as with Meech, these statements were placed not in a

preamble to the constitution (which Meech critics found less objectionable), but in the opening substantive section. Russell, *Constitutional Odyssey*, 101. The proposals regarding the Senate and the Supreme Court also anticipate Meech. In his 1989 defence of Meech, Lowell Murray was able to make these points with good effect. 'Lowell Murray répond à Pierre Trudeau', *La Presse*, 5 Apr. 1989.

61 Russell, *Constitutional Odyssey*, 105.

62 Ibid.

63 These questions are discussed in McRoberts, *Quebec: Social Change and Political Crisis*, chap. 9.

64 *Quebec-Canada: A New Deal* (Quebec City: Éditeur officiel, 1979).

65 Le Directeur général des élections du Québec, *Référendum: Oui—Non* (1980), 2.

66 'La souveraineté-association, ce n'est . . . ni du statu quo, ni du séparatisme. C'est une formule réaliste qui permettra des changements véritables sans devoir tout bouleverser ni recommencer à zero. Nous disons . . . qu'au lieu de ce régime . . . dont tout le monde admet que tel quel il est dépassé . . . et sans renier pour autant une longue tradition de coexistence qui a créé tout un réseau d'échanges, nous nous devons d'arriver avec nos voisins et partenaires du reste du Canada à une nouvelle entente d'égal à égal.' Assemblée nationale, *Journal des Débats*, 4th session, 31st Legislature, 4 March 1980, 4964.

67 McRoberts, *Quebec: Social Change and Political Crisis*, 312.

68 Journalist Denise Bombardier said she had heard such statements ('Noir sur blanc', Radio-Canada, 17 May 1980). See also Gérald Bernier, 'Les Aspects économiques du débat: un dialogue de sourds', in En collaboration, *Québec: Un pays incertain* (Montreal: Québec/Amérique, 1980), 123.

69 According to Maurice Pinard, in 1980 eight polls gave an average of 42 per cent in favour of sovereignty-association, 44 per cent against, and 14 per cent undecided. In the same year, nine polls gave an average of 24 per cent in favour of independence, 64 per cent against, and 12 per cent undecided. See Maurice Pinard, 'The Dramatic Reemergence of the Quebec Independence Movement', *Journal of International Affairs* 45, no. 2 (Winter 1992), Tables 1 and 2.

70 A CROP survey taken between 26 April and 8 May found a solid No lead: Yes, 39.6 per cent; No, 45.5 per cent; don't know or no response, 14.9 per cent, as reproduced in André Blais, 'Le vote: ce que l'on en sait . . . ce que l'on n'en sait pas', in En collaboration, *Québec: Un pays incertain*, Table 2. These figures underestimated the No lead. Most surveyors, including CROP, assumed that the non-responding category was in fact disproportionately inclined to vote No.

71 See the account of the three speeches in Laforest, *Trudeau et la fin d'un rêve canadien*, 42–8.

72 'Je n'en connais pas parmi eux qui ne veuillent pas profiter de ce tourbillon actuel pour renouveler la constitution. Monsieur Ryan a proposé un Livre beige. Les gouvernements des autres provinces, de l'Ontario à la Colombie, ont présenté plusieurs projets. Notre gouvernement, après avoir établi le Commission Pepin-Robarts, a proposé une formule qui s'appelait *Le Temps d'agir*, un bill, un projet de loi qui s'appelait le bill C-60 qui contenait, entre paren-

thèses, beaucoup de propositions pour un renouvellement fondamental. Ceux, donc, qui veulent rester Canadiens, sont prêts à le changer, sont prêts à améliorer le fédéralisme.' See 'Trudeau n'acceptera de négocier qu'après le 2e référendum', *La Presse*, 3 May 1980.

73   'met notre sort entre les mains des autres'.

74   'Nous allions à Ottawa parce que c'est comme ça que les Québécois ont toujours vu leur place dans ce pays. Ils l'ont vue comme étant fiers d'être Québécois, se battant ici pour la défense de leurs droits, mais affirmant aussi leurs droits d'être Canadiens en envoyant parmi leurs meilleurs représentants à Ottawa pour affirmer la place des Québécois au sein du Canada.'

75   My translation of 'je sais parce que je leur en ai parlé ce matin à ces députés, je sais que je peux prendre l'engagement le plus solennel qu'à la suite d'un NON, nous allons mettre en place immédiatement le mécanisme de renouvellement de la Constitution et nous n'arrêtons pas avant que ça soit fait . . . nous mettons nôtre tête en jeu, nous, députés québécois, parce que nous le disons aux Québécois de voter NON, et nous vous disons à vous des autres provinces que nous n'accepterons pas ensuite que ce NON soit interprété par vous comme une indication que tout va bien puis que tout peut rester comme c'était auparavant.

Nous voulons du changement, nous mettons nos sièges en jeu pour avoir du changement.' Prime Minister's Office, Transcription de l'allocution du Très Honorable Pierre Elliott Trudeau du centre Paul Sauvé, Montréal, Québec, le 14 mai 1980, 6–7.

76   McRoberts, *Quebec: Social Change and Political Crisis*, 327.

77   Clarkson and McCall write: 'It was an inspired performance, probably the crucial act that secured the soft neo-federalist vote, directing it away from the Oui and towards the Non.' See Stephen Clarkson and Christina McCall, *Trudeau and Our Times* (Toronto: McClelland & Stewart, 1990), 239.

78   One firm, IQOP, conducted surveys just before and after Trudeau's 14 May speech. The result on 11 May was Yes, 37 per cent; No, 40 per cent; don't know or no response, 23 per cent. The 18 May survey actually indicated a slight surge for the PQ option: Yes, 40.4 per cent; No, 36.5 per cent; don't know or no response, 23.1 per cent. See André Blais, 'Le vote: ce que l'on en sait . . . ce que l'on n'en sait pas', in En collaboration, *Québec: Un pays incertain*, Table 2.

79   Claude Forget, who had been closely involved with the Beige Paper, has recently written that when Ryan was chosen party leader, Trudeau invited him to his residence in Ottawa. There Ryan agreed with Trudeau's suggestion that no mention should be made of the document during the referendum campaign. This had the effect of marginalizing both Ryan and the Beige Paper during the campaign and enabling Trudeau to take control of the constitutional question after the referendum had been won. See Claude E. Forget, 'Référendum: les conséquences méconnues d'un vote négatif', *La Presse*, 29 Mar. 1995. Ryan, however, says there had never been any question of promoting the Beige Paper during the referendum campaign; he had said as much in his closing address to the Liberal convention that adopted the document. See Claude Ryan,

'Référendum de 1980: Ryan en désaccord avec Forget', *La Presse*, 31 Mar. 1995.

80 House of Commons, *Debates*, 1st session, 32nd Parliament, 21 May 1980, 1263.

81 Ibid. (emphasis added).

82 The basic components are the same, but they did undergo some modification. In the case of the amending formula, a referendum mechanism was dropped, and Ontario and Quebec lost their automatic vetoes. (Ottawa had in fact allowed for agreement on an alternative scheme within two years. See Milne, *The Canadian Constitution*, 100.) In the case of the Charter, the notwithstanding clause was added, application of mobility rights was qualified, and interpretative clauses dealing with aboriginal peoples, multiculturalism, and gender were added. The final version still does not deal with central institutions, and the division of powers is ignored except for a section, added to the final version, affirming provincial jurisdiction over non-renewable natural resources, forestry resources, and electrical energy. See the discussion in McWhinney, *Canada and the Constitution*, 94–100. The texts of the original resolution and the final version appear in Appendices A and E. It should be noted that some of the modifications had already been inserted in the revised version of Ottawa's initial resolution. See Milne, *The Canadian Constitution*, 109–12.

83 Pierre Elliott Trudeau, 'The Values of a Just Society', in Thomas S. Axworthy and Pierre Elliott Trudeau, eds, *Towards a Just Society* (Markham, Ont: Viking, 1990), 368.

84 Under this scheme patriation must be linked to a substantial revision of the division of powers, any constitutional declaration of principles must contain a recognition of Quebec's distinctiveness, there must be no entrenchment of language rights (at least with respect to Quebec), and the Supreme Court should be reorganized to give Quebec justices equality on a constitutional bench or 'near equality' in the court as a whole. The Quebec government's position was reproduced in a two-page advertisement in *La Presse*, 21 Aug. 1980.

85 Under the Beige Paper all provinces were to receive exclusive jurisdiction over such matters as manpower training, family law, social insurance (including unemployment insurance), and health and social services. (In effect, the change exceeded the Bourassa government's proposals to the Victoria Conference.) The provinces would be given exclusive jurisdiction over offshore resources (although this would be subject to the federal emergency power). They were to be allowed access to any means of taxation and were to be assigned the residual power. As we have seen, the Pepin-Robarts Report had also envisaged a transfer of jurisdictions to the provinces but with the provision whereby provincial governments would not necessarily exercise them, with the result that Quebec could well emerge with a *de facto* special status. Both proposals also abolished the reservation, disallowance, and declaratory powers of the federal government. Both reports called for a new upper chamber, whose members would be chosen exclusively by the provincial governments and that would have such powers as a suspensive veto over federal legislation in concurrent jurisdictions, a permanent veto over bills involving the spending and emergency powers, and the

power to approve appointments to key federal agencies and the Supreme Court. In this upper chamber, Quebec would be entitled to 25 per cent of the voting seats under the Quebec Liberal Party's proposal and 20 per cent under the Task Force's proposal. As for the Supreme Court, Pepin-Robarts would have established a 'near equality' in the number of justices from Quebec and the rest of the country; the Beige Paper would have established a 'constitutional' bench on which half of the justices would be from Quebec. See Task Force, *A Future Together*; and Le Comité constitutionnelle du Parti libéral du Québec, *Une Nouvelle fédération canadienne* (Montreal: le Parti libéral du Quebec, 1980). As McWhinney documents, some Quebec intellectuals did criticize the Beige Paper for not stressing enough the uniqueness of Quebec. See McWhinney, *Canada and the Constitution*, 30–7.

86 *Constitution Act, 1982*, s. 23. This provision clearly contradicted Bill 101's 'Quebec clause', which restricted access to English-language schools to children whose parents had themselves been educated in English in Quebec or who had a sibling who had been educated in English in Quebec. But it even contradicted the Canada clause to the extent that it covers children who have received, or have a sibling who has received, education in English anywhere in Canada— whatever the status of the parent. At the same time, a special provision in the Charter prevents the language-of-education provisions from applying to children of any Canadian whose first language is English until this is authorized by the Quebec government or the National Assembly.

87 *Constitution Act, 1982*, s. 6. This provision is inoperable so long as a province's employment is below the national average.

88 Bernard Descôteaux, 'L'Assemblée adopte la motion Lévesque sans l'appui du PLQ', *Le Devoir*, 22 Nov. 1980. The PQ government had in fact sought a commitment to unanimous support from the Liberal opposition, but the Liberals were divided on the matter. In particular, some anglophone members voted against the measure. Jean-Pierre Proulx, 'Servir deux maîtres', *Le Devoir*, 24 Nov. 1980.

89 'regrettait profondément que des décisions importantes soient prises à Ottawa sans le consentement du Québec'. See Jean-Claude Picard, 'La Tristesse à l'Assemblée nationale', *Le Devoir*, 3 Dec. 1981. The Liberals refused to support a PQ resolution, passed on 1 Dec. 1981, condemning the agreement and invoking Quebec's right to veto it. Ryan attacked the Lévesque government for sacrificing the veto in the first place and called on the government to pursue further negotiations with Ottawa.

90 Ryan said, 'The absence of a person like myself will serve as a reminder that there are still important issues to resolve: this agreement [on the constitution] was arrived at without Quebec's consent,' as quoted in McWhinney, *Canada and the Constitution*, 137.

91 Quebec Veto Reference, 'Re: Objection to a resolution to amend the constitution' [1982], 2 S.C.R., 813.

92 See Andrew Petter, 'Maître chez Who? The Quebec Veto Reference', *Supreme*

Court Law 6 (1984): 387–99; and G.J. Brandt, 'The Quebec Veto Reference: A Constitutional Postscript', *University of Western Ontario Law Review* 21, no. 1 (1983): 163–71. Whereas Petter is highly critical of this use of a more exacting standard in the Quebec case, Brandt defends it; he argues that, confronted by the 'crisis' raised by the patriation case, namely a deadlock between governments, the court was quite correct in inferring acceptance from conduct. The situation required the court to involve itself in 'the creation of convention'. Now that the crisis had passed, it was proper for the court to retreat to a more traditional judicial approach. The latter argument exaggerates the exceptional aspects of the crisis behind the first reference and ignores the profound crisis behind the second.

93 See Donald V. Smiley, 'A Dangerous Deed: The Constitution Act, 1982', in Keith Banting and Richard Simeon, eds, *And No One Cheered* (Toronto: Methuen, 1983), 77; and Andrew Petter, 'Maître chez Who?'

94 Quebec Veto Reference, 'Re: Resolution to amend the constitution' [1981], 1 S.C.R., 893–4.

95 Quebec Veto Reference [1982], 817.

96 McWhinney, *Canada and the Constitution*, 126.

97 As quoted in Petter, 'Maître chez Who?', 390.

98 Russell, *Constitutional Odyssey*, 129.

99 Claude Ryan, *Regards sur le fédéralisme canadien* (Montreal: Boréal, 1995), 194.

100 *Debates of the Senate*, 2nd session, 33rd Parliament, 30 Mar. 1988, 2996.

101 Ryan, *Regards sur le fédéralisme canadien*, 137.

102 The Fulton-Favreau formula and the Victoria Charter had both given Quebec a veto over all forms of constitutional change. The Quebec Liberal Party's *A New Canadian Federation* adopted the Victoria Charter formula. In the federal government's own proposed resolution of October 1980, all amendments would have to be approved by the Quebec National Assembly. In the case of the Pepin-Robarts Report, Quebec representatives on the Council of the Federation would not have a veto over constitutional amendments (only a majority would be necessary), but a proposed amendment would have to be ratified by a major-ity of Quebec electors voting in a Canada-wide referendum.

103 Alternative explanations are assessed in Peter N. Ropke, 'A Tactically Uncontrollable Strategy: The PQ and the Patriation Struggle', unpublished paper, 67–71.

104 Over the years Trudeau has placed great stock in the contention that Lévesque betrayed the other dissident premiers by initially agreeing to a referendum. On this basis, Trudeau can blame Quebec for isolation. See, for instance, Pierre Elliott Trudeau, 'J'accuse Lucien Bouchard!', *La Presse*, 3 Feb. 1996.

105 Clarkson and McCall, *Trudeau and Our Times*, 377.

106 Though not part of the original agreement among Trudeau and the nine pre-miers, this was later added by the federal government.

107 This provision had not been part of the agreement among Trudeau and the nine premiers. It emerged from a subsequent attempt by the federal government to

obtain Quebec's consent. See *Canadian Annual Review, 1981* (Toronto: University of Toronto Press, 1984), 74–6.

108 The qualification to mobility rights had been added to placate Newfoundland Premier Brian Peckford.

109 Milne, *The Canadian Constitution*, 70; and Clarkson and McCall, *Trudeau and Our Times*, 280.

110 In the first quotation, Lyon was quoting from a paper by Carleton University professor G.P. Browne. All these quotations are taken from Milne, *The Canadian Constitution*, 89–91.

111 Ibid., 76.

112 Donald V. Smiley, 'The Case against the Canadian Charter of Human Rights', *Canadian Journal of Political Science* 2, no. 3 (Sept. 1969): 278–91.

113 Donald V. Smiley, *The Canadian Charter of Rights and Freedoms, 1981* (Toronto: Ontario Economic Council, 1981), 14–5.

114 Cynthia Williams, 'The Changing Nature of Citizen Rights', in Alan Cairns and Cynthia Williams, eds, *Constitutionalism, Citizenship and Society in Canada*, Collected Research Studies of the Royal Commission on the Economic Union and Development Prospects for Canada, vol. 33 (Toronto: University of Toronto Press, 1985), 111–23.

115 The list of groups is drawn from Russell, *Constitutional Odyssey*, 114. See also Milne, *The Canadian Constitution*, 107; Williams, 'Changing Nature of Citizen Rights'; and Rainer Knopf and F.L. Morton, 'Nation-Building and the Canadian Charter of Rights and Freedoms', in Cairns and Williams, *Constitutionalism, Citizenship and Society in Canada*, 150–7.

116 Russell, *Constitutional Odyssey*, 113.

117 Ibid., 116.

118 Milne, *The Canadian Constitution*, 95.

119 See the discussion of the proposals of the Ontario Advisory Committee on Confederation and the BC government in McWhinney, *Quebec and the Constitution*, chap. 7.

120 Ibid., 90.

121 Quoted in Clarkson and McCall, *Trudeau and Our Times*, 280–1.

122 Ibid., 249–53.

123 'Des provinces ont prié Ottawa de leur imposer le respect du français', *Le Devoir*, 23 Oct. 1980.

124 Milne recounts how in the final negotiations Trudeau 'lashed out' at the proposal by the eight dissident premiers that minority-language educational rights be subject to a provincial opting-in clause, accusing them of being 'duped' by the PQ. See Milne, *The Canadian Constitution*, 165. As for the notwithstanding clause, language rights are one of the few provisions to which it does not apply.

125 Canada, House of Commons, *Debates*, 1st session, 32nd Parliament, 15 April 1980, 32–3.

126 Pierre Elliott Trudeau, *Federalism and the French Canadians* (Toronto: Macmillan, 1968), 165.

127 Ibid., 191.

128 Ibid., 151–81.

129 Sheppard and Valpy recount: 'The referendum win, where Ottawa believed it had stepped in and rescued the situation from the foundering provincial Liberals, produced an enormous sense of self-confidence in the Trudeau government at the outset of its mandate. . . . They were almost drunk with a new sense of power and accomplishment.' See Robert Sheppard and Michael Valpy, *The National Deal* (Toronto: Fleet Books, 1982), 40.

130 The nationalism of the last Trudeau administration is analysed in David Milne, *Tug of War* (Toronto: Lorimer, 1986), 200–18.

131 Ian Mulgrew, 'Provinces Using Federal Money but Ottawa is Not Credited: PM', *Globe and Mail*, 25 Nov. 1981.

132 This discussion draws on McRoberts, 'Unilateralism, Bilateralism and Multilateralism', 98–9.

133 Ibid., 104–5.

134 Ibid., 102–3.

135 As quoted in Stanbury, Gorn, and Weinberg, 'Federal Advertising Expenditures', 135.

136 Ibid., 145.

137 Trudeau, *Federalism and the French Canadians*, 202.

138 Laforest, *Trudeau et la fin d'un rêve canadien*, 44–8.

139 'Si la réponse à la question référendaire est Non, nous avons tous dit que ce Non sera interprété comme un mandat pour changer la Constitution, pour renouveler le fédéralisme.' Transcription de l'allocution du Très Honorable Pierre Elliott Trudeau, le 14 mai 1980, 6.

140 'L'accord constitutionnel de 1982 n'a pas été un marché de dupes pour le Québec', *La Presse*, 10 March 1989.

Chapter 7

1   Clarkson and McCall say of the Charter that its 'bitter core—the minority-language education rights that were to be imposed on Quebec for anglophones and on the other provinces where numbers warranted for francophones—was to be coated with layer upon layer of sweetener. . . . With all these favourable aspects of the package diverting attention, the "constitutionalization" of the official languages law and the entrenchment of minority-language education rights would be camouflaged.' See Stephen Clarkson and Christina McCall, *Trudeau and Our Times*, vol. 1 (Toronto: McClelland & Stewart, 1990), 292 and 293.

2   Dominique Clift, *Le Déclin du nationalisme au Québec* (Montreal: Libre expression, 1981).

3   This was contained in his 6 August speech at Sept-Îsles, which in fact was written by Lucien Bouchard.

4   See, for instance, Jean-Louis Roy, 'Le PC, Parti québécois', *Le Devoir*, 6 September 1984, and Solange Chaput-Rolland, 'Après le déluge: Brian Mulroney', *Le Devoir*, 7 Sept. 1984.

5   Donald M. Taylor and Lise Dubé-Simard, 'Language Planning and Intergroup Relations: Anglophone and Francophone Attitudes toward the Charter of the French Language', in Richard J. Bourhis, ed., *Conflict and Language Planning in Quebec* (Clevedon, UK: Multilingual Matters, 1984), 148–73; and Stéphane Dion, 'Explaining Quebec Nationalism', in R. Kent Weaver, ed., *The Collapse of Canada?* (Washington, DC: Brookings Institution, 1992), 93.

6   In a 1977 survey Quebec respondents were asked: 'If French-speaking Canadians were treated as equals to English-speaking Canadians outside Quebec would this affect your attitude towards independence for Quebec?' Only 17 per cent said yes; 81 per cent said no. Affirmative responses were apparently somewhat more frequent among francophones (as opposed to anglophones) while remaining a small minority. See 'What Quebec *Really* Wants: English Consider Us Inferior, Quebec Feels', *Toronto Star*, 17 May 1977.

7   A recent statement of the point is in André Burelle, *Le Mal canadien* (Montreal: Fides, 1995), 44.

8   'Meech Lake Accord Gains General Support, Polls Show', *Toronto Star*, 1 June 1987.

9   After a careful examination of data on public attitudes, four researchers conclude: 'Our findings, though not conclusive, are suggestive. Very briefly, with respect to ideas about basic rights and freedoms, the attitudes of French Canadians and English Canadians are virtually indistinguishable. This is the more impressive considering the social and economic differences between anglophones and francophones—for example, in years of formal schooling—that might misleadingly give the impression their cultures differ.' See Paul M. Sniderman, Joseph F. Fletcher, Peter H. Russell, and Philip E. Tetlock, 'Liberty, Authority and Community: Civil Liberties and the Canadian Political Culture', paper presented at the annual meeting of the Canadian Political Science Association, Windsor, 1988, 31.

10   Joseph Fletcher, 'What Do Canadians Think about Civil Liberties? The Politics of the Canadian Charter'. Paper presented to the Association for Canadian Studies in Australia and New Zealand, Canberra, 23 June 1988. The study even finds that 52.4 per cent of PQ members of the National Assembly agreed that the Charter would strengthen Canadian national identity (p. 19)—presumably, they agreed that this was the *intent* of the Charter.

11   When it comes to supporting the collective rights of other groups, French Canadians seem to be no more disposed to collective rights than are English Canadians. On questions of native rights, for example, English-Canadian and French-Canadian attitudes are quite similar. See Paul M. Sniderman, Joseph F. Fletcher, Peter H. Russell, and Philip E. Tetlock, 'Reply: Strategic Calculation and Political Values—The Dynamics of Language Rights', *Canadian Journal of Political Science* 23, no. 3 (Sept. 1990): 541.

Relying upon data collected in 1981, Richard Johnston and André Blais found that, compared with other Canadians, Quebec francophones were more supportive of political and legal rights and of equality rights. Conversely, they were less sympathetic to the claims of Quebec anglophones as well as the position of immigrants. See Richard Johnston and André Blais, 'Meech Lake and Mass Politics: The "Distinct Society" Clause', *Canadian Public Policy* 14, supplement (Sept. 1988), S29–S33.

12 André Burelle, *Le Mal canadien* (Montreal: Fides, 1995), 65–78.

13 In the fall of 1980 the Quebec Liberal caucus was reportedly anxious that the Charter should undermine Bill 101 and thus be revenge for the Péquiste attacks on members of the caucus during the referendum campaign. See Clarkson and McCall, *Trudeau and Our Times*, 291, and David Milne, *The Canadian Constitution* (Toronto: Lorimer, 1991), 99.

14 See the discussion in Michael Mandel, *The Charter of Rights and the Legalization of Politics in Canada*, rev. edn (Toronto: Thompson, 1994), 143–5. Reciprocal agreements are covered in section 86 of the Quebec *Charter of the French Language*, Quebec City: Éditeur officiel, 1977. To be sure, section 23 of the Charter goes beyond the 'Canada clause' represented by the reciprocal agreement offer. That section covers not just children of anglophone parents but all children who were educated, or whose siblings were educated, in English anywhere in Canada. This latter provision did provoke opposition among Quebec cabinet members during discussions leading up to Quebec's 1985 constitutional proposals. See Gilles Lesage, 'Johnson: *L'actuelle* clause Canada demeure inacceptable', *Le Devoir*, 2 May 1985, and Lise Bissonnette, 'La Confusion des clauses', *Le Devoir*, 3 May 1985.

15 Gilles Lesage, 'Québec souscrit à la "clause Canada" en échange de la primauté de sa Charte', *Le Devoir*, 18 May 1985.

16 Patrick Monahan develops a separate explanation of the difference in reactions: in the case of the minority-language education provisions there was no action to be taken in Quebec, and the court's action was beyond remedy; in the case of the sign law the notwithstanding clause offered a remedy, and there was mobilization of public pressure upon the Bourassa government to use it. See Patrick J. Monahan, *Meech Lake: The Inside Story* (Toronto: University of Toronto Press, 1991), 168.

17 Guy Laforest, *Trudeau et la fin d'un rêve canadien* (Sillery, Quebec: Septentrion, 1992), 175–80.

18 See the analysis of the statements of Ryan and other Liberals in ibid., 194–5.

19 Gérard Bergeron, 'Quebec in Isolation', in Keith Banting and Richard Simeon, eds, *And No One Cheered* (Toronto: Methuen, 1983), 61.

20 Guy Trudel, 'Trois sondages sur le Québec d'après-novembre', *Le Devoir*, 20 Jan. 1982.

21 Robert Sheppard, 'Both Governments Losing Favour in Quebec', *Globe and Mail*, 5 May 1981; and Jacques Bouchard and Pierre Vennat, 'Lévesque n'a pas la majorité pour réaliser son projet de souveraineté-association', *La Presse*, 30 Mar. 1982.

22 Sheppard, 'Both Governments Losing Favour'.

23 '75 p. cent des Canadiens appuient la nouvelle Constitution', *La Presse*, 19 June

1982. Trudeau cites it, among other places, in Pierre Elliott Trudeau, 'J'accuse Lucien Bouchard!', *La Presse*, 3 Feb. 1996.

24   Pierre Fournier, *Autopsie du lac Meech* (Montreal: VLB, 1990), 21.

25   'Lévesque n'a pas la majorité'. The 1981 figures were 27 per cent agree and 54 per cent disagree. In his many interventions, Trudeau has never referred to those findings. See also Max Nemni, 'Le "Dés"accord du Lac Meech et la construction de l'imaginaire symbolique des Québécois', in Louis Balthazar, Guy Laforest, and Vincent Lemieux, eds, *Le Québec et la restructuration du Canada, 1980–1992* (Sillery, Quebec: Septentrion, 1991), 182.

26   See Larry Pratt and John Richards, *Prairie Capitalism: Power and Influence in the New West* (Toronto: McClelland & Stewart, 1979).

27   F.L. Morton, 'The Effect of the Charter of Rights on Canadian Federalism', *Publius* 25, no. 3 (Summer 1995), 183.

28   Alan C. Cairns, 'Reflections on the Political Purposes of the Charter: The First Decade', in Douglas E. Williams, ed., *Reconfigurations* (Toronto: McClelland & Stewart, 1995), 194–214.

29   Morton, 'The Effect of the Charter of Rights'.

Chapter 8

1   Patrick J. Monahan, *Meech Lake: The Inside Story* (Toronto: University of Toronto Press, 1991), 47.

2   As quoted in Robert Sheppard and Michael Valpy, *The National Deal* (Toronto: Fleet Books, 1982), 317–18.

3   Monahan, *Meech Lake*, 46.

4   My translation of 'Nous, notre principe, c'est que nous sommes fédéralistes.' 'Pas une adhésion à la Constitution', *Le Devoir*, 7 Mar. 1986. The price paid by the government for this decision was the resignation of its special constitutional adviser, Léon Dion, who considered it a strategic error to make this gesture independently of any agreement on a revised constitution. See Gilles Lesage, 'Opposé à l'adhésion à la charte canadienne, Léon Dion quitte le gouvernement Bourassa', *Le Devoir*, 17 Mar. 1986.

5   From the text of Rémillard's address as reproduced in Peter M. Leslie, *Rebuilding the Relationship: Quebec and Its Confederation Partners* (Kingston: Institute of Intergovernmental Relations, Queen's University, 1987), 47.

6   Ibid., 37. At the same time, Leslie acknowledges that the conference tended to draw people who were sympathetic to the underlying premise that Quebec's constitutional status needed to be resolved. See ibid., 9.

7   Indeed, the reaction to the proposals among those attending the conference was uniformly positive. See ibid., 57.

8   Monahan, *Meech Lake*, 61.

9   Ibid., 45.

10   These processes are detailed in ibid., chaps. 4 and 5.

11   *Constitutional Amendment, 1987*, s. 2(1b) and s. 2(3) as reproduced in P.W. Hogg, *Meech Lake*, Appendix IV.

12 Ibid., s. 2(1a) and 2(2).

13 Ibid., s. 2(4).

14 Peter W. Hogg, *Meech Lake Constitutional Accord Annotated* (Toronto: Carswell, 1988), 12. This judgement may be excessively narrow; see Jeremy Webber, *Reimagining Canada* (Montreal and Kingston: McGill-Queen's University Press, 1994), 128.

15 *Constitutional Amendment, 1987*, s. 95, and *1987 Constitutional Accord*, s. 2 (as reproduced in Hogg, *Meech Lake*, Appendix II). Quebec would have been allowed to exceed by 5 per cent its proportionate share of immigrants. Agreements with a number of other provinces would also have been constitutionalized.

16 *Constitutional Amendment, 1987*, s. 106A.

17 Ibid., s. 101.

18 Ibid., s. 25.

19 'At the outset, what is required in principle is a statement in the preamble of the Constitution which might be worded along the following lines: "Recognizing the distinctive character of Quebec society as the principal though not exclusive centre of Canadian francophones, and accepting as fundamental the duality of the Canadian federation . . ."' See Royal Commission on the Economic Union and Development Prospects for Canada, *Report*, vol. III (Ottawa: Supply and Services, Canada, 1985), 333.

20 Acknowledging that the preamble he had submitted to the premiers 'can be improved', Trudeau declared, 'All I ask is that any changes in its wording reflect even more accurately the existence of two principal linguistic *and cultural* communities in Canada, *with the French community having its focus and centre of gravity in Quebec,* but at the same time extending across the country' [emphasis added]. See Prime Minister's Office, 'An Open Letter to the People of Quebec', Translation, 11 July 1980, 2. This does not square with Trudeau's claim to the Senate that 'We did not use the expression "French-speaking Canadians" and "English-speaking Canadians" in any of our constitutions.' See Trudeau, 'Who Speaks for Canada? Defining and Sustaining a National Vision', in Michael D. Behiels, ed., *The Meech Lake Primer* (Ottawa: University of Ottawa Press, 1989), 84. At a minimum, he had expressed an openness to terminology that went considerably further than the phrases he found so objectionable in Meech.

21 Chap. 6, 154.

22 The use of the federal spending power would have required approval by a two-thirds majority of the new provincially appointed upper chamber under both Pepin-Robarts and under the Beige Paper. To be sure, as Trudeau pointed out in his Senate presentation on Meech, the 1969 federal proposal provided for direct distribution of funds to *citizens* rather than the governments of opting-out provinces. See Pierre Elliott Trudeau, 'Who Speaks for Canada?', 77.

23 In his Senate presentation, Trudeau insisted the Victoria procedure, by which disputes would be submitted to an electoral college, was different. See Trudeau, 'Who Speaks for Canada?', 78.

24   'Voice of the People', *Maclean's*, 15 June 1987.

25   Chaput-Rolland said, '[The agreement] largely exceeds our hopes.' See 'Il n'y a pas de monstre au lac Meech', *Le Devoir*, 8 May 1987. Claude Ryan issued a spirited defence of the agreement in response to Pierre Trudeau's attack. See Bernard Descôteaux, 'L'accord du lac Meech permettra au Québec de faire des gains importants et incontestables', *Le Devoir*, 30 May 1987.

26   Robert Lévesque, 'Lévesque fait bande à part', *Le Devoir*, 4 May 1987.

27   Milne, *The Canadian Constitution*, 214.

28   'L'accord du lac Meech confirmera le statut du Québec dans les relations internationales', *Le Devoir*, 10 June 1987. Rémillard did not argue that the distinct-society clause, *per se*, gave new powers to Quebec. Rather he contended that with the distinct-society clause the courts might be more sympathetic to Quebec's arguments about the international role that derived from Quebec's jurisdiction over education and culture.

29   Jacques-Yvan Morin, 'Nous sommes devant un nouveau piège', *Le Devoir*, 20 May 1987.

30   Pierre O'Neill, 'Parizeau incite Bourassa à ne pas signer l'accord du lac Meech', *Le Devoir*, 15 May 1987.

31   Pierre O'Neill, 'Le lac Meach [*sic*] a rallié les péquistes de toutes tendances', *Le Devoir*, 4 May 1987. Indeed, Max Nemni argues that the Accord was opposed by the majority of constitutional experts, groups, and associations that presented briefs to the Bourassa government between April and June 1987. See Max Nemni, 'Le "Dés"accord du Lac Meech et. . . ', in Louis Balthazar et al., eds, *Le Québec et la restructuration du Canada, 1980–1992* (Sillery, Quebec: Septentrion, 1991), 188–9. Yet, in a book which is highly critical of Meech and sympathetic to the sovereigntist cause, Pierre Fournier ruefully acknowledges that during the early days of Meech these criticisms had little popular impact and that nationalist critics were 'crying in the desert'. See Pierre Fournier, *A Meech Lake Post-Mortem* (Montreal and Kingston: McGill-Queen's University Press, 1991), 34.

32   The June 1987 survey is reported in 'Voice of the People', *Maclean's*, 15 June 1987, 13. The proportions disapproving of Meech in that survey were: Atlantic Canada, 18 per cent; Ontario, 33 per cent; west, 32 per cent. All the other survey results are from André Blais and Jean Crête, 'Pourquoi l'opinion publique au Canada anglais a-t-elle rejeté l'Accord du Lac Meech?' in Raymond Hudon and Réjean Pelletier, eds, *L'Engagement intellectuel: Mélanges en l'honneur de Léon Dion* (Sainte-Foy: Presses de l'Université Laval, 1991), 386.

33   Blais and Crête, 'Pourquoi l'opinion publique'.

34   Monahan, *Meech Lake*, 32–6. See also Richard Simeon, 'Why Did the Meech Lake Accord Fail?' in Ronald L. Watts and Douglas M. Brown, eds, *Canada: The State of the Federation 1990* (Kingston: Institute of Intergovernmental Relations, Queen's University, 1990), 30.

35   Alan C. Cairns, *Charter versus Federalism* (Montreal and Kingston: McGill-Queen's University Press, 1992), 62–95.

36   Alan C. Cairns, 'Citizens (Outsiders) and Governments (Insiders) in

Constitution-Making: The Case of Meech Lake', *Canadian Public Policy*, 14, supplement (Sept. 1988): S135.

37　Deborah Coyne, 'The Meech Lake Accord and the Spending Power Proposals: Fundamentally Flawed', in M. Behiels, ed., *Meech Lake Primer*, 245–71.

38　Deborah Coyne, 'Beyond the Meech Lake Accord', in David Schneiderman, ed., *Language and the State: The Law and Politics of Identity* (Cowansville, Que.: Yvon Blais, 1991), 445 and 449.

39　Serge Denis, *Le Long Malentendu: le Québec vu par les intellectuels progressistes au Canada anglais, 1970–1991* (Montreal: Boréal, 1992), chap. 6; and Philip Resnick, *Letter to a Québécois Friend* (Montreal and Kingston: McGill-Queen's University Press, 1990).

40　'Voice of the People', *Maclean's*, 15 June 1987, 12.

41　Blais and Crête, 'Pourquoi l'opinion publique', 389.

42　'If somebody says it [Wells's position on the distinct-society clause] resembles Mr Trudeau's thinking, believe me, I take it as a great compliment.' (Clyde Wells quoted in Glen Allen, 'Grit Stands Fast', *Maclean's*, 20 Nov. 1989, 25).

43　As quoted in Jeffrey Simpson, *Fault Lines: Struggling for a Canadian Vision* (Toronto: HarperCollins, 1993), 165.

44　Allan Cairns, 'Political Science, Ethnicity, and the Canadian Constitution', in David Shugarman and Reg Whitaker, eds, *Federalism and Political Community: Essays in Honour of Donald Smiley* (Peterborough, Ont.: Broadview, 1989), 124.

45　Kathleen Mahoney, 'Women's Rights', in Roger Gibbins, ed., *Meech Lake and Canada: Perspectives from the West* (Edmonton: Academic, 1988), 159.

46　See the discussion in Barbara Roberts, 'Smooth Sailing or Storm Warning? Canadian and Québec Women's Groups and the Meech Lake Accord', *Feminist Perspectives féministes*, no. 12a, CRIAW, n.d., 12ff.

47　Special Joint Committee of the Senate and the House of Commons on the 1987 Constitutional Accord, *Minutes of Proceedings and Evidence*, 2nd session, 33rd Parliament, 31 Aug. 1987, issue 15, 82.

48　Ibid., 4 Aug. 1987, issue 4, 43.

49　Guy Laforest analyses at length Trudeau's part in turning English-Canadian opinion against Meech, both through his speeches and his influence on various opinion leaders. See Laforest, *Trudeau et la fin d'un rêve canadien*, chap. 5. See also David M. Thomas, 'Edmund Burke's Ghost, an Abeyance Exhumed, and Pierre Trudeau's Undertaking', paper presented to the Canadian Political Science Association, June 1995.

50　Pierre Elliott Trudeau, '"Say Goodbye to the Dream" of One Canada', *Toronto Star*, 27 May 1987.

51　Pierre Fournier, *Autopsie du lac Meech* (Montreal: VLB, 1990), 90.

52　Monahan, *Meech Lake*, 125.

53　Trudeau, 'Who Speaks for Canada?', 84.

54　Ibid., 94.

55　Ibid., 96.

56　Blais and Crête, 'Pourquoi l'opinion publique', Tables 1 and 4.

57 Jean-H. Guay, Richard Nadeau, and Édouard Cloutier, 'La Crise linguistique au Québec: une étude du mouvement de l'opinion publique engendré par le jugement de la Cour suprême sur l'affichage commercial', paper presented at the annual meeting of the Canadian Political Science Association, May 1990. In their survey of university students, the authors found support for a proposal on commercial signs that was framed explicitly in terms of collective rights: 'Dans le domaine de la langue d'affichage, les droits collectifs de la majorité francophone doivent avoir la priorité sur les droits individuels.' ('With regard to the language of signs, the collective rights of the francophone majority should have priority over individual rights.') Before the Supreme Court judgement on the issue, 46 per cent of the sample supported this proposition; afterwards, 57 per cent did (ibid., 17).

58 For instance, a survey in January 1989 found that 69 per cent of francophone respondents agreed that 'le gouvernement du Québec a raison de restreindre le droit d'afficher en anglais ou dans une autre langue pour assurer la protection du français.' ('The Quebec government is justified in restricting the right to post signs in English or another language in order to protect French.') Twenty-six per cent disagreed. Among non-francophones the percentages were 15 per cent and 81 per cent, respectively. See Louis Falardeau, 'Francophones et anglophones sont insatisfaits de la loi 178', *La Presse*, 21 Jan. 1989.

59 Blais and Crête, 'Pourquoi l'opinion publique', 394.

60 Richard Nadeau, 'Le Virage souverainiste des Québécois, 1980–1990,' *Recherches sociographiques*, 23, no. 1 (Jan.–Apr. 1992): 24.

61 See Simpson, *Fault Lines*, 173.

62 Results of an Environics survey cited in Simpson, *Fault Lines*, 171.

63 'Portrait des Québécois', *L'Actualité*, Jan. 1991, 13–16. Maurice Pinard, in his list of surveys using the terms 'independence' or 'sovereignty', reports 56 per cent for November–December, 1990. See Pinard, 'The Dramatic Reemergence', 480. To be sure, he and others report a decline in support for sovereignty at the beginning of 1991.

64 Citizens' Forum on Canada's Future, *Report to the People and Government of Canada* (Ottawa: Supply and Services Canada, 1991), 126 and 129.

65 'Le Québec est aujourd'hui et pour toujours une société distincte, libre d'assumer son destin et son développement.' As quoted in Rapport du Comité constitutionnel du Parti libéral du Québec, *Un Québec libre de ses choix*, 28 Jan. 1991.

66 Ibid., 47–9. The provision concerning appeals from Quebec courts reads: 'Les décisions des tribunaux supérieurs du Québec ne feront plus l'objet d'appels auprès de la Cour Suprême du Canada mais plutôt auprès d'une nouvelle instance ultime complètement québécoise' (49). ('Decisions of Quebec superior courts will no longer be subject to appeal to the Canadian Supreme Court but rather to a new body of final appeal that will be totally Québécois.') There is no suggestion that this elimination of appeals would be restricted to cases involving Quebec law, as opposed to federal law.

67 Comité constitutionnel, *Un Québec libre de ses choix*, 57.

68 An amendment specified that the Charter of Rights and Freedoms would continue to apply in Quebec. See Pierre O'Neill, 'Bourassa choisit d'abord le Canada', *Le Devoir*, 11 Mar. 1991.

69 Ibid.

70 *Rapport de la Commission sur l'avenir politique et constitutionnel du Québec*, Mar. 1991.

71 See the analysis in François Rocher, 'Le Dossier constitutionnel: l'année des consultations et des valse-hesitations', in Denis Monière, ed., *L'Année politique au Québec, 1991* (Montreal: Québec/Amérique, 1992), 91.

72 Jean-François Lisée tries to show that at the height of the crisis Bourassa hid his intentions from nationalists so as to buy time. See Lisée, *Le Tricheur* (Montreal: Boréal, 1994).

73 My translation. See Michel Venne, 'Robert Bourassa flaire un "féderalisme dominateur"', *Le Devoir*, 4 Mar. 1992.

74 Apparently Mulroney was counting on the talks to fail; that would allow him to draw up unilaterally a package of revisions in close collaboration with Bourassa. Just before the final agreement was reached, he had in fact instructed his Constitutional Affairs Minister Joe Clark to terminate the proceedings. See Jean-François Lisée, *Le Naufrageur* (Montreal: Boréal, 1994), 249.

75 Various participants in the multilateral talks did speak to Quebec officials to determine the acceptability of various proposals, but the process was very haphazard and it produced confused, even contradictory, interpretations of Quebec's position, especially as it bore upon the idea of a triple-E Senate.

76 The following discussion of the 7 July agreement and the Charlottetown Accord draws upon my 'Disagreeing on Fundamentals: English Canada and Quebec', in Kenneth McRoberts and Patrick J. Monahan, eds, *The Charlottetown Accord, the Referendum, and the Future of Canada* (Toronto: University of Toronto Press, 1993), 249–63.

77 Jim Horsman, as quoted in Lisée, *Le Naufrageur*, 219 (my translation from Lisée's French rendition of Horsman's words).

78 Canada, *Status Report: The Multilateral Meetings on the Constitution* (Final Version, 16 July 1992), s. 28.

79 Ibid., s. 29.

80 Ibid., s. 12.

81 'une vision qui est celle du Canada anglophone, fondée sur l'égalité des provinces; un contrôle accru des petites provinces sur le pouvoir central et, malgré les apparences, un raffermissement du pouvoir central. . . . À mon avis, on a régressé.' As quoted in Lisée, *Le Naufrageur*, 263.

82 Ibid., 263–4.

83 Ibid., 247.

84 See the account in ibid., 342–55.

85 Peter H. Russell, *Constitutional Odyssey*, 2nd edn (Toronto: University of Toronto Press, 1993), 217.

86   Canada, *Draft Legal Text, October 9, 1992* (best-efforts text based on the Charlottetown Accord), 3–13.

87   The proposal specified that in all provincial jurisdictions (1) Ottawa could use its spending power only upon agreement with provincial governments; (2) existing arrangements for the use of this power could be renegotiated should a province wish; and (3) in the absence of an agreement, all provinces would be entitled to federal withdrawal with compensation if they undertook to introduce a measure compatible with national objectives defined at a first ministers' conference. This is based upon a text reproduced in Lisée, *Le Naufrageur*, 363.

88   The discussions of the division of powers are related in Lisée, *Le Naufrageur*, 369–82.

89   *Draft Legal Text*, 16 and 47.

90   See Jacques Frémont's analysis of how the Charlottetown Accord falls short of Quebec's minimal demands regarding the division of powers, in Jacques Frémont, 'The Charlottetown Accord and the End of the Exclusiveness of Provincial Jurisdictions', in Kenneth McRoberts and Patrick J. Monahan, eds, *The Charlottetown Accord, the Referendum, and the Future of Canada*, 93–101.

91   *Draft Legal Text*, s. 2(1c).

92   Ibid., s. 2(3). In their comparison of the 7 July and Charlottetown texts, Brown and Young point out that, unlike the 7 July text, Charlottetown does not link 'distinct society' specifically to the Charter; it appears only in the Canada clause and thus applies to the Accord as a whole. See Robert Young and Douglas Brown, 'Overview', in Douglas Brown and Robert Young, eds, *Canada: The State of the Federation 1992* (Kingston: Institute of Intergovernmental Relations, Queen's University, 1992), 16. However, any gain this might represent for Quebec is very much circumscribed by the more restrictive terms of the clause itself.

93   Ibid., s. 2(1d).

94   Lisée, *Le Naufrageur*, 394.

95   Russell, *Constitutional Odyssey*, 217.

96   Susan Delacourt, *United We Fall* (Toronto: Penguin, 1994), 174; and Lisée, *Le Naufrageur*, 319.

97   Atlantic Provinces Economic Council, Renewal of Canada: Division of Powers, *Conference Report*, Halifax, 17–19 Jan. 1992, 12.

98   Ibid., 10.

99   Compare ibid., 16, 21, and 22. See also David Milne, 'Innovative Constitutional Processes', in Douglas Brown and Robert Young, eds, *Canada: The State of the Federation 1992* (Kingston: Institute of Intergovernmental Relations, 1992), 45 and n. 21.

100 Ibid., 16.

101 Tom Kent, 'Recasting Federalism', *Policy Options* 12, no. 3 (April 1992): 3–6. See also Reg Whitaker, 'The Dog That Never Barked: Who Killed Asymmetrical Federalism?' in McRoberts and Monahan, *The Charlottetown Accord*, chap. 8.

102 See, for instance, Gordon Laxer, 'Distinct Status for Québec: A Benefit to English Canada', *Constitutional Forum constitutionnel* 3, no. 3 (Winter 1992), 60.

103 'En raison de son caractère distinct, le Québec peut difficilement accepter une réforme du Sénat où sa représentation serait sensiblement amoindrie. Seule l'obtention d'un statut particulier—réformant au gré du Québec le partage des pouvoirs—pourrait hypothétiquement justifier une diminution sensible de sa représentation au Sénat.' See Jean François-Lisée, 'Dossiers secrets de Bourassa', *L'Actualité*, 1 Nov. 1992, 64.

104 Delacourt, *United We Fall*, 133–6, 402–3; and Lisée, *Le Naufrageur*, 216–25.

105 André Blais, 'The Quebec Referendum: Quebeckers Say No', in McRoberts and Monahan, *The Charlottetown Accord*, 203.

106 This is demonstrated by Lawrence LeDuc and Jon H. Pammet, 'Attitudes and Behaviour in the 1992 Constitutional Referendum', *Canadian Journal of Political Science* 28, no. 1 (Mar. 1995): 31. See also Alain Noël, 'Deliberating a Constitution: The Meaning of the Canadian Referendum of 1992', in Curtis Cook, ed., *Constitutional Predicament* (Montreal and Kingston: McGill-Queen's University Press, 1994), 64–81; and Peter H. Russell, *Constitutional Odyssey*, 2nd edn (Toronto: University of Toronto Press, 1993), 226.

107 Michel Venne, 'Il fallait pas accepter ça', *Le Devoir*, 1 Oct. 1992 (my translation).

108 Richard Johnston and André Blais, as cited by Lisée, *Le Naufrageur*, 593.

109 André Blais, 'The Quebec Referendum: Quebeckers Say No', 203.

110 In fact, even some experts were not impressed. Professor David Elton, of the University of Lethbridge, one of the originators of the concept of the triple-E Senate, campaigned against the Accord. His critical evaluation is contained in 'The Charlottetown Accord Senate: Effective or Emasculated?' in McRoberts and Monahan, *Charlottetown Accord*, chap. 2. This assessment was shared by Professor Roger Gibbins, of the University of Calgary, who declared the Accord to be nothing less than a 'humiliation'. In Gibbins's words, 'it is bitterly ironic that the new agreement on Senate reform will strengthen central Canadian dominance, and more specifically Quebec's dominance, of the national political process.' See Roger Gibbins, 'Something Not So Funny Happened on the Way to Senate Reform', *Canada Watch* 1, no. 2 (Sept. 1992): 22.

111 Richard Johnston, André Blais, Elisabeth Gidengil, and Neil Nevitte, 'The People and the Charlottetown Accord', in Ronald L. Watts and Douglas M. Brown, eds, *Canada: The State of the Federation 1993* (Kingston: Institute of Intergovernmental Relations, Queen's University, 1993), 27.

112 LeDuc and Pammet, 'Attitudes and Behaviour in the 1992 Constitutional Referendum', 27; and Russell, *Constitutional Odyssey*, 2nd edn, 226. Whereas LeDuc and Pammet find that opposition to the measure was not a 'significant' factor in western Canada, the data cited by Russell suggest otherwise.

113 The results of an Angus Reid poll cited in Canada West Foundation, *Canada 2000: Towards a New Canada*, Jan. 1993, 4.

114 According to LeDuc and Pammet, the distinct-society clause was the element

of the agreement that had the greatest impact on voting. See LeDuc and Pammet, 'Attitudes and Behaviour in the 1992 Constitutional Referendum', 27.

115 Pierre Elliott Trudeau, 'A Mess That Deserves a Big No' (Toronto: Robert Davies, 1992), 33.

116 Johnston et al., 'The People and the Charlottetown Accord,' 30. Allan Gregg recorded a similar reaction according to Lisée, *Le Naufrageur*, 589. On the other hand, LeDuc and Pammet argue that Trudeau had no net effect on the vote. See LeDuc and Pammet, 'Attitudes and Behaviour in the 1992 Constitutional Referendum', 23.

117 Alain Noël, 'The Bloc Québécois as Official Opposition,' in Douglas M. Brown and Janet Hiebert, eds, *Canada: The State of the Federation 1994* (Kingston: Institute of Intergovernmental Relations, Queen's University, 1994), 22.

118 Noël argues that the Bloc vote was based largely upon identification with Quebec, as opposed to economic protest: 'Most Quebeckers voted quite naturally for the party that best represented their vision of themselves and the country' (ibid., 23–4). Similarly, Blais and his colleagues conclude that the Bloc's success was due to the support of sovereigntists and of non-sovereigntists who were motivated primarily by identification with Quebec. See André Blais et al., 'L'Élection fédérale de 1993: le comportement électoral des québécois', *Revue québécoise de science politique*, no. 27 (Spring 1995): 46.

119 Thérèse Arseneau, 'The Reform Party of Canada: Past, Present and Future', in Brown and Hiebert, eds, *Canada: The State of the Federation 1994*, 37–57.

Chapter 9

1   See the data on support both for 'sovereignty' and for 'independence' in Maurice Pinard, 'The Secessionist Option and Quebec Public Opinion, 1988–1993', *Canada: Opinion* 2, no. 3 (June 1994): 2.

2   André Blais and Richard Nadeau, 'To Be or Not to Be Sovereigntist: Quebeckers' Perennial Dilemma', *Canadian Public Policy* 18, no. 1 (1991): 89–103.

3   André Blais, Pierre Martin, and Richard Nadeau, 'Attentes économiques et linguistiques et appui à la souveraineté du Québec: une analyse prospective et comparative', *Canadian Journal of Political Science* 28, no. 4 (Dec. 1995): 637–57; and Pierre Martin, 'Générations politiques, rationalité économique et appui à la souveraineté au Québec', *Canadian Journal of Political Science* 27, no. 2 (June 1994): 345–59.

4   See the analysis of the election in François Rocher, 'Les Aléas de la stratégie préréférendaire: Chronique d'une mort annoncée', in Douglas M. Brown and Jonathan W. Rose, eds, *Canada: The State of the Federation 1995* (Kingston: Institute of Intergovernmental Relations, Queen's University, 1995), 19–45.

5   The ADQ proposed a Quebec-Canada union, similar to the European Union, in which Quebec and Canada would hold most government functions but would have a common elected parliament responsible for a limited set of jurisdictions.

The party program did not specify whether Quebec would be formally sovereign. See Action démocratique du Québec, *Québec-Canada: A New Partnership*, n.d.

6   Quebec National Assembly, *An Act respecting the sovereignty of Quebec*, 1st session, 35th Legislature, Bill 1 (Quebec City: Éditeur officiel, 1994).

7   Rocher, 'Les Aléas de la stratégie', 31.

8   Jean Paré, 'Noui au Canada; Non à Ottawa', *L'Actualité*, 15 Mar. 1995, 56.

9   Pierre O'Neill, 'Bouchard entraîne le Bloc dans son "virage"', *Le Devoir*, 10 Apr. 1995.

10   'La souveraineté sera, pour le Québec, le signal d'un nouveau départ dans un partenariat avec le Canada qui n'exclurait pas éventuellement une forme d'union politique.' See Rocher, 'Les Aléas de la stratégie', 36.

11   'L'Entente tripartite du 12 juin', as reproduced in Guy Lachapelle, Pierre P. Tremblay, and John E. Trent, eds, *L'Impact référendaire* (Sainte-Foy: Presses de l'Université du Québec, 1995), 405–9. The negotiations leading to the agreement are recounted in Michel Vastel, *Lucien Bouchard: en attendant la suite* (Outremont: Lanctôt, 1996), 210–1.

12   Robert Howse, 'Sovereignty . . . But Where's the Association?' *Canada Watch* 3, no. 7 (May/June 1995): 97–102. Reportedly, PQ leaders saw the proposal as entailing no more than what already existed under US–Canada free trade (Vastel, *Lucien Bouchard*, 210).

13   'L'Entente tripartite du 12 juin'.

14   The text of the bill appeared in *Le Devoir*, 8 Sept. 1996. There were two main changes from the 1994 version. First, Quebec's accession to sovereignty was no longer to be automatic in one year; it would depend upon a proclamation by the National Assembly. Second, any such proclamation 'must be preceded by a formal offer of economic and political partnership with Canada'.

15   Jean Dion, 'Le Canada "suppliera" Québec de négocier, affirme Bouchard', *Le Devoir*, 28 Sept. 1995.

16   Harold D. Clarke and Allan Kornberg, 'Choosing Canada? The 1995 Quebec Sovereignty Referendum', paper delivered to the Canadian Political Science Association, June 1996, 5.

17   On the Garcia and Beaudoin statements, see Pierre O'Neill, 'L'UQAM se dissocie des propos de Garcia', *Le Devoir*, 27 Sept. 1995; and Michel Laliberté and Jean Dion, 'Les patrons pour le NON ripostent', *Le Devoir*, 4 Oct. 1995. The survey data are presented by Édouard Cloutier, 'The Quebec Referendum: From polls to ballots', *Canada Watch* 4, no. 2 (Nov./Dec. 1995): 37–9; and Pierre Drouilly, 'La Progression du OUI dans les sondages', *La Presse*, 21 Oct. 1996.

18   Cloutier, 'The Quebec Referendum', 39.

19   André Blais, 'Pourquoi le oui a-t-il fait des gains pendant la campagne référendaire?' in John E. Trent, Robert A. Young, and Guy Lachapelle, eds, *Quebec-Canada: Challenges and Opportunities* (Ottawa: University of Ottawa Press, 1996), 71–6. Blais insists that it is incorrect to suggest that the Yes side gained support because the Québécois stopped worrying about the economic

consequences of sovereignty. They simply changed their assessment of these consequences.

20   Personal communication from André Blais, 27 Sept. 1996.

21   'L'aspect le plus déterminant des positionnements dans l'espace identitaire fut sans doute l'incapacité du camp fédéraliste et de Jean Chrétien, en particulier, de convaincre les non-croyants qu'ils pouvaient demeurer canadiens sans restreindre pour autant leur identité québécoise, c'est-à-dire que l'identification à la nation québécoise n'était pas incompatible avec l'identification à la nation canadienne.' ('The most critical aspect of positioning with respect to identity was undoubtedly the inability of the federalist camp and of Jean Chrétien, in particular, to convince the non-believers [not clearly committed to either federalism or sovereignty] that they could remain Canadian without having to limit their identification with Quebec, in other words that identification with the Quebec nation is not incompatible with identification with the Canadian nation.') See Vincent Lemieux, 'Le Référendum de 1995: quelques pistes d'explication', in Trent et al., *Québec-Canada*, 67.

22   For example, at a Yes rally during the last week of the campaign, Bouchard criticized at length Chrétien's involvement in patriation without Quebec's consent. While avoiding the word traitor, he displayed a newspaper headline that read, 'Lévesque trahi par ses alliés'. See Jean Dion, 'Bouchard', *Le Devoir*, 26 Oct. 1995.

23   Jean Dion, 'Trudeau accuse Lucien Bouchard d'avoir menti aux Québécois', *Le Devoir*, 7 Nov. 1995.

24   'Tout changement des compétences constitutionnelles du Québec ne se fera qu'avec le consentement des Québécois'; 'J'ai appuyé cette position dans le passé, je l'appuie aujourd'hui et je l'appuierai dans l'avenir, en toute circonstance.' See Jean Dion, 'Aucun moyen n'est exclu pour assurer le changement, dit Chrétien', *Le Devoir*, 25 Oct. 1995. Statements also drawn from Richard Mackie and Rhéal Séguin, 'Chrétien, Bouchard to Address Nation', *Globe and Mail*, 25 Oct. 1995.

25   This public opposition to Meech apparently reflected Trudeau's personal influence; privately, Chrétien's position was more equivocal. See Cohen, *A Deal Undone*, 263. Chrétien did support the Charlottetown Accord.

26   After Chrétien's speech, the No side was ahead for the first time since early October, according to one survey. See Hugh Winsor, 'Poll Disputes No Rally's Success', *Globe and Mail*, 11 Nov. 1995.

27   My translation of 'Le Canada mon pays, le Québec ma patrie.' See Dion, 'Aucun moyen n'est exclu.'

28   After the rally, the No lead had declined, according to one survey. See Winsor, 'Poll Disputes No Rally's Success.'

29   Michel Venne, '67 p. cent des Québécois sont profondément attachés au Canada', *Le Devoir*, 3 Oct. 1996.

30   Richard Mackie, 'Poll Finds Quebeckers Proud of Canada', *Globe and Mail*, 24 Feb. 1996.

31 Venne, '67 p. cent des Québécois'.

32 Lemieux, 'Le Référendum de 1995', 66; and Vincent Lemieux and Robert Bernier, 'Voters' Questions in the 1995 Québec Referendum', paper presented to the Canadian Political Science Association, St Catharines, Ont., June 1996, 3.

33 'Chrétien: Why Destroy Canada?', Globe and Mail, 26 Oct. 1996.

34 Pierre Drouilly, 'An Exemplary Referendum', Canada Watch 4, no. 2 (Nov./Dec. 1995): 25–7.

35 See the account of the Cree referendum in Grand Chief Matthew Coon Come, 'Dishonourable Conduct: The Crown in Right of Canada and Quebec, and the James Bay Cree', Constitutional Forum constitutionnel 7, nos 2 and 3 (Winter and Spring 1996): 81–3.

36 Norman Delisle, 'La fin ne justifie pas les moyens', Le Devoir, 11 May 1996.

37 Marie-Claude Lortie, 'Vote hors Québec: le directeur des élections durement critiqué', La Presse, 26 Oct. 1996.

38 'A porté atteinte dans un certain sens à la démocratie en général au Québec.' See Delisle, 'La fin ne justifie pas les moyens'.

39 Pierre O'Neill, 'Pas d'élections avant longtemps', Le Devoir, 17 Jan. 1996.

40 Chrétien did not simply support the demand that merchants give English the full visibility allowed by Bill 101. He criticized the law itself, stating that he did not like certain restrictions in it and did not like its 'language police'. See Jean Chartier, 'Affichage: Chrétien approuve le boycottage anglophone', Le Devoir, 2 Aug. 1996. For his endorsement of the principle of partition, see Ross Howard, 'Quebec Divisible, Chrétien Says', Globe and Mail, 30 Jan. 1996.

41 See Grand Council of the Crees, Sovereign Injustice: Forcible Inclusion of the James Bay Crees and Crees Territory into a Sovereign Quebec (Nemaska, Que., 1995). See also Mary Ellen Turpel, 'Does the Road to Quebec Sovereignty Run through Aboriginal Territory?' in Daniel Drache and Roberto Perin, eds, Negotiating with a Sovereign Quebec (Toronto: Lorimer, 1992), 93–106; and Kent McNeil, 'Aboriginal Nations and Quebec's Boundaries: Canada Couldn't Give What It Didn't Have', in ibid., 107–23.

42 While he was premier, Daniel Johnson declared that 'the position of all those elected to the Quebec legislature, the premier, the government and obviously the opposition is to defend everywhere and forever the territorial integrity of Quebec', Montreal Gazette, 19 May 1994, as quoted in Robert A. Young, The Secession of Quebec and the Future of Canada (Montreal and Kingston: McGill-Queen's University Press, 1995), 214.

43 Jean Chartier, 'Le Taux de chômage monte en flèche', Le Devoir, 6 and 7 July 1996; and Tu Thanh Ha, 'Landry Lashes Out at Federalists', Globe and Mail, 27 Aug. 1996.

44 Alan C. Cairns, 'Looking Back from the Future', in Trent et al., Québec-Canada, 77–9.

45 Alan C. Cairns, 'The Legacy of the Referendum: Who Are We Now?', Constitutional Forum constitutionnel 7, nos 2 and 3 (Winter and Spring 1996): 35–9; Reg Whitaker, 'Thinking about the Unthinkable: Planning for a Possible

Secession', ibid., 58–64; and Jeff Rose, 'Beginning to Think about the Next Referendum', occasional paper, Faculty of Law, University of Toronto, 21 Nov. 1995.

46   The No responses to the four propositions, in order, were 6.7 per cent, 13.1 per cent, 15.3 per cent, and 22.4 per cent. See Pierre O'Neill, 'Le Référendum a rendu les Québécois plus revendicateurs que jamais', *Le Devoir*, 12 Nov. 1995.

47   Hugh Winsor, 'Quebeckers Prefer Canada 2–1, Poll Says', *Globe and Mail*, 26 Mar. 1996. In a June survey, 58.9 per cent of respondents wanted Bouchard to put aside sovereignty and partnership and to work for a renewed federalism; 34.6 per cent were opposed. See Richard Mackie, 'Quebeckers Favour Canada, Poll Finds', *Globe and Mail*, 20 June 1996.

48   Edward Greenspon and Anthony Wildon-Smith, 'Secret Summit', *Maclean's* (21 Oct. 1996), 28–9.

49   House of Commons, *Journals*, 1st session, 35th Parliament, no. 273, 11 Dec. 1995, 2232.

50   'An Act Respecting Constitutional Amendments', *Statutes of Canada 1996*, 1st session, 35th Parliament, Bill C–110.

51   F.L. Morton, 'Why Chrétien's Proposal Won't Wash in the West', *Globe and Mail*, 30 Nov. 1995.

52   Stéphane Dion, 'The Constitution Must Recognize Quebec's "Special Distinction"', *Globe and Mail*, 26 Jan. 1996.

53   In a March 1996 survey, 55 per cent of respondents outside Quebec opposed constitutional recognition of Quebec as a 'distinct society'; 43 per cent were in favour. See Hugh Winsor, 'Quebeckers Prefer Canada 2–1, Poll Says', *Globe and Mail*, 26 Mar. 1996.

54   Pierre O'Neill, 'Ottawa annule la réforme constitutionnelle', *Le Devoir*, 15 Apr. 1996. The distinct-society provision requires the support of seven provinces, representing half the Canadian population.

55   Michel Venne, 'Chrétien se libère de l'échéance de 1997', *Le Devoir*, 23 June 1996.

56   Prime Minister's Office, 'Speech from the Throne: 27 February 1996'. The items listed in the second and third provisions, other than job training, largely parallel the 'six sisters' of the Charlottetown Accord, in which Ottawa is already relatively inactive.

57   'Chrétien fait des ouvertures', *Le Devoir*, 31 May 1996.

58   Susan D. Phillips, 'The Canada Health and Social Transfer: Fiscal Federalism in Search of a Vision', in Douglas M. Brown and Jonathan W. Rose, eds, *Canada: The State of the Federation, 1995* (Kingston: Institute of Intergovernmental Relations, Queen's University, 1995), 65–96.

59   Edward Greenspon, 'Provinces Challenged on Safety Net', *Globe and Mail*, 22 Aug. 1996. Bouchard had insisted, over the objections of several other premiers, that the conference discuss a proposal by the economist Thomas Courchene that could entail the elimination of any federal role in setting standards for social policy. See Edward Greenspon and Brian Laghi, 'Premiers Give Ottawa Deadline', *Globe and Mail*, 23 Aug. 1996.

60 Ibid. Warning of federal intrusion into provincial jurisdictions, Bouchard refused to join the child-benefit program despite a mechanism allowing opting out with compensation.

61 Jean Dion, 'Un Bureau d'information vantera les vertus du Canada', *Le Devoir*, 10 July 1996.

62 Hugh Winsor, 'Ottawa Caught Short by Flag Fever', *Globe and Mail*, 29 Aug. 1996.

63 Confederation 2000, *Today and Tomorrow: An Agenda for Action* (Ottawa: 3 and 4 May 1996), 15.

64 Ibid., 21.

65 Group of 22, *Making Canada Work Better*, 1 May 1996, 20.

66 Ibid., 19–21. Most of the group did not support the second alternative: provincial jurisdiction over language.

67 On this basis, the statement assigned Quebec 'jurisdiction over immigration and exclusive jurisdiction over culture, language, and training for employment'. See Canadian Broadcasting Corporation, 'Remaking Canada: "Group of 25 Statement"', unpublished document, 1996.

68 Statement to the House of Commons on 26 Sept. 1996, as reproduced in 'Rock: Does the Law Permit Quebec's Unilateral Secession?' *Globe and Mail*, 27 Sept. 1996.

69 Ibid.

70 To be sure, Quebec government lawyers at the Bertrand hearing have argued that Quebec is not bound by the Canadian constitution since: (1) the Quebec National Assembly did not sign it and (2) an authoritative French-language version has not been prepared. This appears to reverse the position taken in the 1980s by the Lévesque government, which regularly invoked the Charter's notwithstanding clause when passing legislation. However, Quebec government officials have not said that they would not observe Canadian law up to the point that Quebec became sovereign. Section 18 of the Parizeau government's Bill 1 (as reproduced in *Le Devoir*, 8 September 1996) provided for the continuity of Canadian laws beyond this point, unless a sovereign Quebec should decide to alter them. Even if Canada should have refused to discuss the 'partnership' proposal, Quebec was still committed to reaching an agreement with Canada regarding Quebec's accession to sovereignty. Parizeau had always recognized that before becoming sovereign, Quebec would want to reach an agreement on the division of assets and the debt. This is indicated in Bill 1 (s. 25) and the 12 June agreement. Of course, the Quebec government saw no need to discuss the boundaries of a sovereign Quebec. In the speech that he had prepared to deliver in the event of a Yes vote, Parizeau stressed the finality of the referendum result but also insisted that Quebec's accession to sovereignty would not be proclaimed immediately; up to a year could pass. This would give needed time both for Quebec to prepare itself for sovereignty and to negotiate a partnership offer with Canada. (Jacques Parizeau, 'Si le Québec avait dit Oui', *Le Devoir*, 22 Feb. 1996.) Journalist Benoit Aubin claims that the Parizeau government had in fact planned to move far more rapidly (Benoit Aubin, *Chroniques de mauvaise humeur*

[Montreal: Boréal, 1996], 215–18). Presumably, this could have meant a quick declaration of sovereignty without any prior agreement with Canada. However, Parizeau's collaborators claim that the planned speech proves that he did not intend to move precipitously. (Michel Venne, 'Qu'aurait dit Parizeau si le OUI l'avait emporté?', *Le Devoir*, 18 Feb. 1996).

71   The possibility of a unilateral declaration of sovereignty under these conditions is discussed in José Woehrling, 'Ground Rules for the Next Referendum on Quebec's Sovereignty', *Canada Watch* 4, nos. 5 and 6 (Aug. 1996): 95.

72   Rhéal Séguin, 'Federalists Split Over Call For Court Ruling', *Globe and Mail*, 28 Sept. 1996. See also 'Chrétien devrait s'attacher à améliorer le fédéralisme', *La Presse*, 28 Sept. 1996. Claude Ryan had similar comments after Ottawa's initial decision to enter the Bertrand case. See Manon Cornellier, 'Le plan B: une vision électoraliste, déplore Ryan', *La Presse*, 21 May 1996. In late February 1996 Daniel Johnson had said that sovereignty was a political matter; it was not appropriate to make sovereignty a legal question. See Jean Dion, 'Le plan B refait surface', *Le Devoir*, 27 Feb. 1996.

73   Apparently the decision to secure a Supreme Court reference had been opposed by most of the Quebec members of the Chrétien cabinet, excluding Chrétien himself. See Chantal Hébert, 'Droit de sécession: Ottawa s'adresse à la Cour suprême', *La Presse*, 25 Sept. 1996.

74   Ross Howard, 'Quebec Divisible, Chrétien Says', *Globe and Mail*, 30 Jan. 1996.

75   Jean Dion, 'Les Territoires autochtones n'appartiennent pas au Québec, dit Irwin', *Le Devoir*, 14 Feb. 1996. Irwin's position was denounced by Robert Bourassa, as well as by the Bouchard government. See Manon Cornellier, 'Bourassa contredit Irwin', *Le Devoir*, 15 Feb. 1996.

76   Ross Howard, 'Slim Vote Can't Split Canada, PM Says', *Globe and Mail*, 31 Jan. 1996.

77   Hugh Winsor and Tu Thanh Ha, 'Chrétien Signals New Resolve on Quebec', *Globe and Mail*, 12 Dec. 1995; and Jean Dion, 'Chrétien refuse de définir ses "pouvoirs"', *Le Devoir*, 13 Dec. 1995.

78   'C'est absolument à côté de la *track*' (Pierre O'Neill, 'Les discours des ténors fédéraux irritent Johnson', *Le Devoir*, 2 Feb. 1996). The idea of partition was also dismissed by Liberal constitution critic Jean-Marc Fournier; see 'L'intégrité du territoire fait consensus à Québec', *Le Devoir*, 23 Jan. 1996.

79   Andrew Coyne, 'Making Offers to Quebec is Part of the Problem, Not the Solution', *Globe and Mail*, 29 Jan. 1996; and Diane Francis, 'Children Suffer While Their Parents Bicker', *Maclean's*, 14 Oct. 1996, 9. See also Diane Francis, *Fighting for Canada* (Toronto: Key Porter, 1996).

80   Robert Lecker, 'The Writing's on the Wall', *Saturday Night*, July–August 1996, 15–51.

81   Hugh Winsor and Edward Greenspon, 'Hard Line on Separatism Popular Outside Quebec', *Globe and Mail*, 16 Nov. 1996. The survey also showed that only 34 per cent of Canadians outside Quebec would 'support recognizing Quebec as a distinct society in the constitution if it meant that Quebec would stay in Canada'; 52 per cent were opposed.

82   A survey taken on 23–29 January 1997 found that if a referendum on sover-
      eignty were held then, 51.9 per cent of decided Quebeckers would have voted
      Yes with 48.1 per cent voting No. This represented a gain over previous months
      that was attributed both to a sharp rise in satisfaction with the Bouchard gov-
      ernment and a rise in the proportion of Quebeckers who believe that sover-
      eignty will never happen, thus reducing the risks of voting Yes. (Richard Mackie,
      'Belief in Sovereign Quebec Falters', *Globe and Mail*, 1 Feb. 1997.)

Chapter 10

1   See Michael Bliss, 'Let's Shut Up and Keep the Status Quo', *Globe and Mail*, 17
     Jan. 1992.
2   The popular votes in the first three elections were 1968, 53.6 per cent; 1972,
     49.1 per cent; and 1974, 54.1 per cent. Apparently Liberal support was much
     lower among francophones than anglophones. In 1979 the popular vote surged
     to 61.6 per cent; in 1980 it was 68.2 per cent. During the 1960s and 1970s, a
     significant share of the francophone vote went to Social Credit, whose overall
     popular vote reached 24.3 per cent in 1972. While leader Réal Caouette shared
     Trudeau's unqualified federalist beliefs, other party figures did not. Indeed, under
     Fabien Roy the party was tacitly allied with the Lévesque government. Some
     observers claimed that French-Canadian nationalism played a role in the initial
     rise of the party in the 1960s, but apparently economic protest was the primary
     factor. Maurice Pinard, *The Rise of a Third Party: A Study in Crisis Politics*,
     enlarged edition (Montreal and Kingston: McGill-Queen's University Press,
     1975), chap. 5.
3   Vincent Lemieux and Jean Crête, 'Quebec', in Howard Penniman, ed., *Canada
     at the Polls* (Washington, DC: American Enterprise Institute for Public Policy
     Research, 1981), 215. Of course, 20 per cent to 30 per cent of PQ voters would
     represent a substantial share of *francophone* supporters of the federal Liberal Party.
4   Lemieux and Crête comment: 'The Liberals put forward a nationalistic slogan:
     "Speak Up, Quebec!" The slogan was especially surprising since Quebec
     Liberals had an ideological commitment to equal rights for individuals all across
     Canada rather than to equal rights for communities. Their slogan clearly
     appealed to the local community only' (ibid., 219). The Liberal surge was facil-
     itated by the collapse of the Créditistes, who were unprepared for the campaign
     and lacked funding (217). It may have been reinforced by francophone resent-
     ment over English-Canadian hostility to Trudeau, a fellow francophone (225).
5   Maurice Pinard, 'The Dramatic Reemergence of the Quebec Independence
     Movement', *Journal of International Affairs*, 45, no. 2 (Winter 1992): Table 3. The
     table is reproduced in chap. 7 of this book, as Table 4. In Pinard's data, respon-
     dents chose a single referent among 'French Canadian', 'Quebecker', and
     'Canadian'.
6   The figures are derived from 1971 and 1991 Census of Canada data presented
     in Brian R. Harrison and Louise Marmen, *Languages in Canada* (Scarborough,
     Ont.: Prentice-Hall, 1994), Table A.2. The data have been modified to accom-
     modate multiple responses to home language.

7   In 1971 even the Montreal *Gazette* said that the strategy could never work: 'The idea that French-Canadian society can be sustained in geographical pockets from coast to coast by federal laws and policies is impractical. People in Quebec will not buy it anyway. The principal instrument of French-Canadian survival is the Quebec government. If it cannot be done by Quebec, it cannot be done.' See 'Search for Survival', Montreal *Gazette*, 23 June 1971.

8   B&B Commission, Book I: *The Official Languages*, xlvii.

9   See Janine Brodie, 'The Women's Movement Outside Quebec: Shifting Relations with the Canadian State', in Kenneth McRoberts, ed., *Beyond Quebec: Taking Stock of Canada* (Montreal and Kingston: McGill-Queen's University Press, 1995), 333–57.

10   On Quebec and ethnic nationalism see, for instance, William Johnson, *A Canadian Myth* (Montreal: Robert Davies, 1994); and Max Nemni, 'Le "Dés"accord du Lac Meech et la construction de l'imaginaire symbolique des Québécois', in Louis Balthazar, Guy Laforest, and Vincent Lemieux, eds, *Le Québec et la restructuration du Canada, 1980–1992* (Sillery: Septentrion, 1991), 167–97; and Diane Francis, *Fighting for Canada* (Toronto: Key Porter, 1996).

11   David J. Bercuson and Barry Cooper, *Deconfederation* (Toronto: Key Porter, 1991), 16.

12   Charles Taylor, *Reconciling the Solitudes* (Montreal and Kingston: McGill-Queen's University Press, 1993), 177.

13   See Raymond Breton, 'From Ethnic to Civic Nationalism: English Canada and Quebec', *Ethnic and Racial Studies*, no. 11 (1988): 85–102; and Kenneth McRoberts, 'English-Canadian Perceptions of Quebec', in Alain G. Gagnon, ed., *Quebec: State and Society*, 2nd edn (Scarborough, Ont.: Nelson, 1993), 116–29.

14   See Joseph H. Carens, ed., 'Immigration, Political Community, and the Transformation of Identity: Quebec's Immigration Policies in Critical Perspective', in Joseph H. Carens, ed., *Is Quebec Nationalism Just?* (Montreal and Kingston: McGill-Queen's University Press, 1995) 21–81.

15   See the analysis of Parizeau's statement by Charles Taylor, claiming that such sentiments reflect, not racism or rejection of immigrants, but a Jacobin model of society that allows too little recognition of cultural diversity (Charles Taylor, 'Les Ethnies dans une société "normale"', *La Presse*, 21 and 22 Nov. 1995).

16   'Bouchard s'excuse', *Le Devoir*, 18 Oct. 1995.

17   Jeremy Webber, 'The Response to Parizeau's "Ethnic Vote"', *Canada Watch* 4, no. 3 (Nov./Dec. 1995): 34–5.

18   See the argument in Gilles Bréton and Jane Jenson, 'After Free Trade and Meech Lake: Quoi de neuf?', *Studies in Political Economy* 34 (Spring 1991): 199–218.

19   None the less, the shifts may not be as great as is often assumed. See Melville L. McMillan, 'Economic Threats to National Unity: From Within and Without', in McRoberts, *Beyond Quebec*, Table 1.

20   Alan C. Cairns, 'The Embedded State: State-Society Relations in Canada', in Keith Banting, ed., *State and Society: Canada in Comparative Perspective*, Collected

Research Studies of the Royal Commission on the Economic Union and Development Prospects for Canada, vol. 31 (Toronto: University of Toronto Press, 1986), 53–86; Leslie A. Pal, *Interests of State* (Montreal and Kingston: McGill-Queen's University Press, 1993); Eric A. Nordlinger, *On the Autonomy of the Democratic State* (Cambridge, Mass.: Harvard University Press, 1981); and Peter B. Evans, Dietrich Rueschemeyer, and Theda Skocpol, eds, *Bringing the State Back In* (Cambridge: Cambridge University Press, 1985).

21　At the same time, the ability of these groups to mobilize around the Charter is itself partly due to the support they had previously received from the Canadian state; especially the programs of the secretary of state designed to strengthen the sense of Canadian identity and citizenship. See Leslie Pal, *Interests of State*; and F.L. Morton, 'The Effect of the Charter of Rights on Canadian Federalism', *Publius* 25, no. 3 (Summer 1995): 181.

22　See the data in Michel Sarra-Bournet, '"French Power, Québec Power": La place des francophones québécois à Ottawa', in François Rocher, ed., *Bilan québécois du fédéralisme canadien* (Montreal: VLB, 1992), 199–225. The list of Trudeau's colleagues who supported Meech is from Cohen, *A Deal Undone* (Vancouver/Toronto: Douglas & McIntyre, 1990), 176. Marc Lalonde and Jean Chrétien did support Trudeau's position. For information on the support of Meech by Quebec business people see Jean-H. Guay, 'Le Patronat: une année de transition', in Denis Monière, ed., *L'Année politique au Québec, 1989 au 1990* (Montreal: Québec/Amérique, 1990), 137–8.

23　Cairns, 'The Embedded State', 81.

24　In the opinion of the commission, native peoples did not fall within either of the two phrases that appear in their terms of reference: 'two founding races' and 'other ethnic groups'. Accordingly, it could not have been the government's intention that the commission address the question of native populations. At the same time, the commission did affirm the need 'to help the native populations preserve their cultural heritage, which is an essential part of the patrimony of all Canadians' and 'to assist the survival of the Eskimo language and the most common Indian dialects' (B&B Commission, Book I: *The Official Languages*, xxvi–xxvii).

25　Task Force on Canadian Unity, *A Future Together* (Hull: Dept. of Supply and Services, 1979), 122.

26　Pat Armstrong et al., 'Three Nations in a Delicate Balance', *Toronto Star*, 4 Feb. 1992.

27　Charles Taylor, 'Shared and Divergent Values', in Charles Taylor, *Reconciling the Solitudes*, chap. 8.

28　Daiva Stasiulis, '"Deep Diversity": Race and Ethnicity in Canadian Politics', in Michael S. Whittington and Glen Williams, eds, *Canadian Politics in the 1990s*, 4th edn (Toronto: Nelson, 1995), 211–12.

29　Gordon Laxer, 'Distinct Status for Quebec: A Benefit to English Canada', *Constitutional Forum constitutionnel* 3, no. 3 (Winter 1992), 62–6; and Philip Resnick, 'Toward a Multinational Federalism: Asymmetrical and Confederal

Alternatives', in F. Leslie Seidle, ed., *Seeking a New Canadian Partnership* (Montreal: Institute for Research on Public Policy, 1994), 71–101. On the other hand, Jeremy Webber argues against depriving MPs of the vote. See Jeremy Webber, *Reimagining Canada* (Montreal and Kingston: McGill-Queen's University Press, 1994), 279–84.

30 Donald G. Lenihan, Gordon Robertson, and Roger Tassé, *Canada: Reclaiming the Middle Ground* (Montreal: Institute for Research on Public Policy, 1994), 134.

31 André Burelle, *Le Mal canadien* (Montreal: Fides, 1995), chap. 5. See the critique in François Rocher and Miriam Smith, 'The New Boundaries of the Canadian Political Culture', paper presented at a conference organized by the Centre of Canadian Studies, University of Edinburgh, 1996.

32 Roger Gibbins, 'Decentralization and National Standards: "This Dog Won't Hunt"', *Policy Options politiques* 17, no. 5 (June 1996): 7–10: and Robert Howse, 'Find New Ways to Secure Our Social Union', ibid., 11–14.

33 *Shaping Canada's Future Together: Proposals* (Ottawa: Supply and Services Canada, 1991).

34 David C. Hawkes, 'Reconfederating Canada', in John E. Trent, Robert A. Young, and Guy Lachapelle, eds, *Québec-Canada: Challenges and Opportunities* (Ottawa: University of Ottawa Press, 1996), 316, n. 3.

35 Lenihan, Robertson, and Tassé, *Canada: Reclaiming the Middle Ground*, 96–7.

36 The federal and provincial responsibilities that would probably continue are discussed in Webber, *Reimagining Canada*, 267.

37 In particular the Native Women's Association of Canada argued for unqualified application of the Charter. See the discussion of the Accord and debate surrounding it in Mary Ellen Turpel, 'The Charlottetown Accord and Aboriginal Peoples' Struggle for Fundamental Political Change', in McRoberts and Monahan, *The Charlottetown Accord*, 111–51.

38 Burelle, *Le Mal canadien*, 76.

39 A model is provided by the recent constitutional amendment, applying to New Brunswick alone, stating that 'the English linguistic community and the French linguistic community in New Brunswick have equality of status and equal rights and privileges, including the right to distinct educational institutions and such distinct cultural institutions as are necessary for the preservation and promotion of those communities', *House of Commons Debates*, 3rd session, 34th Parliament, vol. 132, 15084, as cited by Don Desserud, 'The Exercise of Community Rights in the Liberal-Federal State: Language Rights and New Brunswick's Bill 88', unpublished paper, 6 Dec. 1994. Desserud analyses the theoretical issues raised by such a recognition of 'linguistic communities'.

40 Indeed, in 1989 the Fédération des francophones hors Québec (FFHQ), representing francophones outside Quebec, formally ended its support for a pan-Canadian official bilingualism, claiming that it had not produced the results that had been hoped for. Instead, the FFHQ called for recognition of linguistic duality, as defined in the Meech Lake Accord and for the creation of 'protected institutional zones' in which the full range of French-language educational and

social services would be available. (Guy Taillefer, 'Mise au rancart du bilinguisme officiel par la Fédération des francophones hors Québec', *La Presse*, 25 June 1989; and 'Official Bilingualism Let Us Down, Francophones Outside Quebec Say', Montreal *Gazette*, 25 June 1989.)

41 See Philip Resnick, *Thinking English Canada* (Toronto: Stoddart, 1994); and 'English Canada: The Nation That Dares Not Speak Its Name', in McRoberts, *Beyond Quebec*, 81–92.

42 Gordon Gibson, *Plan B: The Future of the Rest of Canada* (Vancouver: Fraser Institute, 1994).

43 Richard Mackie, 'Federalist Fortunes Get Boost in Latest Survey', *Globe and Mail*, 21 Oct. 1996; and Richard Mackie, 'Belief in Sovereign Quebec Falters', *Globe and Mail*, 1 Feb. 1997.

44 Mario Fontaine, 'Référendum: les Québécois veulent un sursis de 10 ans', *La Presse*, 28 Sept. 1996; and Richard Mackie, 'Quebeckers Want Votes Delayed', *Globe and Mail*, 4 Oct. 1996.

45 John Robert Colombo, *Colombo's All-Time Great Canadian Quotations* (Toronto: Stoddart, 1994), 220.

46 Senate of Canada, *Debates*, 2nd session, 33rd Parliament, 1986–87–88, 2999.

47 This discussion draws upon Kenneth McRoberts, 'After the Referendum: Canada with or without Quebec', in McRoberts, *Beyond Quebec*, 403–49. A very thorough treatment appears in Robert A. Young, *The Secession of Quebec and the Future of Canada* (Montreal and Kingston: McGill-Queen's University Press, 1995).

48 As quoted in Jeffrey Simpson, 'Legal Arguments against Secession Avoid the Unthinkable', *Globe and Mail*, 6 Jan. 1995. This was explicitly or tacitly acknowledged by all three parties in the last Parliament and has been affirmed by the Reform Party. See Reg Whitaker, 'Quebec's Self-determination and Aboriginal Self-government', in Carens, ed., *Is Quebec Nationalism Just?*, 205. As we saw in Chapter 9, Justice Minister Allan Rock took great pains when announcing his government's intention to submit a Supreme Court reference on a unilateral declaration of independence to insist that 'the leading political figures of all our provinces and the Canadian public have long agreed that the country cannot be held together against the clear will of Quebeckers'. Intergovernmental Affairs Minister Stéphane Dion said recently, 'In Canada, there is a convention that exists that we cannot keep a people against its will.' See 'Next Referendum Question Must Be Clear, Dion Says', *Globe and Mail*, 1 Oct. 1996.

49 At the time of the 1995 referendum, Daniel Johnson, leader of the No forces, had made it clear that if a majority voted Yes he would support the Quebec government's attempt to begin negotiations.

50 Some commentators have claimed that, whatever majority should be necessary in a Quebec referendum, a vote for sovereignty would have to be approved by a similar referendum in the rest of Canada. Yet, in the case of Newfoundland a majority vote of Parliament was judged to be sufficient. Nor was provincial approval deemed necessary; in fact, Quebec was formally opposed. On the basis

of Canadian practice in particular, the 50 per cent plus 1 threshold is proposed in Patrick J. Monahan and Michael J. Bryant, 'Coming to Terms with Plan B: Ten Principles Governing Secession', *C.D. Howe Institute Commentary*, 83, June 1996 (Toronto: C.D. Howe Institute, 1996), 29–31. At the same time, they insist that the referendum must be 'on a clear question conducted according to a transparent and fair procedure' (p. 19). They do not call for approval by a referendum in the rest of the country but do argue that the terms of secession, as agreed to in negotiations between Quebec and the rest of Canada, would have to be approved by Quebeckers in a second referendum (pp. 33–4).

51   See José Woehrling, 'Ground Rules for the Next Referendum on Quebec's Sovereignty', *Canada Watch* 4, nos. 5 and 6 (Aug. 1996): 95; and Monahan and Bryant, 'Coming to Terms with Plan B', 33–5. The Lévesque government was committed to a second referendum in 1980; apparently Lucien Bouchard had argued for such a referendum in his negotiations with Jacques Parizeau and Mario Dumont in the spring of 1995. See Michel Vastel, *Lucien Bouchard: en attendant la suite* (Outremont: Lanctôt, 1996) 210–1.

52   Monahan and Bryant propose a 'Canadian negotiating authority' (ibid., 31–3). Also, see Young, *The Secession of Quebec*, 197.

53   Kenneth McRoberts, 'Protecting the Rights of Linguistic Minorities', in Daniel Drache and Roberto Perin, *Negotiating with a Sovereign Quebec* (Toronto: Lorimer, 1992), 183–5. Partition is also rejected in Young, *The Secession of Quebec*, 213, as well as in Gordon Gibson, *Plan B*, 119–22. None the less, the possibility of partition is advocated in Scott Reid, *Canada Remapped* (Vancouver: Arsenal Pulp, 1992) and in Monahan and Bryant, 'Coming to Terms with Plan B', 35–7.

54   See McRoberts, 'Protecting the Rights of Linguistic Minorities', 186–8.

55   While affirming that boundaries should remain intact, Young is dubious about the feasibility of reciprocal agreements. See Young, *The Secession of Quebec*, 223–9.

56   McRoberts, 'After the Referendum', 407–18.

57   The most recent formulation of the notion is Philip Resnick, *Toward a Canada-Quebec Union* (Montreal and Kingston: McGill-Queen's University Press, 1991). Earlier presentations are Douglas V. Verney and Diana M. Verney, 'A Canadian Political Community? The Case for Tripartite Confederalism', *Journal of Commonwealth and Comparative Politics* 12, no. 1 (Mar. 1974): 1–19; Hugh Thorburn, 'Needed! A New Look at the Two-Nations Theory', *Queen's Quarterly* 80 (Summer 1974): 268–73; and Gérard Bergeron, *L'Indépendance: oui, mais . . .* (Montreal: Quinze, 1977).

BIBLIOGRAPHY

Abu-Labon, Y., and D. Stasiulis
    1992   'Ethnic Pluralism under Seige: Popular and Partisan Opposition to Multiculturalism', *Canadian Public Policy*, 18, no. 4: 365–86.

Action démocratique du Québec
    n.d.   *Québec-Canada: A New Partnership.*

L'Actualité
    1991   'Portrait des Québécois'. Jan., 13–16.

d'Aillon, P.G.
    1979   *Daniel Johnson: l'égalité avant l'indépendance.* Montreal: Stanké.

Ajzenstat, J.
    1988   *The Political Thought of Lord Durham.* Montreal and Kingston: McGill-Queen's University Press.

Allen, G.
    1989   'Grit Stands Fast'. *Maclean's*, 20 Nov., 25.

Andrew, J.B.
    1977   *Bilingual Today, French Tomorrow: Trudeau's Master Plan and How It Can Be Stopped.* Richmond Hill: BMG.

Arès, R.
    1967   *Dossier sur le pacte fédératif de 1867.* Montreal: Bellarmin.

Armstrong, P., et al.
    1992   'Three Nations in a Delicate Balance'. *Toronto Star*, 4 Feb.

Arsenau, T.
    1994   'The Reform Party of Canada: Past, Present and Future'. Pp. 35–57 in D. Brown and J. Hiebert (eds), *Canada: The State of the Federation 1994.* Kingston: Institute of Intergovernmental Relations, Queen's University.

Atlantic Provinces Economic Council
    1992   Renewal of Canada: Division of Powers, *Conference Report.* Halifax, 17–19 Jan.

Aubin, B.
    1996   *Chroniques de mauvaise humeur.* Montreal: Boréal.

Balthazar, L.
    1989   'Pour un multiculturalisme québécois'. *Action nationale* 79 (Oct.): 942–53.

Behiels, M.
  1985   *Prelude to Quebec's Quiet Revolution: Liberalism Versus Neo-nationalism,*
          1945–1960. Montreal and Kingston: McGill-Queen's University Press.

Behiels, M. (ed.)
  1989   *The Meech Lake Primer: Conflicting Views of the 1987 Constitutional Accord.*
          Ottawa: University of Ottawa Press.

Bercuson, D.J., and B. Cooper
  1991   *Deconfederation: Canada without Quebec.* Toronto: Key Porter.

Bergeron, G.
  1977   *L'Indépendance: oui, mais. . . .* Montreal: Quinze.
  1983   'Quebec in Isolation'. Pp. 59–73 in K. Banting and R. Simeon (eds),
          And No One Cheered: Federalism, Democracy and the Constitution Act.
          Agincourt, Ont.: Methuen.
  1985   *Notre Miroir à deux faces.* Montreal: Québec/Amérique.

Bergeron, M-H., D. Brown, and R. Simeon
  1980   *The Question: The Debate on the Referendum Question, Quebec National*
          Assembly, March 4–20, 1980. Kingston: Institute of Intergovernmental
          Relations, Queen's University.

Bernard, J-P.
  1971   *Les Rouges.* Montreal: Presses de l'Université du Québec.

Bernier, G.
  1980   'Les Aspects économiques du débat: un dialogue de sourds'. Pp. 111–34
          in En Collaboration, *Québec: Un pays incertain* (Montreal: Québec/
          Amérique).

Bibby, R.W.
  1990   *Mosaic Madness: The Poverty and Potential of Life in Canada.* Toronto:
          Stoddart.

Bibeau, G.
  1984   'No Easy Road to Bilingualism'. *Language and Society* 12 (Winter):
          44–7.

Bissonnette, L.
  1985   'La Confusion des clauses'. *Le Devoir*, 3 May.

Bissoondath, N.
  1994   *Selling Illusions: The Cult of Multiculturalism in Canada.* Toronto: Penguin.

Black, E.R.
  1975   *Divided Loyalties: Canadian Concepts of Federalism.* Montreal and
          Kingston: McGill-Queen's University Press.

Blais, A.
1980 'Le vote: ce que l'on en sait . . . ce que l'on n'en sait pas'. Pp. 157–82 in
En Collaboration, *Québec: Un pays incertain.*
1993 'The Quebec Referendum: Quebeckers Say No'. Pp. 200–7 in
McRoberts and Monahan, *The Charlottetown Accord, the Referendum, and
the Future of Canada.*
1996 'Pourquoi le oui a-t-il fait des gains pendant la campagne référendaire?'
Pp. 71–7 in J.E. Trent, R. Young, and G. Lachapelle (eds), *Québec-
Canada: Challenges and Opportunities.*

Blais, A., and J. Crête
1991 'Pourquoi l'opinion publique au Canada anglais a-t-elle rejeté l'Accord
du Lac Meech?' Pp. 385–400 in R. Hudon and R. Pelletier (eds),
L'Engagement intellectuel: Mélanges en l'honneur de Léon Dion. Sainte-Foy:
Presses de l'Université Laval.

Blais, A., P. Martin, and R. Nadeau
1995 'Attentes économiques et linguistiques et appui à la souveraineté du
Québec: une analyse prospective et comparative'. *Canadian Journal of
Political Science* 28, no. 4 (Dec.): 637–57.

Blais, A., and R. Nadeau
1991 'To Be or Not to Be Sovereigntist: Quebeckers' Perennial Dilemma'.
Canadian Public Policy 18, no. 1: 89–103.

Blais, A., et al.
1995 'L'Élection fédérale de 1993: le comportement électoral des québécois'.
Revue québécoise de science politique 27 (Spring): 15–47.

Bliss, M.
1992 'Let's Shut Up and Keep the Status Quo'. *Globe and Mail,* 17 Jan.

Boismenu, G.
1989 'La Pensée constitutionnelle de Jean Lesage'. Pp. 96–104 in R. Comeau
(ed.), *Jean Lesage et l'éveil d'une nation.* Sillery, Que.: Presses de
l'Université du Québec.

Bombardier, D.
1980 'Noir sur blanc'. Radio-Canada, 17 May.

Bonenfant, J.-C.
1969 *La Naissance de la Confédération.* Montreal: Leméac.

Bonin, D. (ed.)
1992 *Towards Reconciliation? The Language Issue in Canada in the 1990s.*
Kingston, Ont.: Institute of Intergovernmental Relations, Queen's
University.

Bothwell, R.
  1995   *Canada and Quebec: One Country, Two Histories.* Vancouver: UBC Press.

Bouchard, J., and P. Vennat
  1982   'Lévesque n'a pas la majorité pour réaliser son projet de souveraineté-association'. *La Presse*, 30 Mar.

Bourassa, H.
  1970   'Réponse amicale à la Vérité', as translated and reproduced in J. Levitt (ed.), *Henri Bourassa on Imperialism and Biculturalism, 1900–1918.* Toronto: Copp Clark.

Brandt, G.J.
  1983   'The Quebec Veto Reference: A Constitutional Postscript'. *University of Western Ontario Law Review* 21, no. 1: 163–71.

Bréton, A., et al.
  1964   'Manifeste pour une politique fonctionnelle'. *Cité libre*, May: 11–17.

Bréton G., and J. Jenson
  1991   'After Free Trade and Meech Lake: Quoi de neuf?' *Studies in Political Economy* 34 (Spring): 199–218.

Breton, R.
  1986   'Multiculturalism and Canadian Nation-Building'. Pp. 27–66 in A. Cairns and C. Williams (eds), *The Politics of Gender, Ethnicity and Language in Canada.* Collected Research Studies of the Royal Commission on the Economic Union and Development Prospects for Canada, vol. 34. Toronto: University of Toronto Press.
  1988   'From Ethnic to Civic Nationalism: English Canada and Quebec'. *Ethnic and Racial Studies* 11: 85–102.

Brodie, J.
  1995   'The Women's Movement Outside Quebec: Shifting Relationships with the Canadian State'. Pp. 333–57 in McRoberts, *Beyond Quebec.*

Brunet, M.
  1964   *La Présence anglaise et les canadiens.* Montreal: Beauchemin.

Burelle, A.
  1995   *Le Mal canadien: Essai de diagnostic et esquisse d'une thérapie.* Montreal: Fides.
  1996   Interview, 9 July.

Cairns, A.C.
  1986   'The Embedded State: State-Society Relations in Canada'. Pp. 53–86 in K. Banting (ed.), *State and Society: Canada in Comparative Perspective.* Collected Research Studies of the Royal Commission on the

Economic Union and Development Prospects for Canada, vol. 31.
Toronto: University of Toronto Press.

1988 'Citizens (Outsiders) and Governments (Insiders) in Constitution-
Making: The Case of Meech Lake'. *Canadian Public Policy* 14,
supplement (Sept.): S121–45.

1989 'Political Science, Ethnicity, and the Canadian Constitution'. Pp.
113–40 in D.P. Shugarman and R. Whitaker (eds), *Federalism and
Political Community: Essays in Honour of Donald Smiley*. Peterborough,
Ont.: Broadview.

1992 *Charter versus Federalism: The Dilemmas of Constitutional Reform*. Montreal
and Kingston: McGill-Queen's University Press.

1995 'Reflections on the Political Purposes of the Charter: The First
Decade'. Pp. 194–214 in Douglas E. Williams (ed.), *Reconfigurations:
Canadian Citizenship and Constitutional Change*. Toronto: McClelland &
Stewart.

1996 'The Legacy of the Referendum: Who Are We Now?' *Constitutional
Forum constitutionnel* 7, nos 2 and 3 (Winter–Spring): 35–9.

1996 'Looking Back from the Future'. Pp. 77–80 in J.E. Trent, et al. *Québec-
Canada*.

Cameron, D.R.
1993 'Not Spicer and Not the B&B: Reflections of an Insider on the
Workings of the Pepin-Robarts Task Force on Canadian Unity'.
International Journal of Canadian Studies 7–8 (Spring–Fall): 331–45.

Camp, D.
1968 'Reflections on the Montmorency Conference'. *Queen's Quarterly* 76,
no. 2 (Summer): 185–99.

Canada
1867 *British North America Act*.
1969 *Official Languages Act*, 1st session, 28th Parliament, C-120.
1973 Department of Health and Welfare, *Working Paper on Social Security for
Canadians*. Ottawa: Information Canada.
1982 *Constitution Act, 1982*.
1987 Special Joint Committee of the Senate and House of Commons on the
1987 Constitutional Accord, *Minutes of Proceedings and Evidence*. Various
issues.
1988 *Canadian Multiculturalism Act*, 2nd session, 33rd Parliament, C-93.
1988 *Official Languages Act*, amended, 2nd session, 33rd Parliament, C-72.
1991 *Shaping Canada's Future Together: Proposals*. Ottawa: Supply and Services
Canada.
1992 *Status Report: The Multilateral Meetings on the Constitution*, Final Version,
16 July.
1992 *Draft Legal Text, October 9, 1992*. [Charlottetown Accord].

1996   'An Act Respecting Constitutional Amendments'. *Statutes of Canada 1996*, 1st session, 35th Parliament, C-110.
House of Commons, *Debates*. Various years.
Senate, *Debates*. Various years.

Canada, Royal Commission on Bilingualism and Biculturalism
1965   *Preliminary Report*. Ottawa: Queen's Printer.
1967   *General Introduction*. Ottawa: Queen's Printer.
1967   Book I: *The Official Languages*. Ottawa: Queen's Printer.
1968   Book II: *Education*. Ottawa: Queen's Printer.
1966   Book III: *The Work World*. Ottawa: Queen's Printer.
1970   Book IV: *The Cultural Contribution of the Other Ethnic Groups*. Ottawa: Queen's Printer.

Canada, Royal Commission on the Economic Union and Development Prospects for Canada
1985   *Report*, vol. III. Ottawa: Supply and Services Canada.

Canada, Supreme Court
1981   Re: Resolution to amend the Constitution. 1 S.C.R.
1982   Re: Objection to a Resolution to amend the Constitution. 2 S.C.R.

Canada West Foundation
1993   *Canada 2000: Towards a New Canada*. Calgary.

Canadian Annual Review
Toronto: University of Toronto Press. Various issues.

Canadian Broadcasting Corporation
1996   'Remaking Canada: "Group of 25 Statement"'. Unpublished document.

Canadian Dimension
1967   'The NDP Federal Convention—1967', Sept.–Oct.: 4 and 37–8.
1969   'For an Independent Socialist Canada'. Aug.–Sept.: 8–10.

Careless, A.G.S.
1977   *Initiative and Response: The Adaptation of Canadian Federalism to Regional Economic Development*. Montreal and Kingston: McGill-Queen's University Press.

Carens, J.H. (ed.)
1995   'Immigration, Political Community, and the Transformation of Identity: Quebec's Immigration Policies in Critical Perspective'. Pp. 21–81 in Carens (ed.), *Is Quebec Nationalism Just?*
1995   *Is Quebec Nationalism Just? Perspectives from Anglophone Canada*. Montreal and Kingston: McGill-Queen's University Press.

Chaput-Rolland, S.
1984   'Après le déluge: Brian Mulroney'. *Le Devoir*, 7 Sept.
1987   'Il n'y a pas de monstre au lac Meech'. *Le Devoir*, 8 May.

Charbonneau, H., J. Henripin, and J. Legaré
1974   'L'Avenir démographique des francophones au Québec et à Montréal en l'absence de politiques adéquates'. *Revue de géographie de Montréal* 24: 199–202.

Chartier, J.
1996   'Le Taux de chômage monte en flèche'. *Le Devoir*, 6 and 7 July.
1996   'Affichage: Chrétien approuve le boycottage anglophone'. *Le Devoir*, 2 Aug.

Chevrier, R.
1983   *Français au Canada: situation à l'extérieur du Québec.* Montreal: Conseil de la langue française.

Christian, T.J.
1991   'L'Affaire Piquette'. Pp. 107–21 in D. Schneiderman, *Language and the State.* Cowansville, Que.: Yvon Blais.

Christiano, K.J.
1994   *Pierre Elliott Trudeau: Reason Before Passion.* Toronto: ECW Press.

Citizens' Forum on Canada's Future
1991   *Report to the People and Government of Canada.* Ottawa: Supply and Services Canada.

Clarke, H.D., and A. Kornberg
1996   'Choosing Canada? The 1995 Quebec Sovereignty Referendum'. Paper delivered to the Canadian Political Science Association, June 1996.

Clarkson, S., and C. McCall
1990   *Trudeau and Our Times*, vol. 1, *The Magnificent Obsession.* Toronto: McClelland & Stewart.

Clift, D.
1981   *Le Déclin du nationalisme au Québec.* Montreal: Libre expression.

Cloutier, É.
1995   'The Quebec Referendum: From polls to ballots'. *Canada Watch* 4, no. 2 (Nov./Dec.): 37–9.

Cohen, A.
1990   *A Deal Undone: The Making and Breaking of the Meech Lake Accord.* Vancouver/Toronto: Douglas & McIntyre.

Coleman, W.D.
  1984   *The Independence Movement in Quebec, 1945–1980.* Toronto: University of Toronto Press.

Colombo, J.R.
  1994   *Colombo's All-Time Great Canadian Quotations.* Toronto: Stoddart.

Le Comité constitutionnel du Parti libéral du Québec
  1980   *Une Nouvelle fédération canadienne.*
  1991   *Un Québec libre de ses choix.*

Comité pour une politique fonctionelle
  1965   'Bizarre algèbre'. *Cité libre* 15, no. 82 (Dec.): 13–20.

Commissioner of Official Languages
      Annual Reports. Ottawa: Information Canada or Supply and Services. Various years.

Confederation 2000
  1996   *Today and Tomorrow: An Agenda for Action.* Ottawa.

Conway, J.F.
  1992   *Debts to Pay: English Canada and Quebec from the Conquest to the Referendum.* Toronto: Lorimer.

Cook, R.
  1969   *Provincial Autonomy, Minority Rights and the Compact Theory, 1867–1921.* Studies of the Royal Commission on Bilingualism and Biculturalism, no. 4. Ottawa: Queen's Printer.
  1971   *The Maple Leaf Forever: Essays on Nationalism and Politics in Canada.* Toronto: Macmillan.

Cook, R., with J.T. Saywell and J.C. Ricker
  1963   *Canada: A Modern Study.* Toronto: Clarke Irwin.

Coon Come, M.
  1996   'Dishonourable Conduct: The Crown in Right of Canada and Quebec, and the James Bay Cree'. *Constitutional Forum constitutionnel* 7, nos 2 and 3 (Winter and Spring): 81–3.

Cornellier, M.
  1995   *The Bloc.* Toronto: Lorimer.
  1996   'Bourassa contredit Irwin'. *Le Devoir,* 15 Feb.
  1996   'Le plan B: une vision électoraliste, déplore Ryan'. *La Presse,* 21 May.

Coyne, A.
  1996   'Making Offers to Quebec is Part of the Problem, Not the Solution'. *Globe and Mail,* 29 Jan.

Coyne, D.
  1989   'The Meech Lake Accord and the Spending Power Proposals:
          Fundamentally Flawed'. Pp. 245–71 in M. Behiels (ed.), *Meech Lake
          Primer*. Ottawa: University of Ottawa Press.
  1991   'Beyond the Meech Lake Accord'. Pp. 437–67 in D. Schneiderman
          (ed.), *Language and the State*. Cowansville, Que.: Yvon Blais.

Craig, G.M. (ed.)
  1963   *Lord Durham's Report*. Carleton Library no. 1. Toronto: McClelland &
          Stewart.

Creighton, D.
  1964   *The Road to Confederation*. Toronto: Macmillan.
  1970   *Canada's First Century*. Toronto: Macmillan.
  1972   'The Myth of Biculturalism'. Pp. 256–70 in D. Creighton, *Towards the
          Discovery of Canada*. Toronto: Macmillan.

Cummins, J., and M. Danesi
  1990   *Heritage Languages: The Development and Denial of Canada's Linguistic
          Resources*. Toronto: Our Schools/Our Selves Foundation.

Dahl, R.A. (ed.)
  1966   *Political Oppositions in Western Democracies*. New Haven: Yale University
          Press.

Daignault, R.
  1981   *Lesage*. Quebec City: Libre expression.

Delacourt, S.
  1994   *United We Fall: In Search of a New Canada*. Toronto: Penguin.

Delisle, N.
  1996   'La fin ne justifie pas les moyens'. *Le Devoir*, 11 May.

Denis, S.
  1992   *Le Long Malentendu: le Québec vu par les intellectuels progressistes au Canada
          anglais, 1970–1991*. Montreal: Boréal.

Denis, W.B.
  1990   'The Politics of Language'. Pp. 148–85 in Peter S. Li (ed.), *Race and
          Ethnic Relations in Canada*. Toronto: Oxford University Press.

Descôteaux, B.
  1980   'Les provinces ont prié Ottawa de leur imposer le respect du français'.
          Le Devoir, 23 Oct.
  1980   'L'Assemblée adopte la motion Lévesque sans l'appui du PLQ'. *Le
          Devoir*, 22 Nov.

1987   'L'accord du lac Meech permettra au Québec de faire des gains importants et incontestables'. *Le Devoir*, 30 May.

1987   'L'accord du lac Meech confirmera le statut du Québec dans les relations internationales'. *Le Devoir*, 10 June.

1988   'Ottawa négociera avec le Québec sur la loi des langues'. *Le Devoir*, 8 June.

1988   'Ottawa et Québec s'entendent sur les langues officielles'. *Le Devoir*, 18 Aug.

Desserud, D.

1996   'The Exercise of Community Rights in the Liberal-Federal State'. *International Journal of Canadian Studies* 14, 215–36.

Le Devoir

1967   'Stanfield: gare aux mots'. 1 Sept.

1968   'Léo Cadieux donne son appui à Paul Hellyer'. 14 Mar.

1968   'Trudeau est assuré de l'appui de 23 députés du Québec'. 20 Mar.

1968   'Isabelle appuie plutôt Winters; Lessard, Hellyer'. 28 Mar.

1968   'Le sénateur Lamontagne appuie Trudeau dont il dit partager "en gros" les positions constitutionnelles'. 29 Mar.

1968   'La course au leadership accentue les divisions dans le caucus du Québec'. 11 Apr.

1976   'Le séparatisme est mort, pense Trudeau'. 11 May.

1980   'Des provinces ont prié Ottawa de leur imposer le respect du français'. 23 Oct.

1986   'Pas une adhésion à la Constitution'. 7 Mar.

1995   'Bouchard s'excuse'. 18 Oct.

1996   'Chrétien fait des ouvertures'. 31 May.

Diefenbaker, J.G.

1976   *One Canada*, vol. 2: *The Years of Achievement, 1957–1962*. Toronto: Macmillan.

Dion, J.

1995   'Le Canada "suppliera" Québec de négocier, affirme Bouchard'. *Le Devoir*, 28 Sept.

1995   'Aucun moyen n'est exclu pour assurer le changement, dit Chrétien'. *Le Devoir*, 25 Oct.

1995   'Trudeau accuse Lucien Bouchard d'avoir menti aux Québécois'. *Le Devoir*, 7 Nov.

1995   'Chrétien refuse de définir ses "pouvoirs"'. *Le Devoir*, 13 Dec.

1996   'Les Territoires autochtones n'appartiennent pas au Québec, dit Irwin'. *Le Devoir*, 14 Feb.

1996   'Le plan B refait surface'. *Le Devoir*, 27 Feb.

1996   'Ottawa n'aurait pas dû intervenir dans l'affaire Bertrand, selon le député libéral McWhinney'. *Le Devoir*, 23 May.

1996   'Un Bureau d'information vantera les vertus du Canada'. *Le Devoir*, 10 July.

Dion, L.
1975   *Nationalismes et politique au Québec*. Montreal: Hurtubise HMH.
1989   'The Impact of Demolinguistic Trends on Canadian Institutions'. In *Demolinguistic Trends and the Evolution of Canadian Institutions*, special issue of *Canadian Issues* of the Association of Canadian Studies, pp. 57–71.

Dion, S.
1992   'Explaining Quebec Nationalism'. Pp. 77–121 in R. Kent Weaver (ed.), *The Collapse of Canada?* Washington, DC: Brookings Institution.
1996   'The Constitution Must Recognize Quebec's "Special Distinction"'. *Globe and Mail*, 26 Jan.

Directeur général des élections du Québec
1980   *Référendum: Oui—Non.*

Donneur, A.
1975   'La Solution territoriale au problème du multilinguisme'. J.-G. Savard and R. Vigneault (eds), *Les États multilingues: problèmes et solutions*. Quebec City: Presses de l'Université Laval.

Drache, D., and R. Perin (eds)
1992   *Negotiating with a Sovereign Quebec*. Toronto: Lorimer.

Drolet, J.
1974   'Henri Bourassa: une analyse de sa pensée'. Pp. 223–50 in F. Dumont, et al., *Idéologies au Canada français, 1900–1929*. Quebec City: Presses de l'Université Laval.

Drouilly, P.
1995   'An Exemplary Referendum'. *Canada Watch* 4, no. 2 (Nov./Dec. 1995): 25–7.
1996   'La Progression du OUI dans les sondages'. *La Presse*, 21 Oct.

Dufour, C.
1990   *A Canadian Challenge/Le Défis québécois*. Lantzville, BC, and Halifax: Oolichan Books and IRRP.

Elliott, J.L., and A. Fleras
1990   'Immigration and the Canadian Ethnic Mosaic'. Pp. 69–90 in Peter S. Li (ed.), *Race and Ethnic Relations in Canada*. Toronto: Oxford University Press.

Elton, D.
1993   'The Charlottetown Accord Senate: Effective or Emasculated?' Pp. 37–55 in McRoberts and Monahan, *The Charlottetown Accord, the Referendum, and the Future of Canada*.

En Collaboration
    1980   *Québec: un pays incertain: réflexions sur le Québec post-référendaire*. Montreal: Québec/Amérique.

English, J.
    1992   *The Life of Lester Pearson*, vol. 2, *The Worldly Years*. Toronto: Knopf.

Evans, P.B., D. Rueschemeyer, and T. Skocpol (eds)
    1985   *Bringing the State Back In*. Cambridge: Cambridge University Press.

Falardeau, J.-C.
    1960   'Les Canadiens français et leur idéologie'. Pp. 20–38 in M. Wade (ed.), *Canadian Dualism*. Toronto: University of Toronto Press.

Falardeau, L.
    1989   'Francophones et anglophones sont insatisfaits de la loi 178'. *La Presse*, 21 Jan.

Ferguson, D.
    1990   'Tory Blames Bilingualism for Backlash'. *Toronto Star*, 26 Mar.

Fletcher, J.
    1988   'What Do Canadians Think about Civil Liberties? The Politics of the Canadian Charter'. Paper presented to the Association for Canadian Studies in Australia and New Zealand, Canberra, 23 June.

Fontaine, M.
    1996   'Référendum: les Québécois veulent un sursis de 10 ans'. *La Presse*, 28 Sept.

Forbes, H.D.
    1993   'Canada: From Bilingualism to Biculturalism', *Journal of Democracy*, 4, no. 4: 69–84.
    1996   'Trudeau's Moral Vision'. Pp. 17–39 in A.A. Peacock (ed.), *Rethinking the Constitution: Perspectives on Canadian Constitutional Reform, Interpretation, and Theory*. Toronto: Oxford University Press.

Forget, C.E.
    1995   'Référendum: les conséquences méconnues d'un vote négatif'. *La Presse*, 29 Mar.

Forsey, E.
    1962   'Canada: Two Nations or One?' *Canadian Journal of Economics and Political Science* 28, no. 4: 485–501.

Fortier, D.
    1988   'Breaking Old Habits'. *Language and Society* 24 (Fall): 12–3.

Fournier, J.-M.
    1996   'L'intégrité du territoire fait consensus à Québec'. *Le Devoir*, 23 Jan.

Fournier, P.
1990   *Autopsie du lac Meech: La souveraineté est-elle inévitable?*, Montreal: VLB.
1991   *A Meech Lake Post-Mortem: Is Quebec Sovereignty Inevitable?* Montreal and Kingston: McGill-Queen's University Press.

Francis, D.
1996   'Children Suffer While Their Parents Bicker'. *Maclean's*, 14 Oct.
1996   *Fighting for Canada.* Toronto: Key Porter.

Frémont, J.
1993   'The Charlottetown Accord and the End of the Exclusiveness of Provincial Jurisdictions'. Pp. 93–101 in K. McRoberts and P.J. Monahan (eds), *The Charlottetown Accord, the Referendum, and the Future of Canada.*

Gagnon, A. G., and M.B. Montcalm
1990   *Quebec: Beyond the Quiet Revolution.* Scarborough, Ont.: Nelson.

Gairdner, W. D.
1990   *The Trouble with Canada.* Toronto: Stoddart.

Gibbins, R.
1992   'Something Not So Funny Happened on the Way to Senate Reform'. *Canada Watch* 1, no. 2 (Sept): 22–3.
1996   'Decentralization and National Standards: "This Dog Won't Hunt"'. *Policy Options politiques* 17, no. 5 (June): 7–10.

Gibson, F.W. (ed.)
1970   *Cabinet Formation and Bicultural Relations.* Studies of the Royal Commission on Bilingualism and Biculturalism, no. 6. Ottawa: Queen's Printer.

Gibson, G.
1994   *Plan B: The Future of the Rest of Canada.* Vancouver: Fraser Institute.

The Globe and Mail
1969   'Back to the Solitudes'. 18 Dec.
1977   'Trudeau: Unity in Canada Won't Be Fractured'. 23 Feb.
1988   'Francophones Urge PM to Protect Their Rights'. 5 Apr.
1988   'Peterson Disappointed by Decision on New Act'. 6 Apr.
1996   'Rock: Does the Law Permit Quebec's Unilateral Secession?' 27 Sept.
1996   'Chrétien: Why Destroy Canada?' 26 Oct.
1996   'Next Referendum Question Must Be Clear, Dion Says'. 1 Oct.

Graefe, P.
1996   'From Coherence to Confusion: The CCF–NDP Confronts Federalism'. Major research paper, M.A. Program in Political Science, York University.

Granatstein, J.L.
    1986   *Canada 1957–1967: The Years of Uncertainty and Innovation*. Toronto: McClelland & Stewart.

Grand Council of the Crees
    1995   *Sovereign Injustice: Forcible Inclusion of the James Bay and Crees Territory into a Sovereign Quebec*. Nemaska, Quebec.

Grant, George
    1965   *Lament for a Nation*. Toronto: McClelland & Stewart.

Greenspon, E.
    1996   'Provinces Challenged on Safety Net'. *Globe and Mail*, 22 Aug.

Greenspon, E., and B. Laghi
    1996   'Premiers Give Ottawa Deadline'. *Globe and Mail*, 23 Aug.

Greenspon, E., and A. Wildon-Smith
    1996   'Secret Summit'. *Maclean's*, 21 Oct., 28–9.

Group of 22
    1996   *Making Canada Work Better*. 1 May.

Guay, J.-H.
    1990   'Le Patronat: une année de transition'. Pp. 137–44 in Denis Monière (ed.), *L'Année politique au Québec, 1989 au 1990*. Montreal: Québec/Amérique.

Guay, J.-H., R. Nadeau, and E. Cloutier
    1990   'La Crise linguistique au Québec: une étude du mouvement de l'opinion publique engendré par le jugement de la Cour suprême sur l'affichage commercial'. Paper presented at the annual meeting of the Canadian Political Science Association, May.

Guindon, Hubert
    1988   *Quebec Society: Tradition, Modernity, and Nationhood*. Toronto: University of Toronto Press.

Gwyn, R.
    1980   *The Northern Magus*. Toronto: McClelland & Stewart.

Ha, T.T.
    1996   'Landry Lashes Out at Federalists'. *Globe and Mail*, 27 Aug.

Haggart, R., and A.E. Golden
    1971   *Rumours of War*. Toronto: New Press.

Hamelin, J., and L. Beaudoin
    1972   'Les Cabinets provinciaux, 1867–1967'. Pp. 91–115 in R. Desrosiers (ed.), *Le Personnel politique québécois*. Montreal: Boréal.

Harles, J.C.
  n.d.   'Integration *before* Assimilation: Immigration, Multiculturalism and the
          Canadian Polity'. Unpublished paper.
  n.d.   'Making a Virtue of Necessity: National Integration and
          Multiculturalism in Canada'. Unpublished paper.

Harrison, B.R., and L. Marmen
  1994   *Languages in Canada*. Scarborough, Ont.: Prentice-Hall. Published
          jointly with Statistics Canada.

Hawkes, D.C.
  1996   'Reconfederating Canada'. Pp. 309–16 in J.E. Trent, et al., *Québec-
          Canada: Challenges and Opportunities*. Ottawa: University of Ottawa
          Press.

Hébert, C.
  1996   'Droit de sécession: Ottawa s'adresse à la Cour suprême'. *La Presse*, 25
          Sept.

Heintzman, R.
  1971   'In the Bosom of a Single State'. *Journal of Canadian Studies* 6, no. 4
          (Nov.): 1–2, 63–4.

Henripin, J.
  1993   'Population Trends and Policies in Quebec'. Pp. 304–18 in A. Gagnon
          (ed.), *Quebec: State and Society*. 2nd edn. Scarborough, Ont.: Nelson.

Hodgetts, J.E.
  1955   *Pioneer Public Service*. Toronto: University of Toronto Press.

Hogg, P.W.
  1988   *Meech Lake Constitutional Accord Annotated*. Toronto: Carswell.

Horowitz, G.
  1965   'The Future of English Canada'. *Canadian Dimension*, July–Aug., 12 and
          25.

Horton, D.J.
  1992   *André Laurendeau: French-Canadian Nationalist, 1912–1968*. Toronto:
          Oxford University Press.

House of Commons
  Journals. Various years.

Howard, F.
  1967   'Davis Assures Quebec Areas of Agreement Remain Ontario's Goal'.
          Globe and Mail, 8 Aug.

Howard, R.
  1996   'Quebec Divisible, Chrétien Says'. *Globe and Mail*, 30 Jan.

1996   'Slim Vote Can't Split Canada, PM Says'. *Globe and Mail*, 31 Jan.

Howse, R.
 1995   'Sovereignty . . . But Where's the Association?' *Canada Watch* 3, no. 7
         (May/June): 97–102.
 1996   'Find New Ways to Secure Our Social Union'. *Policy Options politiques*
         17, no. 5 (June): 11–14.

Jaworsky, J.
 1979   'A Case Study of the Canadian Federal Government's Multiculturalism
         Policy'. M.A. thesis, Department of Political Science, Carleton
         University.

Johnson, D.
 1965   *Egalité ou indépendance*. Montreal: Éditions de l'homme.

Johnson, W.
 1994   *A Canadian Myth: Quebec, Between Canada and the Illusion of Utopia*.
         Montreal: Robert Davies.

Johnston, R., and A. Blais
 1988   'Meech Lake and Mass Politics: The "Distinct Society" Clause'.
         Canadian Public Policy 14, supplement (Sept.): S25–S42.

Johnston, R., et al.
 1993   'The People and the Charlottetown Accord'. Pp. 19–43 in R.L. Watts
         and D.M. Brown (eds), *Canada: The State of the Federation 1993*.
         Kingston: Institute of Intergovernmental Relations, Queen's University.

Joy, R.J.
 1972   *Languages in Conflict: The Canadian Experience*. Toronto: McClelland &
         Stewart.
 1992   *Canada's Official Languages: The Progress of Bilingualism*. Toronto:
         University of Toronto Press.

Juteau, D.
 1990   'The Canadian Experiment: Multiculturalism as Ideology and Policy'.
         Paper presented to Conference on Cultural Diversity in Europe, Berlin.

Juteau, D., and M. McAndrew
 1992   'Projet national, immigration et intégration dans un Québec souverain'.
         Sociologie et sociétés 24, no. 2 (Autumn): 161–80.

Juteau, D., M. McAndrew, and L. Pietrantonio
 n.d.   'Multiculturalism à la Canadian and Intégration à la Québécoise:
         Transcending Their Limits'. Unpublished paper.

Kallen, E.
 1982   'Multiculturalism: Ideology, Policy and Reality'. *Journal of Canadian
         Studies* 17, no. 1 (Spring): 51–63.

Kelly, S.
    1995   'Les imaginaires canadiens du 19e siècle'. Thèse de doctorat,
            Département de sociologie, l'Université de Montréal.

Kent, T.
    1988   *A Public Purpose: An Experience of Liberal Opposition and Canadian
            Government.* Kingston and Montreal: McGill-Queen's University Press.
    1992   'Recasting Federalism'. *Policy Options* 12, no. 3 (April): 3–6.
    1996   Interview, 20 June.

Knopf, R., and F.L. Morton
    1985   'Nation-Building and the Canadian Charter of Rights and Freedoms'.
            Pp. 133–82 in A. Cairns and C. Williams, *Constitutionalism, Citizenship
            and Society in Canada.* Collected Research Studies of the Royal
            Commission on the Economic Union and Development Prospects for
            Canada, vol. 33. Toronto: University of Toronto Press.

Lachapelle, G., P.P. Tremblay, and J.E. Trent (eds)
    1995   *L'Impact référendaire.* Sainte-Foy: Presses de l'Université du Québec.

Lachapelle, R.
    1992   'Demography and Official Languages in Canada'. Pp. 86–9 in D. Bonin
            (ed.), *Towards Reconciliation? The Language Issue in Canada in the 1990s.*
            Kingston: Institute of Intergovernmental Relations, Queen's University.

Lachapelle, R., and J. Henripin
    1980   *La Situation démolinguistique au Canada: Evolution passée et prospectives.*
            Montreal: Institut de recherches politiques.

Lacoste, P.
    1990   'André Laurendeau et la Commission sur le bilinguisme et le
            biculturalisme'. Pp. 207–13 in R. Comeau and L. Beaudry (eds), *André
            Laurendeau: Un intellectuel d'ici.* Sillery, Que.: Presses de l'Université du
            Québec.

Lacoursière, J., and C. Bouchard. *Notre histoire Québec–Canada.*
    1972   Montreal: Éditions Format.

Laforest, G.
    1992   *Trudeau et la fin d'un rêve canadien.* Sillery, Que.: Septentrion.
    1995   *Trudeau and the End of a Canadian Dream.* Montreal and Kingston:
            McGill-Queen's University Press.

Laliberté, M., and J. Dion
    1995   'Les patrons pour le NON ripostent'. *Le Devoir*, 4 Oct.

Lalonde, G.
    1987   'Back to the B and B'. *Language and Society* 19 (Apr.), 22–4.

Lamoureux, A.
    1985   *Le NPD et le Québec, 1958–1985*. Montreal: Les Éditions du Parc.

Laponce, J.A.
    1987   *Languages and Their Territories.* Toronto: University of Toronto Press.
    1992   'Reducing the Tensions Resulting from Language Contacts: Personal or
            Territorial Solutions?' Pp. 125–39 in D. Bonin (ed.), *Towards
            Reconciliation? The Language Issue in Canada in the 1990s.* Kingston:
            Institute of Intergovernmental Relations, Queen's University.

LaSelva, S.V.
    1996   *The Moral Foundations of Canadian Federalism: Paradoxes, Achievements and
            Tragedies of Nationhood.* Montreal and Kingston: McGill-Queen's
            University Press.

La Terreur, M.
    1973   *Les Tribulations des conservateurs au Québec de Bennett à Diefenbaker.*
            Quebec City: Presses de l'Université Laval.

Laurendeau, A.
    1962   'Pour une enquête sur le bilinguisme'. *Le Devoir,* 20 Jan.
    1990   *Journal tenu pendant la Commission royale d'enquête sur le bilinguisme et le
            biculturalisme.* Montreal: VLB/Septentrion.
    1991   *The Diary of André Laurendeau: Written During the Royal Commission on
            Bilingualism and Biculturalism, 1964–1967.* Toronto: Lorimer.

Laurendeau, M.
    1974   *Les Québécois violents: un ouvrage sur les causes et la rentabilité de la violence
            d'inspiration politique au Quebec.* Montreal: Boréal.

Laxer, G.
    1992   'Distinct Status for Quebec: A Benefit to English Canada'. *Constitutional
            Forum constitutionnel* 3, no. 3 (Winter): 62–6.

Lebel, R.
    1968   'PM Creating Great Division'. *Globe and Mail,* 21 June.

Lecker, R.
    1996   'The Writing's on the Wall'. *Saturday Night,* Jul.–Aug., 15–51.

Le Cours, R.
    1986   'Pas une adhésion à la Constitution'. *Le Devoir,* 7 Mar.

Leduc, L., and J.H. Pammet
    1995   'Attitudes and Behaviour in the 1992 Constitutional Referendum'.
            Canadian Journal of Political Science 28, no. 1 (Mar.): 3–33.

Lemelin, C.
    1968   'Sharp: Ottawa devra faire preuve de souplesse sur la question
            constitutionnelle'. *Le Devoir,* 23 Mar.

Lemieux, V.
  1996   'Le Référendum de 1995: quelques pistes d'explication'. Pp. 65–9 in
          Trent, et al., *Québec-Canada*.

Lemieux, V., and R. Bernier
  1996   'Voters' Questions in the 1995 Québec Referendum'. Paper presented
          to the Canadian Political Science Association, June.

Lemieux, V., and J. Crête
  1981   'Quebec'. Pp. 208–25 in H. Penniman (ed.), *Canada at the Polls, 1979
          and 1980*. Washington, DC: American Enterprise Institute for Public
          Policy Research.

Lenihan, D.G., G. Robertson, and R. Tassé
  1994   *Canada: Reclaiming the Middle Ground*. Montreal: Institute for Research
          on Public Policy.

Lesage, G.
  1985   'Johnson: L'*actuelle* clause Canada demeure inacceptable'. *Le Devoir*, 2
          May.
  1985   'Québec souscrit à la "clause Canada" en échange de la primauté de sa
          Charte'. *Le Devoir*, 18 May.
  1986   'Opposé à l'adhésion à la charte canadienne, Léon Dion quitte le
          gouvernement Bourassa'. *Le Devoir*, 17 Mar.

Leslie, P.M.
  1987   *Rebuilding the Relationship: Quebec and Its Confederation Partners*.
          Kingston: Institute of Intergovernmental Relations, Queen's University.

Lévesque, René
  1968   *An Option for Quebec*. Toronto: McClelland & Stewart.
  1968   *Option Québec*. Montreal: Éditions de l'homme.

Lévesque, Robert
  1987   'Lévesque fait bande à part'. *Le Devoir*, 4 May.

Levitt, K.
  1970   *Silent Surrender: The Multinational Corporation in Canada*. Toronto:
          Macmillan.

Linteau, P.-A., R. Durocher, and J.-C. Robert
  1979   *Histoire du Québec contemporain: de la Confédération à la crise*. Montreal:
          Boréal.
  1983   *Quebec: A History 1867–1929*. Toronto: Lorimer.

Linteau, P.-A., et al.
  1986   *Histoire du Québec contemporain: Le Québec depuis 1930*. Montreal: Boréal.
  1991   *Quebec since 1930*. Toronto: Lorimer.

Lijphart, A.
   1968   *The Politics of Accommodation: Pluralism and Democracy in the Netherlands.*
           Berkeley: University of California Press.

Lisée, J.-F.
   1992   'Dossiers secrets de Bourassa'. *L'Actualité*, 1 Nov.
   1994   *Le Tricheur: Robert Bourassa et les Québécois, 1990–1991.* Montreal:
           Boréal.
   1994   *Le Naufrageur: Robert Bourassa et les Québécois, 1991–1992.* Montreal:
           Boréal.
   1994   *The Trickster: Robert Bourassa and the Québécois, 1990–1992.* Toronto:
           Lorimer.

Litt, P.
   1991   'The Massey Commission, Americanization, and Canadian
           Nationalism'. *Queen's Quarterly* 98, no. 2 (Summer): 375–87.

Lortie, M.-C.
   1996   'Vote hors Québec: le directeur des élections durement critiqué'. *La
           Presse*, 26 Oct.

Lumsden, Ian (ed.)
   1970   *Close the 49th Parallel.* Toronto: University of Toronto Press.

Lupul, M.R.
   1982   'The Political Implementation of Multiculturalism'. *Journal of Canadian
           Studies* 17, no. 1 (Spring): 96–7.

McAndrew, M.
   n.d.   'Multiculturalisme canadien et interculturalisme québécois: mythes et
           réalités'. Unpublished paper.

McCall, C., and S. Clarkson
   1994   *Trudeau and Our Times*, vol. 2, *The Heroic Delusion.* Toronto: McClelland
           & Stewart.

McDowell, S.
   1971   'Governments All Water Down Aims to Create Basis of New
           Constitution'. *Globe and Mail*, 18 June.

Mackie, R.
   1996   'Poll Finds Quebeckers Proud of Canada'. *Globe and Mail*, 24 Feb.
   1996   'Quebeckers Favour Canada, Poll Finds'. *Globe and Mail*, 20 June.
   1996   'Quebeckers Want Votes Delayed'. *Globe and Mail*, 4 Oct.
   1996   'Federalist Fortunes Get Boost in Latest Survey'. *Globe and Mail*, 21
           Oct.
   1997   'Belief in Sovereign Quebec Falters'. *Globe and Mail*, 1 Feb.

Mackie, R., and R. Séguin
  1995   'Chrétien, Bouchard to Address Nation'. *Globe and Mail*, 25 Oct.

Maclean's
  1987   'Voice of the People'. 15 June, 12–13.
  1990   'Cross–Canada Checkup'. 12 Nov., 18–19.

MacMillan, C.M.
  1996   'Contemporary Challenges to National Language Policy: The
          Territorial Imperative'. Paper presented to the Canadian Political
          Science Association, Brock University, June.

McMillan, M.L.
  1995   'Economic Threats to National Unity: From Within and Without'. Pp.
          275–94 in McRoberts, *Beyond Quebec*.

McNeil, K.
  1992   'Aboriginal Nations and Quebec's Boundaries: Canada Couldn't Give
          What It Didn't Have'. Pp. 107–23 in D. Drache and R. Perin,
          Negotiating with a Sovereign Quebec.

McRae, K.
  1975   'The Principle of Territoriality and the Principle of Personality in
          Multilingual States'. *International Journal of the Sociology of Language* 4:
          35–45.
  1978   'Bilingual Language Districts in Finland and Canada: Adventures in the
          Transplanting of an Institution'. *Canadian Public Policy* 4, no. 3
          (Summer): 331–51.
  Forth- 'Official Bilingualism: From the 1960s to the 1990s', in J. Edwards
  coming (ed.), *Language in Canada*. Cambridge: Cambridge University Press.

McRoberts, K.
  1984   'The Sources of Neo-Nationalism in Quebec'. *Ethnic and Racial Studies*
          7, no. 1 (Jan.): 55–85.
  1985   'Unilateralism, Bilateralism and Multilateralism: Approaches to
          Canadian Federalism'. Pp. 71–129 in R. Simeon (ed.), *Intergovernmental
          Relations*. Collected Research Studies of the Royal Commission on the
          Economic Union and Development Prospects for Canada, vol. 63,
          Toronto: University of Toronto Press.
  1989   'Making Canada Bilingual: Illusions and Delusions of Federal Language
          Policy'. Pp. 141–71 in D.P. Shugarman and R. Whitaker (eds), *Federalism
          and the Political Community: Essays in Honour of Donald Smiley*.
          Peterborough, Ont.: Broadview.
  1991   *English Canada and Quebec: Avoiding the Question*. North York, Ont.:
          Robarts Centre for Canadian Studies, York University.
  1992   'Protecting the Rights of Linguistic Minorities'. Pp. 173–88 in D.

Drache and R. Perin, *Negotiating with a Sovereign Quebec*. Toronto: Lorimer.

1993   'Disagreeing on Fundamentals: English Canada and Quebec'. Pp. 249–63 in McRoberts and Monahan, *The Charlottetown Accord, the Referendum, and the Future of Canada*.

1993   'English-Canadian Perceptions of Quebec'. Pp. 116–29 in A.G. Gagnon (ed.), *Quebec: State and Society*, 2nd edn. Scarborough, Ont.: Nelson.

1993   *Quebec: Social Change and Political Crisis*, 3rd edn with postscript. Toronto: McClelland & Stewart.

1995   'After the Referendum: Canada with or without Quebec'. Pp. 403–49 in McRoberts, *Beyond Quebec*.

1996   'La Thèse tradition-modernité: l'historique québécois'. Pp. 29–45 in Mikhael Elbaz, Andrée Fortin, and Guy Laforest (eds), *Les Frontières de l'identité: modernité et postmodernisme au Québec*. Sainte-Foy: Presses de l'Université Laval.

McRoberts, K. (ed.)
1995   *Beyond Quebec: Taking Stock of Canada*. Montreal and Kingston: McGill-Queen's University Press.

McRoberts, K., and P.J. Monahan (eds)
1993   *The Charlottetown Accord, the Referendum, and the Future of Canada*. Toronto: University of Toronto Press.

McWhinney, E.
1979   *Quebec and the Constitution, 1960–1978*. Toronto: University of Toronto Press.
1982   *Canada and the Constitution, 1979–1982: Patriation and the Charter of Rights*. Toronto: University of Toronto Press.

Mahoney, K.
1988   'Women's Rights'. Pp. 159–70 in R. Gibbins (ed.), *Meech Lake and Canada: Perspectives from the West*. Edmonton: Academic.

Mandel, M.
1994   *The Charter of Rights and the Legalization of Politics in Canada*, rev. edn. Toronto: Thompson.

Manning, P.
1992   *The New Canada*. Toronto: Macmillan.

Martel, M.
1994   'Les Relations entre le Québec et les francophones de l'Ontario: De la survivance aux *Dead Ducks*, 1937–1969'. Ph.D. dissertation, History Department, York University.

Martin, P.
1994   'Générations politiques, rationalité économique et appui à la

souveraineté au Québec'. *Canadian Journal of Political Science* 27, no. 2 (June): 345–59.

1995　'Association after Sovereignty: Canadian Views on Economic Asociation with a Sovereign Quebec'. *Canadian Public Policy* 21, no. 1: 53–71.

Meisel, J.

1972　*Working Papers on Canadian Politics*. Montreal and Kingston: McGill-Queen's University Press.

Milne, D.

1986　*Tug of War: Ottawa and the Provinces under Trudeau and Mulroney*. Toronto: Lorimer.

1991　*The Canadian Constitution*. Toronto: Lorimer.

1992　'Innovative Constitutional Processes'. Pp. 27–51 in D. Brown and R. Young, *Canada: State of the Federation, 1992*. Kingston: Institute of Intergovernmental Relations, Queen's University.

Monahan, P.J.

1991　*Meech Lake: The Inside Story*. Toronto: University of Toronto Press.

Monahan, P.J., and M.J. Bryant

1996　'Coming to Terms with Plan B: Ten Principles Governing Secession'. *C.D. Howe Institute Commentary*, 83 (June). Toronto: C.D. Howe Institute.

Montreal *Gazette*

1971　'If Quebec Says No to Victoria Charter'. 19 June.

1971　'Search for Survival'. 23 June.

1989　'Official Bilingualism Let Us Down, Francophones Outside Quebec Say'. 25 June.

Morin, J.-Y.

1987　'Nous sommes devant un nouveau piège'. *Le Devoir*, 20 May.

Morrison, N.M.

1989　'Bilingualism and Biculturalism'. *Language and Society*, Special Report (Summer): R–7–R–8.

Morton, D.

1972　'The NDP and Quebec: A Sad Tale of Unrequited Love'. *Saturday Night*, June, 17–20.

1974　*NDP: The Dream of Power*. Toronto: Hakkert.

1986　*The New Democrats, 1961–1986: The Politics of Change*. Toronto: Copp Clark Pitman.

Morton, F.L.

1995　'The Effect of the Charter of Rights on Canadian Federalism'. *Publius* 25, no. 3 (Summer): 173–88.

1995   'Why Chrétien's Proposal Won't Wash in the West'. *Globe and Mail*, 30
        Nov.

Morton, W.L.
1970   'The Cabinet of 1867'. Pp. 1–17 in F.W. Gibson (ed.), *Cabinet Formation
        and Bicultural Relations*. Studies of the Royal Commission on
        Bilingualism and Biculturalism, no. 6. Ottawa: Queen's Printer.

Mosimann-Barbier, M.-C.
1992   *Immersion et bilinguisme en Ontario*. Rouen: l'Université de Rouen.

Mulgrew, I.
1981   'Provinces Using Federal Money but Ottawa is Not Credited: PM'.
        Globe and Mail, 25 Nov.

Murray, Lowell
1989   'Lowell Murray répond à Pierre Trudeau'. *La Presse*, 5 Apr.

Nadeau, R.
1992   'Le Virage souverainiste des Québécois, 1980–1990'. *Recherches
        sociographiques* 23, no. 1 (Jan.–Apr.): 9–28.

Nemni, M.
1991   'Le "Dés"accord du Lac Meech et la construction de l'imaginaire
        symbolique des Québécois'. Pp. 167–97 in L. Balthazar, G. Laforest, and
        V. Lemieux (eds), *Le Québec et la restructuration du Canada, 1980–1992:
        enjeux et perspectives*. Sillery, Que.: Septentrion.

New Democratic Party
1976   'Towards a New Canada: A New Canadian Constitution'. In *New
        Democratic Policies, 1961–1976*. Ottawa: New Democratic Party.

Newman, P.C.
1963   *Renegade in Power: The Diefenbaker Years*. Toronto: McClelland & Stewart.
1966   'Now There's a Third Viewpoint in the French-English Dialogue'.
        Toronto Star, 2 Apr.
1968   *The Distemper of Our Times: Canadian Politics in Transition, 1963–1968*.
        Toronto: McClelland & Stewart.

Noël, A.
1994   'The Bloc Québécois as Official Opposition'. Pp. 19–35 in D.M.
        Brown and J. Hiebert (eds), *Canada: The State of the Federation 1994*.
        Kingston, Ont.: Institute of Intergovernmental Relations, Queen's
        University.
1994   'Deliberating a Constitution: The Meaning of the Canadian
        Referendum of 1992'. Pp. 64–81 in C. Cook (ed.), *Constitutional
        Predicament: Canada after the Referendum of 1992*. Montreal and
        Kingston: McGill-Queen's University Press.

Nordlinger, E.A.
1981   *On the Autonomy of the Democratic State.* Cambridge, Mass.: Harvard
        University Press.

Norman, W.
1995   'The Ideology of Shared Values: A Myopic Vision of Unity in the
        Multi-nation State'. Pp. 137–59 in J.H. Carens (ed.), *Is Quebec
        Nationalism Just? Perspectives from Anglophone Canada.* Montreal and
        Kingston: McGill-Queen's University Press.

Ogmundson, R.
1992   'On the Right to Be Canadian'. Pp. 45–55 in S. Hryniuk, *Twenty Years
        of Multiculturalism: Successes and Failures.* Winnipeg: St John's College
        Press.

Oliver, M.
1991   'Laurendeau et Trudeau: leurs opinions sur le Canada'. Pp. 339–68 in
        R. Hudon and R. Pelletier (eds), *L'Engagement intellectuel: Mélanges en
        l'honneur de Léon Dion.* Sainte-Foy: Presses de l'Université Laval.
1991   *The Passionate Debate: The Social and Political Ideas of Quebec Nationalism,
        1920–1945.* Montreal: Véhicule.
1993   'The Impact of the Royal Commission on Bilingualism and
        Biculturalism on Constitutional Theory and Practice'. *International
        Journal of Canadian Studies* 7–8 (Spring–Fall): 315–32.

O'Neill, P.
1968   'La Course au leadership accentue les divisions dans le caucus du
        Québec'. *Le Devoir*, 11 Apr.
1987   'Le lac Meach [*sic*] a rallié les péquistes de toutes tendances'. *Le Devoir*,
        4 May.
1987   'Parizeau incite Bourassa à ne pas signer l'accord du lac Meech'. 15
        May.
1991   'Bourassa choisit d'abord le Canada'. *Le Devoir*, 11 Mar.
1995   'Bouchard entraîne le Bloc dans son "virage"'. *Le Devoir*, 10 Apr.
1995   'L'UQAM se dissocie des propos de Garcia'. *Le Devoir*, 27 Sept.
1995   'Le Référendum a rendu les Québécois plus revendicateurs que jamais'.
        Le Devoir, 12 Nov.
1996   'Pas d'élections avant longtemps'. *Le Devoir*, 17 Jan.
1996   'Les discours des ténors fédéraux irritent Johnson'. *Le Devoir*, 2 Feb.
1996   'L'intégrité du territoire fait consensus à Québec'. *Le Devoir*, 23 Jan.
1996   'Ottawa annule la réforme constitutionnelle'. *Le Devoir*, 15 Apr.

Ontario
1986   *An Act to Provide French Language Services in the Government of Ontario,*
        2nd session, 33rd Parliament, Bill 8.

Ormsby, W.
1969   *The Emergence of the Federal Concept in Canada, 1839–1845.* Toronto: University of Toronto Press.

Pal, L.A.
1993   *Interests of State: The Politics of Language, Multiculturalism and Feminism in Canada.* Montreal and Kingston: McGill-Queen's University Press.

Pâquet, M.
1994   'Le Fleuve et la cité: Représentations de l'immigration et esquisses d'une action de l'État québécois, 1945–1968'. Ph.D. dissertation, History Department, l'Université Laval.

Paré, J.
1986   'Pas une adhésion à la Constitution'. *Le Devoir,* 7 Mar.
1995   'Noui au Canada; Non à Ottawa'. *L'Actualité,* 15 Mar.

Parizeau, J.
1996   'Si le Québec avait dit Oui'. *Le Devoir,* 22 Feb.

Parti libéral du Québec
1991   *Un Québec libre de ses choix.* Rapport du Comité constitutionnel. 28 Jan.

Patry, A.
1989   'Témoignage'. Pp. 137–9 in R. Comeau (ed.), *Jean Lesage et l'éveil d'une nation.* Sillery, Que.: Presses de l'Université du Québec.

Peacock, D.
1968   *Journey to Power: The Story of a Canadian Election.* Toronto: Ryerson.

Pearson, L.B.
1975   *Mike: The Memoirs of the Right Honourable Lester B. Pearson.* J.A. Munro and A.I. Inglis (eds). Toronto: University of Toronto Press.

Pelletier, G.
1974   'The Cultural Anguish of Quebec'. Notes for a speech to la Chambre de commerce de Montréal, 19 Feb.

Pépin, J.-L.
1964   'Cooperative Federalism'. *Canadian Forum,* Dec., 206–10.

Pepin, M.
1976   'Si Québec ne collabore pas, Trudeau rapatriera tout seul la constitution'. *La Presse,* 6 Mar.

Petter, A.
1984   'Maître chez Who? The Quebec Veto Reference'. *Supreme Court Law* 6: 387–99.

Phillips, S.D.
1995   'The Canada Health and Social Transfer: Fiscal Federalism in Search of

a Vision'. Pp. 65–96 in D.M. Brown and J.W. Rose (eds), *Canada: The State of the Federation, 1995*. Kingston: Institute of Intergovernmental Relations, Queen's University.

Picard, J.-C.
1981   'La Tristesse à l'Assemblée nationale'. *Le Devoir*, 3 Dec.

Pickersgill, J. W.
1975   *My Years with Louis St Laurent: A Political Memoir*. Toronto: University of Toronto Press.

Pinard, M.
1975   *The Rise of a Third Party: A Study in Crisis Politics*, enlarged edn. Montreal and Kingston: McGill–Queen's University Press.
1992   'The Dramatic Reemergence of the Quebec Independence Movement'. *Journal of International Affairs* 45, no. 2 (Winter): 472–95.
1994   'The Secessionist Option and Quebec Public Opinion, 1988–1993'. *Canada: Opinion* 2, no. 3 (June): 1–5.

La Presse
1980   'Trudeau n'acceptera de négocier qu'après le 2e référendum'. 3 May.
1980   'Trudeau accuse le Parti Québécois de lâcheté'. 8 May.
1982   '75 p. cent des Canadiens appuient la nouvelle Constitution'. 19 June.
1989   'L'accord constitutionnel de 1982 n'a pas été un marché de dupes pour le Québec'. 10 Mar.
1996   'Chrétien devrait s'attacher à améliorer le fédéralisme'. 28 Sept.

Pratt, L., and J. Richards
1979   *Prairie Capitalism: Power and Influence in the New West*. Toronto: McClelland & Stewart.

Prime Minister's Office
1980   An Open Letter to the People of Quebec. Translation, 11 July.
1996   Speech from the Throne: 27 Feb.

Progressive Conservative Policy Advisory Conference of the Centennial Convention
n.d.   *Report on the Montmorency Conference, Courville, Quebec, August 7–10, 1967.*

Proulx, J.-P.
1980   'Servir deux maîtres'. *Le Devoir*, 24 Nov.
1988   'L'Histoire d'un échec qui combla d'aise Pierre Elliott Trudeau'. *Le Devoir*, 5 Nov.

Quebec
1956   *Rapport de la commission royale d'enquête sur les problèmes constitutionnels*, 5 vols.
1972   *Rapport de la commission d'enquête sur la situation de la langue française et*

sur les droits linguistiques au Québec, vol. 1, *La Langue de travail*; vol. 2, *Les Droits linguistiques*. Quebec City.

1991   *Rapport de la Commission sur l'avenir politique et constitutionnel du Québec.* Quebec City: Secrétariat de la Commission.

Quebec, Ministère de l'Immigration
1978   *Accord entre le gouvernement du Canada et le gouvernement du Québec portant sur la collaboration en matière d'immigration et sur la sélection des ressortissants étrangers qui souhaitent s'établir au Québec à titre permanent ou temporaire.* Montreal.

Quebec, National Assembly
1977   *Charter of the French Language*, 2nd session, 31st Legislature, Bill 101.
1979   *Quebec-Canada: A New Deal.* Quebec City: Éditeur officiel.
1994   *An Act respecting the sovereignty of Quebec*, 1st session, 35th Legislature, Bill 1.
       Journal des débats. Various years.

Radawanski, G.
1978   *Trudeau.* Scarborough, Ont.: Macmillan—NAL.

Ramirez, B., and S. Taschereau
1988   'Les Minorités: le multiculturalisme appliqué'. Pp. 384–404 in Y. Bélanger, et al., *L'Ère des libéraux: le pouvoir fédéral de 1963 à 1984.* Sillery, Que.: Presses de l'Université du Québec.

Regenstreif, P.
1969   'Note on the "Alternation" of French and English Leaders in the Liberal Party of Canada'. *Canadian Journal of Political Science* 2 (Mar.): 118–22.

Reid, S.
1992   *Canada Remapped: How the Partition of Quebec Will Reshape the Nation.* Vancouver: Arsenal Pulp.
1993   *Lament for a Notion: The Life and Death of Canada's Bilingual Dream.* Vancouver: Arsenal Pulp.

Reitz, J.G., and R. Breton
1994   *The Illusion of Difference: Realities of Ethnicity in Canada and the United States.* Toronto: C.D. Howe Institute.

Rempel, H.D.
1975   'The Practice and Theory of the Fragile State: Trudeau's Conception of Authority'. *Journal of Canadian Studies* 10, no. 4 (Nov.): 24–38.

Resnick, P.
1977   *The Land of Cain: Class and Nationalism in English Canada, 1945–1975.* Vancouver: New Star.

1990   *Letter to a Québécois Friend*. Montreal and Kingston: McGill-Queen's University Press.

1990   *The Masks of Proteus*. Montreal and Kingston: McGill-Queen's University Press.

1991   *Toward a Canada-Quebec Union*. Montreal and Kingston: McGill-Queen's University Press.

1994   *Thinking English Canada*. Toronto: Stoddart.

1994   'Toward a Multinational Federalism: Asymmetrical and Confederal Alternatives'. Pp. 71–90 in F.L. Seidle (ed.), *Seeking a New Canadian Partnership: Asymmetrical and Confederal Options*. Montreal: Institute for Research on Public Policy.

1995   'English Canada: The Nation That Dares Not Speak Its Name'. Pp. 81–92 in McRoberts, *Beyond Quebec*.

Roberts, B.

n.d.   'Smooth Sailing or Storm Warning? Canada and Québec Women's Groups and the Meech Lake Accord'. *Feminist Perspectives féministes* 12a, CRIAW.

Robertson, G.

1996   Interview, 22 Aug.

Rocher, F.

1992   'Le Dossier constitutionnel: l'année des consultations et des valse-hesitations'. Pp. 85–114 in D. Monière (ed.), *L'Année politique au Québec, 1991*. Montreal: Québec/Amérique.

1995   'Les Aléas de la stratégie pré-référendaire: Chronique d'une mort annoncée'. Pp. 19–45 in D.M. Brown and J.W. Rose (eds), *Canada: The State of the Federation 1995*. Kingston: Institute of Intergovernmental Relations, Queen's University.

1996   'Is a Neo-Jacobin Vision of the "Canadian Nation" Compatible with Democracy?' *McGill Études sur le Québec*, Mar.

Rocher, F., and M. Smith

1996   'The New Boundaries of the Canadian Political Culture'. Paper presented at a conference organized by the Centre of Canadian Studies, University of Edinburgh.

Rocher, G.

1976   'Multiculturalism: The Doubts of a Francophone', in *Multiculturalism as State Policy: Conference Report*, Second Canadian Conference on Multiculturalism, Canadian Consultative Council on Multiculturalism (ed.). Ottawa: Dept. of Supply and Services.

Ropke, P.N.

n.d.   'A Tactically Uncontrollable Strategy: The PQ and the Patriation Struggle'. Unpublished paper.

Rose, J.
1995   'Beginning to Think about the Next Referendum'. Occasional paper,
        Faculty of Law, University of Toronto, 21 Nov.

Roy, J.-L.
1976   *La Marche des Québécois: le temps des ruptures, 1945–1960*. Montreal:
        Leméac.
1978   *Le Choix d'un pays: le débat constitutionnel Québec-Canada, 1960–1976*.
        Montreal: Leméac.
1984   'Le PC, Parti québécois'. *Le Devoir*, 6 Sept.

Russell, P.H.
1993   *Constitutional Odyssey: Can Canadians Become a Sovereign People?* 2nd
        edn. Toronto: University of Toronto Press.

Ryan, C.
1967   'Le Congrès conservateur de Toronto'. *Le Devoir*, 7 Sept.
1968   'Vieille tentation du Canada anglais'. *Le Devoir*, 1 Feb.
1968   'Le Choix du 25 juin'. *Le Devoir*, 19 June.
1970   'Les Mesures de guerre: trois questions'. *Le Devoir*, 17 Oct.
1971   'Le Dilemme de M. Bourassa'. *Le Devoir*, 22 June.
1971   'L'Aide aux groupes ethniques exige-t-elle l'abandon du
        biculturalisme?' *Le Devoir*, 9 Oct.
1976   'Le Rêve vain de M. Trudeau'. *Le Devoir*, 8 Mar.
1987   'L'Accord du lac Meech permettra au Québec de faire des gains
        importants et incontestables'. *La Presse*, 30 May.
1990   'Il a soulevé les vraies questions et refuté les réponses toutes faites'. Pp.
        277–81 in R. Comeau and L. Beaudry (eds), *André Laurendeau: Un
        intellectuel d'ici*. Montreal: Presses de l'Université du Québec.
1995   'Référendum de 1980: Ryan en désaccord avec Forget'. *La Presse*, 31
        Mar.
1995   *Regards sur le fédéralisme canadien*. Montreal: Boréal.

Ryerson, S.B.
1968   *Unequal Union: Confederation and the Roots of Conflict in the Canadas,
        1815–1873*. Toronto: Progress.

Sarra-Bournet, M.
1992   '"French Power, Québec Power": La place des francophones québécois
        à Ottawa'. Pp. 195–225 in F. Rocher (ed.), *Bilan québécois du fédéralisme
        canadien*. Montreal: VLB.

Savoie, D.J.
1991   *The Politics of Language*. Kingston: Institute of Intergovernmental
        Relations, Queen's University.

Schneiderman, D. (ed.)

1991   *Language and the State: The Law and Politics of Identity*. Cowansville, Que.: Yvon Blais.

Secretary of State

1990   *Annual Report to Parliament, 1989–1990: Official Languages*. Ottawa.

1991   *Annual Report, 1990–91: Official Languages*. Ottawa.

Séguin, R.

1996   'Federalists Split Over Call for Court Ruling'. *Globe and Mail*, 28 Sept.

Sharp, M.

1994   *Which Reminds Me . . . A Memoir*. Toronto: University of Toronto Press.

Sheppard, R.

1981   'Both Governments Losing Favour in Quebec'. *Globe and Mail*, 5 May.

Sheppard, R., and M. Valpy

1982   *The National Deal: The Fight for a Canadian Constitution*. Toronto: Fleet Books.

Silver, A.I.

1982   *The French-Canadian Idea of Confederation, 1864–1900*. Toronto: University of Toronto Press.

Simeon, R.

1972   *Federal-Provincial Diplomacy: The Making of Recent Policy in Canada*. Toronto: University of Toronto Press.

1990   'Why Did the Meech Lake Accord Fail?' Pp. 16–40 in R.L. Watts and D.M. Brown (eds), *Canada: The State of the Federation 1990*. Kingston: Institute of Intergovernmental Relations, Queen's University.

Simeon, R., and Ian Robinson

1990   *State, Society and the Development of Canadian Federalism*. Collected Research Studies of the Royal Commission on the Economic Union and Development Prospects for Canada, vol. 71. Toronto: University of Toronto Press.

Simpson, J.

1993   *Fault Lines: Struggling for a Canadian Vision*. Toronto: HarperCollins.

1995   'Legal Arguments against Secession Avoid the Unthinkable'. *Globe and Mail*, 6 Jan.

Smiley, D.V.

1967   *The Canadian Political Nationality*. Toronto: Methuen.

1969   'The Case against the Canadian Charter of Human Rights'. *Canadian Journal of Political Science* 2, no. 3 (Sept.): 278–91.

1970   *Constitutional Adaptation and Canadian Federalism Since 1945*. Documents

of the Royal Commission on Bilingualism and Biculturalism, no. 4.
Ottawa: Queen's Printer.

1977   'French-English Relations in Canada and Consociational Democracy'.
Pp. 179–203 in M.J. Esman (ed.), *Ethnic Conflict in the Western World*.
Ithaca: Cornell University Press.

1980   *Canada in Question: Federalism in the Eighties*, 3rd edn. Toronto:
McGraw-Hill Ryerson.

1980   'Reflections on Cultural Nationhood and Political Community in
Canada'. Pp. 20–43 in R.K. Carty and P. Ward (eds), *Entering the
Eighties: Canada in Crisis*. Toronto: Oxford University Press.

1981   *The Canadian Charter of Rights and Freedoms, 1981*. Toronto: Ontario
Economic Council.

1983   'A Dangerous Deed: The Constitution Act, 1982'. Pp. 74–95 in K.
Banting and R. Simeon (eds), *And No One Cheered: Federalism,
Democracy and the Constitution Act*. Toronto: Methuen.

1987   *The Federal Condition in Canada*. Toronto: McGraw-Hill Ryerson.

Smith, D.
1971   *Bleeding Hearts . . . Bleeding Country: Canada and the Quebec Crisis*.
Edmonton: Hurtig.

Sniderman, P.M., et al.
1988   'Liberty, Authority and Community: Civil Liberties and the Canadian
Political Culture'. Paper presented at the annual meeting of the
Canadian Political Science Association, Windsor.

1990   'Reply: Strategic Calculation and Political Values—The Dynamics of
Language Rights'. *Canadian Journal of Political Science* 23, no. 3 (Sept.):
537–44.

Spicer, K.
1989   'How the Linguistic World Looked in 1970'. *Languages and Society*,
Special Edition (Summer): R–10–R–12.

Stanbury, W.T., G.J. Gorn, and C.B. Weinberg
1983   'Federal Advertising Expenditures'. Pp. 66–92 in G.B. Doern (ed.), *How
Ottawa Spends: The Liberals, the Opposition and Federal Priorities, 1983*.
Toronto: Lorimer.

Stanley, G.F.C.
1956   'Act or Pact: Another Look at Confederation'. Proceedings of the
Canadian Historical Association.

Staples, J.
1974   'Consociationalism at Provincial Level: The Erosion of Dualism in
Manitoba'. Pp. 288–302 in K. McRae (ed.), *Consociational Democracy:
Political Accommodation in Segmented Societies*. Toronto: McClelland &
Stewart.

Stasiulis, D.K.
  1988   'The Symbolic Mosaic Reaffirmed: Multiculturalism Policy'. Pp.
          81–111 in K.A. Graham (ed.), *How Ottawa Spends, 1988–89*. Ottawa:
          Carleton University Press.
  1995   '"Deep Diversity": Race and Ethnicity in Canadian Politics'. Pp.
          191–217 in M.S. Whittington and G. Williams (eds), *Canadian Politics in
          the 1990s*, 4th edn. Toronto: Nelson.

Statistics Canada
  1961   *Census of Canada*
  1971   *Census of Canada*
  1981   *Census of Canada*
  1985   *Languages in Canada*. Hull: Minister of Supply and Services.
  1991   *Census of Canada*
  1991   *Home Language and Mother Tongue*

Stevenson, D.
  n.d.   'What Is an Official Language?' Unpublished paper.

Stevenson, G.
  1989   *Unfulfilled Union: Canadian Federalism and National Unity*, 3rd edn.
          Toronto: Gage.
  1995   'Multiculturalism: As Canadian as Apple Pie'. *Inroads* 4: 72–87.

Stursberg, P.
  1975   *Diefenbaker: Leadership Gained, 1956–62*. Toronto: University of Toronto
          Press.
  1978   *Lester Pearson and the Dream of Unity*. Toronto: Doubleday.

Sullivan, M.
  1968   *Mandate '68*. Toronto: Doubleday.

Taillefer, G.
  1989   'Mise au rancart du bilinguisme officiel par la Fédération des
          francophones hors Québec'. *La Presse*, 25 June.

Tanguay, A.B., and A.-G. Gagnon
  1996   *Canadian Parties in Transition*, 2nd edn. Scarborough, Ont.: Nelson.

Task Force on Canadian Unity
  1979   *A Future Together: Observations and Recommendations*. Hull: Dept. of
          Supply and Services.

Taylor, C.
  1993   *Reconciling the Solitudes: Essays on Canadian Federalism and Nationalism*.
          Montreal and Kingston: McGill-Queen's University Press.
  1995   'Les Ethnies dans un société "normale"'. *La Presse*, 21 and 22 Nov.

Taylor, D.M., and L. Dubé-Simard
  1984   'Language Planning and Intergroup Relations: Anglophone and
          Francophone Attitudes toward the Charter of the French Language'.
          Pp. 148–73 in R.J. Bourhis (ed.), *Conflict and Language Planning in
          Quebec*. Clevedon, UK: Multilingual Matters.

Termote, M.
  1991   'L'Évolution démolinguistique du Québec et du Canada'. Pp. 239–329
          in Commission sur l'avenir politique et constitutionnel du Québec,
          *Éléments d'analyse institutionnelle, juridique et démolinguistique pertinents à la
          révision du statut politique et constitutionnel du Québec*. Document de
          travail, numéro 2 (n.p.).

Thomas, D.M.
  1995   'Edmund Burke's Ghost, an Abeyance Exhumed, and Pierre Trudeau's
          Undertaking'. Paper presented to the Canadian Political Science
          Association, June.
  1995   'The Second Time Around: Pepin-Robarts Then and Now'. Paper
          presented to the Association for Canadian Studies in the United States,
          Seattle, 18–19 Nov.

Thomson, D.C.
  1967   *Louis St Laurent: Canadian*. Toronto: Macmillan.
  1984   *Jean Lesage and the Quiet Revolution*. Toronto: Macmillan.

Thorburn, H.
  1974   'Needed! A New Look at the Two-Nations Theory'. *Queen's Quarterly*
          80 (Summer): 268–73.

Thordarson, B.
  1972   *Trudeau and Foreign Policy*. Toronto: Oxford University Press.

Thorson, J.T.
  1973   *Wanted: A Single Canada*. Toronto: McClelland & Stewart.

The Toronto Star
  1969   'Back to the Solitudes'. 19 Dec.
  1977   'What Quebec *Really* Wants: English Consider Us Inferior, Quebec
          Feels'. 17 May.
  1987   'Meech Lake Accord Gains General Support, Polls Show'. 1 June.

Trent, J.E., R.A. Young, and G. Lachapelle (eds)
  1996   *Québec-Canada: What is the Path Ahead? Nouveaux sentiers vers l'avenir*.
          Ottawa: University of Ottawa Press.

Trudeau, P.E.
  1968   *Federalism and the French Canadians*. Toronto: Macmillan.
  1969   *Federal-Provincial Grants and the Spending Power of Parliament*. Ottawa:
          Queen's Printer.

1976   'Il faut qu'on se parle dans le blanc des yeux'. *La Presse*, 8 Mar.

1977   *Pierre Elliott Trudeau à la Chambre de commerce de Québec, 18 janvier 1977.* Montreal: *La Presse.*

1980a   'Trudeau n'acceptera de négocier qu'après le 2e référendum'. [Transcript of Pierre Trudeau's first referendum address.] *La Presse*, 2 May.

1980b   Transcription de l'allocution du Très Honorable Pierre Elliott Trudeau du centre municipal des Congrès à Québec, 7 May.

1980c   Transcription de l'allocution du Très Honorable Pierre Trudeau au centre Paul Sauvé, Montréal, 14 May.

1987   '"Say Goodbye to the Dream" of One Canada'. *Toronto Star*, 27 May.

1987   Special Joint Committee of the Senate and the House of Commons on the 1987 Constitutional Accord, *Minutes of Proceedings and Evidence*, 2nd session, 33rd Parliament, Issue no. 14, 27 Aug. 1987, 116–58.

1988   *Debates* of the Senate, 2nd session, 33rd Parliament, 1986–87–88, 30 Mar 1988, 2982–3023. Edited version appears in Behiels, *The Meech Lake Primer*, 60–99.

1990   'The Values of a Just Society'. Pp. 357–85 in T.S. Axworthy and P.E. Trudeau (eds), *Towards a Just Society: The Trudeau Years*. Markham, Ont.: Viking.

1992   'A Mess That Deserves a Big No'. Toronto: Robert Davies.

1993   *Memoirs.* Toronto: McClelland & Stewart.

1996   'J'accuse Lucien Bouchard!'. *La Presse*, 3 Feb.

Trudeau, P.E. (ed.)
1970   *La Grève de l'amiante.* Montreal: Éditions du jour.

Trudel, G.
1982   'Trois sondages sur le Québec d'après–novembre'. *Le Devoir*, 20 Jan.

Turpel, M.E.
1992   'Does the Road to Quebec Sovereignty Run through Aboriginal Territory?' Pp. 93–106 in D. Drache and R. Perin (eds), *Negotiating with a Sovereign Quebec.* Toronto: Lorimer.

1993   'The Charlottetown Accord and Aboriginal Peoples' Struggle for Fundamental Political Change'. Pp. 111–51 in K. McRoberts and P.J. Monahan, *The Charlottetown Accord, the Referendum, and the Future of Canada.*

Vaillancourt, Y.
1992   'Le Régime d'assistance publique du Canada: perspective québécoise'. Thèse de doctorat en science politique, l'Université de Montréal.

1993   'Quebec and the Federal Government: The Struggle Over Opting Out'. Pp. 168–89 in D. Glenday and A. Duffy (eds), *Canadian Society: Understanding and Surviving in the 1990s.* Toronto: McClelland & Stewart.

Vastel, M.
 1989   *Trudeau: le Québécois*. Montreal: Éditions de l'homme.
 1990   *The Outsider*, trans. Hubert Bauch. Toronto: Macmillan.
 1996   *Lucien Bouchard: en attendant la suite*. Outremont: Lanctôt.

Venne, M.
 1992   'Robert Bourassa flaire un "féderalisme dominateur"'. *Le Devoir*, 4 Mar.
 1992   'Il fallait pas accepter ça'. *Le Devoir*, 1 Oct.
 1996   'Qu'aurait dit Parizeau si le OUI l'avait emporté?' *Le Devoir*, 18 Feb.
 1996   'Chrétien se libère de l'échéance de 1997'. *Le Devoir*, 23 June.
 1996   '67 p. cent des Québécois sont profondément attachés au Canada'. *Le Devoir*, 3 Oct.

Verney, D.V.
 1986   *Three Civilizations, Two Cultures, One State: Canada's Political Traditions*. Durham, NC: Duke University Press.

Verney, D.V., and D.M. Verney
 1974   'A Canadian Political Community? The Case for Tripartite Confederalism'. *Journal of Commonwealth and Comparative Politics* 12, no. 1 (Mar.): 1–19.

Vineberg, M.
 1968   'The Progressive Conservative Leadership Convention of 1967'. M.A. thesis, Dept. of Economics and Political Science, McGill University.

Vipond, R.C.
 1991   *Liberty and Community: Canadian Federalism and the Failure of the Constitution*. Albany, NY: State University of New York Press.
 1989   'Whatever Became of the Compact Theory? Meech Lake and the New Politics of Constitutional Amendment in Canada'. *Queen's Quarterly* 96, no. 4: 793–811.
 1996   'Citizenship and the Charter of Rights: Two Sides of Pierre Trudeau'. *International Journal of Canadian Studies* 14 (Fall): 179–91.

Waddell, E.
 1991   'Some Thoughts on the Implications of French Immersion for English Canada'. Pp. 423–32 in D. Schneiderman (ed.), *Language and the State: The Law and Politics of identity*. Cowansville, Que.: Yvon Blais.

Waite, P.B.
 1962   *The Life and Times of Confederation, 1864–1867: Politics, Newspapers and the Union of British North America*. Toronto: University of Toronto Press.
 1963   *The Confederation Debates in the Province of Canada, 1865*. Carleton Library, no. 2. Toronto: McClelland & Stewart.

Weaver, S.M.
 1981   *Making Canadian Indian Policy: The Hidden Agenda 1968–1970*. Toronto: University of Toronto Press.

Webber, J.
    1994   *Reimagining Canada: Language, Culture, Community and the Canadian Constitution*. Montreal and Kingston: McGill-Queen's University Press.
    1995   'The Response to Parizeau's "Ethnic Vote"'. *Canada Watch* 4, no. 3 (Nov./Dec.): 34–5.

Westell, A.
    1967   'Diefenbaker Won't Continue; Tories Back 2-Nation Plan'. *Globe and Mail*, 8 Sept.
    1968   'PM challenges Quebec Tories on Two Nations'. *Globe and Mail*, 21 June.
    1969   'If Canada doesn't want bilingualism, I want out'. *Toronto Star*, 8 Feb.
    1972   *Paradox: Trudeau as Prime Minister*. Scarborough, Ont.: Prentice-Hall.

Whitaker, R.
    1992   'Reason, Passion and Interest: Pierre Trudeau's Eternal Liberal Triangle'. Pp. 132–62 in R. Whitaker (ed.), *A Sovereign Idea*. Montreal and Kingston: McGill-Queen's University Press.
    1993   'The Dog That Never Barked: Who Killed Asymmetrical Federalism?' Pp. 107–14 in McRoberts and Monahan, *The Charlottetown Accord, the Referendum, and the Future of Canada*.
    1993   'Apprehended Insurrection? RCMP Intelligence and the October Crisis'. *Queen's Quarterly* 100, no. 2 (Summer): 383–406.
    1995   'Quebec's Self-determination and Aboriginal Self-government'. Pp. 193–220 in Carens (ed.), *Is Quebec Nationalism Just?*
    1996   'Thinking about the Unthinkable: Planning for a Possible Secession'. *Constitutional Forum constitutionnel* 7, nos 2 and 3 (Winter–Spring): 58–64.

Whitehorn, A.
    1992   *Canadian Socialism: Essays on the CCF–NDP*. Toronto: Oxford University Press.

Williams, C.
    1985   'The Changing Nature of Citizen Rights'. Pp. 111–23 in A. Cairns and C. Williams (eds), *Constitutionalism, Citizenship and Society in Canada*. Collected Research Studies of the Royal Commission on the Economic Union and Development Prospects for Canada, vol. 33. Toronto: University of Toronto Press.

Winsor, H.
    1995   'Poll Disputes No Rally's Success'. *Globe and Mail*, 11 Nov.
    1996   'Quebeckers Prefer Canada 2–1, Poll Says'. *Globe and Mail*, 26 Mar.
    1996   'Ottawa Caught Short by Flag Fever'. *Globe and Mail*, 29 Aug.

Winsor, H., and E. Greenspon
    1996   'Hard Line on Separatism Popular Outside Quebec'. *Globe and Mail*, 16 Nov.

Winsor, H., and T.T. Ha
    1995   'Chrétien Signals New Resolve on Quebec'. *Globe and Mail*, 12 Dec.

Woehrling, J.
    1996   'Ground Rules for the Next Referendum on Quebec's Sovereignty'. *Canada Watch* 4, nos 5 and 6 (Aug.).

Young, R.
    1995   *The Secession of Quebec and the Future of Canada*. Montreal and Kingston: McGill-Queen's University Press.

Young, R., and D. Brown
    1992   'Overview'. Pp. 1–24 in D. Brown and R. Young (eds), *Canada: The State of the Federation 1992*. Kingston: Institute of Intergovernmental Relations, Queen's University.

Zemans, J.
    1995   'The Essential Role of National Cultural Institutions'. Pp. 138–62 in McRoberts, *Beyond Quebec*.

INDEX